Operations Management in Business

Operations Management in Business

Andrew Greasley

Stanley Thornes (Publishers) Ltd

First published in 1999 by
Stanley Thornes (Publishers) Ltd
Ellenborough House
Wellington Street
Cheltenham
Glos. GL50 1YW
UK

A catalogue record for this book is available from The British Library.

ISBN 0 7487 2084 7

Typeset by Northern Phototypesetting Co. Ltd, Bolton
Printed and bound in Great Britain by TJ International Ltd, Padstow, Cornwall

Contents

Part 3 Improvement

Preface

Operations management deals with the creation of goods and the delivery of services to the customer. It thus plays an essential role in the success of any organisation. At the basic level the operations *activity* is defined as that which is concerned with the transformation of inputs into outputs, and thus occurs throughout the organisation. The operations *function* itself is defined as being concerned with those transformation processes that provide goods and services for *external* customers.

The aim of this book is to provide a clear and concise treatment of operations management as it relates to the organisation. The text aims to cover the main areas of the design of the operations system, the management of the system over time and the need for improvement of the system. The text will incorporate the following key developments in the field:

- the development of production systems from the mass to the lean era;
- the increasing importance of operations strategy formulation;
- the increasing importance of service operations;
- the increasing impact of globalisation on the link between operations systems across organisations.

Acknowledgements

The author and publishers would like to thank the following organisations for permission to reproduce material:

Blackwell Publishers, The Financial Times Ltd, The McGraw-Hill Companies Inc., Pearson Education Ltd and Simon and Schuster Inc. Every effort has been made to contact copyright holders, and we apologise if any have been overlooked.

I would also like to thank the following people for their support of this book: for the contributions of Professor David Bennett at Aston University, Mark Teale at the University of Lincolnshire and Humberside, and Joe Marshall at the University of Derby many thanks; to Professor David Gowland at the University of Derby who encouraged me to undertake the task; to the reviewers for their constructive comments and to Francis Dodds, Sarah Wilman and Sandy Marshall at Stanley Thornes. Finally I would like to thank my wife, Kay, for her support.

Andrew Greasley
January 1999

Part 1   Concepts and design

1 Concepts

Objectives

By the end of this chapter, you should be able to:

- understand the concepts of operations management, the operations function and operations activities;
- understand the main areas of difference between service and manufacturing operations;
- understand the operations system as a transformation process;
- understand how operations relates to other sub-systems in the organisation;
- understand the relationship between the organisation and stakeholder needs;
- understand how the stakeholder model can be used to meet organisational objectives.

Organisations will not succeed if they cannot consistently deliver goods or services at the right time and the right place. Operations decisions directly affect the size, shape, quantity, quality, price, profitability and speed of delivery of a company's output, whether the company produces a manufactured product such as a car or delivers a service such as fast food.

This chapter introduces the concept of the operations functions and describes some of the decision areas in the subject of operations management. A key issue in operations is the management of service facilities and differences in manufacturing and service organisation are introduced. Operations is examined in terms if its components and its role in the organisation. The operations activity is defined as a transformation process and as such occurs throughout the organisation. The operations function itself is defined as being concerned with those transformation processes that provide goods and services for external customers. By considering the relationship of the organisation and its stakeholders it can be seen that the operations function will need to deal with a wide range of issues including management of employees, meeting customer needs, ensuring profitability and providing links with distributors and suppliers.

What is operations management?

Operations Management is about how organisations produce or deliver the goods and services that provide the reason for their existence. This chapter will look at some of the tasks involved in managing operations activities and then look in detail at operations from a systems viewpoint.

Operations can be seen as one of many functions (e.g. marketing, finance, personnel) within the organisation. The operations function can be described as that part of the organisation devoted to the production or delivery of goods and services. Not every organisation will have a functional department called 'operations', but they will all undertake operations activities because every organisation produces goods and/or services.

The operations manager will have responsibility for managing resources involved in the operations function. Positions involved in operations have a variety of names, and may differ between the manufacturing and service sectors. Examples of job titles involved in manufacturing include supervisor, logistics manager, and industrial engineer. Examples in service industry include office supervisor and quality manager. The operations role participates in a wide variety of decision areas in the organisation, examples of which are given below:

- **Business planning:** What strategy should be followed?
- **Product design:** What product/service should the organisation provide?
- **Resource planning:** What labour, materials and plant are required?
- **Location and layout:** Where and how do we operate?
- **Job design:** How do people and technology work together?
- **Quality control:** Are standards being met?

Manufacturing and service operations

One of the key developments in operations is the increasing importance of service operations as service industry accounts for an increasing proportion of the output of industrialised economies.

> 'The United States has by far the biggest service sector, accounting for 72 percent of its gross domestic product (GDP). At the other extreme, the service sector provides only 57 percent of Germany's GDP, thanks partly to a multitude of restrictive practices that have hindered expansion. Meanwhile, manufacturing's share of the GDP has fallen in the big economies. It now only accounts for 23 percent of the US's GDP. In Britain and Canada, manufacturing has tumbled to less than 20 percent of total output. Even in Japan and Germany, the strongholds of industry, manufacturing is now no more than 30 percent of GDP' (Rosen, 1998).

Services are defined in terms of the tangibility of the output of the operations system. Basically goods are tangible and services are not. A service is intangible and should be seen as a process that is activated on demand. The main areas of difference between service and manufacturing organisations are as follows.

Customer contact

Because a service cannot be stored its production and consumption will occur at the same time; that implies that the producer of the service will come into contact with the customer. In fact the customer will be involved to a greater or lesser extent in the actual delivery of the operation. For instance a supermarket requires the customer to choose and transport the goods around the store and queue at an appropriate checkout till. However it should not be assumed that all employees in a service operation have to deal directly with a customer. For the supermarket example, the checkout till is an example of high customer contact, but stores personnel may not have to deal directly with the customer at all. This distinction in services is denoted by 'back office' tasks which add value to the inputs of the service operation (e.g. stocktaking) and 'front office' tasks which deal with the customer both as an input and output of the operation.

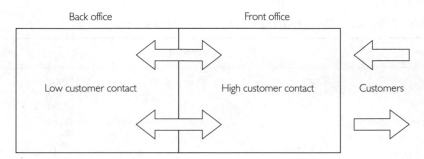

Figure 1.1 Front office and back office in service operations

Finished goods inventory

Because services are intangible then it follows that they cannot have a store of finished goods. Manufacturing operations will often compensate for fluctuations in demand by fulfilling demand from finished goods inventory produced during a slack period. This option is not open to service operations and they must focus on trying to alter the demand pattern to meet capacity by such strategies as discounting the price of the service during periods of low demand.

Measuring performance

Because the output of a service is intangible it is more difficult to assess performance by such measures as productivity or output. For example a manufacturer can simply count the volume of output of its product range, but an administration service for example will have more difficulty in measuring the productivity of their employees.

Quality

The quality of a service will be judged by the process of delivering that service as well as the quality of any tangible goods that are involved. This leads to the problem that it is more difficult to measure the quality of service delivery than the quality of manufactured goods. Rosen (1998) provides some additional comment about the nature of services.

'Since services supposedly do not create value, produce a tangible product, or incur large capital costs, it has been argued that savings in these sectors will be hard to accomplish. This argument sounds good on the surface, but it is untrue. Services such as communications, transportation, pipelines, and utilities are among the most capital intensive of all industries. If services do not create value, why are we, as consumers, willing to pay for them?'

In reality most operations systems produce a mixture of goods and services. Most goods have some supporting service element (e.g. a maintenance facility), called a **facilitating service**, while many services will have supporting goods (e.g. a management consultancy report), termed facilitating goods. The expenses and revenues of many nominal manufacturing industries actually represent pre- and post-purchase services in the form of systems planning, pre-installation support, software, repair, maintenance, delivery, collection and bookkeeping (Rosen, 1998). Examples of production of goods and services by manufacturing and services operations are given in Table 1.1.

Table 1.1 Examples of production of goods and services by operations systems

Goods		Services	
Agriculture	Crops Livestock Fishing	Transportation	Postal Airlines Trucks
Mining	Coal Oil Minerals	Utilities	Electric Gas Water
Construction	Building	Retail	Food Furniture Eating
Manufacturing	Furniture Electronic Equip. Cars, Aircraft	Financial	Banks Insurance Estate Agents
		Services	Hotels Cinema Garage Repair
		Government Bodies	Health Education Legal

Operations as a system

To understand operations, it is necessary to see organisations as systems. A system is shown in Figure 1.2.

A system is a group of interrelated items in which no item studied in isolation will act in the same way as it would in the system. A system is divided into a series of parts or subsystems, and any system is a part of a larger system. The system's boundary defines what is inside the system and what is outside. A system's **environment** is everything outside the system boundary that may have an impact on the behaviour of the system. A system's inputs are the physical objects of information that enter it from the environment and its outputs are the same which leave it for the environment.

This chapter will examine the following relationships:

- activities within the operations system;
- operations within the business system;
- the business system within the environment.

This chapter will explore the relationship between the organisation and its environment, through a discussion of the need for the organisation to meet the need of its stakeholders. It will explore the relationship of operations to other functions in the business e.g. marketing, and to look at the sub-systems within the operations system.

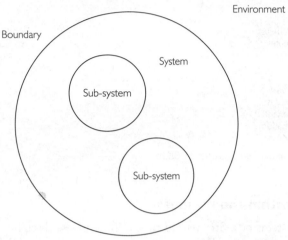

Figure 1.2 A system

Activities within the operations system

The activities in an operations system can be classified as input, transformation process and output. The input activity involves two categories of resources. **Transforming resources** are the elements that act on, or carry out, the transformation process on other elements. These include such elements as labour, equipment/plant and energy. The nature and mix of these resources will differ between operations. The transformed resources are the elements which give the operations system its purpose or goal. The operations system is concerned with converting the transformed resources from inputs into outputs in the form of goods and services. Slack (1995) outlines three main types of transformed resources:

- **Materials.** These can be transformed either physically (e.g. manufacturing), by location (e.g. transportation), by ownership (e.g. retail) or by storage (e.g. warehousing).
- **Information.** This can be transformed by property (e.g. accountants), by possession (e.g. market research), by storage (e.g. libraries), or by location (e.g. telecommunications).
- **Customer.** They can be transformed either physically (hairdresser), by storage (e.g. hotels), by location (e.g. airlines), by physiological state (e.g. hospitals), or by psychological state (e.g. entertainment).

Two types of transforming resources are defined (Slack, 1995):

- **Facilities** – e.g. building and equipment.
- **Staff** – all the people involved in the operations process.

Figure 1.3 shows the components of an operations system.

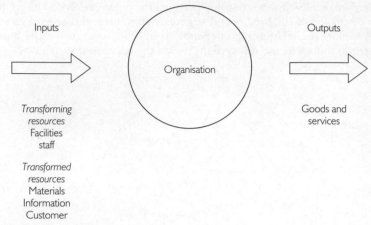

Figure 1.3 Components of an operations system

Operations within the business

The three sub-systems of a firm related to specific business disciplines are termed the functional areas of a business. The three main functional activities in a business are:

- operations
- sales and marketing
- finance.

The **sales and marketing function** work to find and create demand for the company's goods and services by understanding customer needs and developing new markets. The need for marketing and operations to work closely together is particularly important as the marketing function will provide the forecast of demand from which operations can plan sufficient capacity in order to deliver goods and services on time.

The **finance function** is responsible for the obtaining and controlling of funds and covering decisions such as investment in equipment and price-volume decisions.

Other functions which play a supporting role in the organisation include the personnel function which will play a role on the recruitment and labour relations, the research and development **R&D function** which generates and investigates the potential of new ideas and the **information technology** (IT) department which supplies and co-ordinates the computer-based information needs of the organisation.

The relationship between functions can be seen as a number of sub-systems within the system called the 'organisation'. Thus each function (e.g. marketing) can be treated using the same input/process/output transformation model as the operations function. In other words each function within the organisation can be treated as performing an operations activity, as they are transforming inputs into outputs. This implies every part of the organisation is involved in the operations activity (to an external or internal customer) and thus the theory of operations covered in this book is relevant to them. When operations is cited as a function in itself however it is referring to the part of the organisation which provides goods and services for *external* customers.

The **operations function** itself is involved in all parts of the firm and thus has a major impact on the competitive position of the organisation. The traditional view of the operations sub-system is that it is one function within a linear sequence of processes and is thus 'buffered' from the actions of the marketplace. Thus both physical stocks and allocation of responsibility within functions outside of operations are used to protect the operations system from the external environment. For example the R&D function will carry responsibility for the development of new product ideas which are then 'passed on' to the operations function and the purchasing function will take responsibility for the sourcing of materials and bought-in services. Physical **buffers** include stocks of materials before and after the operations function to ensure stability of supply and ability to meet fluctuating demand respectively. The idea behind this model is that the operations function can concentrate solely on transforming inputs of raw materials into goods and services without the need to consider the external environment outside of the organisational system.

The disadvantage of this model includes the slowness of response to changes in the environment as they are transmitted through various connected functions and the inability of operations to develop in response to the needs of customers. In fact the operations function is critical in meeting customer needs and is deeply involved in the performance of the organisation. For example the parameters under which a product/service can be marketed is directly consequent on inputs from the operations functions such as shown in Table 1.2.

Table 1.2

Operations input	Marketing parameter
Cost of delivery of goods/service	Price
Ability to schedule	Deliver on time
Flexibility	Product range available
Quality	Repeat orders

Thus instead of being seen as simply a 'black box' which takes raw materials and transforms then into a product/service, the operations function should be seen as critical to the marketing position and competitive advantage of the organisation. Brown (1996) explains how the need for operations to improve performance across a number of attributes (e.g. quality, delivery, cost) means that competitive improvements will require long-term commitment and thus a strategic view of operations. The approach requires a commitment to quality improvement and then an improvement in other competitive factors that together lead to a reduction in cost. This contrasts with the direct approach to cost reduction of cutting the labour force or '**downsizing**'. Apart from failing to tackle the underlying problems and increase performance across the competitive factors, this approach is limited by the fact that direct labour costs typically account for a small proportion of overall costs.

The process view of organisations
Recently there has been a move away from considering business as a set of discrete functional areas towards a view of the organisation as consisting of sets of processes which link together in order to meet customer needs. Processes can be related in one functional area (e.g. production), but could relate to cross-functional activities (e.g. fulfilling customer orders) or even occur in all functional areas (e.g. planning activities).

An example of a process view of an organisation is shown in Figure 1.4.

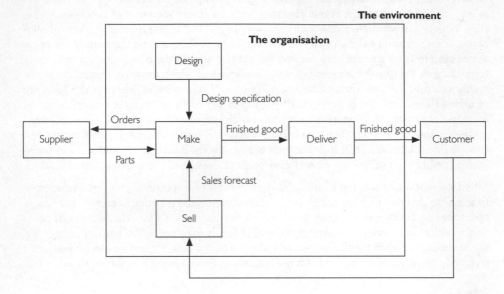

Figure 1.4 Process view of an organisation

In functional terms the processes would be situated in areas such as operations, marketing and finance, but from the customer's view the value they gain is dependent on the performance of the set of linked processes involved in the delivery of the product/service. The term 'value added' is used to denote the amount of value a process creates for its internal or external customer.

The set of processes used to create value for a customer is often called the value chain (Porter, 1985). The **value chain** includes primary processes that directly create the value the customer perceives and support processes that assist the primary process in adding value. The key issue is that the configuration of the value chain should be aligned with the particular way the organisation provides value to the customer.

Organisations and stakeholders

If the organisation is seen as a sub-system within the business environment, then it can be seen that an whole range of interested parties (called stakeholders) will be involved in the direction and success of the organisation. The organisation and thus the operations function, will need to be aware and take appropriate account of a range of stakeholder needs in order to be successful. This section will look more closely at the role of stakeholders and the organisation. The purpose of the organisation can be defined in terms of its need to meet the needs of stakeholders. A stakeholder can be defined as 'anyone with a legitimate interest in the activities of an organisation'.

As Figure 1.5 shows, businesses need to deal with a wide range of stakeholders. These can be divided into three basic groups:

● internal stakeholders
● connected stakeholders
● external stakeholders.

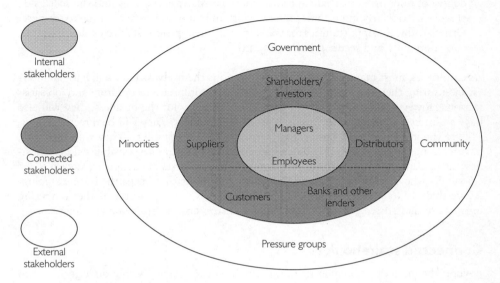

Figure 1.5 Organisational stakeholders

Internal stakeholders

The internal stakeholders of a business are its managers and employees. In many companies, the managers will themselves be employees of the business, responsible to its owner. If the company is a public or private limited company, the management team will be responsible to shareholders. A company's **managers** will act on behalf of its owners in managing the workforce to meet the objectives set by the owners. Their interests will, therefore, overlap with but be distinct from those of the rest of the workforce.

Employees will have a number of interests in the business. These include two obvious concerns:

● **Job Security:** employees will want to ensure that jobs are secure. This concern will include securing continuity of employment of individuals, sustaining the overall number of jobs in the business and protecting employees from arbitrary or unfair dismissal. It will also include protecting the content of jobs from changes which might make them more insecure or difficult.
● **Rewards:** those working in a business want the best pay and conditions they can achieve. They will want rewards that they feel reflect the value of their work and the market rate for the job compared to other workers in comparable jobs.

However, a workforce may well have a number of wider interests which managers need also to take account of:

- **Recognition:** employees want to be respected and treated fairly by management. Individual workers need to feel that they are valued, their status and contribution recognised, and that mangers consult them.
- **Fulfilment (job satisfaction):** most employees prefer jobs that give them some degree of responsibility, challenge and creativity. Many employees find the social side of work particularly important, prefer to work in teams and have the time to socialise. Others will want opportunities for training and career progression to exploit their talents more fully and secure greater recognition, rewards and security.

As employees, most managers share these aspirations themselves. They will have an interest in ensuring their own security, levels of reward, appropriate recognition and job satisfaction. However, as managers with overall responsibility for the business, they will also have an interest in meeting the needs of other stakeholders. They will be directly responsible to the investors in the business for its success and profitability. They will, therefore, have a strong interest in meeting the investors' goals. The same responsibility for the business also means they need to look very closely to the interests of customers, since it is the customers who create the sales, and ultimately, the profit that keeps the business going. As we shall see, one of the key roles of management is to try to reconcile the competing interests of these three groups of stakeholders: customers, investors and employees.

Connected stakeholders

Beyond the immediate boundaries of the firm are other parties with a direct connection with the business. Amongst these the most important are the following.

Customers

Customers have a number of interests in the activities of a business. Broadly, these are concerned with:

- price
- fit to customer's needs
- quality and reliability
- availability
- service.

In general, customers will look for the best price when they shop for a product or service. The need to be competitive on price puts an obvious pressure on **profits**, creating a potential area of conflict with investors. Investors in turn will expect managers to keep a tight control on costs. Since a major element of business costs may be **labour costs**, pressure from customers and investors may impact on wages and on employees' productivity. Pressures on prices, profits and costs may mean lower wage increases and workers having to work harder to improve productivity.

However, customers may not judge a product or service solely on price. They will choose one which best suits their needs. In some cases, bread for instance, competing products or services from differing firms may be identical, in which case price becomes the deciding issue. In others, preserves for example, customers may want something tailored to their specific requirements. In this case they may be prepared to pay a higher price for a customised product. If so, businesses will need to be particularly sensitive to customer needs. Managers and employees may need to show extra flexibility, perhaps in developing a wide range of product types or in researching customer likes and dislikes. They will need to balance producing customised products with the higher costs involved in these types of operations and its resulting pressure on prices. In doing so they will need to get the right balance of price and fit to give the customer value for money, whilst providing investors with the returns they expect.

Increasingly customers are also looking for high levels of quality and reliability in the goods and services they buy. **Quality** has been one of the major weapons in the success of Japanese firms in entering western markets on the post-war era. This emphasis on quality puts pressure on costs and on higher levels of commitment and skill from both management and staff in improving production methods and eradicating errors.

There is, of course, little point in having a good product to sell if it is not available when and where the customer needs it. As markets have become more competitive and customer expectations have increased, consumers have become less tolerant of shortages and delays in availability. In the past, businesses overcame any problems in supply by holding large levels of stock, despite the costs of storage and depreciation and pressures on working capital. The need to reduce costs together with competition from Japanese companies in particular have pushed more and more firms into keeping stocks low and developing 'just-in-time' delivery and production systems. These systems, which need to react quickly to changes in demand, require flexibility and skill from both management and workforce.

Just as customers have come to expect more in such areas as price, quality and availability, so they increasingly expect higher standards of service, when they buy it, or in the support they receive after purchasing the product. They expect businesses to adapt their needs rather than the other way round. High standards of service require motivated and well-trained staff with the authority to deal effectively with customer queries and needs.

Investors

Businesses can call on a wide range of sources of finance, from government grants to ploughing back part of their own profits into the business. However, the two main sources of finance for most public limited companies (PLCs) are:

- shares bought by shareholders
- loans provided by banks.

Private limited companies also depend on **shares** as a main source of finance, although these shares cannot be sold on the Stock Exchange. Both these and small businesses are often also reliant on banks for finance. We will look at shareholding first.

Shareholders

Shareholders are those individuals or groups who have bought shares in the company. There are two main financial benefits to holding shares:

- Depending on the amount of profit earned in a particular year, a business will set aside a proportion of its profit to pay out as an annual **dividend** to shareholders.
- Shares can be bought and sold on the Stock Market. If a business is doing well, the value of its shares will tend to increase beyond the price originally paid shareholders, giving them the opportunity to sell shares to other investors at a profit.

In return for providing the business with finance through the purchase of shares, most shareholders are able to elect the firm's board of directors at annual meetings of shareholders (some classes of shares do not give their owners voting rights). Shareholders would not usually be involved in the day-to-day running of the business, which is left to management. The managers of a business need to keep shareholders satisfied for two reasons:

● Shareholders can vote to remove the board of directors if they are unhappy with the company's performance.
● If shareholders are concerned about the business's poor performance, they may sell their shares to avoid losses incurred in any fall in the share price. Selling shares in such circumstances would be seen by the Stock Market as a danger signal, accelerating the fall in the value of shares. A serious collapse in the share price of a company would undermine its ability to raise further finance, and worry remaining shareholders. Other investors (for instance, banks) and creditors (the people to whom it owed money) could force a business into bankruptcy by demanding the immediate repayment of outstanding debts and forcing the sale of the business's assets to achieve this.

Banks and other lenders

Businesses depend on a variety of organisations, such as banks and other lending institutions to maintain and expand their activities. Organisations may borrow on a short-term basis to finance current operations or on a long-term basis for new equipment or to acquire or build new facilities. Lending institutions will need to be convinced that any money can be repaid before moneys are lent.

Distributors and suppliers

The final groups of connected stakeholders are distributors and suppliers. Like customers, both suppliers and distributors will look for the best price they can get from a business. The supplier will want to charge the highest price for supplying raw materials or components, for example, to a business. Suppliers may also want to produce as cheaply as possible to get the maximum return from the prices they charge. Distributors will want to buy as cheaply as they can so that they have the greatest scope for marking up the final price they charge to the end user. Complex distribution arrangements can lead to high prices for consumers as they bear the brunt of attempts by individuals in the distribution chain to mark up the price successively so each person gets their 'cut'.

Both suppliers and distributors will want to control the flow of materials and goods in a way that suits them. A supplier wants a secure and stable pattern of demand, so will look to develop long-term relationships with businesses. Suppliers may sometimes be resistant to just-in-time (JIT) systems. These have been developed by businesses to allow them to order raw materials and components only when they need them, rather than stockpile materials. JIT systems reduce the costs and risks of holding large amounts of raw materials and components. However, because they depend on supplying small amounts at frequent intervals, they require more time and expertise to operate well, and will tend to leave the supplier holding on to the stock and, therefore, taking more of a risk if demand drops. JIT systems may also lead to less certainty and predictability for suppliers as supply rises and falls in direct relation to production levels, themselves changing in tune with each fluctuation in market demand.

Distributors, on the other hand, might well welcome a JIT system since it means that they may not need to hold much stock themselves. They will want a supply to fit their needs, and push for the right to return what is not sold, keeping any risk with the producer and not with them. Both suppliers and distributors will also bargain with a business for the best credit terms, delaying payment for as long as possible to help their cash flow. Powerful suppliers and distributors, charging high prices for raw materials on the one hand, and, on the other, forcing manufacturers to sell at a low price for resale by the distributor to the consumer, can significantly reduce a company's profitability.

External stakeholders

There is a wide range of external stakeholders, the most important one usually being the government. Governments are involved in the organisation in many ways, including setting regulations in areas such as **health and safety**, and the **environment** in creating an economic policy which provides the framework within which business operates. The availability and level of **government grants** available in different geographical areas may affect the operations location decision (Chapter 2). Other external stakeholders include the local community, minorities and pressure groups.

Meeting stakeholder needs

Using the stakeholder model the question which organisations must address is how they can deal with this wide range of stakeholder needs. Wilson (1985) deals with this by the idea that an organisation is made up of diverse individuals and groups, each with their own needs and reasons for participating in the organisation. Each individual or group has a set of demands or inducements to ensure their continued membership of the organisation and in return they contribute services or resources which are necessary for the organisation to function. In order for the organisation to be viable at any point in time there must be a minimum level of inducement to remain within the organisation and provide a contribution to the satisfaction of all groups. This is called the feasible set. Given this definition of purpose, an effective organisation is one in which members choose feasible strategies that ensure genuine satisfaction of members in the long term. In other words the goal of the organisation should be to genuinely satisfy the needs of members (i.e. stakeholders) which are necessary for the success of the organisation in the long run. An example of this is in paying low wages to a section of workers. In the short run this may save labour costs, but in the long run it may cause a general move to strike action by members of the organisation. Thus the organisational goals can be seen as satisfying the stakeholder needs. The system is thus represented by the complete **feasible set** of human demands and contributions which requires adequate satisfaction (Figure 1.6) (Wilson, 1985).

Using the stakeholder model to meet organisational objectives

Doyle (1998) recognises the need for a business to adopt a multiple perspective and to satisfy different groups of stakeholders. He states that the companies that have competed successfully over a number of years are not outstanding on any single measure of performance but recognise the trade-offs involved in maximising measures such as profits, growth and shareholder value. Thus they aim to achieve a satisfactory level of performance across a multiple, competing set of criteria. Doyle (1998) outlines three mechanisms for developing a balanced set of objectives.

Balanced organisational representation
This involves having representation of various stakeholder groups at the highest level. The Japanese kieretsu structure ensures the involvement of internal and external stake-

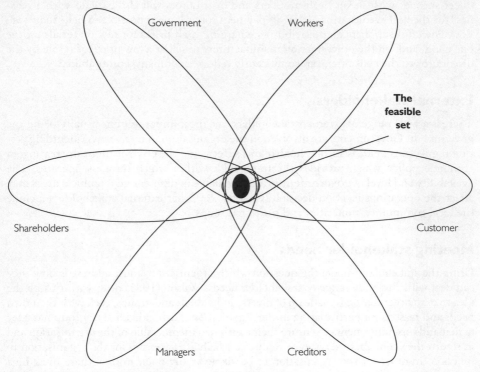

Figure 1.6 The stakeholder model showing the feasible set

holders such as customers, suppliers and employees in the success of the organisation. This means that mutually agreed objectives can result in each of the parties accepting long-term investment decisions and the occasional short-term economic sacrifice on the understanding that everyone can gain from organisational success. This contrasts with the typical British approach in which the only stakeholder group represented at board level is the senior managers, with a consequent risk of moving out of alignment with other stakeholder groups.

Defining the organisation's mission
Doyle (1998) states 'the major function of the **mission statement** should be to define the key stakeholders whom the corporation will seek to satisfy and, in broad terms, describe what strategy it will pursue to meet their objectives'. The aim is to ensure management evaluates their policies in the light of stakeholder expectations.

Creating the balanced scorecard
In order to translate strategic objectives into action, performance measures are required to provide an indication of progress towards goals. Traditionally the main performance indicators have been financial but the balanced scorecard approach (Kaplan, 1996) incorporates the interests of a broader range of stakeholders through performance measures across four perspectives.

- **Financial:** shareholder objectives.
- **Customer:** meeting customer needs.
- **Operational:** achieving on key levers, which driver performance excellence.
- **Internal:** meeting expectations and building up the capabilities of employees.

The idea of the scorecard is to provide managers with a multiple perspective of the goals that need to be met for organisational success.

Summary of key points

1. Operations management is about how organisations produce or deliver goods and services.
2. The output of service operations are intangible
3. The operations system can be seen as a transformation process, converting inputs into outputs in the form of goods and service.
4. The three main sub-systems or functional areas in a business are the operations, marketing and finance functions.
5. An alternative to the functional perspective is a process view in which the organisation is seen as consisting of a set of processes which link together to meet customer needs.
6. The organisation and thus the operations function will need to be aware and take appropriate account of a range of stakeholder needs.
7. The goal of the organisation should be to genuinely satisfy the needs of members (i.e. stakeholders) which are necessary for the success of the organisation in the long run.
8. The balanced scorecard approach incorporates the interests of a broad range of stakeholders through performance measures across different perspectives.

Exercises

1 Locate operations roles in job advertisements in the manufacturing and service sectors.
2 Identify the mix of goods and services in the following organisations:
   a) Fast food restaurant
   b) Hotel
   c) University
   d) Food retailer
   e) Car manufacturer
3 Identify the transformed and transforming resources for the organisations stated in Question 2.
4 What is the relationship between the operations and marketing functions?
5 Identify the stakeholders of an organisation with which you are familiar.

References

Brown, S., *Strategic Manufacturing for Competitive Advantage: Transforming Operations from Shop Floor to Strategy*, Prentice-Hall (1996).

Doyle, P., *Marketing Management and Strategy*, Second Ed., Prentice-Hall (1998).

Kaplan, R.S. and Norton, D.P., Using the balanced scorecard as a strategic measurement system, *Harvard Business Review*, (Jan–Feb 1996).

Porter, M.E. and Millar, V.E., How information gives you competitive advantage, *Harvard Business Review*, (Jul–Aug 1985) pp. 149–160.

Rosen, L.D., Service: manufacturing's new frontier, *National Productivity Review*, 16, No. 4, (Autumn 1998) pp. 1–3.

Slack, N., Chambers, S., Harland, C., Harrison, A. and Johnston, R., *Operations Management*, 2nd Ed., Pitman Publishing, London (1998).

Wilson, R.M.S. and Chau, W.F., *Managerial Accounting: Method and Meaning*, 2nd Ed., Chapman & Hall, London. (1985).

Further Reading

Hope, C. and Mühlemann, A., *Service Operations Management: Strategy, Design and Delivery*, Prentice-Hall (1997).

Krajewski, L. and Ritzman, L.P., *Operations Management: Strategy and Analysis*, 2nd Ed., Addison-Wesley (1990).

Steadman, M., Albright, T. and Dunn, K., Stakeholder group interest in the new manufacturing environment, *Managerial Auditing Journal*, 11, 2, (1996) pp. 4–9.

Vonderembse, M.A. and White, G.P., *Operations Management: Concepts, Methods and Strategies*, 2nd Ed., West Publishing (1991).

Waters, D., *Operations Management: Producing Goods and Services*, Addison-Wesley. (1996).

2 Facility design

Objectives

By the end of this chapter you should be able to:

- identify the three main issues involved in facility design;
- understand the concept of vertical integration;
- understand the concept of strategic alliances;
- relate the factors involved in a facility location decision;
- undertake qualitative techniques for location selection;
- understand issues of volume and timing in long-term capacity planning decisions;
- understand the impact of globalisation on facility location decisions;
- understand the impact of the virtual organisation on facility design.

In this book facility design is taken in a broad sense to mean the decisions surrounding how capacity will be supplied by the organisation to meet market demand. This may be achieved internally by the organisation by the construction of facilities or externally by agreement with suppliers. There are three main issues involved in decisions regarding this area:

1. **Vertical integration** – how will the capacity be supplied? This will address the topic of vertical integration; which is deciding what activities the organisation should undertake internally and what should be subcontracted to other agencies. The strategy of sharing activities with other organisations through strategic alliances will also be discussed.
2. **Facility location** – where will the capacity be located? This covers the question of the geographical location of capacity supplied by the organisation.
3. **Long-term capacity planning** – how much capacity should be supplied? This covers the question of how much long-term capacity should be supplied by the organisation.

The issue of how large organisations can supply goods and services to many countries competitively has been affected by increasing competitiveness and developments in transportation networks and telecommunications technology. These issues are discussed in the sections on globalisation and the virtual organisation.

Vertical integration

Vertical integration is the extent of activities the organisation is involved in from raw materials to delivery of the goods/services to the customer. These activities are termed the **supply chain** which is shown in Figure 2.1

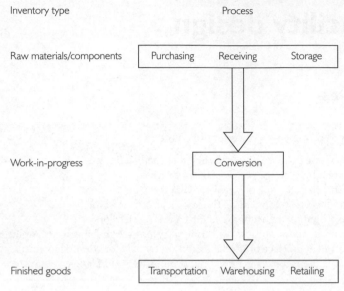

Figure 2.1 The supply chain

Few organisations will be fully vertically integrated (i.e. do everything from extract raw materials, to the process of transformation into goods, to the distribution and sales to the customer) but the amount of vertical integration should be dependent on the competitive priorities of the organisation. Note that a firm can either vertically integrate backwards to take control of its inputs provided by suppliers or vertically integrate forwards to take control of the delivery of the goods to the customer. Figure 2.2 shows backward and forward integration for an assembly maker.

The effects of vertical integration can be measured against the operations performance objectives of quality, speed, dependability, flexibility and cost (Slack, 1995).

- **Quality.** The advantage of vertical integration is that it is easier to conduct quality improvement programmes with an in-house function than an independent one. Against this is that the lack of a commercial relationship may mean there is a lack of incentive to improve performance.
- **Speed.** Delivery speed can be improved by better co-ordination and control of schedules. However there can be a tendency to give priority to outside customers for components that may be needed in-house (and eventually by other outside customers).
- **Dependability.** Close communication in a vertically integrated structure should allow better forecasts and thus more accurate delivery promises. Again the problem of supply to outside customers and consequent disruption to a scheduled supply, may occur.
- **Flexibility.** Vertical Integration allows new products to be developed specifically to customer needs while being in control of the component or even raw material elements of the product. Against this is a potential loss of focus on core competencies (e.g. assembly) if the organisation has to deal with issues across the supply chain. Vertical integration ownership should facilitate volume and delivery flexibility although there may be a reluctance to change volumes to in-house suppliers, rather than with an independent company.

- **Cost.** Costs can be reduced in a vertically integrated structure by savings on bought-in parts and services by integrating all aspects of the supply chain together. However there is the problem of high exposure as demand increases and the potential for loss of focus on core competencies.

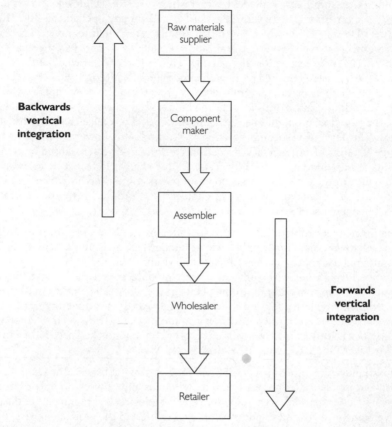

Figure 2.2 Backwards and forwards vertical integration for an assembler

Strategic alliances

In recent years the issue of vertical integration has become less important in many firms who have formed strategic alliances instead of the outright ownership of supply chain activities. Strategic alliances can take a number of forms including joint ventures, franchising agreements and buyer/seller relationships such as those practised in just-in-time production systems. Alliances should be on a long-term basis and be of benefit to both parties so an atmosphere of mutual trust can be fostered. An ideal alliance should allow an organisation to concentrate on core activities and enable a transfer of learning between the parties. Alliances are particularly common in research and development activities, which may be particularly expensive, and so collaboration allows costs to be shared. In fact the need for constant innovation and the requirement to quickly bring new designs to market is one of the reasons behind the increase in the number of strategic alliances.

CASE STUDY

Vertical integration in the car industry

Examining the car industry provides an interesting case study of developments in vertical integration strategies. In 1927 the Ford Car Company opened the River Rouge plant (near Detroit, USA) which was nearly totally vertically integrated. Rubber, silicon and iron ore flowed in one end and Model T cars flowed out the other end (Krafcik 1988). The main reason for this was that Henry Ford, who owned and ran every aspect of the business, required parts with close tolerances to tight delivery schedules and he thought that relying on arm's length purchases in the open market would be fraught with difficulties. Ford's idea, termed mass production, was that by making a standard product at high volume, he could dramatically reduce the unit cost of the product. This level of vertical integration led to problems however, which included the large amount of bureaucracy needed to co-ordinate the centralised system, the problems of shipping large goods (i.e. cars) around the world from one location, and government import trade barriers stopping exports to markets in which he did not manufacture. This led Ford to design, engineer and produce his parts centrally in Detroit but then assemble them in remote locations (Womack, 1990).

In time however a problem arose with the different needs of customers in different countries that were all being supplied with a standard product. In particular the Europeans required a smaller car than did the Americans. This led in the early 1930s to further decentralisation with fully integrated manufacturing facilities in England, Germany and France in addition to the plants in the USA. The world's mass production assembler ended up adopting widely varying degrees of formal integration ranging from about 25% in-house production at some specialist firms such as Porsche and Saab, to about 70% at General Motors (GM). The amount at Ford, fell from near 100% at River Rouge to about 50% after World War II.

The next innovation came in the 1950s when Toyota established a new approach to components supply under the lean production philosophy. Toyota organised suppliers into tiers; first tier suppliers were responsible for working as an integral part of the product development team, and second tier suppliers fabricated the individual parts. Rather than vertically integrate its suppliers into a single large bureaucracy it created a network of quasi-independent companies in which it holds a minority of the equity, sometimes providing loans to finance new machinery and sharing personnel to disseminate knowledge. The idea is to create a 'lean' supply chain in which long-term partnerships are formed. The issue of 'make-or-buy' in traditionally vertically integrated firms becomes one of assembler and suppliers working together to reduce costs and improve quality, whatever formal legal relationship they may have (Womack, 1990).

Source: Excerpted with permission of Rawson Associates/Scribner, a division of Simon & Schuster Inc., from *The Machine that Changed the World* by James P. Womack, Daniel T. Jones and Daniel Roos. Copyright © 1990 by James P. Womack, Daniel T. Jones, Daniel Roos and Dana Sammons Carponter.

Facility location

The location decision

The organisation's strategy will need to address the issue of facility location. This must be considered in terms of the need to serve customer markets effectively and to meet long-range demand forecasts. The issues can be considered in terms of the competition and cost of the location decision and the size of the facility.

- **Competition.** A company's competitiveness will be affected by its locations as it will impact on costs such as for transportation and labour. In service operations when the facility may not only produce the good but also deliver it to the customer from the facility, the convenience of the location for the customer is vital.
- **Cost.** A location decision is costly and time consuming to change. The costs include the purchase of land and construction of buildings. An organisation may be located inappropriately due to a previous poor location decision and an unwillingness to face the costs of a subsequent relocation. A change in input costs, such as materials or labour, may also lead to a need to change location.
- **Size of facility.** In order to meet the long-term demand forecast it is necessary to consider the size of the facility. Within a medium term planning cycle the size of the facility will impose an upper limit on the organisation's capacity. Purchasing additional components from suppliers or subcontracting work can however increase this level. However these strategies may lead to higher costs and thus a loss of competitiveness. The ability to supplement capacity is most restricted in service operations when contact with the customer is required.

A procedure for making aggregate estimates of resource requirements can be made using a **resource requirements plan** (RRP), which is associated with operation planning and control systems such as **materials requirements planning** (MRP). This assists in planning resources such as machine capacity and work-force size, which will impact on the space required to meet forecast demand. To anticipate inaccuracies in the forecast of demand and ensure that sufficient capacity is available, the organisation may plan some reserve capacity or select a site that is suitable for expansion. To anticipate a fall in demand the building might be designed so that it could be converted to other uses if the market changes significantly. **Work measurement** techniques can be used to estimate the amount of worker-hours required and thus the work-force size needed for a specified capacity.

Location factors

The location decision can be considered in terms of factors that vary in such a way as to influence cost as location varies (supply-side factors) and factors that vary in such a way as to influence customer service as location varies (demand-side factors). The location decision can be seen as a trade-off between these factors. In service organisations a need for customer contact may mean that demand-side influences will dominate while in a mineral extraction company, for example, land costs may mean supply-side influences dominate.

Supply-side influences
Distribution costs
Distribution and transportation costs can be considerable, especially for a manufactu-

ring organisation that deals in tangible products. The sheer volume of the raw material involved in operations such as steel production means that a location decision will tend to favour areas near to raw materials. A manufacturer and seller of custom-built furniture however will need to be near potential customers. For service companies such as supermarkets and restaurants the need to be in market-oriented locations means that the cost of transportation of goods will not be a major factor in the location decision. Distribution across country borders means that a whole series of additional costs and delays must be taken into account, including import duties and delays in moving freight between different transportation methods (e.g. air, rail, truck, ocean). A site near to an airport or a rail link to an airport may be an important factor if delivery speed is important.

Labour costs
Labour costs have generally become less important as the proportion of direct labour cost in high volume manufacturing have fallen. What is becoming more important is the skills and flexibility of the labour force to adapt to new working methods and to engage in continuous improvement efforts. The wage rate of labour can be a factor in location decisions, especially when the service can be provided easily in alternative locations. Information technology companies involved in data entry can locate in alternative countries without the customer being aware.

Energy costs
Some manufacturing companies use large amounts of power to operate production processes. Thus energy costs and the availability of enough energy to meet forecast demand can be important factors in the location decision.

Site and construction costs
Both the cost of the land and the cost of purchasing materials and building a facility are directly related to the location decision. These costs should be considered together as relatively low-cost land may require substantial preparation to make it suitable for building development.

Intangible factors
There are also a number of factors that are not financial but may have an effect on the location decision. These include the potential for objections to development on environmental grounds, to local regulations regarding business developments and to the necessary quality of life in the area needed to attract skilled employees.

Demand-side influences
Labour skills
The need for a pool of skilled labour is becoming increasingly important. However it may be possible in some instances to use skilled labour from a remote location. e.g. the use of computer programmers in India for American software companies.

Location image
Retail outlets in particular will wish to locate in an area which 'fits' with the image they are trying to project. Often shopping districts will be associated with a particular type of retail outlet e.g. designer clothing.

Customer convenience

For many service organisations in particular the location of the facility must be convenient for the potential customer. This can range from restaurants where customers may be prepared to travel a short distance to hospitals where the speed of response is vital to the service.

Location selection

The location selection process consists of identifying a suitable region/country, identifying an appropriate area within that region and finally comparing and selecting a suitable site from that area. A number of techniques for location selection are described at the end of this chapter.

Long-term capacity planning

The level at which management sets the level of capacity (or the potential number of units the organisation can produce at any one time) is a key determinant of the competitiveness of the organisation. Capacity planning decisions need to take into account both the volume and timing of capacity increases or decreases.

Capacity volume

In determining the optimum capacity level the concept of economies of scale is considered. This classifies production costs as either fixed or variable. Thus as a facility is expanded and fixed costs remain the same the average cost of producing each unit will fall. However fixed costs are likely to be incurred as capacity is increased at what are called fixed cost 'breaks'. These may occur, for example, when new equipment is required to increase capacity further. Another factor is that at a certain capacity level for a particular location, diseconomies of scale (i.e. increased costs related to an increase in volume) may set in. These may include the transportation costs incurred in supplying a large geographical area from a single location and the complexity a large organisation may add to the communication and co-ordination problems.

Balancing capacity

Another factor to take into account is that the total capacity of any system is dependent on the stage with the smallest capacity, called the **bottleneck**. Thus in order for the system to operate at its most efficient it is necessary to equalise the capacity between production stages. The capacity of subsequent stages can be visualised as a series of pipes of varying capacity, with the smallest pipe limiting the capacity of the whole system (Figure 2.3).

Figure 2.3 Visualising capacity

In Figure 2.3 the total capacity of the system is limited by the capacity at stage 2. One measure that can be used to assess the balance of the system is the **cycle efficiency** where:

Cycle efficiency = 100% − Percentage idle time
Percentage idle time = Idle time per cycle/Total cycle time

The cycle time is a measure of the time between production of each unit, and is related to output as follows:

Cycle time = 1/Output rate

Thus for a output rate of 30 products an hour the cycle time is 2 minutes.

Capacity timing

There are two major strategies for the timing of capacity changes to meet market demand:

- *Capacity leads demand.* Here the organisation ensures that there is sufficient capacity to meet demand, ensuring revenue is maximised and thus insuring that the organisation is in a position to supply increases in market demand. This strategy also ensures that demand from customers can always be met. The problem with this strategy is that the capacity utilisation will be relatively low and return on investment in plant may be delayed.
- *Capacity lags demand.* This strategy ensures that capacity is adjusted to meet demand, but not to exceed it. This ensures that utilisation is high, minimising unit costs and ensuring that return on investment in plant is secured as soon as possible. The disadvantage of this strategy is that revenue is not maximised if demand exceeds supply and customer service will suffer as the product cannot be supplied.

Most organisations will follow a strategy between capacity leading and capacity lagging. In manufacturing organisations capacity utilisation can be maximised by producing **inventory** when demand is lower than supply in order that inventory can be used to supplement capacity when demand exceeds supply. This in effect smoothes demand fluctuations, but has the disadvantage of the costs of holding inventory and even of inventory becoming obsolete.

Globalisation

Facility design decisions may often be taken in the context of the integrated global strategy of an organisation. This section describes the development of **multinational organisations** into global companies and provides guidelines for the implementation of a global organisation. The main strategy of the multinational corporation was either market or resource led. One strategy was to enter a new market in which it had a product advantage and then keep barriers to entry high for competitors. The operations strategy was then aligned to fit the strategic advantage on which the firm would compete. The other strategy was based on either the exploitation of a countries' natural resource or its use as a source of cheap labour.

The main difference between multinationals and globalised firms is that the global firm is organised into a network. This means that operations at several locations could perform tasks for a given customer group and/or a single facility could perform a task for several downstream groups. Networks can improve delivery and cost performance relative to fixed supply facilities because the network can pool demand and increase volume to reduce cost and choose different facilities to provide product for a given customer under different conditions.

The use of a network should lead to a more robust system that avoids capacity bottlenecks through the use of close co-ordination facilitated by the use of communications technology. The global organisation will attempt to extend and co-ordinate internal operations to create new value through a consolidation of manufacturing, reduced delivery costs and economies of scale. The aim is to create an international network of operations which will sell the same products in several countries, increase overall sales thereby reducing the cost per unit of development, co-ordinate the work of subsidiaries to provide a product/service to the global customer and shift production in response to exchange rate fluctuations

To achieve the global firm the operations function will require the use of cross-functional continuous improvement teams (Chapter 11) extended in a continuous improvement programme across countries. An international network also requires an improvement of global supply chain performance which co-ordinates the location and capacity of plants as well as the purchasing function. The improvements will aim to secure economies of scale and scope by using a global supply chain to reduce unit costs through lower transportation expenses.

The use of global alliances across continents will lead to competition between combined groups of firms to compete across a global marketplace. Because of the many and complex nature of alliances between organisations it is increasingly difficult to determine the national identity of a product. Indeed global competition is increasingly about competition between global alliances of organisations rather than competition between nationally based companies.

Strategy for globalisation

McGrath and Hoole (1992) provide three general guidelines for the move from a multinational to a globally integrated manufacturing organisation.

Affirm a global manufacturing mission
This requires that the manufacturing strategy supports the company's global business strategy and is consistent across all facilities. A study of the manufacturing infrastructure in the context of a world-wide business strategy can provide a foundation for a meaningful manufacturing mission. Senior management must then publicly declare its commitment to global integration outlining the mission to employees, customers and suppliers.

Develop a profile of capabilities
Managers need to have a realistic idea of the company's current strength and weaknesses in order to assess what capabilities the companies require and to provide a focus for a plan of action. Capabilities crucial to creating an integrated organisation include telecommunications technology such as e-mail and electronic data interchange (EDI) which is compatible across the organisation. A universal set of management practices and

measurement systems is also crucial to communication. Once global communication skills have been developed, issues such as rationalisation of output can be taken on a global basis rather than considering single plants in isolation. For plants undertaking similar operations in different locations, performance should be measured and benchmarks of best practice developed. Knowledge should then be transferred between plants in order to increase overall performance.

Identify options, pick a plan of action, and target specific results
Implementation of a global integration strategy may involve closure of plants, re-deployment of resources and re-engineering of critical processes. It is important that the company targets and achieves specific results quickly in order to build momentum for the achievement of long term goals.

    CASE STUDY
The 'networked' firm: Asea Brown Boveri (ABB)

Tom Peters (1992) argues for a move away from large organisations to small to medium sized units that are able to respond to the ever-increasing variety of products demanded by consumers world-wide. The growth of the service sector and the service component of manufacturing means that employee initiative and imagination in meeting customer needs are paramount. Peters argues these forces can only be released by a radical decentralisation of the corporate structure first.

Firms will achieve global reach not through the formal multinational structure but through the use of an informal network, facilitated by telecommunications technology, providing scale power without vertical integration. Asea Brown Boveri (ABB) is cited as a global manufacturing company attempting to combine the advantages of a global organisation with the flexibility and innovation possible from small localised units.

ABB was created in 1987 through the merger of the Swedish firm Asea and the Swiss firm Brown Boveri. Since then it has acquired or taken a minority position in 60 companies representing investments worth $6 billion. In 1991 ABB grossed $28.9 billion revenue across 140 countries and employed 240,000 people world-wide (Taylor, 1991). The company operates in eight business segments: Power Plants, Power Transmission, Power Distribution, Industry, Transportation, Environmental Control, Financial Services and Various Activities (e.g. robotics).

It has undergone a radical restructuring programme under the leadership of Percy Barnevik. He sees the company has having three internal contradictions.

'We want to be global and local, big and small, radically decentralised with centralised reporting and control. If we resolve these contradictions, we create real organisational advantage.' Taylor (1991)

This is to be achieved through the framework of a matrix structure that is designed to enable businesses to be optimised on a global scale and maximise performance in each market location.

Matrix structure

Along one dimension of the matrix the company is a distributed global network. Business area leaders around the world make decisions on product strategy and performance without regard for national borders. Along a second dimension country managers run a traditionally organised national company, serving its home markets as effectively as possible. Each national company is divided into profit centres of approximately 50 personnel that are accountable to their own profit and loss account and serve external customers directly. Each profit centre manager reports to both the business area and country manager who in turn refer to the executive committee of 13 who decide global strategy and performance. Thus there are only three layers of management in total.

Scale economics

Most business area teams are pursuing economies of scale, but mostly learning scale, not production scale.

'We are not a global business, we are a collection of local businesses with intense global co-ordination. This makes us unique. We want our local companies to think small, to worry about their home market and a handful of export markets, and to learn to make money on smaller volumes.' Sune Karlsson, Business Area Manager, Power Transformers, Taylor (1991)

ABB's global scale ($500 million spent on raw materials each year) allows it to leverage suppliers on price, quality and delivery schedules, with strategic purchasing a priority. But Karlsson believes these 'hard' advantages may be less than the advantages of global co-ordination:

'Our most important strength is that we have 25 factories around the world, each with its own president, design manager, marketing manager and production manager. These people are working on the same problems and opportunities day after day, year after year, and learning a tremendous amount. We want to create a process of continuous expertise transfer. If we do, that's a source of advantage none of our rivals can match.'

Decentralisation

To ensure real responsibility within the organisation the 240,000 employees are organised into small legally separate companies with their own profit and loss accounts. To ensure the advantages of size are retained the company is simultaneously monitored by the 13 member executive committee which are each responsible for business segments, countries and staff functions. To achieve this a management information system collates monthly performance figures for all 4,500 profit centres which is used to monitor trends and provide feedback to local managers.

The virtual organisation

The need for innovation and flexibility in the marketplace has made some organisations consider reducing the amount of vertical integration and focusing on their core skills or core competencies. This move has been facilitated by improvements in transportation networks and especially communication technologies. The idea is that the key to successful organisations is the ability to generate and share knowledge both internally and externally among a network of partner organisations. The term 'virtual' organisation refers to the use of **information technology** (IT) to blur organisational boundaries in the production of goods and services.

Peters (1992) suggests that success is not just dependent on the size of the organisation in terms of its level of vertical integration, but proportional to the knowledge and ability to use knowledge. This is a function of:

- the reach of the firm's network;
- the density of the network in terms of the variety of partners and intensity of relationships;
- the network's flexibility and skill at quickly reconfiguring.

Examples of IT which facilitates this process are:

EDI

Electronic data interchange (EDI) is the electronic transfer of formal business transactions in a standard format between organisations. The fact that the information is structured enables it to be used more powerfully than free-format electronic communication such as e-mail. EDI takes its form in four areas of business.

- Electronic funds transfer – EFTPOS, banking clearing
- Trade data exchange – Purchase order, delivery advices, invoices
- Technical data interchange – technical drawings, scientific data
- Interactive query/response – travel bookings, customers' access.

The use of structured data enables information to be sent between computers internationally and actions taken on that data. For example, purchase orders can be sent automatically when the stock level for a certain part drops below a certain level. The supplier will then send the required parts and invoice the company automatically through the EDI system. Thus the main advantage of EDI can be seen in the reduced time for information exchange and increased accuracy of data. The benefits of EDI can be seen more strategically in that it can enable closer links with suppliers and forge establishment of long-term partnerships. These benefits will be proportional to the number of partners and the number of EDI documents exchanged between these partners. Any process between organisations, which relies on a paper format will inevitably slow the whole transaction cycle down. Thus all parties in the system must work together to ensure the highest usage of EDI possible and thus maximise the potential benefits.

EPOS / EFTPOS

EPOS (**electronic point-of-sale**) data capture allows the tracking of material movements and is extensively used to plan inventory replenishment schedules in retailer-operated warehouse facilities and to communicate inventory requirements to suppliers. The suppliers can then in turn use this information to plan production schedules and formulate their own component supply needs. EFTPOS (**electronic funds transfer at point-of-sale**) links transaction data with a customers' source of funds. This allows checking of customer credit during payment transactions and improves the suppliers' cash flow by reducing the payment time.

 CASE STUDY
Using EDI and EPOS systems

Food companies, such as supermarkets, have extremely efficient logistics systems that enable their stores to stock a huge variety of products. For example, Sainsbury's have a product line of 16,000 items and a single store may stock up to 9,000 of these. Boots the chemist has up to 40,000 items in their larger stores. They can only do this profitably by accurate information on the purchases of the customers and rapid delivery of stock, to keep stock as low as possible and still satisfy customer needs. Innovation in retail logistics has been an important agent in the development of logistics information systems for many other businesses. The development of bar-coding systems enables items, labelled with a product code, to have their details easily read by a scanner linked to a computer. For example, libraries have kept bar code information on books for many years. The development of Electronic Data Interchange (EDI) systems enables companies to exchange information electronically. Orders placed by the firm can be instantaneously received by the supplier (or within the few seconds it takes for electronic signals to travel along a telephone wire). These two systems together give us Electronic Point of Sale (EPOS) systems. EPOS enables the firm to have accurate up-to-date information on stock levels. This information is used to monitor in store stock levels at stores and is transmitted to district warehouses and suppliers. Loyalty cards, which contain personal customer data, enhance the system further by providing real-time market research that does not lie. In the past firms have had to rely on surveys to determine buying patterns. The increase of information has led to new concepts such as data warehousing, where vast quantities of data are stored then analysed according to business requirements. Customers benefit from greater availability of products, promotions based on their own interests and better reporting systems from the cash tills (such as targeted promotions). Retailers are now allowing customers to scan goods as they place them in the trolley. This speeds up the checkout process, allowing stores to reduce staff levels and customers are happy that they are not waiting in checkout queues.

Quantitative techniques for location selection
Locational cost-volume analysis

Locational cost-volume analysis will indicate when a particular location is superior for a particular volume level by analysing the mix of fixed and variable costs. Some costs such as the costs of building the facility will be fixed, while others such as the level of demand will vary with the location. The relationship between both of these factors will vary for each location being considered. The procedure for graphical cost-volume analysis is as follows (refer to Figure 2.4):

1. Determine the fixed and variable costs for each location.
2. Plot the total cost (i.e. fixed + variable) lines for the location alternatives on the graph.
3. Choose the location with the lowest total cost line at the expected volume level.

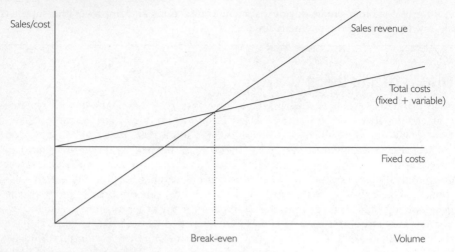

Figure 2.4 *Cost-volume graph*

The equation for expressing costs in terms of location is:

$$TC = VC \times X + FC$$

where:
TC = total cost
VC = variable cost per unit
X = number of units produced
FC = fixed costs

WORKED EXAMPLE

A manufacturing organisation is considering the following locations for its plant.

	Barcelona	*Madrid*
Variable costs	£1.75/unit	£1.25/unit
Annual fixed costs	£200,000	£180,000
Initial fixed costs	£1,400,000	£1,600,000

a) Draw a cost-volume graph for both locations over a 5-year period at a volume of 200,000 units per year.
b) Which location has the lowest cost?
c) At what volume do the locations have equal costs?

SOLUTION
a) Cost at year 0: Barcelona = 1,400,000; Madrid = 1,600,000.

Cost at year 5:
Barcelona = 1,400,000 + (5 × 200,000) + (5 × 200,000 × 1.75) = £4,150,000.

Madrid = 1,600,000 + (5 × 180,000) + (5 × 200,000 × 1.25) = £3,750,000.

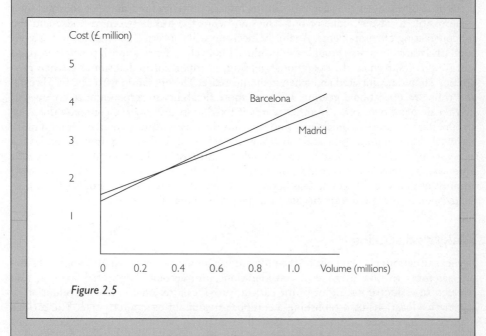

Figure 2.5

b) From the graph Madrid has the lowest costs after 5 years (1,000,000 units).
c) Let X equal the number of years until costs are equal. Then using subscript B for Barcelona and M for Madrid:

$TC_B = TC_M$

1,400,000 + 200,000X + (200,000 × 1.75)X = 1,600,000 + 180,000X + (200,000 × 1.25)X

1,600,000 – 1,400,000 + 180,000X – 200,000X + 250,000X – 350,000X = 0

200,000 – 120,000X = 0

X = 200,000/120,000 = 1.6 years

Volume = 200,000 × 1.6 = 320,000 units

This method has assumed that fixed costs are constant for the volume range when in fact step changes may occur in fixed cost expenditure to meet certain volume levels. Also variable costs are assumed to have a linear (straight-line) relationship with volume, when this may not be so. Some cost-volume models may incorporate a nonlinear (curved) relationship. Another assumption is that output of the facility has also been aggregated into one product that may not reflect the complexity of how a mix of products affects costs over a range of volumes.

If the analysis includes the economics of the logistics activity for a range of volumes then it is possible to review make-or-buy issues and thus the mix between in-house and the subcontracting of components. Again the decision will concern the relationship between fixed and variable costs through the product life cycle. The relationship between fixed and total costs, termed the operational gearing, is important in determining when production should be initiated and when it should cease. The operation with low fixed costs, and thus low operational gearing will have more flexibility in responding to changes in market demand over time. In other words if fixed costs are low the company does not require high volumes to break-even and can thus decrease output to match demand more easily. A high volume producer however invests in specialised equipment and thus increases operational gearing in order to reduce unit costs and thus create greater profit potential. Thereby an increase in volume for a high volume producer will only add a small amount of unit variable costs. This approach means the high volume producer will prefer to operate as close to capacity limits as possible to maximise profit.

Weighted scoring

In most situations cost will not be the only criteria for a location decision. Weighted scoring attempts to take a range of considerations into account. Weighted scoring, also referred to as **factor rating** or **point rating**, provides a rational basis for evaluation of alternative locations by establishing a composite value for each alternative. The ratings include factors based on qualitative as well as quantitative factors. The procedure consists of determining a list of factors that are relevant to the location decision. This may include convenience to customers, labour skills, transportation facilities etc. Each factor is then given a weighting that indicates its relative importance compared to the other factors. Each location is then scored on each factor and this score is multiplied by the factor value. The alternative with the highest score is then chosen. The usefulness of the method is dependent on identifying the appropriate location factors and devising a suitable weighting for each. One approach is to use the method to assess the intangible factors (e.g. quality of life) only and then determine if the difference between the intangible scores is worth the cost of the difference in tangible costs between the locations.

WORKED EXAMPLE

New Technologies Ltd. are an organisation that specialise in simulation modelling consultancy. They have identified three sites on the West Coast of the USA which have approximately equal initial and operating costs. The sites have been evaluated on a score of 1 to 10 (10 being best) against the following criteria and weighting assigned by management. Rank the three cities in order of their total weighted points score.

	Weighting	Los Angeles	Portland	Seattle
Pool of skilled system modellers	0.5	6	4	5
University research in modelling	0.3	3	5	3
Recreational and cultural activities	0.2	5	3	4

SOLUTION

Los Angeles = $(6 \times 0.5) + (3 \times 0.3) + (5 \times 0.2) = 4.9$

Seattle = $(5 \times 0.5) + (3 \times 0.3) + (4 \times 0.2) = 4.2$

Portland = $(4 \times 0.5) + (5 \times 0.3) + (3 \times 0.2) = 4.1$

The centre of gravity method

The centre of gravity method can be used to determine the location of a distribution centre by minimising distribution costs. This method assumes distribution costs change in a linear fashion with the distance and the quantity transported. The method also assumes the quantity transported is fixed for the duration of the journey. The relative co-ordinates of the distribution points are placed on a map and the location of the distribution point should be at the centre of gravity of the co-ordinates. To find this point the average of the x co-ordinates and y co-ordinates are found using the following equations.

$$\bar{x} = \sum x_i Q_i / \sum Qi$$

$$\bar{y} = \sum y_i Q_i / \sum Q_i$$

where:
Q_i = quantity to be transported to destination i
x_i = x co-ordinate of destination i
y_i = y co-ordinate of destination i
$\bar{x}$ = x co-ordinate of centre of gravity
$\bar{y}$ = y co-ordinate of centre of gravity

WORKED EXAMPLE

A manufacturing organisation wishes to build a centralised warehouse system which will serve a number of production facilities in Germany. The expected demand and relative grid references for the facility are given below.

Location	Demand (units/year)	Relative grid reference
Hamburg	40,000	(3,7)
Cologne	20,000	(1,4)
Stuttgart	35,000	(3,2)
Munich	70,000	(4,1)
Dresden	45,000	(6,5)
Berlin	110,000	(5,6)

At what location, in terms of grid reference, should the warehouse be situated?

SOLUTION

$\bar{x} = (3 \times 40,000) + (1 \times 20,000) + (3 \times 35,000) + (4 \times 70,000) + (6 \times 45,000) + (5 \times 110,000)/(40,000 + 20,000 + 35,000 + 70,000 + 45,000 + 110,000) = 4,2$

$\bar{y} = (7 \times 40,000) + (4 \times 20,000) + (2 \times 35,000) + (1 \times 70,000) + (5 \times 45,000) + (6 \times 110,000)/(40,000 + 20,000 + 35,000 + 70,000 + 45,000 + 110,000) = 4,3$

Quantitative decision making in transportation

Vehicle scheduling

Many quantitative models have been developed to help firms decide where to site warehouses and the design of them, as illustrated. One of the more complex issues is connected with vehicle scheduling. For example, how do we decide on the route of a delivery van to maximise the number of customers visited in a certain period? Whilst there are mathematical methods for the solution of this type of problem; other methods can be used that are more easily understood. For example, take the scenario illustrated in Figure 2.6a.

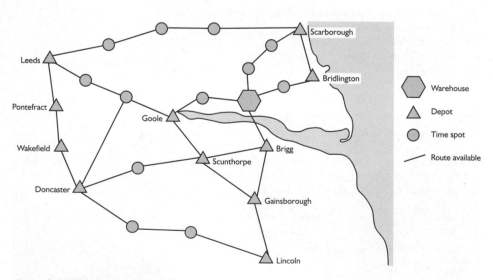

Figure 2.6a Vehicle routeing problem

We could apply a mathematical model, but one way to get a good quick answer would be to redraw the routes highlighting the depots joined by a nominal time. In this simple case, 30 minutes (Figure 2.6b).

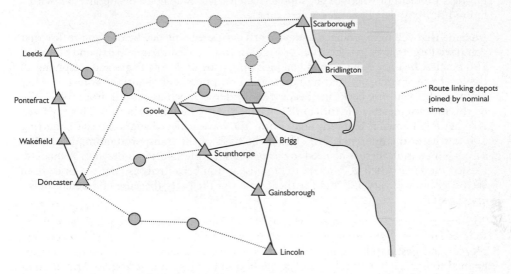

Figure 2.6b Vehicle routeing problem

All we need to do now is join up the ends of the three networks. In this case, it is not possible to visit all of the depots (Figure 2.6c).

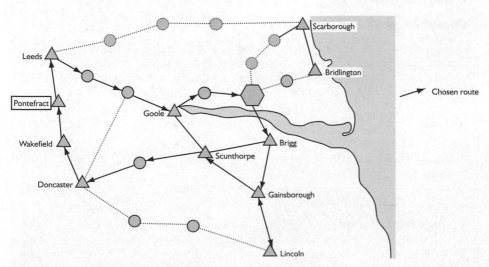

Figure 2.6c Vehicle routeing problem

Transportation models

Transportation models are a special form of **linear programme**. They address a common business problem of where to get supplies when there is a choice of suppliers all with a limited capacity. The basic idea is very simple.

Imagine that you have arranged a New Year's eve party. The day before, you realise that you have forgotten to get the wine. It is going to be a Champagne party and you need 100 bottles. Being a canny person you pick up a copy of Yellow Pages and telephone all the local wine merchants, getting information on prices and quantities available. After making a list you ring back the cheapest and order as much as you can from them. You do this for each merchant in turn until you have your required 100 bottles. This approach is sometimes known as a **greedy algorithm**. You have achieved your objective of getting 100 bottles at the minimum cost. This is the basis of the transportation model. In this simple illustration there is no need to create a model, the solution is obvious. A model is needed, however when you intend to organise a number of parties, and the price from each supplier will vary according to the location of the party (because of different delivery charges).

To solve transportation problems you need to know the capacity requirements of the sources and the destinations, and an estimation of the costs of transport between the sources and destinations. Once this data is available, a number of techniques can be applied to find a low-cost solution. The method to be illustrated is **Vogel's Approximation Method** (VAM), which can quickly generate low cost solutions. To illustrate the use of VAM we will extend the Champagne illustration as a worked example.

WORKED EXAMPLE

Vineyard problem

You are a wine producer with three vineyards in France, Italy and Romania. The vineyards supply, amongst other products, Champagne-style white wine to four main warehouses, in Germany, Spain, England and Denmark. The table shows the annual capacities of the vineyards and the demand at the warehouses.

Vineyards	Capacity (litres)	Warehouse	Demand
France	1,000	Denmark	450
Italy	750	Spain	600
Romania	500	England	350
		Germany	650
Total	2,250	Total	2,000

A transportation matrix, Figure 2.7, shows the transportation costs associated with each destination. The transportation matrix also includes a dummy column. This needs to be added because the total capacity of the vineyards is greater than the anticipated demand. The transportation costs for the dummy destinations are set to zero.

Source	Denmark	Spain	England	Germany	Dummy	Capacity	Row penalty
France	85	75	95	60	0	1000	
Italy	95	115	105	75	0	750	
Romania	125	135	110	85	00	500	
Demand	450	600	300	650	250	2,250	
Column penalty							

Figure 2.7   Transportation matrix – vineyard problem

In Vogel's Approximation Method, we evaluate the difference between the transportation costs between the various destinations and sources. The objective is to minimise the effect of large differences in costs and to choose the best source, to give the lowest cost for a particular destination.

SOLUTION

An individual buyer in Denmark would, if possible, buy all their supply from France; this could be to the detriment of the other parts of the company. We evaluate the best options by assigning a row and column penalty. The row penalty is the difference between the lowest and next lowest costs in that row. In the case of France this is 60 (60–0).

The column penalty is worked out in the same way, in the case of Denmark it is 10 (95–85). A row or column with a high penalty would be a high priority assignment, because if that option is not chosen then a much higher cost will be encountered. Figure 2.8 shows the penalties for the initial set-up of the transportation matrix.

Source	Denmark	Spain	England	Germany	Dummy	Capacity	Row penalty
France	85	75	95	60	0	1000	60
Italy	95	115	105	75	0	750	75
Romania	125	135	110	85	00 **250**	500	85
Supply	450	600	300	650	**250**	2,250	
Column penalty	10	40	10	15	0		

Figure 2.8   Row/column penalties and first assignment

Figure 2.8 also shows the first assignment of two hundred bottles of wine from the source with the highest penalty – Romania, to the destination with the lowest cost – Dummy. After each assignment we can delete the row or column, if that assignment has met the required demand or capacity.

Source	Denmark	Spain	England	Germany	Dummy	Capacity	Row penalty
France	85	75 ⟨600⟩	95	60	0̶	1000	6̶0̶, 15
Italy	95	115	105	75	0̶	750	7̶5̶, 20
Romania	125	135	110	85	0̶0̶ ⟨250⟩	5̶0̶0̶, 250	8̶5̶, 25
Supply	450	600	300	650	2̶5̶0̶		
Column penalty	10	40	10	15	0̶		

Figure 2.9   Row/column penalties and second assignment

Figure 2.9 shows that demand has been satisfied at the dummy destination, the dotted line indicates that we can now ignore this column. The totals are adjusted and new penalties calculated. We only need calculate the row penalties, as the column penalties remain unchanged. The largest this time is in the Spain column and we allocate 600 bottles from the French brewery.

Source	Denmark	Spain	England	Germany	Dummy	Capacity	Row penalty
France	85	7̶5̶ ⟨600⟩	95	60 ⟨400⟩	0̶	1̶0̶0̶0̶, 400	6̶0̶,1̶5̶, 25
Italy	95	1̶1̶5̶	105	75	0̶	750	7̶5̶,2̶0̶, 20
Romania	125	1̶3̶5̶	110	85	0̶0̶ ⟨250⟩	5̶0̶0̶, 250	8̶5̶,2̶5̶, 25
Supply	450	6̶0̶0̶	300	650	2̶5̶0̶		
Column penalty	10	4̶0̶	10	15	0̶		

Figure 2.10   Row/column penalties and third assignment

Figure 2.10 shows the third assignment and Figure 2.11 the final matrix. There is a tie between the penalties for Romania and France. In the case of a tie, the analyst can pick one at random. We have chosen France as this removes them from further consideration.

Source	Denmark	Spain	England	Germany	Dummy	Capacity	Row penalty
France	85	75	95	60	0	1000, 400	60, 15, 25
		600		400			
Italy	95	115	105	75	0	750, 300, 50	75, 20, 20, 20, 30
	450		50	250			
Romania	125	135	110	85	00	500, 250	85, 25, 25. 25, 25
			250		250		
Supply	450	600	300	650, 250	250		
Column penalty	10, 30	40	10, 5	15, 10	0		

Figure 2.11 Final matrix – vineyard problem

The cost of the final solution is:

$600 \times 75 + 400 \times 60 + 450 \times 95 + 50 \times 105 + 75 \times 250 + 110 \times 250 =$
£163,250

Summary of key points

- The three main issues in facility design are vertical integration, facility location and long-term capacity planning.
- The effects of vertical integration should be measured against the operations performance objectives
- Strategic alliances should be assessed as an alternative to a vertical integration strategy.
- Facility location factors can be considered as influencing cost as location varies (supply-side factors) and influencing customer service as location varies (demand-side factors).
- Quantitative techniques that can be used to assist in the facility location decision include cost-volume analysis, weighted scoring and the centre of gravity method.
- Long-term capacity planning decisions need to take into account both the volume and timing of capacity increases or decreases.
- Facility design decisions may be affected by globalisation strategies.
- The idea of the virtual organisation requires a re-assessment of facility design issues.

Exercises

1 For a retail outlet discuss the issues involved in deciding how capacity will be supplied, where capacity will be located and how much capacity should be supplied.
2 Discuss the advantages and disadvantages of a vertical integration strategy.
3 For an organisation with which you are familiar discuss the location decision in terms of supply-side influences and demand-side influences.
4 A manufacturing organisation is looking at the following two locations.
   a) Draw a cost-volume graph for both locations over a 10 year period at a volume of 750,000 units per year.
   b) Which location has the lowest cost at the end of the 10 year period?
   c) At what volume do these locations have equal costs?

	Birmingham	Manchester
Variable costs	£14/unit	£16/unit
Annual fixed costs	£12,000,000	£11,000,000
Initial fixed costs	£165,000,000	£145,000,000

5 The following table lists the weightings representing the relative importance of factors for the location of a retail site. Four potential sites have been given a score out of 100 for each factor. Rank the four sites in order of their total weighted points score for suitability for the proposed location.

		Site			
Factor	Weight	A	B	C	D
Construction cost	0.1	90	60	80	70
Operating cost	0.1	90	80	90	85
Population density	0.4	70	90	80	75
Convenient access	0.2	75	80	90	90
Parking area	0.2	60	70	85	75

6 A retail chain has four major stores in the East Midlands area which have monthly demands rates as listed. The following map shows the relative co-ordinates of the four outlets. The organisation has decided to find a 'central' location in which to build a warehouse. Find the co-ordinates of the centre that will minimise distribution costs.

Store location	Monthly demand (units)
Derby	2000
Nottingham	1000
Leicester	1000
Sheffield	2000

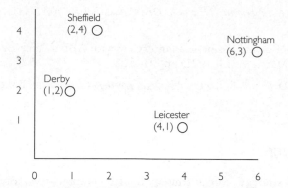

Figure Ex. 2.1

7 The following information provides the specification for a line process.
a) What is the total system capacity?
b) Which stage is the bottleneck?
c) What is the level that system capacity can be increased to by increasing the bottleneck capacity only?
d) Calculate the current cycle efficiency.
e) Calculate the cycle efficiency when the bottleneck capacity is increased as in (c).

Figure Ex. 2.2

Stage	Capacity (units/hr)
A	120
B	140
C	110
D	150

8 Outline how a strategy of globalisation will impact on a policy of pursuing economies of scale advantages.
9 Describe how an organisation with which you are familiar with could move towards the concept of becoming a virtual organisation.

References

Krafcik, J.F., Triumph of the lean production system, *Sloan Management Review*, (Fall, 1988) pp. 41–52.

McGrath, M.E. and Hoole, R.W., Manufacturing's new economics of scale, *Harvard Business Review*, (May–June 1992).

Peters, T., *Liberation Management: Necessary Disorganisation for the Nanosecond Nineties*, Macmillan (1992).

Taylor, W., The logic of global business: an interview with ABB's Percy Barnevik, *Harvard Business Review*, (March–April, 1991) pp. 91–105.

Womack, J.P., Jones, D.T. and Roos, D., *The Machine that Changed the World*, Macmillan (1990).

Further reading

Egelhoff, W.G., Great strategy or great strategy implementation – two ways of competing in global markets, *Sloan Management Review*, (Winter, 1993) pp. 37–50.

Elgar, T. and Smith, C., *Global Japanization: The Transnational Transformation of the Labour Process*, Routledge (1994).

Flaherty, M.T., *Global Operations Management*, McGraw-Hill (1996).

Lei, D. and Slocum, J.W., Global strategy, competence building and strategic alliances, *California Management Review*, (Fall, 1992) pp. 81–97.

Mair, A., *Honda's Global Local Corporation*, Macmillan (1994).

Murray, E.A. and Mahon, J.F., Strategic alliances: gateway to the new Europe? *Long Range Planning*, **26**, 4, (1993) pp. 102–111.

Ohmae, K., Managing in a borderless world, *Harvard Business Review*, (May–June 1989).

Porter, M.E., The competitive advantage of nations, *Harvard Business Review*, (March–April, 1990) pp. 73–93

Susaki, T., What the Japanese have learned from strategic alliances, *Long Range Planning*, **26**, 6, (1993) pp. 41–53.

3 Process design

Objectives

By the end of this chapter, you should be able to:

- understand what operations managers mean by processes in manufacturing and service operations;
- be familiar with the links between product and process design;
- understand how process types are determined by a combination of work organisation and facility arrangement;
- identify the main characteristics of the conventional process types;
- appreciate the benefits and drawbacks of the conventional process types;
- understand how trade-offs can be used to manage the constraints associated with conventional processes;
- be aware of the way in which cellular organisations exhibit the beneficial features of conventional processes while having fewer of their drawbacks;
- understand how technology can be used to improve the efficiency of processes;
- appreciate the main purpose and features of process re-engineering.

What are processes?

When engineers refer to 'processes' they are usually talking about the specific technologies for changing the shape or form of materials or assembling component parts into finished products. These are what are usually called 'manufacturing processes'. They include casting, forging, cutting, grinding, pressing and welding as well as more recently developed processes such as electrochemical machining, surface mount technology for electronic components etc. (Ostwald and Muñoz, 1997).

To the operations manager there is another meaning to the word 'processes'. Instead of referring to the specific technological means of converting or assembling materials they mean the wider system or arrangement of physical facilities and human resources for transforming materials into finished products or providing services. Rather than examining the technologies themselves, operations managers are therefore concerned with the organisation of the equipment and personnel in implementing that technology, the management systems used in its operation, major operations strategies and policies and common problems (decisions) confronted in manufacturing and service organisations (Fogarty *et al.*, 1989).

Under this use of the term there are, relatively, far fewer 'process types' compared with the engineers' perspective. As we will see later the number of process types is typically fewer than five or six, depending on the particular typology being adopted. Moreover, process choice is not based on technical or engineering criteria but on factors relating to volume and variety of products demanded by the market.

Processes in manufacturing and service operations

Operations management is concerned both with the manufacture of goods and the provision of services. Equally, processes are relevant in both manufacturing and service delivery systems. Clearly the technologies for delivering services are quite different from those used in manufacturing, however, there is an argument that the typology used in operations management for classifying process types can be equally appropriate to both. Hill, for example suggests that there are five process types which he calls:

- project
- jobbing
- batch
- line
- continuous.

Although these are derived from manufacturing concepts he argues that they are also appropriate to service operations and gives examples from both sectors to illustrate the point (Hill, 1991).

While many writers, like Hill, refer to only one typology, regardless of context, others recognise the distinction between manufacturing and service. For example, Slack and colleagues use a similar means to Hill for classifying manufacturing processes but for services they identify different process types (Slack, et al., 1995). They state there is less consensus on the terms of the process types for services but propose three that follow a similar sequence in terms of volume and variety. These they call:

- professional services
- service shops
- mass services.

The links between product and process design

It is rare for processes to be designed in isolation of the products or services they are intended to manufacture or deliver. Sometimes there may be uncertainty about the precise nature of a product and its demand, as for example with general subcontracting. However, even in such cases as these there will be a general assumption made concerning the nature and range of products that are likely to be required and the expected demand quantities. A process would then be designed that has much greater flexibility than one intended for products which are well-known with a predictable and stable demand.

In practice, therefore, there is a close link between product and process design, the management of which has been identified by many authors as a key to achieving greater competitiveness. There are essentially three links, the first is between the changes made to product and process as part of development projects. The second is between the stages of the product and process life cycle. The third is between the nature of product demand and process type.

Product and process changes

To illustrate the first link Hayes et al. have identified different kinds of development project against the degree of product and process change involved (Hayes et al., 1998). The relationships are shown in Figure 3.1.

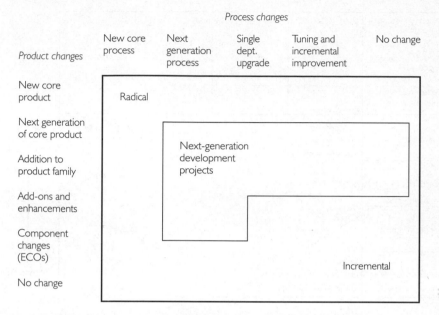

Figure 3.1 Range of product and process development combinations (Hayes, Wheelwright and Clark, 1988)

Product changes and process changes are shown along each axis of the diagram. Each have been classified according to their type on an incremental scale. A project designed to create a whole new market or industry based on its own production technology (such as genetic engineering) would fall into the upper left-hand corner of the figure, i.e. where there is the simultaneous development of a new core product and a new core process. A small incremental change to an existing product or process, something that could be implemented through a routine engineering change order, would fall in the lower right hand corner. It is the major 'next generation' projects, those that fall in the shaded area, that consume the bulk of resources spent on product and process development at the business unit level and which can have significant competitive leverage.

Product and process life cycles

The link between product and process life cycles has been identified by Hayes and Wheel-wright (1984) and has more recently been revisited by Noori and Radford (1995). It is illustrated in Figure 3.2.

The matrix suggests that as the product progresses through its life cycle from introduction to maturity and decline, the process that best suits the needs of the firm also goes through similar stages. Thus the so-called 'job shop' process is appropriate during a product's introductory stage, when production volumes are low and the product is often customised. As the product progresses through the growth and maturity stages it becomes more standardised and the production volumes increase. The job shop is then replaced by intermittent, and then repetitive, batch production. Continuous flow processes take over as the product becomes a commodity and the competitive focus shifts to price. Thus the diagonal of the product/process life cycle matrix, sometimes called the 'product possibility frontier' represents the best set of product/process combinations.

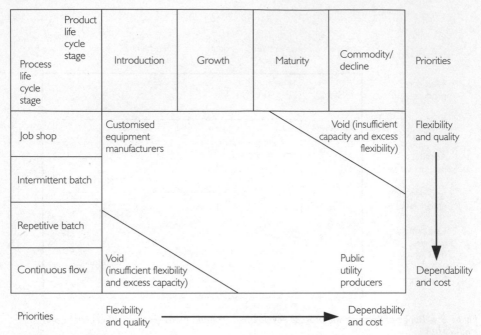

Figure 3.2 The product/process life cycle matrix (adapted from Noori and Radford, 1995 Product and Operations Management: Total Quality and Responsiveness. Reproduced by permission of The McGraw-Hill Companies)

Two types of organisation are shown on the diagonal to illustrate the two extremes. The first, shown in the top left-hand corner, is a customised equipment manufacturer (such as a specialised machine tool company) for which every product is unique and can be representative of the introductory stage of the product life cycle. In this type of organisation an early life cycle 'job shop' process would be commonly used where the priorities both for the product and process would be flexibility and quality. The second example, shown in the bottom right-hand corner, is a public utility producer (such as an electric power company) for which the product has gone beyond the maturity stage and become a commodity. In this type of organisation a late life cycle 'continuous flow' process would be commonly used where priorities both for the product and process would be dependability and cost.

Product demand and process type

Before considering the different process types in relation to the nature of product demand it is first relevant to consider how processes are characterised in terms of the resources employed in the transformation of materials.

Previously in this chapter the idea of process typologies was introduced and several have already been mentioned such as the classification of Hill and of Slack and colleagues (Hill, 1991; Slack *et al.*, 1995). However, the underlying basis of these typologies is often unexplained and taken for granted. By analysing the resources used in the physical transformation system an understanding can be provided of the rationale behind the typologies as well as helping to explain the features of the different process types.

The transformation system is that part of the total production system which is necessary to physically transform materials into finished products (or indeed to deliver services). So, in manufacturing it comprises all the machines, tools and equipment needed to cut, mould, assemble, inspect, move and store all the direct materials and consumables used in the production process. In service provision there will similarly be equipment and devices used, for example, to transport, treat, process, inform or entertain customers (or their property/organisation). Together these items can be referred to as the physical facilities. Apart from the **physical facilities** there are, of course, all the people needed to set, operate and maintain the machines, move the material, inspect the products etc. These can be called the **human resources** (Bennett and Forrester, 1993).

Thus, process types can be characterised by:

1. Organisation of work (the way the human resources are organised), and
2. The choice and arrangement of the physical facilities.

In the past, much of the effort to enhance the performance of production processes has been directed towards planning and control. The result has been the development of a plethora of techniques and software packages aimed at improving capacity planning, work scheduling, inventory control, etc. However, many of the weaknesses associated with a production process are a result of the limitations in the underlying transformation system and any benefit to be derived from implementing better control systems will be determined by the inherent constraints on material flow efficiency imposed by the choice of work organisation or arrangement of physical facilities. By directing attention towards the less fashionable, but perhaps more important, question of the design of transformation systems many of the constraints on improving planning and control can be removed.

Process types – the organisational options

It was stated previously that there were two broad parameters that characterise a type of process:

● the physical facilities
● the human resources.

So an examination of the choices open to the designers of processes can be carried out within these two broad parameters. Taking first the human resources. Based on, and extending, the ideas of Hayes and Schmenner work organisation can take one of three forms (Hayes and Schmenner, 1978). It can be:

● product orientated
● process orientated
● task orientated.

Product-orientated work organisation
This is based on the idea of a worker or team performing all the work elements required to manufacture a product. The work elements are performed as a set, though not necessarily together nor in a particular order. It is represented conceptually in Figure 3.3. It might be speculated that this was the original way in which workers organised

themselves. Its attraction lies in the fact that it does not necessarily require the preparation of formal production plans. Individuals or groups can work independently and different products can be manufactured in parallel. However it does not make the most efficient use of resources and workers do not have the opportunity of becoming specialised.

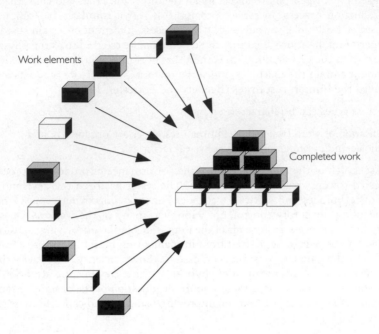

Figure 3.3 Product-orientated work organisation

Process-orientated organisation

This is a means of enabling some specialisation to be achieved. It does this by enabling similar operations to be performed repeatedly on a whole range of components and products and thereby exploits the principle of division of labour. However, it requires more planning and co-ordination. Figure 3.4 illustrates the general concept.

Task-orientated organisation

This takes the idea of specialisation to its logical conclusion. It involves repeatedly carrying out small work tasks on part-completed components and products which are manufactured continuously as represented in Figure 3.5. Task-orientated work organisation requires a considerable amount of planning but the economies of scale can be considerable.

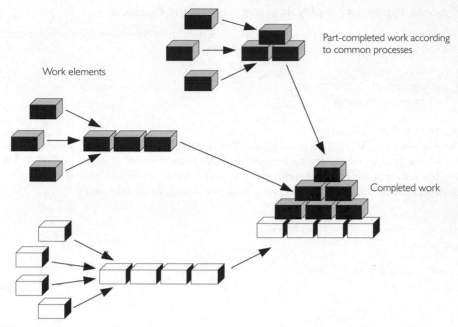

Work elements

Part-completed work according to common processes

Completed work

Figure 3.4 Process-orientated work organisation

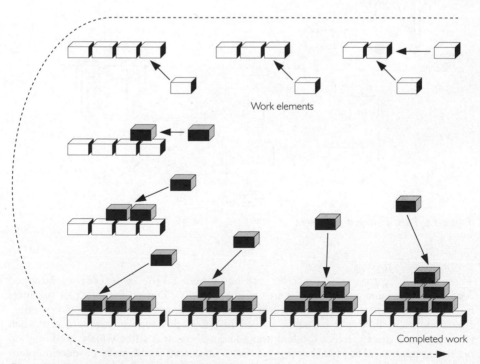

Work elements

Completed work

Figure 3.5 Task-orientated work organisation

Process types – the physical arrangement options

Considering now the arrangement of facilities. Again there are three alternative options which this time can be attributed to Wild (1990). These are:

- by fixed position
- by function
- by operation sequence.

Fixed position arrangements

These are where the product remains stationary and all the productive resources (materials, equipment, labour etc.) are brought to the place of work as shown in Figure 3.6. By their nature some products naturally need to be manufactured in a fixed position but for others this arrangement represents just one of the available options.

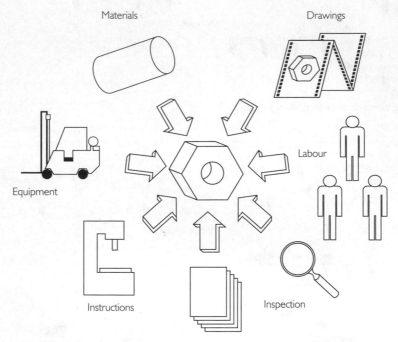

Figure 3.6 Fixed position arrangement

Arrangements by function

These are where machines, processes and equipment of the same type are grouped together in the same department or area as in Figure 3.7. During manufacture products move from one department to another according to the operations required. In the industrial revolution there was probably a need to adopt this type of arrangement when machines were driven from a single power source. Today it is still a widely used method of arranging physical facilities but it gives rise to numerous problems of production planning and control.

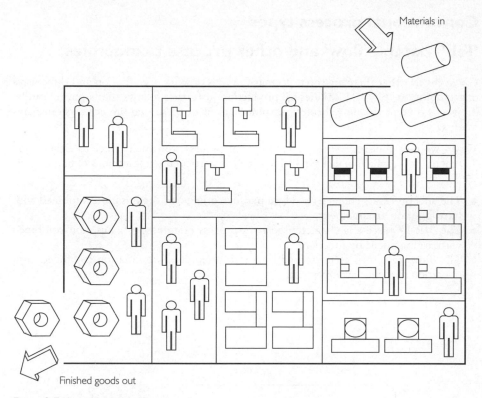

Figure 3.7 Arrangement by function

Operation sequence arrangements

These are **product layouts** where machines, equipment and workplaces are arranged according to the order in which operations need to be carried out to produce a complete component, product or sub-assembly. An example of this type of arrangement is given in Figure 3.8. They usually take the form of unidirectional lines although there are other means of arranging facilities according to sequence. In some ways the planning of production is relatively uncomplicated since product flow is straightforward. When used for assembly, however, the scheduling of material supplies to each stage of production can still be a complex problem.

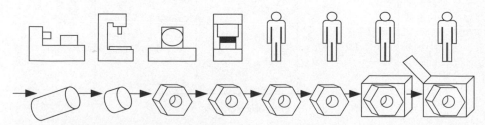

Figure 3.8 Operation sequence arrangement

Conventional process types

'Job' 'batch', 'flow' and other process taxonomies

Given the fact that there are three alternative types of work organisation and three ways of arranging the physical facilities for production, it further follows that a matrix can be drawn to contain the nine theoretical combinations of these two physical system parameters.

When we talk about a *conventional* production process we usually refer to either 'job', 'batch' or 'flow', which in fact can be identified as particular combinations of parameters, see Figure 3.9.

- The 'job' process is characterised by a product-orientated organisation combined with fixed position arrangement.
- The 'batch' process is characterised by a process-orientated organisation combined with arrangement by function.
- The 'flow' system is characterised by a task-orientated organisation combined with operation sequence arrangement.

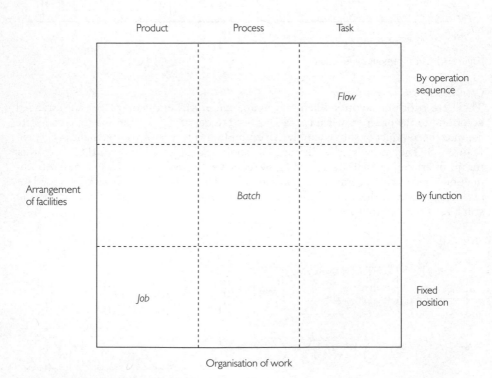

Figure 3.9 The conventional production system types

The third factor which must be considered within the context of the design of processes, which must also be considered alongside the combinations of productive resources, is demand (in terms of quantity or pattern). This again could be viewed as being divided into three types, shown in the table.

	Type 1	Type 2	Type 3
Demand quantity	low	medium	high
Demand pattern	unique	intermittent	continuous

When demand is considered alongside the other parameters there are also conventions which normally prevail, i.e.

- The job process is characterised by a combination of product-orientated organisation with fixed position arrangement and also low or unique demand.
- The batch process is characterised by a combination of process-orientated organisation with arrangement by function and also medium or intermittent demand.
- The flow process is characterised by a combination of task-orientated organisation with operation sequence arrangement and also high or continuous demand.

A question that arises from the preceding discussion relates to the number of process types that it is possible to identify. In this analysis just three have been recognised ('job', 'batch' and 'flow'), whereas other typologies recognise more; for example five in the case of Hill's interpretation ('project', 'jobbing', 'batch', 'line' and 'continuous'). In fact there

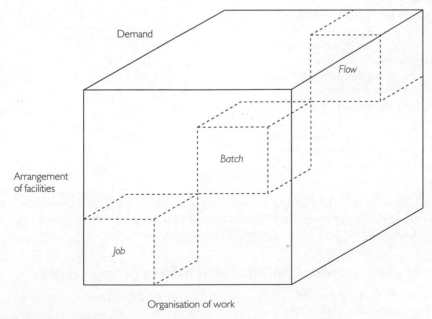

Figure 3.10 The process cube

is no inconsistency here because in practice there is a continuum on which these process types lie. 'Project' and 'continuous' processes can be regarded as lying at the extremes of the continuum although they are essentially similar to the 'job' and 'flow' processes discussed above.

With three parameters now describing the three types of process they can be positioned within a **process cube**. The edges of this cube are defined by the three characterising parameters (work organisation, facility arrangement, demand). Since each of these was categorised into three types then the total number of combinations (i.e. spaces within the cube) are 27 of which the conventional processes represent just three. Later, some additional process types will be described which occupy more novel positions within the process cube. To understand the rationale behind these alternative systems, however, it is first necessary to examine the characteristics, benefits and drawbacks of the conventional systems.

Characteristics of the conventional process types – their capability (volume/variety) and cost implications

The three conventional process types differ in many respects and each has its distinctive advantages and disadvantages which derive from their characteristics. These characteristics can be itemised according to their relationship with the three resources (physical facilities; human resources; materials). They are as follows:

Characteristics relating to the physical facilities
- types of layout
- types of plant and equipment.

Characteristics relating to the human resources
- proportion of managers
- number of levels of management
- skills, number and type
- training requirements.

Characteristics relating to materials control
- amount of product movement
- queuing and work in progress
- throughput time.

The nature of each of the characteristics is shown in Figure 3.11. This figure also indicates the capability of the system types in terms of product range and volumes together with the implications for fixed and variable production costs.

Benefits and drawbacks of the conventional process types

Now let us look at the benefits and drawbacks which are derived from these characteristics. They are shown in the table.

System type / Characteristic	Job production	Batch production	Flow production
Physical facilities			
Type of layout	Fixed position	By function	By operation sequence
Type of plant and equipment	Mainly general purpose	Mixture of general purpose and adapted	Mainly special purpose
Human resources			
Proportion of managers	Relatively few managers	Relatively more managers	Most managers
Number of management levels	Few levels (i.e. shallow hierarchy)	Relatively more levels	Most levels (i.e. deep hierarchy)
Skills, number and type	Large numbers of 'direct' skilled operators	Moderate number and range of skills	Skills confined to 'indirect' functions (setting, maintenance etc)
Training requirements	Extensive training of most direct operators	Moderate training needs	Most training aimed at indirect workers
Materials control			
Amount of product movement	Negligible movement of product	Extensive movement of part-finished products	Minimum movement
Queuing and work in progress	Dependent on resource availability and allocation	Long queues at facilities High work in progress	Limited queuing and lower work in progress levels
Throughput time	Dependent on resource availability and allocation	Long throughput time compared with total operation time	Short throughput time
System capability and cost implications			
Product range and quantities	High variety/ low volume		Low variety/ high volume
Production costs	Low fixed/ high variable costs		High fixed/ low variable costs

Figure 3.11 Characteristics of the conventional production systems

Benefits	Drawbacks
For job process:	
• flexibility (product)	• low resource utilisation
• low fixed costs	• duplication of facilities
• job enlargement	• high training costs
• planning can be simplified	• no skill specialisation benefits
For batch process:	
• flexibility (process)	
• specialisation (of operational tasks and supervision)	• high working capital costs
• isolation of processes where necessary	• frequent set ups
• ability to make priority changes	• high material handling costs
	• long delivery lead times
For flow process:	
• few set ups	'human' problems:
• low working capital costs	• recruitment difficulty
• low material handling costs	• high absenteeism
• low direct training costs	• high labour turnover
• specialisation enables reduction in task times and application of direct incentives	'physical' problems:
• high capital cost	• interdependency can cause unreliability
• easily automated	• inflexibility (product and process)

To overcome the drawbacks associated with the processes described above it may be necessary to adopt alternative approaches using different combinations of work organisation and facility arrangement. If such process types can extend the limits on the efficiency of material flow there will be clear strategic benefits and the control system will not be constrained by the previous restrictions imposed. The ideas behind how such alternatives can be developed are now explained.

The use of trade-offs to manage constraints

How process constraints limit the capability of operations systems

To explain the reasoning behind the development of alternative process types it is first necessary to understand that the design of processes is normally influenced by a number of underlying assumptions. The main such assumption is that trade-offs must be reached both within and between the customer service and resource efficiency objectives, which in turn influence its design parameters. (For a seminal discussion of trade-off decisions in manufacturing see Skinner, 1969). The existence of trade-offs means that optimum solutions must be sought within the inherent limits (or constraints) of the process. These optimum solutions in turn keep the system in 'balance' as shown in Figure 3.12.

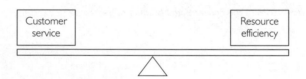

Figure 3.12 The balance or trade-off between customer service and resource efficiency in a production system

To explain this idea further it is necessary to understand that the resource efficiency of the system determines the cost of producing a product while customer service will influence its selling price. Profitability is a function of both total production cost and sales revenues and the elements which go to make up each are represented in Figure 3.13.

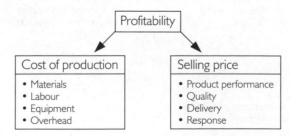

Figure 3.13 The determinants of profitability leading to the trade-off assumptions

The need for trade-offs can be demonstrated within this model. It is assumed that to gain an improvement on one side of the profitability model there will be a consequent penalty to be paid on the other. Alternatively the improvement and the penalty may both lie on the same side of the model. However, this makes no difference to the general idea which may be illustrated with the examples shown in the table. Examples 1 to 3 are of trade-offs between factors on either side of the profitability model while the factors in Example 4 both lie on the same side.

- *Example 1: Trade-off between delivery performance and material cost*. Conventional trade-off assumption ... Improved delivery is achieved by holding high stocks of work in progress, conversely low stocks make delivery performance worse.
- *Example 2: Trade-off between quality and overhead cost*. Conventional trade-off assumption ... Better quality is achieved by investing in inspection equipment and procedures, conversely reducing the inspection overhead has an adverse effect on quality.
- *Example 3: Trade-off between response and equipment cost*. Conventional trade-off assumption ... Greater customer response can be obtained by investing in more flexible machinery, conversely reduced capital investment leads to poorer response.
- *Example 4: Trade-off between overhead and materials cost*. Conventional trade-off assumption ... Machine overheads can be reduced by increasing their utilisation and building stocks of materials; conversely reducing material stocks adversely effects utilisation and increases overheads.

The optimisation of trade-offs

Although the idea of trade-offs has been widely discussed, there is considerable debate about their real importance and the extent to which it is necessary to manage them. Where the management of trade-offs is accepted there are number of approaches designed to optimise objectives within the constraints imposed by the influencing factors.

Examples of the **optimisation approach** include the 'economic batch quantity', 'optimum maintenance policies' and 'the cost of quality concept'. Each of these assumes that the increasing and decreasing cost functions of the opposing trade-off factors, when added together, produce a total cost function which has a readily identifiable minimum. This then determines the 'economic' level of activity (batch size, maintenance effort, amount of quality control etc.)

The idea behind any optimisation approach to managing trade-offs is that the underlying process constraints are identified and accepted. No attempt is made to reduce or remove the constraints; a balance is simply struck which minimises (or maximises) the total effect. A limit to the solution is thereby imposed by the strength of the constraints. If these constraints could be reduced or even removed then it may be possible to develop alternative processes which yield significantly better levels of performance than can be achieved by optimising the 'conventional' processes described earlier. Thus it is possible to think in terms of a different paradigm for process design that overcomes the deficiencies of conventional systems. This can be termed the **improvement approach**, which is based on the idea of deliberately exposing constraints and finding ways of reducing and removing them rather than simply optimising within them as illustrated in Figure 3.14.

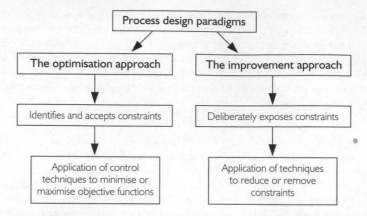

Figure 3.14 The essential differences between the optimisation approach and the improvement approach towards process design

Cellular organisations for manufacture, assembly and service

Loosening the process constraints through alternative system designs

An essential part of the improvement approach is the development of new types of process design which allow the limits on system performance to be extended. The objective here is to design processes based on combinations of work organisation and facility arrangement which will exhibit the beneficial features of conventional processes while having fewer of their drawbacks. In this way many of the intrinsic constraints of conventional processes can be removed and the improvement approach can thereby be facilitated.

Within operations management there is a commonly accepted objective of improving the **customer orientation** of processes. This is usually achieved by designing them with a greater **product orientation**, but this is normally only associated with the 'job' type of processes. The extension of product orientation to include a wider range of situations can be achieved through cellular or modular organisation. There are basically two types of cellular organisation:

- for batch manufacture of components;
- for continuous production (through assembly) of end products.

Although cellular organisation was originally conceived for manufacturing systems it also has applicability in services where, of course, customer orientation is usually more important.

The types of cellular organisation mentioned above are based on two established principles, namely **group technology** and **autonomous working**.

Cellular organisation for batch manufacture of components

Cellular organisation for the production of intermittent batches of components is based on the principles of group technology or GT (Snead, 1989). Group technology has three aspects.

- grouping parts into families;
- grouping physical facilities into cells with the aim of reducing material movement;
- creating groups of multi-skilled workers.

Grouping parts into families

Grouping parts into families has the objective of reducing the amount of setting time between batches and thereby avoids the need to produce in large batches to minimise the unit ordering and setting cost. Parts family formation is based on the idea of grouping parts together according to geometrical or processing similarity. Sometimes a **composite component** is conceived which has all, or most, of the features of the constituent parts. The composite component may be 'real', although more often than not it will probably be hypothetical. If the process is set up to produce the composite component the setting time between all its constituent parts can, by definition, be minimised.

Grouping physical facilities into cells

Physical facilities are grouped into cells with the intention of reducing material movement. Whereas a functional layout involves extensive movement of material between departments with common processes, a cell comprises all the facilities required to manufacture a family of components. Material movement is therefore restricted to within the cell and throughput times are thereby reduced. The change from functional layout to group technology cells is shown in Figure 3.15.

Creating groups of multi-skilled workers

Creating groups of multi-skilled workers enables increased autonomy and flexibility on the part of operators. This enables easier changeovers from one part to another and increases the job enrichment of members of the group. This in turn can improve motivation and have a beneficial effect on quality.

An additional feature of group technology is that cells can be a single planning point rather than individual machines. Production control need therefore only plan down to the level of the cells and becomes more simplified. Planning within the cell is carried out by the group members themselves which enables them to apply their detailed knowledge of process capacity, capability etc.

Earlier the idea of a **process cube** was developed and illustrated in Figure 3.10. The position of the group technology approach to cellular organisation is shown in Figure 3.16. Work organisation is product orientated which is in common with job production. Facility arrangement is by operation sequence so in this way it is similar to flow production. Group Technology is therefore able to derive the advantages of these two types of production system while still being suited to intermittent batch production.

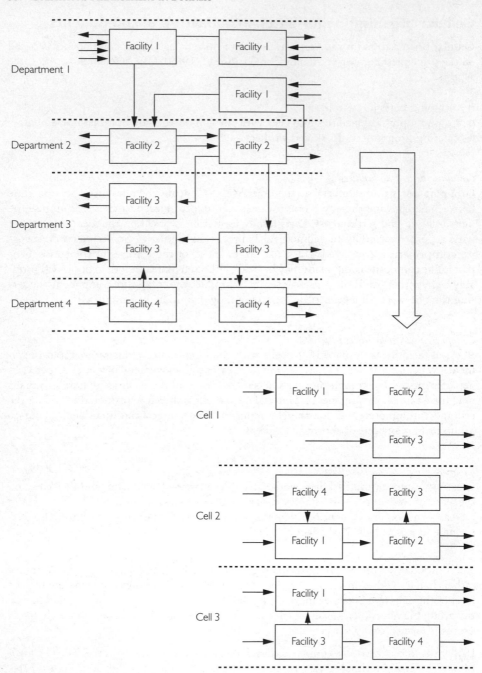

Figure 3.15 The change from functional layout to group technology cells

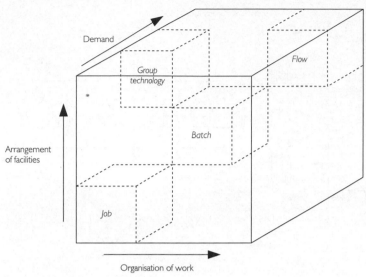

Figure 3.16 Group technology within the process cube

The benefits of **group technology** can be summarised as follows:

- Setting times are reduced due to the similar nature and sequence of machining operations.
- Material handling is reduced due to shorter distances between machines.
- Throughput times are shorter due to the rapid flow of parts through the cell.
- Levels of work-in-progress are reduced because large batches of partly completed items are not waiting between machines.
- A cell is a single planning point which makes scheduling and monitoring easier.
- Greater operator autonomy and responsibility enables job satisfaction and improved quality.

It should be noted that by loosening the constraints associated with the conventional process types all the above benefits, in one way or another, mean that group technology is especially applicable to just-in-time production. Just-in-time production will be explained in more detail in Chapter 8.

Cellular organisation for the assembly of end products

The general approach to cellular organisation for end product assembly is based on the principle of **autonomous working** (Sandberg, 1982). This is an alternative to conventional flow production systems and, like flow production, it is associated with high (continuous) demand. Autonomous working addresses both the human and physical problems associated with conventional flowlines.

To implement autonomous working in a practical environment the broad options available are: parallel assembly cells; or cells based on line assembly.

Each type can be based on assembly being carried out by individual operators or groups. See Figure 3. 17.

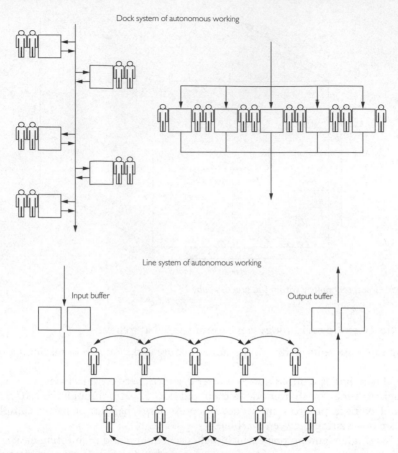

Figure 3.17 Alternative layout options for autonomous working

Both approaches change the work organisation from being task orientated to being product orientated. Parallel assembly, however, uses a fixed position facility arrangement while line assembly retains the operation sequence arrangement usually associated with flowline working (Karlsson and Bennett, 1991). The two types of autonomous working are thus positioned on the production system cube illustrated in Figure 3.18.

The benefits of autonomous working can be summarised as follows:

- The balance and system losses associated with conventional flowlines are reduced or eliminated with the longer cycle times of autonomous working.
- Different products can be produced at the same time in different cells or modules.
- Response and volume flexibility is greater than with flowlines.
- Model changes can be effected more easily.
- The autonomous nature of assembly cells means there is no work station interdependency.
- Job enrichment and autonomy lessens the human problems associated with flowline working.
- Quality tends to improve because responsibilities are more clearly assigned.

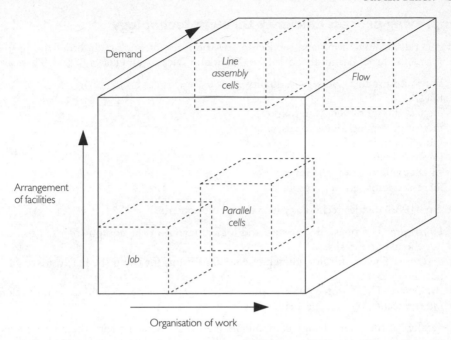

Figure 3.18 Autonomous working within the production system cube

Improving process efficiency

The competitiveness of companies is largely derived from the design of its products, services and processes and, as competition becomes increasingly more severe, continuous improvements will need to be made. One of the means of enabling processes to become more efficient can be derived through the removal of the constraints associated with the conventional process types. This can often be achieved by the use of cellular organisation as has been described previously. However, the use of alternative process types will not in itself be sufficient to ensure greater competitiveness. Companies will also be searching for how to make improvements in terms of the cost, function, quality and speed of delivery of their products and services. The relationship between products and processes which was described earlier means that process improvements are often linked to those made to products.

There are two basic means whereby these process improvements can be achieved. The first is through the application of **technology**. The second is through **re-engineering** the processes by fundamentally examining them and making radical changes to their design. In practice the two approaches should not be separated. The application of technology to a process cannot achieve the best results unless the design of that process has itself been the subject of scrutiny and improvement (otherwise the result may just be automated chaos!). Likewise, any changes to the design of a process should only be made in light of the available technologies that would enable those changes to be put to best effect. The last two sections of this chapter therefore consider the question of how, respectively, technology and business process re-engineering, can be used to improve the efficiency of processes.

Improving process efficiency through technology

In general, manufacturing and service organisations use technology in order to improve performance through a number of means (Markland, Vickery and Davis, 1995). These are:

- improved product and service quality
- lower cost
- increased responsiveness to markets
- increased responsiveness to customers
- more flexibility
- improved safety
- smaller work-in-progress inventories
- increased long-term profitability.

Zeleny (1986) divides technology into three components:

- Hardware. The physical structure and logical layout of the equipment used to carry out the required tasks.
- Software. The set of rules, guidelines and algorithms for using the hardware to carry out the tasks.
- Brainware. The reasons, purpose and justification for using, expanding and developing the technology in a particular way.

Generally, all three technology components are interdependent and, therefore, equally important. However, in recent years the term 'advanced technology' has come into common use to describe the type of technology where the relative emphasis is on software, specifically computer programs, for control purposes. Gerwin and Kolodny (1992) say that **advanced manufacturing technology** is used mainly in the activities of product and process design, manufacturing planning and control, the production process and their integration. Some of the more popular advanced technologies used for process efficiency in manufacturing are given below.

Product and process design technology
- **Computer-aided design** (CAD). Helps create and modify designs and stores the information in an engineering database.
- **Computer-aided engineering** (CAE). Uses simulation and other techniques to analyse the properties of a design such as stress in a mechanical part.
- **Computer-aided process planning** (CAPP). Helps in planning the sequence of operations a part will go through in the production process.

Conversion process technologies
- **Numerical control** (NC). Uses fixed, coded, instructions to control a process.
- **Computer numerical control** (CNC). Controls a process through a program stored in a mini- or micro-computer attached to the process.
- **Programmable robot**. A multi-function manipulator that moves a part, tool or device through variable motions to perform a variety of tasks.
- **Flexible manufacturing systems** (FMS). A system consisting of several processes and automated handling devices controlled by computers.

Automated material handling technologies
- **Automated storage and retrieval systems** AS/RS. Computer-controlled stocking

systems in which parts are stored on racks and received and retrieved using computerised robots, cranes and/or similar devices.
- **Automated Guided Vehicles** (AGVs). Provide driverless transportation of products, materials etc. using vehicles equipped with automatic guidance devices.

Process control technologies
- **Computer-aided inspection** (CAI). Helps check conformance to specifications, typically using an automated programmable device for measuring co-ordinates and other parameters.
- **Programmable logic controllers** (PLCs). Electronic process control devices with programmable memories that execute the steps of a logical sequence of process operations and collect information.

Process integration technologies
- **Local area network** (LAN). Telecommunications linkages for exchanging information between different points in the production process or between departments.
- **Intercompany or wide area network** (WAN). Telecommunications links for exchanging information between production, subcontractors, suppliers and/or customers.
- **Computer-aided design and manufacture** (CAD/CAM). Technologies for using design information to automatically generate parts programs that are electronically downloaded to control production processes.
- **Computer-integrated manufacturing** (CIM). Technologies that bring together the individual advanced manufacturing technologies used in product and process design, operations planning and control, and the production process under unified computer control using information technology.

A general description of the main technologies used in production can be found in Bennett (1986) while more specialised texts provide detailed descriptions of the individual technologies. For example Waldner (1992) described the general principles and elements of **computer-integrated manufacturing**, Maus and Allsup (1986) provide a guide for managers on the use of **robotics**, and Tempelmeier and Kuhn (1993) provide an account of the application of **flexible manufacturing systems**.

Although most of the descriptions of advanced technology relate to manufacturing operations its use in improving the efficiency of service processes is becoming increasingly common. Finch and Luebbe (1995) describe how technology can be used in financial services, communications, health care, education, hotel services, telemarketing and leisure services. However, they emphasise that the use of technology to replace the role of a human in service is not always successful. They say that customers must believe they gain some benefit from using the technology or they will resist or possible reject it.

To assist in determining where, and how, to apply technology in services it is relevant to recognise that service delivery processes can be categorised into:

- front office processes, and
- back office processes.

Front office service processes are those involving interaction between the customer and the service delivery system. Therefore technology should be implemented with the aim of making this interaction more effective. Consequently the emphasis will be on information technologies for assisting with such activities as diagnosis, customer order progressing, goods tracking and monitoring (i.e. in the case of a parcel delivery service) etc.

Back office processes are those where there is no interaction between the customer and the service delivery system. Here it is possible to apply the type of automation technology more usually associated with manufacturing because the customer will usually be unaware of its presence and will not reject it or be opposed to its use.

A further way of examining the applicability of technology in a service process is by identifying its position on the **service process matrix** (Schmenner, 1995). This is shown in Figure 3.19. On one side of this matrix is the degree of interaction and customisation, while on the other side is the degree of labour intensity. Four categories of service process are therefore identified on the matrix: the service factory, the service shop, mass service and professional service. Of these the two extremes are the service factory (low interaction and customisation/low labour intensity) and the professional service (high interaction and customisation/high labour intensity). Between these, shown as a shaded arrow, is the diagonal towards which services tend to be drawn as they are segmented and become more diversified. The professional service will, like the front office processes described above, have more information technologies while the service shop, like the back office, will have more automation technologies. Applying technology to mass services will draw them towards the service factory quadrant when it is aimed at reducing labour and towards the professional service quadrant if it is aimed at improving the effectiveness of customer interaction. Similarly, applying technology to service shops will draw them towards the service factory quadrant if it reduces the amount of customer interaction (through more back office activities) and towards the professional quadrant when the technology is aimed at offering a greater degree of personal service to the customer.

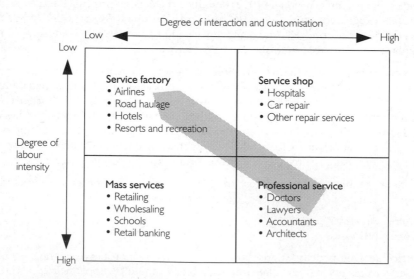

Figure 3.19 The service process matrix

Improving process efficiency through business process re-engineering

In the introduction to this section on process efficiency improvement it was argued that the application of technology and process re-engineering were interdependent. In fact the thinking behind 'business process re-engineering' goes back to the late 1970s when a research programme at the Massachusetts Institute of Technology looked at investment by the US and Europe in technology. It was discovered from this research that despite the billions of dollars spent on technology during the 1970s there had been only a one percent increase in productivity. Further research then showed that instead of breaking down the barriers between business functions and specialisms, information technology departments were reinforcing them, making them higher and damage proof (Towers, 1994).

Business process re-engineering (BPR) is the term that has become accepted for the approach which seeks to adopt a holistic means of improving efficiency which combines technology, people and processes. The model developed by MIT to represent this idea conceptually is shown in Figure 3.20. As an approach for bringing about dramatic improvements in process efficiency it has been brought to prominence by Hammer (1990 and 1993) who has put forward what is probably the most simple and widely accepted definition of BPR which is:

'To fundamentally change the way work is performed in order to achieve radical performance improvements in quality, speed and cost'

BPR applies a standard set of principles to rethink the way processes are designed and create an entirely new sequence of activities. This often involves combining several tasks or jobs into one and giving responsibility for decision-making to the people who actually do the work rather than just managing it (Melnyk and Denzler, 1996).

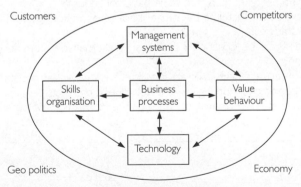

Figure 3.20 The MIT business process model (Towers, 1994)

The ideas behind BPR are not entirely new. Many of the ideas from method study that were developed around fifty years ago remain relevant, such as **process flow analysis and critical examination** (i.e. asking fundamental questions about the process: what? where? when? who? and how?). By not accepting anything about current processes BPR often reduces what is done or even eliminates entire activities. For example, the minimum possible resources are used on checking and control work since this does not add value; instead the need for doing the checking is removed by focusing on quality of design rather than quality of conformance. Also the barriers between functions are removed to avoid problems of duplication and reduce the amount of time and effort lost during handover from one process to another (Kurogane, 1993).

Business process re-engineering is by no means just applicable to manufacturing processes. There are many examples of where it has been effectively applied in services such as hospitals, airlines, banking and insurance (Coulson-Thomas, 1997; Homa, 1995).

From this brief discussion of BPR it can be seen that its essential characteristic is the radical approach to process redesign it seeks to advocate. This is in contrast to the approach whereby improvements are made incrementally. In practice nether approach is correct; the operations manager has a choice of methods for improving process efficiency and will choose the best combination of these that will suit the particular circumstances and achieve the desired degree of competitiveness for the organisation.

Summary of key points

- To the operations manager a process is a system or arrangement of physical facilities and human resources for transforming materials into finished products or providing services.
- There is a close link between product and process design which needs to be managed effectively to achieve greater competitiveness.
- The main links between product and process design relate to the degree of change involved in development projects, life cycles and product demand and process type.
- Process types can be characterised by organisation of work and the choice and arrangement of physical facilities.
- The conventional processes are 'job', 'batch' and 'flow' although different typologies will identify other process types along the same basic continuum.
- The process constraints that limit the capability of an operations system are traditionally managed using trade-offs.
- Process constraints can be loosened with the use of alternative system designs such as cellular organisations.
- The two types of cellular organisation are group technology for batch manufacture of components and autonomous working for assembly of end products.
- Process efficiency can be improved through the application of technology and re-engineering.

Exercises

1 Choose a product that is familiar to you. Based on what you believe might be its likely demand, what work organisation and facility arrangement options do you think could have been used in its manufacture? What are the drawbacks and advantages of the options you have identified for this particular product?
2 What are the similarities and differences in the characteristics of the processes that could

have been used for the following and are there any aspects of process design that these two examples can learn from each other?
a) the manufacture of wooden furniture in medium quantities and
b) the organisation of package holidays?

3 Under the trade-off argument what would be the penalty paid for achieving the following?
a) Minimisation of labour cost.
b) Maximisation of product performance.
c) Minimisation of equipment cost.

4 Why does cellular organisation differ from conventional process types in terms of the way in which the work is organised? What are the advantages that this offers?

5 What are the main reasons for applying technology to manufacturing processes? What factors is it necessary to take into account before automation is applied in service operations?

 CASE STUDY
Cellular manufacturing at GPT

The Business Systems Group of GPT develops and manufactures telecommunications equipment including exchange and switching systems, local area network (LAN) products and computer-supported telephone systems. Its manufacturing processes include automatic and manual component insertion and 'on-sertion' (surface mounting), flow soldering, automatic circuit testing of assembled printed circuit boards (PCBs) and other functional and systems testing.

GPT has recognised the need for 'local ownership' of processes whereby the operators could take increased responsibility for ensuring manufacture under controlled conditions, process and product inspection, maintenance and housekeeping. In terms of production systems design in the Business Systems Group this was helped by changing the conventional herring-bone or 'spine-and-spur' production layout to the U-shaped cells used for the manufacture of telephone products. The previous layout involved operators carrying out an allocated task before moving the product on. Implementation of the U-shaped cells was achieved using existing benches and changeover of individual operations into a cell took as little as 48 hours to complete with a minimum of capital investment.

To communicate the details of the planned changes a series of one-hour presentations was made by the manufacturing engineering team. They started with top management and then moved down through the organisation. Presentations to the workforce were made by their own production managers, but supported by manufacturing engineering personnel. Many questions were asked of this new configuration of production facilities and the consequences of it. A great deal of interest and enthusiasm for the change in manufacturing approach was thus generated from the outset.

GPT called their new production system 'U-shaped (people-based) flexible JIT cells'. The emphasis was on enabling people to have the flexibility and scope to assume more responsibility for their own work and for cells to manage their own operations. With the introduction of cells the company was keen to maximise team working, product ownership and customer focus. The main feature of U-shaped cells was that the work layout should facilitate the introduction of just-in-time production (JIT) to ensure work was pulled through the cells in a continuous flow and production was levelled with a minimum of work-in-progress (WIP) between individual operations. The requirement for JIT and smoothed production demanded the development of multi-skilled operators within the cells to facilitate mobility between tasks so that workloads could be balanced.

Managers at GPT expressed surprise at the enthusiasm with which the workforce greeted the U-shaped cells. Operators freely admitted they had assumed greater pride in their work and their teams. Specific benefits arising from the introduction of U-shaped cells included:

● Product quality was improved to the extent that faulty work shipments became largely a thing of the past.
● Work-in-progress was dramatically reduced, both within and between cells. Cell operators packed the products and shipped them directly, while supplier deliveries direct to point of use were arranged.
● Savings in labour were achieved. Most cells comprised four operators and typically produced the same output as seven people in the old systems. Overall a labour cost saving of 30% was reported.
● Operators could work at their own pace instead of being governed by other operations. When an operator finished a task they would look around the cell and move to those tasks where they would be more gainfully employed instead of waiting for more work as they did in the old system.

CASE STUDY

The cascade system at international computers

An example of autonomous working in assembly operations

The way in which a manufacturer can become more customer-oriented is by focusing on its downstream operations where components, subassemblies and other front-end items are brought together into finished products that are configured to suit customer requirements. The final assembly plant of International Computers was typical of such downstream operations in that it was required to produce mainframe and mini-computer systems strictly to customer order. Volumes were low and varieties high, and its operations consisted primarily of assembly activities using items made in the company's other factories and by external suppliers. Material purchases therefore represented a large proportion of production cost and value added was small. Consequently, greater emphasis needed to be placed on quality, service and inventory management than on trying to reduce production costs. Meeting these demands involved making extensive changes to the plant's production system that had been designed originally when the company's aim was to sell 'boxes'. Its new objective of selling 'solutions' required a more flexible and responsive system, so the 'Modular Assembly Cascade' was developed.

The cascade comprised a number of autonomous modules within each of which part of the total assembly operation could be carried out. These modules, where assembly was carried out manually, were extremely flexible, their main constraint being the overall dimensions of the products or subassemblies they could handle. Both within and between the modules just-in-time principles were applied. Modules manufacturing larger dimensional assemblies 'pulled' their requirements from those manufacturing smaller ones, hence the concept of materials cascading down the various levels of assembly as shown in Figure 3.21. The modules themselves derived their flexibility from making the production activities and material flow system as generalised as possible. This meant re-equipping the assembly areas with more general-purpose tools and investing in an ambitious programme of training to extend the range of operator skills and increase their ability to work in a less structured environment.

The equipment used in the Modular Assembly Cascade included automatic guided vehicles, computer controlled cranes and automatic paternoster and carousel stores together with a hierarchy of computers for controlling the system.

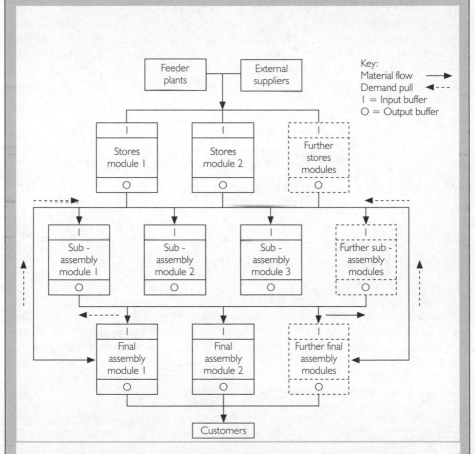

Figure 3.21 The Modular Assembly Cascade Principle

CASE STUDY

Flow production of car bodies at the press and paint facilities of Vauxhall Motors

When Vauxhall Motors commissioned new equipment in its press and paint shop at its Ellesmere Port plant it featured a 'first' in Europe – the application of a sophisticated, computer-integrated control system called Manufacturing Automation Protocol (MAP 3.0). MAP is essentially the means of bridging the gap between different computerised control systems in a manufacturing plant with a fast, reliable and efficient communications system.

When first installed, the paint equipment, which cost £60 million, ran at 35 car bodies per hour (net) but had the capacity to handle 45 bodies per hour to match forecast volume requirements. The latest paint processes, materials and 'clean room' concepts were adopted to enhance paint quality, durability and appearance of the car bodies. This included the first use in the UK of water-borne primer paint technology. This helped reduce manufacturing costs, as paint processes represent a significant factor in the total cost of building a vehicle.

Environmental benefits of the new facilities resulted from:

- the use of water-borne primer;
- efficient management of overspray paint (including pioneering research methods of recycling waste material);
- energy savings through heat recuperation.

Working conditions were improved by:

- glass sidewalls in the paint spray booths;
- temperature controlled working areas;
- extensive use of automated equipment;
- the introduction of team working concepts;
- improved rest areas.

Other equipment investments in the manufacturing facilities of the press and paint shop included a massive 1600 tonne Tri-Axis transfer press and a new high-speed coil cutting line, together involving a total investment of £30 million. Considered to be the most technologically advanced equipment of its kind, the fully automated large transfer press had the capability to produce body panels with a performance equivalent to four conventional press flowlines. The main benefits of the new transfer press were:

- negligible inventory;
- a near-continuous manufacturing capability;
- lower tooling costs;
- greater flexibility of manufacture.

Apart from enhanced productivity, other advantages included:

- further improved body quality from more consistent pressings;
- safer and quieter operation;
- a more pleasant working environment.

References

Bennett, D.J., *Production Systems Design*, Butterworths, London (1986).

Bennett, D.J. and Forrester, P.L., *Market Focused Production Systems: Design and Implementation*, Prentice-Hall, Hemel Hempstead, UK (1993).

Bennett, D.J. and Karlsson, U., Work organisation as a basis for competition: the transition of car assembly in Sweden, *International Studies of Management and Organization* 22, 4 (1992).

Coulson-Thomas, C., Process management in a hospital and healthcare context, *Business Process Management Journal*, 3, 2 (1997).

Fogarty, D.W., Hoffman, T.R. and Stonebraker, P.W., *Production and Operations Management*, South-Western Publishing Co., Cincinnati (1989).

Gerwin, D. and Kolodny, H., *Management of Advanced Manufacturing Technology*, John Wiley, New York (1992).

Hammer, M., Re-engineering work: don't automate; obliterate, *Harvard Business Review*, July/August (1990).

Hammer, M. and Champy, J., *Re-engineering the Corporation*, Nicholas Brealey, London (1993).

Hayes, R.H. and Schmenner, R., How should you organize manufacturing? *Harvard Business Review*, (January–February 1978).

Hayes, R.H. and Wheelwright, S.C., *Restoring our Competitive Edge: Competing Through Manufacturing*, Wiley, New York (1984).

Hayes, R.H., Wheelwright, S.C. and Clark, K.B., *Dynamic Manufacturing: Creating the Learning Organisation*, The Free Press, New York (1988).

Hill, T., *Production/Operations Management: Text and Cases*, Prentice-Hall, Hemel Hempstead, UK (1991).

Homa, P., Business process re-engineering: theory and evidence-based practice, *Business Process Re-engineering and Management Journal*, 1, 3 (1995).

Kurogane, K., *Cross-Functional Management*, Asian Productivity Organization, Tokyo (1993).

Markland, R.E., Vickery, S.K. and Davis R.A., *Operations Management Concepts in Manufacturing and Services*, West Publishing Co., St Paul, Minneapolis (1995).

Maus, R. and Allsup, R., *Robotics: A Manager's Guide*, John Wiley, New York (1986).

Melnyk, S.A. and Denzler, D.R., *Operations Management: A Value Driven Approach*, Richard D. Irwin, Chicago (1996).

Noori, H. and Radford, R., *Production and Operations Management: Total Quality and Responsiveness*, McGraw-Hill, New York (1995).

Ostwald, P.F. and Muñoz J., *Manufacturing Processes and Systems*, 9th Edn, John Wiley, New York (1997).

Sandberg, T., *Work Organisation and Autonomous Groups*, Liber Forlag, Lund, Sweden (1982).

Schmenner, R., *Service Operations Management*, Prentice-Hall International, Englewood Cliffs, New Jersey (1995).

Skinner, W., Manufacturing – missing link in corporate strategy, *Harvard Business Review*, (May–June 1969).

Slack, N., Chambers, S., Harland, C., Harrison, A. and Johnston, R., *Operations Management*, Pitman Publishing, London (1995).

Snead, C., *Group Technology – Foundation for Competitive Manufacturing*, Van Nostrand Reinhold, New York (1989).

Tempelmeier, H. and Kuhn, H., *Flexible Manufacturing Systems*, Wiley, New York (1993).

Towers, S., *Business Process Re-engineering*, Stanley Thornes (Publishers) Ltd, Cheltenham, UK (1994).

Waldner, J-B., *Principles of Computer-Integrated Manufacturing*, John Wiley, Chichester, UK (1992).

Wild, R., *Essentials of Production and Operations Management*, Cassell, London (1990).

Zeleny, M., 'High technology management', *Human System Management*, 6 (1996).

4 Job design

Objectives

By the end of the chapter, you should be able to:

- understand the need for job design to achieve a reasonable compromise of technical, behavioural and economic feasibility;
- understand how job design has developed in response to market demands and individual needs;
- evaluate the scientific management approach to job design;
- understand the steps involved in a method study analysis;
- understand the use of the work measurement technique;
- use the learning curve concept;
- evaluate the behavioural approach to job design;
- understand the techniques of job enlargement and job enrichment;
- understand the use of ergonomics;
- understand the approach of Sociotechnical systems theory;
- evaluate the issues involved in the introduction of new technology;
- understand the approach of empowerment.

Meeting needs through compromise

Job design consists of the formal specifications and informal expectations of an employee's work-related activities. The job design should try to meet the needs of both the jobholder and the organisation. Thus each job must be a reasonable compromise of technical, economic and behavioural feasibility.

- *Technical feasibility*. The person holding the job must be capable of performing the required tasks with the resources available to them. This requires suitable selection of resources, such as equipment, and proper selection and training of employees. This is personal **competence**.
- *Economic feasibility*. The costs of providing a salary to the employees, providing equipment and maintaining the organisational environment must remain within the organisation's capabilities. This is corporate **viability**.
- *Behavioural feasibility*. The feelings that people derive from a job affects their motivation to perform it. Unstructured jobs often require so much of a person's creativity and mental attention that a good attitude is vital for good performance. Even routine, structured jobs require a person to be motivated enough to be present at the job and contribute the necessary effort. In addition informal work groups have a large impact on the effectiveness of an organisation. Peer relations may be responsible for many of the motivational reactions of workers. This is collective **stimulation**.

Traditional approaches to job design have been based on the need to improve **efficiency** and thus have largely been achieved using the principle of specialisation of tasks and centralisation of control and decision making. This approach, which originates from the scientific approach advocated by F.W. Taylor (1911), has in many cases proved unsatisfactory for two main reasons.

The business environment
The increasing dynamism of the business environment in which firms have to operate has increased the need for **flexibility** and **innovation** from the work force. In the manufacturing sector this environment has been variously called 'world class manufacturing' (Schonberger, 1986), 'the fifth wave of manufacturing' (Bessant, 1991), 'mass customisation' (Pine *et. al.*, 1993), 'flexible specialisation' (Piore and Sable, 1984) and 'strategic manufacturing' (Brown, 1996).

The effect of the changing nature of manufacturing on human resource management policies can be traced over time, by considering the craft, mass and the current manufacturing eras, see Table 4.1.

Table 4.1 Characteristics of manufacturing systems

Characteristic	Craft era	Mass era	Current era
Skill level	High	Low	High
Volume	Low	High	Various
Variety	High	Low	Various
Customisation	High	Low	High

Thus the current era in many ways resembles the craft tradition of high variety and skilled work. In the current era however this need is driven by the requirement for rapid new introduction of products with a range of variety, volume and delivery characteristics. This leads to a requirement for flexibility in reacting to market demands with consequences for job design strategies.

Employee performance
Recognition of the problems caused by the scientific management approach by social psychologists such as Maslow and Herzberg have drawn attention to people's need for psychological fulfilment from their work. The importance of such things as responsibility, recognition and the opportunity to develop new skills has been recognised in the motivation of personnel.

Scientific management

This refers to a process of reducing a job to its component parts and then reassembling these parts in order to optimise the work process design. The redesign process is often undertaken, not by the people actually performing the work, but by industrial engineers who use a variety of job design techniques such as time and motion studies. These break down the actions required in order to carry out a task and redesign the work to eliminate unnecessary movements. **Work simplification** often leads to a job design that has the following characteristics:

- repetitive work
- concentration of work on a small part of the product
- limited social interaction among workers
- training in specific skills necessary to undertake the task.

In order to measure the performance of jobs the **work study** method was developed and consists of two elements, method study and work measurement. These devices rely on the characteristics of a job given by the scientific approach. Thus the work should be sufficiently routine and repetitive to make it feasible to derive an average time from a sample of operators and operations. It must also be possible for the worker to vary their rate of work voluntarily in a measurable way. Therefore it can be applied quite readily to routine manual or clerical work but lends itself less well to indirect work such as maintenance or non-repetitive work such as professional and managerial duties.

Method study

Dividing and analysing a job is called method study and was pioneered by Gilbreth (1911). The method takes a systematic approach to reducing waste, time and effort. The approach can be analysed in a six-step procedure:

1. **Select**. Tasks most suitable will probably be repetitive, require extensive labour input and be critical to overall performance.
2. **Record**. This involves observation and documentation of the correct method of performing the selected tasks. Flow process charts are often used to represent a sequence of events graphically. They are intended to highlight unnecessary material movements and unnecessary delay periods.
3. **Examine**. This involves examination of the current method, looking for ways in which tasks can be eliminated, combined, rearranged and simplified. This can be achieved by looking at the flow process chart for example and re-designing the sequence of tasks necessary to perform the activity.
4. **Develop**. Developing the best method and obtaining approval for this method. This means choosing the best alternative considered, taking into account the constraints of the system such as the performance of the firm's equipment. The new method will require adequate documentation in order that procedures can be followed. Specifications may include tooling, operator skill level and working conditions.
5. **Install**. Implement the new method. Changes such as installation of new equipment and operator training will need to be undertaken.
6. **Maintain**. Routinely verify that the new method is being followed correctly.

New methods may not be followed due to inadequate training or support. On the other hand people may find ways to gradually improve the method over time. Learning curves can be used to analyse these effects.

Process charts

A process chart is often used to analysis the steps of a job or show how a set of jobs fit together into the overall flow of the production process. For example the steps involved in processing a customer order received by telephone. There are five main symbols in a process chart as shown in Figure 4.1.

Symbol	Name	Description
⬭	Operation	An activity directly contributing to the product service
⇨	Transportation	Moving of the product or service from one location to another
▭	Inspection	Examining the product or service for quality
D	Delay	Process wait for a time period
▽	Storage	Storage of product or service

Figure 4.1 Symbols for a process chart

An example process chart for a typical administration process is shown in Figure 4.2.

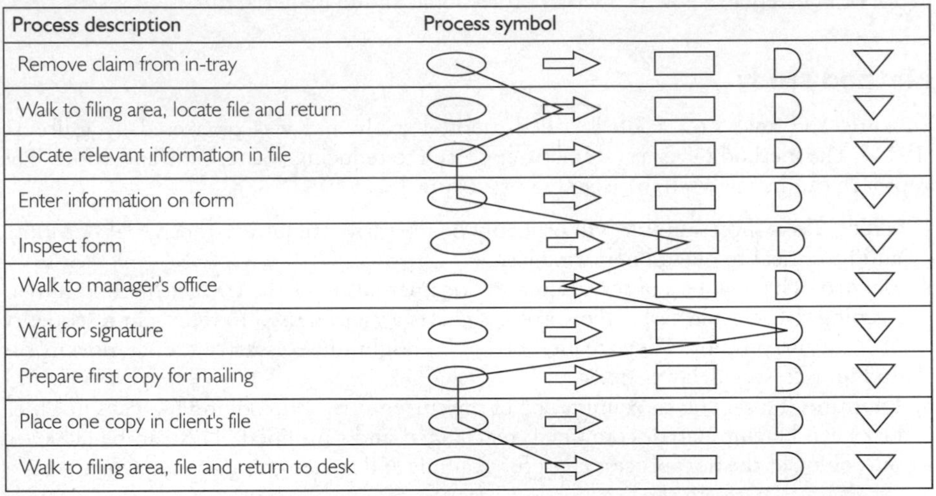

Process description	Process symbol				
Remove claim from in-tray	⬭	⇨	▭	D	▽
Walk to filing area, locate file and return	⬭	⇨	▭	D	▽
Locate relevant information in file	⬭	⇨	▭	D	▽
Enter information on form	⬭	⇨	▭	D	▽
Inspect form	⬭	⇨	▭	D	▽
Walk to manager's office	⬭	⇨	▭	D	▽
Wait for signature	⬭	⇨	▭	D	▽
Prepare first copy for mailing	⬭	⇨	▭	D	▽
Place one copy in client's file	⬭	⇨	▭	D	▽
Walk to filing area, file and return to desk	⬭	⇨	▭	D	▽

Figure 4.2 Process chart for generic administration process

The process chart performs a number of functions including identifying the following:

● task sequence
● task relationships
● task delays
● task movements
● worker assignment to tasks.

The charts can be used in conjunction with a written **job description** to form a detailed outline of a job. The charts can also be useful in the first stage of a **job improvement scheme**.

Motion study

Motion study is the study of the individual human motions that are used in a job task. The purpose of motion study is to try to ensure that the job does not include any unnecessary motion or movement by the worker and to select the sequence of motions that ensure that the job is being carried out in the most efficient manner possible. The technique was originated by Gilbreth (1911) who studied many workers at their jobs and from among them picked the best way to perform each activity. He then combined these elements to form the best way to perform a task. However, Taylor (1911) in his studies selected the best worker from a number of workers and used that worker's methods as the best way to perform the task.

For even more detail videotapes can be used to study individual work motions in slow motion and analyse them to find improvement – a technique termed **micro-motion analysis**. Gilbreth's motion study research and analysis has evolved into a set of widely adopted principles of motion study, which are used by organisations as general guidelines for the efficient design of work. The principles are generally categorised according to the efficient use of the human body, efficient arrangement of the workplace and the efficient use of equipment and machinery. These principles can be summarised into general guidelines:

Efficient use of the human body
- Work should be rhythmic, symmetrical and simplified.
- The full capabilities of the human body should be employed.
- Energy should be conserved by letting machines perform tasks when possible.

Efficient arrangement of the workplace
- Tools, materials and controls should have a defined place and be located to minimise the motions needed to get to them.
- The workplace should be comfortable and healthy.

Efficient use of equipment
- Equipment and mechanised tools enhance worker abilities.
- Controls and foot-operated devices that can relieve the hands/arms of work should be maximised.
- Equipment should be constructed and arranged to fit worker use.

Motion study is seen as one of the fundamental aspects of scientific management and indeed it was effective in the design of repetitive, simplified jobs with the task specialisation which was a feature of the mass production system. The use of motion study has declined as there has been a movement towards greater job responsibility and a wider range of tasks within a job. However the technique is still a useful analysis tool and particularly in the service industries, can help improve process performance.

Work measurement

The second element of work study is work measurement which determines the length of time it will take to undertake a particular task. This is important not only to determine pay rates but also to ensure that each stage in a production line system is of an equal duration (i.e. 'balanced') thus ensuring maximum output. Usually the method study and work measurement activities are undertaken together to develop time as well as method standards. Setting time standards in a structured manner permits the use of benchmarks against which to measure a range of variables such as cost of the product and share of work between team members. However the work measurement technique has been criticised for being misused by management in determining worker compensation. The time needed to perform each work element can be determined by the use of historical data, work sampling or most usually time study.

Time study

The purpose of time study is, through the use of statistical techniques, to arrive at a standard time for performing one cycle of a repetitive job. This is arrived at by observing a task a number of times. The standard time refers to the time allowed for the job under specific circumstances, taking into account allowances for rest and relaxation. The basic steps in a time study are indicated below:

1. *Establish the standard job method*. It is essential that the best method of undertaking the job is determined using method study before a time study is undertaken. If a better method for the job is found then the time study analysis will need to be repeated.
2. *Break down the job into elements*. The job should be broken down into a number of easily measurable tasks. This will permit a more accurate calculation of standard time as varying proficiencies at different parts of the whole job can be taken into account.
3. *Study the job*. This has traditionally been undertaken with a stopwatch, or electronic timer, by observation of the task. Each time element is recorded on an observation sheet. A video camera can be used for observation, which permits study away from the workplace, and in slow motion which permits a higher degree of accuracy of measurement.
4. *Rate the worker's performance*. As the time study is being conducted a rating of the worker's performance is also taken in order to achieve a true time rating for the task. Rating factors are usually between 80% and 120% of normal. This is an important but subjective element in the procedure and is best done if the observer is familiar with the job itself.
5. *Compute the average time*. Once a sufficient sample of job cycles have been undertaken an average is taken of the observed times called the cycle time. The sample size can be determined statistically, but is often around five to fifteen due to cost restrictions.
6. *Compute the normal time*. Adjust the cycle time for the efficiency and speed of the worker who was observed. The normal time is calculated by multiplying the cycle time by the performance rating factors.
7. *Compute the standard time*. The standard time is computed by adjusting the normal time by an allowance factor to take account of unavoidable delays such as machine breakdown and rest periods. The standard time is calculated as follows:

Normal time (NT) = Cycle time (CT) × Rating factor (RF)

Standard time (ST) = Normal time (NT) × Allowance

WORKED EXAMPLE

PCB Limited wants to determine the standard time for a manual solder operation on one of their new circuit boards. From the following task times observed during a time study exercise calculate the standard time for the job. Assume the worker who has been observed is 10% slower than average at this task. Assume an allowance factor of 20%.

Sample No.	1	2	3	4	5	6	7	8	9	10
Time (sec.)	6.7	7.1	7.3	7.0	7.1	6.8	6.9	6.8	7.1	7.0

SOLUTION

Cycle time (CT) = Average of samples = 69.8 /10 = 6.98 s

Normal time (NT) = CT × RT = 6.98 × 0.9 = 6.282 s

Standard time (ST) = NT × Allowance = 6.282 × 1.2 = 7.54 s

Predetermined motion times

One problem with time studies is that workers will not always co-operate with their use, especially if they know the results will be used to set wage rates. Combined with the costs of undertaking a time study, a company may use historical data in the form of time files to construct a new standard job time from a previous job element. This has the disadvantage however of the reliability and applicability of old data.

Another method for calculating standard times without a time study is to use the **predetermined motion time system** (PMTS) which provides generic times for standard micro-motions such as reach, move and release, which are common to many jobs. The standard item for the job is then constructed by breaking down the job into a micro-motions that can then be assigned a time from the motion time database. The standard time for the job is the sum of these micro-motion times. Factors such as load weight for move operations are included in the time motion database.

The advantages of this approach are that standard times can be developed for jobs before they are introduced to the workplace without causing disruption and needing worker compliance. Also performance ratings are factored into the motion times and so the subjective part of the study is eliminated. The timings should also be much more consistent than historical data for instance. Disadvantages include the fact that these times ignore the context of the job in which they are undertaken, i.e. the timings are provided for the micro-motion in isolation and not part of a range of movement. The sample is from a broad range of workers in different industries with different skill levels, which may lead to an unrepresentative time. Also the timings are only available for simple repetitive work which is becoming less common in industry.

Work sampling

Work sampling is useful for analysing the increasing proportion of non-repetitive tasks that are performed in most jobs. It is a method for determining the proportion of time a worker or machine spends on various activities and as such can be very useful in job redesign and estimating levels of worker output. The basic steps in work sampling are indicated below:

1. Define the job activities

All possible activities must be categorised for a particular job, e.g. 'worker idle' and 'worker busy' states could be used to define all possible activities.

2. Determine the number of observations in the work sample

The accuracy of the proportion of time the worker is in a particular state is determined by the observation sample size. Assuming the sample is approximately normally distributed the sample size can be estimated using the following formula:

$$n = (z/e)^2 p(1-p)$$

where:
n = sample size
z = number of standard deviations from the mean for the desired level of confidence
e = the degree of allowable error in the sample estimate
p = the estimated proportion of time spent on a work activity.

The accuracy of the estimated proportion p is usually expressed in terms of an allowable degree of error e (e.g. for a 2% degree of error, $e = 0.02$). The degree of confidence would normally be 95% (giving a z value of 1.96) or 99% (giving a z value of 2.58).

3. Determine the length of the sampling period

There must be sufficient time in order for a random sample of the number of observations given by the equation above to be collected. A random number generator can be used to generate the time between observations in order to achieve a random sample.

4. Conduct the work sampling study and record the observations

Calculate the sample and calculate the proportion (p) by dividing the number of observations for a particular activity by the total number of observations.

5. Periodically recompute the sample size required

It may be that the actual proportion for an activity is different from the proportion used to calculate the sample size in Step 2. Therefore as sampling progresses it is useful to re-compute the sample size based on the proportions actually observed.

WORKED EXAMPLE

The FastCabs Company has a complement of 25 cabs on duty at any one time. The manager of the company wishes to determine the amount of time a cab driver is sitting idle which he estimates at 35%. The cabs were called over a period of a week at random to determine their status. If the manager wants the estimate to be within ± 5% of the actual proportion with a confidence level of 95%, estimate the sample size required.

SOLUTION

$$n = (z/e)^2 p(1-p)$$

At 95% confidence $z = 1.96$ (from Normal Table – see Appendix); $e = 0.05$; $p = 0.35$, thus:

$n = (1.96/0.05)^2 \times 0.35(1 - 0.35) = 350$

Thus 350 samples are required.

Learning curves

Organisations have often used learning curves to predict the improvement in productivity that can occur as experience is gained of a process. Thus learning curves can give an organisation a method of measuring continuous improvement activities. If a firm can estimate the rate at which an operation time will decrease then it can predict the impact on cost and increase in effective capacity over time.

The learning curve is based on the concept of when productivity doubles, the decrease in time per unit is the rate of the learning curve. Thus if the learning curve is at a **learning rate** of say 85%, the second unit takes 85% of the time of the first unit, the fourth unit takes 85% of the second unit and the eighth unit takes 85% of the fourth and so on.

Mathematically the learning curve is represented by the function:

$y = ax^{-b}$

where:
x = number of units produced
a = hours required to produce the first unit
y = time to produce the xth unit
b = constant equal to $-(\ln p)/(\ln 2)$
$\ln = \log_{10}$
p = learning rate (e.g. 80% = 0.8)

Thus for a 80% learning rate:

$b = -(\ln 0.8)/\ln (2) = -(-0.233)/(0.693) = 0.322$

WORKED EXAMPLE

A company is introducing a new product and has determined that an 80% learning rate is applicable. Estimates of demand for the first four years of production are 100, 150, 175 and 200. The time to produce the first unit is estimated at 100 hours. Estimate the labour hours required for each of the first 4 years of production.

SOLUTION

$y = ax^{-b}$

where:
$b = -(\ln p)/(\ln 2)$
$a = 100$
$p = 0.8$
$b = -\ln 0.8/\ln 2 = 0.322$

Thus for year 1: $x = 100$; $y = 100 \times 100^{0.322} = 440$ hours

The results for the first four years of production are shown in the table below.

Year	Labour hours	Cumulative labour hours
1	$100(100)^{0.322}$	440
2	$100(250)^{0.322}$	592
3	$100(425)^{0.322}$	702
4	$100(625)^{0.322}$	795

Learning curves are usually applied to individual operators, but the concept can also be applied in a more aggregate sense, termed an experience or improvement curve, and applied to such areas as manufacturing system performance or cost estimating. Industrial sectors can also be shown to have different rates of learning

It should be noted that improvements along a learning curve do not just happen and the theory is most applicable to new product or process development where scope for improvement is greatest. In addition step changes can occur which can alter the rate of learning, such as organisational change, changes in technology or quality improvement programs. To ensure learning occurs the organisation must invest in factors such as research and development, advanced technology, people and continuous improvement efforts.

Behavioural approach

Work simplification can be beneficial when jobs have become over-complex or require a precise design of tasks and their interrelationships to increase output. However simplification can prevent worker participation in new ideas. Also task simplification can lead to boredom and teamwork can be inhibited.

Some approaches have been taken to reduce job simplification. These have been suggested by such as Herzberg's **two-factor theory** and Hackman and Oldman's **job characteristics model**.

Herzberg (1968) stated that there are two major sets of factors, 'motivators' and 'hygiene' factors, which affect motivation. Hygiene factors should be present to prevent dissatisfaction and consist of extrinsic elements such as working conditions, salary level and relationships with fellow workers. However in order to obtain real motivation in employees the motivator factors must be present. These are more intrinsic factors such as responsibility, recognition and advancement. Thus in order to increase motivation the redesign of jobs should focus on motivators such as increasing accountability and providing feedback on performance.

The Hackman and Oldman (1980) job characteristics model is useful in providing suggestions of how to structure jobs to include more motivators. The model links job characteristics with the desired psychological state of the individual and the outcomes in terms of motivation and job performance. The model takes into account individual differences and provides a structure for analysing motivational problems at work and to predict the effects of change on people's jobs and to help plan new work systems.

The model proposes five desirable characteristics for a job:

- *Skill variety:* The extent to which a job makes use of different skills and abilities.
- *Task identity:* The extent to which a job involves a meaningful piece of work.
- *Task significance:* The extent to which a job affects other people.
- *Autonomy:* The extent to which information about the level of job performance is provided.
- *Feedback:* The extent to which information about the level of job performance is provided.

The model proposes that the presence of these characteristics will lead to desirable mental states in terms of meaningful work and responsibility for outcomes of work, which in turn leads to higher motivation and quality of work performance.

The following are examples of approaches to job design that have been used in an attempt to bring these desirable job characteristics to people's work leading to an improved mental state and thus increased performance.

Job enlargement
This involves the horizontal integration of tasks to expand the range of tasks involved in a particular job. If successfully implemented this can increase task identity, task significance and skill variety through involving the worker in the whole work task either individually or within the context of a group. **Job rotation** is a common form of job enlargement and involves a worker changing job roles with another worker on a periodic basis. If successfully implemented this can help increase task identity, skill variety and autonomy through involvement in a wider range of work task with discretion about when these mix of tasks can be undertaken. However this method does not actually improve the design of the jobs and it can mean that people gravitate to the jobs that suit them and are not interested in initiating rotation with colleagues. At worst it can mean rotation between a number of boring jobs with no acquisition of new skills.

Job enrichment
Job enrichment involves the vertical integration of tasks and the integration of responsibility and decision making. If successfully implemented this can increase all five of the desirable job characteristics by involving the worker in a wider range of tasks and providing responsibility for the successful execution of these tasks. This technique does require feedback so that the success of the work can be judged. The managerial and staff responsibilities potentially given to an employee through enrichment can be seen as a form of empowerment. This should in turn lead to improved productivity and product quality.

Implementation of job enlargement/job enrichment approaches
There are a number of factors which account for the fact that job enlargement and job enrichment are not more widely implemented. Firstly the scope for using different forms of work organisation will be dependent to a large extent on the type of operation in which the work is organised.

Job shop manufacturing will require skilled workers who will be involved in a variety of tasks and will have some discretion in how they undertake these tasks. Sales personnel may also have a high level of discretion in how they undertake their job duties also.

The amount of variety in a batch manufacturing environment will to a large extent depend on the length of the production runs used. Firms producing large batches of a single item will obviously have less scope for job enrichment than firms producing in small batches on a make-to-order basis. One method for providing job enlargement is to use a cellular manufacturing system, which can permit a worker to undertake a range of tasks on a part. When combined with responsibility for cell performance this can lead to job enrichment.

Jobs in mass production industries may be more difficult to enlarge. Car plants must work at a certain rate in order to meet production targets and on a moving line it is only viable for each worker to spend a few minutes on a task before the next worker on the line must take over. A way of overcoming this problem is to use teams. Here tasks are exchanged between team members and performance measurements are supplied for the team as a whole. This provides workers with greater variety and feedback, but also some autonomy and participation in the decisions of the team.

Secondly financial factors may be a constraint on further use. These may include the performance of individuals who actually prefer simple jobs, higher wage rates paid for the higher skills of employees, increasing average wage costs and the capital costs of introducing the approaches. The problem is that many of the benefits associated with the technique, such as an increase in creativity, may be difficult to measure financially.

Finally the political aspects of job design changes have little effect on organisational structures and the role of management. Although job enrichment may affect supervisory levels of management, by replacement with a team leader for example, the power structures in which technology is used to justify decisions for personal objectives is intact.

   CASE STUDY
Job design and just-in-time production

Suzaki (1987) defines just-in-time production (JIT) as a management philosophy aimed at eliminating waste from every aspect of manufacturing and its related activities. Work by Toyota after years of ongoing improvement identified seven key types of waste:

- waste from overproduction
- waste of waiting time
- transportation waste
- processing waste
- inventory waste
- waste of motion
- waste from product defects.

Suzaki (1987) suggests an eighth waste of 'the waste of under-utilised people's skills and capabilities'. The following strategies for utilising peoples skills are given:

- **Job security**. In order to utilise workers' abilities to improve performance a culture of trust and job security is needed. Opportunities to fulfil potential and to find an appropriate role should be provided through education and training programmes.

- **Suggestion schemes**. Suggestion scheme programmes are seen as an essential element in improvement activities. This requires systems that can evaluate suggestions and a feeling of trust.
- **Cell layouts**. These can be used to form teams and improve communication, co-ordination and co-operation between employees.
- **Flexible organisation**. In order to obtain flexibility requires close co-ordination between organisational functions such as engineering, manufacturing and marketing. The basic principles of simplify, combine and eliminate are used to facilitate improvement.
- **Decentralised organisation**. A decentralised organisational structure provides a broader scope of responsibility for all employees and the development of a larger number of people with skills and knowledge. Management roles will change to one of sponsorship and providing vision for the organisation.

Ergonomics

In addition to the psychological effects of work outlined in the Hackman and Oldham (1980) model discussed previously, job design should consider the physical effects of work. Ergonomics uses information about human characteristics and behaviour to understand the effect of design, methods and environment. Two areas of major concern are the interaction with physical devices, such as computer terminals, and with the environment, such as the office.

Physical design

When required to operate a physical device a worker must be able to reach the controls and apply the necessary force to them. Although the average person is capable of a variety of tasks, the speed and accuracy of any actions can be affected by the location of a device. Because the human part of this system cannot obviously be designed, considerable thought must be placed into the location of the device taking into account human capabilities.

Anthropometric data

Anthropometric data is information concerning factors related to the physical attributes of a human being, such as the size, weight and strength of various parts of the human body. From this information it is possible to gather data on the range of motion, sitting height, strength, working height and other variables. The data can then be used to ensure that the vast majority, say 95% of the population, has the capability to use the device efficiently. For instance the reach required to operate equipment should be no greater than the shortest reach of all the persons required to operate it. In some cases equipment may need adjustment devices built in to cater for different needs. The adjustable car seat is an example of this. Other designs are more subtle. For instance the arrangement of a number of dials or gauges so they all point or read in the same direction during normal operation enables much speedier checking by an operative.

Environmental design

This involves the immediate environment in which the job takes place. Some environmental variables to consider include the following.

- **Noise**. Excessive noise levels can not only be distracting but can lead to damage to the worker's hearing. Noise is measured in decibels (dB) on a logarithmic scale which means that a 10dB increase in noise equates to an increase of ten times in noise intensity. Extended periods of exposure above 90dB have been judged to be permanently damaging to hearing. Higher sound intensities may be permitted for short exposures but no sound as high as 130dB should be experienced.
- **Illumination**. The level of illumination depends on the level of work being performed. Jobs requiring precise movements will generally require a higher level of illumination. Other lighting factors such as contrast, glare and shadows are also important.
- **Temperature and humidity**. Although humans can perform under various combinations of temperature, humidity and air movement, performance will suffer outside of an individual's **comfort zone**. Obviously the nature of the task will effect the temperature range under which work can be undertaken.

   CASE STUDY

The QWERTY keyboard – a case for ergonomics?

The layout of the Qwerty keyboard on virtually all computer keyboards, pocket calculators, lap tops, electronic typewriters and diaries etc. and manufactured worldwide is based on a design from 1874 on the mechanical typewriter, in order to prevent an operator keying too quickly and jamming the keys. It is not arranged so that letters correspond to typical sequences of letters in words that are the most frequently used letters grouped together within easy reach.

Ergonomic studies have proved that alternative layouts are quicker to learn, lead to fewer mistakes and cause less fatigue. Maybe it's ignorance or economics rather than ergonomics which maintains the impetus of the present design.

   CASE STUDY

The seated worker – Homo Sedans

Medical and ergonomic research has advocated that workers should be seated wherever possible. The critical arguments are stress on the legs is lessened, unnatural positions can be avoided, energy consumption can be reduced and there is less demand on the blood circulation. The disadvantages include slackened abdominal muscles, rounded back and possible damage to digestive tracts and lungs.

In principle a nearly upright sitting position with slight lumbar lordosis is ideal. This can be achieved best by suitable seats and back rests. Electro-myographic investigations suggest a slightly stooped posture produces less stress in the muscles and is thus more comfortable. Despite years of research and recommendations it is thought that most seating used (domestic and industrial) is inappropriate to the work, leading to inefficiency, discomfort and injury.

Case study

Ergonomics and automation

While the use of automation has made the job of the worker easier, paradoxically it is also harder. Automatic and machine controlled equipment replaces much of the muscular work and demands much less precise psychomotor skill but does not provide much opportunity to practise skills should intervention be needed. Secondly, the natural compatibility between display and control is often lost. The worker is often remote from the process and receives information from displays symbolically. The symbols must be interpreted to find out about the process. The design of jobs in automated systems (e.g. driving, computer terminals, computerised machine tools, CAD/CAM, air traffic control, condition monitoring in maintenance work, process control) particularly in respect to mental loads, is critical if we are to optimise the efficiency and contribution of the human in the system.

In the interests of individual fitness and the popularity of physical exercise, to increase the physical loading of a largely sedentary population we may need to find work and job design projects that increase the energy requirements of the worker!

Sociotechnical systems theory

Sociotechnical systems theory recognises that changes to the technical system are likely to have a significant impact on the social organisation in which they are performed. The idea is to design a work system that fulfils both the human and social needs as well as the technical and economic requirements of the organisation. This will ensure that 'obvious' benefits in terms of productivity from the introduction of technology is not lost by failing to take the social consequences of the change into account.

The sociotechnical approach usually involves the formation of autonomous **work groups**. Here members are responsible for a part of the work, but much of the decision making is taken as a group in order to foster joint commitment to objectives. Thus many of the social relationships between group members are not specified by the formal organisation and members can vary their roles over time with the agreement of the group. This can then help to build a close social group and thus improve effectiveness at the technical task.

The introduction of new technology

The shift from mass production to **computer-integrated manufacturing** (CIM) can lead to greater opportunities or intellectual mastery and cognitive skills for workers, more worker responsibility for results, and greater interdependence among workers, enabling more social interaction and the development of teamwork and co-ordination skills (Daft, 1989).

The introduction of new technology can lead to the simplification of jobs which can mean boring, repetitive work that provides little satisfaction. Management can see this as an advantage if increasing task specialisation and reducing the level of skill required in a job leads to lower wages. The organisation around a technology can be used to control labour costs, as well as ensure greater control over such factors as worker decision making and career progression, thus maintaining the role and status of managers as a controlling group. Thus technology can be used to justify unpopular management decisions. The fact that repetitive work leading from specialisation leads to low worker motivation only confirms management's view of the need for their approach. To change this view will require an examination of the culture of the workplace that leads to a focus on the social as opposed to simply the technical issues of change. Job design has been used to try to overcome the problems of introducing technology by attempting to match organisational, technical and human needs.

In summary, the introduction of technology in the form of computer-based information systems and automation will lead to organisations which are:

- *Small:* small organisations will remain, but large organisations will be subdivided into small groups consisting of multi-skilled people using technology to undertake a variety of tasks using a teamwork approach.
- *Flexible:* organisations will need to become more flexible in how they react to market demands and this will be attained by creating a more flexible workforce. Importantly the idea of the organisation as a system – where the interactions between parts are as important as the parts themselves – will enable people to implement strategies which move the whole company in one direction, not just particular departments.
- *Responsive:* the integration of human and technology systems, through such approaches as sociotechnical systems theory should enable the organisation to rapidly respond to environmental changes. For example, the use of **computer-aided design** (CAD) will enable fast changes to product designs to be made in response to customer needs. However this requires a need for marketing, engineering and manufacturing to be able to collaborate closely in order to ensure designs are suitable for customers and can be manufactured to specification at a competitive cost.

 CASE STUDY

Technology and the future of work

Zuboff (1988) analysed the introduction of information technology and its relationship to the nature of work and the social relationships that organise productive activity. She concluded that technology has not only got the capacity to automate, but to what is termed 'informate'. The term refers to when technology is used to automate, it 'simultaneously generates information about the underlying productive and administrative processes through which an organisation accomplishes its work' Zuboff (1988). When automation occurs this capacity can be utilised or simply ignored. Organisations which pursue an information technology strategy will need to recognise the emergent demand for intellective skills and develop a learning environment in which such skills can develop.

'The organisations described in this book have illustrated how the need to defend and reproduce the legitimacy of managerial authority can challenge potential innovation towards a conventional emphasis on automation. In this context, managers emphasise machine intelligence and managerial control over the knowledge base at the expense of developing knowledge in the operating work force.... In these organisations, the promise of automation seemed to exert a magnetic force, a seduction that promised to fulfil a dream of perfect control and heal egos wounded by their needs for certainty. The dream contains the image of people serving a smart machine, but in the shadow of the dream, human beings have lost the critical judgement that would allow them to no longer simply respond but to know better than, to question, to say no.' (Zuboff, 1988 p. 390)

Empowerment

Empowerment is characterised by an organisation in which employees are given more autonomy, discretion and responsibility in decision making. Empowerment is often associated with teamwork, which is claimed to offer a higher level of responsibility than at the individual level. 'Individuals may argue about who is exactly responsible for what, whereas a team is responsible for the result. How any problem is best resolved becomes an internal matter' (Belbin, 1996). Empowered teams are the basis of what is called high-performance work systems. These systems are defined as performing to an excellent standard across a number of attributes (Viall, 1982). A feature of empowered teams is the change of the first line supervisor position from a supervising to a facilitating role. This implies a loss of direct control of employees, a wider span of worker control and a role as a co-ordinator of ideas for improvement. These changes have led to what have been called high-performance work systems based on empowered, autonomous teamwork in 'new design plants' and have been claimed to represent a new kind of organisation (Lawler, 1986; 1995). The 'new design plants' have attributes such as **self-managing teams** performing 'whole' work processes with elected leaders, a flat management hierarchy and team responsibility for selecting and training of new members (Buchanan, 1997).

Empowerment has been developed in response to an individual need for challenging and meaningful work and the expectations of employers in a marketplace characterised by rapid change and new technologies.

'First, there is an expectation that empowerment develops employee skills, job satisfaction and motivation, and leads to improved decision-making and problem-solving and to the development of a climate of continuous improvement. Second, skilled and motivated employees are expected to produce quality products, to provide customers with high levels of service and to respond in a rapid and flexible way to change' (Buchanan, 1997).

In summary, **job enrichment** approaches attempt to increase worker satisfaction leading to motivation and thus better performance. The sociotechnical approach recognises the need to consider both the human and technological aspects of job design. The empowerment concept aims to meet both the needs of employees for challenging, meaningful work and the needs of rapidly changing markets and new technology.

Summary of key points

- Each job must be designed around a compromise of technical, economic and behavioural feasibility.

- Scientific management often leads to work that is repetitive, narrow in scope and permits limited social interaction among workers.
- Work study is used to measure performance of jobs which have characteristics given by the scientific approach, i.e. routine and repetitive
- Work study consists of two main elements: method study and work measurement.
- Method study consists of dividing and analysing a task in a systematic manner in order to improve the method of carrying out that task.
- Work measurement consists of determining the length of time it will take to undertake a task in order to establish a benchmark against which performance can be measured.
- Learning curves are used to predict the improvement in productivity that can occur as experience is gained at a process.
- The job characteristics model links job characteristics to performance through an intervening variable: motivation.
- Two approaches to job design that have attempted to increase motivation (and thus performance) are job enlargement and job enrichment.
- The scope of introducing job enlargement and job enrichment will depend to a large extent on the type of operation in which the work is organised.
- Ergonomics uses information about human characteristics and behaviour to understand the effect of physical and environmental design.
- Sociotechnical systems theory takes an approach to work design in which both the human and social needs are taken into consideration.
- The workplace culture can determine whether social issues as opposed to solely technical issues are considered in job design.
- Empowerment has been developed in response to an individual need for challenging and meaningful work and the expectations of employers in a marketplace characterised by rapid change and new technologies.

Exercises

1 Investigate and redesign a suitable process with which you are familiar using the method study approach.
2 The following times have been observed for a job consisting of five elements. A performance rating factor has been calculated for each element. Assume an allowance factor of 15%.
   a) Determine the normal time (NT) for each element.
   b) Determine the overall normal time.
   c) Determine the standard time.

Element	Time	Ratings factor
1	3.6	1.05
2	4.8	0.9
3	2.9	1.0
4	4.9	1.1
5	1.7	0.95

3 Calculate the portion of time a supervisor spends in the maintenance department from the following data. Management believe that 50% of the supervisor's time is spent in main-

tenance. They require an estimate to be within ± 5% of the actual proportion with a 95% degree of confidence.

4 An electrical goods manufacturer is producing an electronic component for a washing machine. It is estimated that it will take 150 hours to produce the first unit. The standard learning curve for this type of component is 90%. What are the labour hours required for the 500th (and last) unit produced?

5 Analyse the major drawbacks of job specialisation and show using examples how the techniques of job design can help to overcome them.

6 Locate two newspaper articles referring to empowerment and contrast their implementation.

References

Belbin, M., *The Coming Shape of Organisation*, Butterworth-Heinemann (1996).

Bessant, J., *Managing Advanced Manufacturing Technology*, Blackwell, Oxford (1991).

Brown, S., *Strategic Manufacturing for Competitive Advantage: Transforming Operations from Shop Floor to Strategy*, Prentice-Hall (1996).

Buchanan, D. and Huczynski, A., *Organizational Behaviour: An Introductory Text*, Third Ed., Prentice-Hall (1997).

Daft, R.L., *Organization Theory and Design*, Third Ed., West Publishing Co. (1989).

Gilbreth, F., *Motion Study*, Van Nostrand Co: New York (1911).

Hackman, R.J., Oldman, G. (1980), *Work Redesign*, Addison-Wesley.

Herzberg, F., One more time: how do you motivate employees? *Harvard Business Review* (Sep–Oct 1968).

Lawler, E.E., *High Involvement Management: Participative Strategies for Improving Organizational Performance*, Jossey-Bass (1986).

Lawler, E.E., *The Ultimate Advantage: Creating the High Involvement Organization*, Macmillan (1995).

Pine, B., Best, V. and Boynton, A., Making mass customisation work, *Harvard Business Review*, (September–October 1993) pp. 108–119.

Piore, M., Sable, C., *The Second Industrial Divide: Possibilities for Prosperity*, Basic Books, New York (1984).

Schonberger, R., *World Class Manufacturing*, Free Press, New York (1986).

Suzaki, K., *The New Manufacturing Challenge: Techniques for Continuous Improvement*, Free Press, New York (1987).

Taylor, F.W., *The Principles of Scientific Management*, Harper and Brothers: New York (1911).

Vaill, P.B., The purposing of high performing systems, *Organizational Dynamics*, (Autumn 1982) pp. 23–39.

Zuboff, S., *In the Age of the Smart Machine: The Future of Work and Power*, Heinemann (1988).

Further reading

Bailey, J., *Managing People and Technological Change*, Pitman (1993).

Mullins, L.J., *Management and Organisational Behaviour*, Fourth Ed., Pitman (1996).

Mundel, M.E., *Motion and Time Study: Improving Productivity*, Sixth Ed., Prentice-Hall (1985).

Slack, N., Chambers, S., Harland, C., Harrison, A. and Johnston, R., *Operations Management*, Second Ed., Pitman (1998).

Wagner, J.A. and Hollenbeck, J.R., *Organisational Behavior: Securing Competitive Advantage*, Third Ed., Prentice-Hall (1998).

5 Product and service design

Objectives

By the end of this chapter, you should be able to:

- understand the main steps in product design;
- understand the role of market, economic and technical analysis in assessing the feasibility of a product design;
- utilise the cost-volume-profit model for economic analysis of product design;
- understand the role of reliability and maintainability in functional design;
- understand techniques relevant to improving the product design process;
- understand issues involves in the design of services.

Key functions in design

Good design of products and services is an essential element in satisfying customer needs and therefore ensuring the long-term success of the organisation. The success of the design process is primarily dependent on the relationship between the marketing, design and operations functions of the organisation. These functions need to co-operate in order to identify customer needs and produce a cost-effective and quality design that meets these needs. The roles of the main functions are summarised below:

Marketing
- Conduct market research to evaluate consumer needs.
- Provide a forecast of demand in the marketplace taking into account competitive pressures and the external environment.
- Understand the attributes of the product/service life cycle.

Engineering
- Undertake product/service process design and re-engineering.

Operations
- To produce the product or service as designed using the specified processes.
- To ensure efficient levels of supply while delivering a high quality product or service.

In addition the role of **suppliers** are becoming increasingly important in product/service design to the extent of outsourcing or contracting to another company part of the design or production of the product itself.

Finance will also be involved in providing capacity for development costs and facilities required for production. It will need to evaluate the success of any products introduced into the marketplace and provide estimates of when the investments made to bring the product to market will be paid back. Calculations will need to include factors such as overhead costs as well as costs directly attributable to the product.

Communication between all these functions can be facilitated by the use of **accounting** and **information systems** that allow up-to-date and accurate information to be available across the organisation.

This chapter will outline the steps involved in the process of product design and then discuss some of the techniques that may be used to improve the results of the design process. Many of the techniques are concerned with ensuring that final product quality is high by taking appropriate action at the design stage.

The product design process

The product design process involves the steps shown in Figure 5.1.

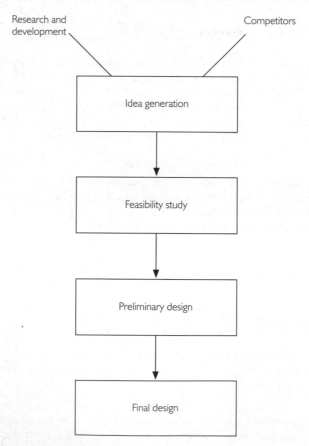

Figure 5.1   The product design process

Ideas generation

Ideas for new products can come from a variety of sources, including the organisation's research and development (R&D) department, suggestions from customers, market research data, salespeople, competitor actions or developments in new technology. The major source of new ideas or innovations will be dependent largely on the organisational strategy.

The research and development function

For an organisation that has a strategy of being first to the market with a new product, ideas will be devised principally from the organisation's own R&D department. For an organisation with a similar product to their competitors, innovation may be primarily in the design and manufacture stages to attain lower production costs. Successful product innovation comes from understanding the customer and identifying their needs. Various data collection methods such as questionnaires, focus groups and interviews should be used to gain sufficient understanding of customer requirements.

Research and development can take one of three forms:

- **Pure research:** knowledge-oriented research to develop new ideas with no specific product in mind.
- **Development:** product-oriented research concerned with turning research ideas into new products.
- **Applied research:** problem-oriented research to discover new and better products with specific commercial applications.

Pure research is often based in universities and funded by government agencies and so it is necessary for organisations to maintain close contact with the relevant institutions. Applied research will be undertaken by most organisations. The cost of undertaking research and development is high and there will be many failed projects, but the payoff from the small number of successes may be vital to the organisation's continued profitability.

Competitors

Competitors can provide a good source of ideas and it is important that the organisation analyses any new products they introduce to the market and make an appropriate response. **Reverse engineering** is a systematic approach to dismantling and inspecting a competitor's product to look for aspects of design that could be incorporated into the organisation's own product. This is especially prevalent when the product is a complex assembly such as a car, where design choices are myriad.

Benchmarking compares a product against what is considered the best in that market segment and then making recommendations on how the product can be improved to meet that standard. Although a reactive strategy, benchmarking can be useful to organisations who have lost ground to innovative competitors.

Feasibility study

The marketing function will take the product ideas and customer needs identified in the idea generation stage and form a series of alternative product concepts on which a feasibility study is undertaken. The product concept refers not to the physical product the person is buying but the overall set of expected benefits that a customer is buying. For instance a restaurant meal consists not only of the meal itself, but the level of attention and the general surroundings. Thus the product concept is referring to a combination of physical product and service referred to as the service package. Once a concept has been formulated it must then be submitted to a number of analyses in order to assess its feasibility.

Market analysis

Market analysis consists of evaluating the product concept with potential customers through interviews, focus groups and other data collection methods. The physical product may be tested by supplying a sample for customer evaluation. The market analysis should identify whether sufficient demand for the proposed product exists and its fit with the existing marketing strategy.

The product life cycle

At a strategic level the organisation can use the product life cycle (PLC) to determine the likely cost and volume characteristics of the product. The product life cycle describes the product sales volume over time (Figure 5.2).

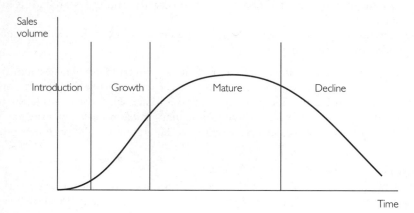

Figure 5.2 The product life cycle

In the early introduction phase production costs are high and design changes may be frequent. However there should be little or no competition for the new product and so a premium price can be charged to customers attracted to innovative products. The growth phase sees a rapid increase in volumes and the possibility of competitors entering the market. At this stage it is important to establish the product in the market as firmly as possible in order to secure future sales. Production costs should be declining as process improvements and standardisation takes place.

In the mature phase competitive pressures will increase and it is important that sales are secured through a branded product to differentiate it from competitors and a competitive price. There should be a continued effort at design improvement to both product and process. Some products, such as consumer durables, may stay in the mature phase almost indefinitely, and techniques such as advertising are used to maintain interest and market share.

If substitute products appear (e.g. CD for records) sales will decline. Before the product is discontinued or modified to meet customer needs the focus should be on optimising profits while minimising new investment. The PLC is a useful tool in developing a port-folio of products to different stages of the life cycle and for identifying when the product will enter the next stage of the life cycle. A particular problem can be when investment is diverted to the development of a new product, on the assumption that a current prod-uct is entering the decline phase, when this may not be the case. If the new product fails, potential sales may have been lost from the current product. The relationship between the product and process life-cycles is covered in Chapter 3.

Economic analysis
Economic analysis consists of developing estimates of production and demand costs and comparing them with estimates of demand. In order to perform the analysis requires an accurate estimate of demand as possible, derived from statistical forecasts of industry sales and estimates of market share in the sector the product is competing in. These estimates will be based on a predicted price range for the product which is compatible with the position of the new product in the market. In order to assess the feasibility of the pro-jected estimates of product costs, such factors as materials, equipment and personnel must be estimated. Techniques such as cost/benefit analysis, decision theory and account-ing measures such as net present value (NPV) and internal rate of return (IRR) may be used to calculate the profitability of a product. Another tool that can be used is the cost-volume-profit model.

The cost-volume-profit model
The cost-volume-profit (CVP) model provides a simplified representation that can be used to estimate the profit level generated by a product at a certain product volume.

Revenue is given by the following formula:

$$TR = SP \times X_s$$

where:
TR = total revenue
SP = selling price
X_s = units sold.

Cost is given by the following formula:

$$TC = FC + (VC \times X_p)$$

where:
TC = total cost
FC = fixed cost
VC = variable cost per unit
X_p = number of units produced.

Profit can then be given by the following formula:

$P = TR - TC$

where:
P = profit
TR = total revenue
TC = total cost.

Assuming $X_s = X_p$ (i.e. all products made are sold) then the volume for a certain profit can be given by the following formula:

$X = (P + FC)/(SP - VC)$

where:
X = volume (units)
P = profit
FC = fixed costs
SP = selling price
VC = variable costs.

When profit = 0 (i.e. selling costs = production costs) this is called the **break-even point** and can be given by the following formula:

$X = FC/(SP - VC)$

If contribution (C) is defined as (*Selling price – Variable cost*) ($SP - VC$) then the formula can be given as follows:

$X = FC/C$

A graphical representation of the model is shown as in Figure 5.3.

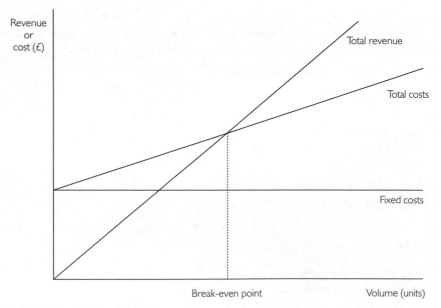

Figure 5.3 Cost-volume-profit model

WORKED EXAMPLE

A manufacturer produces a product with the following parameters.

a) What is the break-even point?
b) How many do they need to sell to make £15,000 profit a week.

Selling price (SP) = £7/unit
Variable cost (VC) = £4/unit
Fixed costs (FC) = £15,000/week

SOLUTION
a) At break-even point, $P = 0$:

$X = FC/(SP - VC) = 15,000/(7 - 4) = 5,000$ units/week

b) At $P = 15,000$:

$X = (P + FC)/(SP - VC) = (15,000 + 15,000)/(7 - 4) = 10,000$ units/week

When using the CVP model it must be remembered that it makes certain simplifications including an assumption of a linear relationship of cost and revenue to volume.

Using the CVP model for multiple products

If a firm produces more than one product using the same fixed costs the total profit can be calculated. The weighted contribution (Selling price − Variable cost) is calculated as follows:

$$WC = \sum_{i=1}^{n} M_i (SP_i - Vc_i)$$

where:
WC = weighted contribution
M_i = product mix as a percentage of the total sales for product i (where $i = 1$ to n, n = number of products)
SP_i = Selling price for product i
VC_i = Variable cost for product i

The volume for a certain profit level is given by the following formula:

$X = (P + FC)/WC$

where:
X = volume (units)
P = profit
FC = Fixed costs
WC = Weighted contribution

WORKED EXAMPLE

The following product mix is planned. Annual fixed cost = £20,000. What is the break-even point?

	Pliers	Saws
Product mix	0.75	0.25
Selling price/unit	£1.50	£3.20
Variable cost	£1.20	£1.80

SOLUTION

$$WC = \sum_{i=1}^{n} M_i (SP_i - VC_i) = 0.75 \times (1.50 - 1.20) + 0.25 \times (3.2 - 1.8) =$$
$$0.75 \times 0.3 + 0.25 \times 1.4 = 0.575$$

At profit = 0:

$X = FC/WC = 20{,}000/0.575 = 34{,}783$ units.

Technical analysis

Technical analysis consists of determining whether technical capability to manufacture the product exists. This covers such issues as ensuring materials are available to make the product to the specification required, and ensuring the appropriate machinery and skills are available to work with these materials. The technical analysis must take into account the target market and so product designers have to consider the costs of manufacturing and distributing the product in order to ensure it can be sold at a competitive price.

Strategic analysis involves ensuring that the product provides a competitive edge for the organisation, drawing on its competitive strengths and is compatible with the core business.

Preliminary design

Product concepts that pass the feasibility stage enter preliminary design. The specification of the concept – what the product should do to satisfy customer needs – is translated into a technical specification of the components of the package (the product and service components that satisfy the customer needs defined in the concept) and the process by which the package is created.

The specification of the components of the package requires a product/service structure which describes the relationship between the components and a bill of materials (BOM) or list of component quantities derived from the product structure. The process by which the package is created must also be specified in terms of mapping out the sequence of activities which are undertaken. This can be achieved with the aid of such devices as process flow charts (see Chapter 4).

Final design

The final design stage involves refining the preliminary design through the use of a prototype until a viable final design can be made. **Computer-aided design** (CAD) and **simulation modelling** can be used at this stage to build a computer-based prototype and refine the product and process design. The final design will be assessed in three main areas:

- functional design
- form design
- production design.

Functional design

Functional design is ensuring that the design meets the performance characteristics that are specified in the product concept. Two aspects of these are reliability and maintainability.

Reliability

Reliability is an important performance characteristic and measures the probability that a product will perform its intended function for a specified period of time under normal conditions of use. The reliability will refer the parts of the product and the reliability of each part must be determined by reference to the criteria of 'failure' and 'normal' service. These criteria are determined by reference to customer expectations and cost levels. Reliability can be determined by either the probability of failure at a given test level or the probability of failure during a given time.

The probability of failure during a given test is a function of the reliability of component parts and the relationship of those parts. For a product of two component parts as shown in Figure 5.4, the reliability is the product of the probabilities:

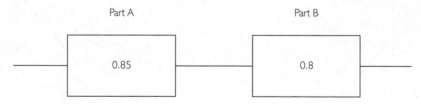

Figure 5.4 *Product reliability (serial)*

Reliability = 0.85 × 0.8 = 0.68

Note that the product reliability (0.68) is much less than the component parts and will continue to decline as the number of parts increases. For a product with backup (redundant) components however, as in Figure 5.5, the following applies:

Reliability = (0.8 + 0.85) × (1 − 0.8) = 0.97

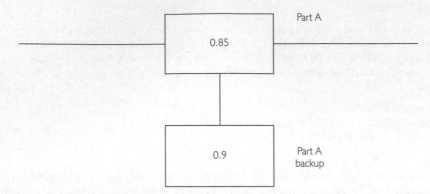

Figure 5.5 Product reliability (parallel or backup)

Note that the product reliability (0.97) is much higher than the component parts, but the cost of providing a backup makes its use relevant in only critical components or applications.

The probability of failure during a given time is often expressed diagramatically as a distribution of failures over time. Failure rates tend to follow the distribution pattern shown in Figure 5.6 which is often referred to as the **bathtub curve**. Defective parts fail early and then the failure rate rises again towards the end of a product's life after a period of infrequent random failures in mid-life.

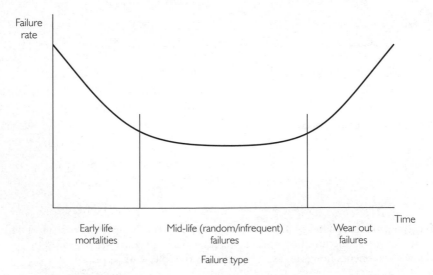

Figure 5.6 Failure pattern (derived from the distribution of failures) over time

The reciprocal of the actual failure rate, found by product testing, is called the **mean time between failures** (MTBF) and if it is found to follow a negative exponential law. The reliability (or probability that the product will not fail before a time T) can be found as follows:

P (no failure before T) $= e^{-T/MTBF}$

where:
e $= 2.7183$
$T =$ time period
$MTBF =$ mean time between failures

WORKED EXAMPLE

If the life of a product follows a negative exponential distribution and the average lifespan $= 10$ years, what is the probability that the product will fail after 5 years?

SOLUTION

$P(5) = e^{-5/10} = 0.61$

Thus here is a 61% chance of lasting 5 years. Conversely there is a 39% chance of failure during this time period.

It can be seen from the affect on reliability of serial and paralleled components that simplified product design (i.e. fewer parts), improved reliability of individual parts and the adoption of redundant parts will all improve overall product reliability.

Maintainability
Maintainability considers the cost of servicing the product at the design stage. This may include such issues as the ability of the customer to service the product or the need for trained personnel to undertake maintenance or repair activities. Maintainability is connected to issues such as the cost of the product (it may be cheaper to throw away rather than to repair the product) and its reliability (very high reliability will reduce the importance of maintainability).

Maintainability can be expressed as the mean time to repair (MTTR). Thus the **availability** of a product (i.e. uptime for a machine) can be calculated by combining the MTBF measure, along with the time taken to repair these failures (MTTR).

Availability $= MTBF/(MTBF + MTTR)$

Maintainability can be improved by modular design to enable whole modules to be replaced rather than pursue a lengthy investigation of faults. Maintenance schedules should also be specified to help prevent problems from occurring. An improved ability to perform under adverse conditions (termed the **design robustness**) will improve maintainability.

Form design
Form design refers to the product **aesthetics** such as look, feel and sound if applicable. This is particularly important for consumer durables but even industrial appliances should at least project an image of quality.

Production design

This involves ensuring that the design takes into consideration the ease and cost of manufacture of a product. Good design will take into consideration the present manufacturing capabilities in terms of material supplies, equipment and personnel skills available.

The cost of production can be reduced by:

- **simplification** – reducing the number of assemblies
- **standardisation** – enabling the use of components for different products and modules
- **modularisation** – combining standardised building blocks in different ways to create a range of products.

Improving product design

The text will now explore a number of techniques that have been developed in an attempt to improve the design process.

Concurrent design

Concurrent design, also known as simultaneous engineering, is when contributors to the stages of the design effort provide their expertise together throughout the design process as a team. This contrasts with the traditional sequential design process when work is undertaken within functional specialisms. The problem with the traditional approach is the cost and time involved in bringing the product to market. In some business sectors (e.g. Information Technology) shrinking product life cycles have meant that new products or improvements to existing products are required in an ever shorter time scale. Concurrent design reduces the time wasted when each stage in the design process waits for the previous stage to finish completely before it can commence.

Another problem of the traditional approach to design is the lack of communication between functional specialists involved in the different stages of design. This can lead to an attitude of 'throwing the design over the wall' without any consideration of problems that may be encountered by later stages. An example of this is decisions made at the preliminary design stage that adversely effect choices at the product build stage. This can cause the design to be repeatedly passed between departments to satisfy everyone's needs, increasing time and costs. By facilitating communication through the establishment of a **project team**, problems of this type can be reduced.

Design for manufacture

An important aspect of good design is that the product designed can be produced easily and at low cost. Design for manufacture (DFM) is a concept which views product design as the first step in the manufacture of that product. DFM incorporates guidelines on such aspects as simplification, standardisation and modularisation but also techniques such as failure mode and effect analysis (FMEA) and value engineering (VE).

Failure mode and effect analysis

Failure mode and effect analysis (FMEA) is a systematic approach to identifying the cause and effect of product failures. The approach involves the following:

- list the function of the component parts of the product;
- define the failure modes (e.g. leakage, fatigue) for all parts;
- rank the failures in order of likelihood and seriousness;
- address each failure in rank order, making design changes where necessary.

The idea of FMEA is to anticipate failures and deal with them at the design stage. The term **failure mode, effect** and **criticality analysis** (FMECA) is used when a criticality index is used to rank the failures. The criticality index is the product of the following three values on a scale of 1 to 10.

P = probability of failure occurring (1 = unlikely, 10 = definitely)
S = seriousness of failure (1 = unimportant; 10 = danger to life and limb)
D = difficulty of detection before use by the consumer (1 = will be found; 10 = will not be found)

Thus:

Critical factor $= P \times S \times D$

Value engineering and value analysis

Value engineering (VE) aims to eliminate unnecessary features and functions that do not contribute to the value or performance of the product. It is derived from the idea of value analysis (VA) which was developed to improve the actual design, particularly taking into account the use of new technology. The technique uses a **team approach** and follows a formal procedure which has the following core activities:

- *Define function:* this involves defining each function of the product and its cost.
- *Gather alternatives:* a team will brainstorm new ways to accomplish the functions.
- *Evaluate alternatives:* each idea generated is evaluated for feasibility and cost

The technique can be used during design or as a continuous improvement tool during production when a flexible design specification is needed to accommodate suggestions at the production stage.

Quality functional deployment

Quality functional deployment (QFD) is a structured process that translates the voice of the customer (what the customer needs) into technical design requirements (how these needs are met). It is particularly relevant to the concept of **concurrent design** as it complements the use of teams in attempting to co-ordinate design objectives. The technique consists of a series of tables which translate requirements at successive design stages as follows:

- **The 'House of Quality':** Customer requirements → Product characteristics
- **Parts deployment:** Product characteristics → Part characteristics
- **Process planning:** Part characteristics → Process characteristics
- **Operating requirements:** Process characteristics → Operations

The most used matrix is the House of Quality that converts customer requirements into product characteristics. The House of Quality matrix is shown in Figure 5.7.

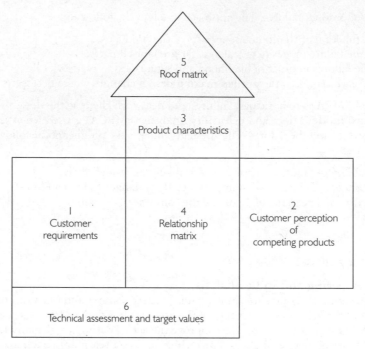

Figure 5.7 House of Quality matrix

The elements of the House of Quality are described below:

1. *Customer requirements.* This links the attributes of the product that are important to the customer along with their relative importance.
2. *Customer perceptions of competitive products.* This compares customer perceptions of the organisation and competitors', performance for each of the customer requirements. It provides information on relative performance and also identifies where competitive advantage can be attained by improving relative performance on a highly ranked customer requirement.
3. *Product characteristics.* This lists the product characteristics, expressed in engineering terms and grouped where appropriate.
4. *Relationship matrix.* The matrix correlates the attributes of customer requirements with product characteristics. The relationship may be a positive or negative one and assists in identifying design changes to product characteristics to meet customer requirements.
5. *Roof matrix.* This explores the interaction between product characteristics. This assists identification of an adverse change in product characteristic as a consequence of a change in another characteristic.
6. *Technical assessments and design targets.* This includes performance measures to compare the product with competitors. It also contains chosen critical design factors such as cost and importance.

Any change in product characteristic as a result of analysis of customer requirements in then carried forward to the parts deployment matrix and then converted to the process planning and finally operating requirements matrix. In this way QFD enables the full consequences of any design change to be assessed and operationalised. The technology provides a method of communicating the effect of change quickly amongst all the members of the design team.

Taguchi methods

Taguchi suggests that product failure is mainly a function of design. Three of the techniques for imposing design quality are:

- robust design
- quality loss function (QLF)
- design of experiments (DOE).

Robust design

The robustness of a product is defined by its ability to withstand variations in environmental and operating conditions. Robust design is the process of designing in the ability of the product to perform under a variety of conditions and so reducing the chance of product failure. In order to achieve this Taguchi suggests a focus on consistency of parts rather than just requiring manufacture within a tolerance. The tolerance arbitrarily defines a cut-off point between poor quality and good quality which may not be recognised by the customer. Taguchi has formalised the effect on customer dissatisfaction as the actual value deviates from the target value (i.e. the distance from the tolerance limit) called the Quality Loss Function (QLF). Taguchi argues that consistency is especially important is assembled products were parts at either end of their tolerance limit can result in a poor quality product. Thus the ability to produce a part to a consistent specification through design is important.

Quality loss function

The quality loss function (QLF) is a simple cost estimate which shows how customer preferences are oriented towards consistently meeting quality expectations and that a customer's dissatisfaction (i.e. quality loss) increases geometrically as the actual value deviates from the target value. See Figure 5.8 overleaf.

The quality loss function can be expressed mathematically:

$$L = kd^2$$

where:
L = quality loss
k = cost coefficient = consumer loss/(functional tolerance)^2
d = deviation from target value = $x_i - T$
x_i = measure of item i
T = target value.

Consumer loss consists of factors such as the cost of repair, the cost of correcting the results of a failure and the cost of not being able to use the product while it is being repaired. Functional tolerance is the deviation from a target value at which most customers will demand a repair or replacement.

Design of experiments

Design of experiments (DOE) aims to identify factors which affect a product's performance by providing a way of testing a number of design options under various

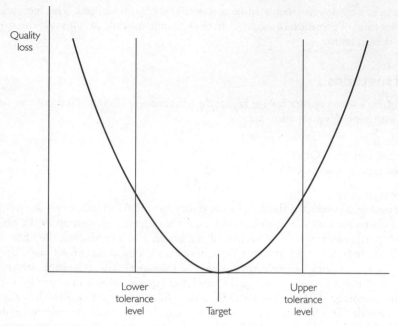

Figure 5.8 Quality loss function

operating and environmental conditions. In other words DOE provides a method of achieving robust design. The conditions that cause a poor product performance are separated into controllable and uncontrollable factors. In a design situation controllable factors are design parameters such as material type or dimensions. Uncontrollable factors derive from the wear of the product, such as the length of use or settings, or are environmental such as heat and humidity. A good design will have variables that act in a robust fashion to the possible occurrence of uncontrollable factors.

Service design

The service design process follows the steps in design outlined earlier in this chapter. The organisation must ensure that the service both fills a customer's need and can be provided competitively in the market place. One complication may be that the consumers of the service may not necessarily be the ones who purchase it. For example commercial TV stations provide a service to organisations wishing to advertise their goods. However the consumers of the service are the actual TV viewers. In services the design process includes both service design and service delivery.

Design of service

Once a market has been identified the service enters the design phase. The overall set of expected benefits that the customer is buying is termed the service concept. The service will actually usually consist of a combination of goods and services and is termed the service package. Fitzsimmons (1994) defines the service package as a bundle of goods and services consisting of the following four features.

1. *Supporting facility:* the physical resources that must be in place before a service can be offered.
2. *Facilitating goods:* the material purchased or consumed by the buyer or items provided by the customer.
3. *Explicit services:* the benefits that are readily observable by the senses and consist of the essential or intrinsic features of the service.
4. *Implicit services:* psychological benefits that the customer may sense only vaguely or extrinsic features of the service.

Because the service is intangible it is often difficult to test the quality levels before the service is provided. From the customer's point of view quality may only be assessed when the service is provided or perhaps an indication of service quality may be gained by seeking the views of others who have experience of the service required. Quality can be designed into the service by taking the design features and implementing a quality system to maintain conformance to design requirements. The techniques of QFD and Taguchi discussed earlier in this chapter are relevant in ensuring service design quality.

Design of service delivery

The role of service design is closely tied to the idea of maximising customer perception of the benefit of the service which will be balanced against the cost of providing that service. Since services are delivered as they are produced the roles of operations and marketing are closely tied and the design must consider both the delivery by the operations system and the distribution of the service to the customer. Once the service package has been specified for the target market the requirements of the service delivery system can be more fully determined. Design of the service delivery system is considered under service process design in Chapter 3 and capacity planning in services in Chapter 6.

 CASE STUDY

Car designers: the man who saved Chrysler's skin

Many of the best car designers develop from stylists to supervisors as they climb the corporate ladder. At best, they gain responsibility for a brand – or, better still, an entire group's design.

Few, however, reach the dizzy heights of Tom Gale, Chrysler's head of styling and much else. And none has done so while retaining his identity as a designer.

Isolating Gale's origins would be hard from his visiting card. It tells you he is executive vice-president (product strategy, design and external affairs), and general manager of the Jeep division. Design seems to be seriously diluted in his job description.

Yet, in spite of the heap of titles he has accumulated in three decades with America's most creative and resourceful car-maker, it is for design that he remains best known.

Ask about his proudest achievements at Chrysler – the smallest of Detroit's Big Three, which has twice been near bankruptcy – and he cites the Voyager, the world's first multipurpose vehicle (MPV). Now in its second incarnation. It was one of the milestones in the company's financial recovery after a roller-coaster ride under the larger-than-life Lee Iacocca, its previous chairman. By combining the attributes of a comfortable family saloon with the flexibility and carrying capacity of a van, it created a new niche and saved Chrysler's skin.

Mini-vans are not the only products of which 54-year-old Gale feels proud. He played a central role in reviving Jeep, the brand bought by Renault as part of American Motors and sold by the French to Chrysler in 1987 – a decision still rued in Paris.

All the latest generation of Jeeps was influenced by Gale's pen after he took over as vice-president of design in 1985. The honest, timeless lines of the Cherokee, barely changed in last year's face-lift, and the elegant Grand Cherokee played a significant part in reviving Chrysler's fortunes by moving it into the then nascent market for high-margin sports utility vehicles.

It was not only production cars which guided Chrysler's financial recovery. Gale helped put the company, written off by many potential customers, back on the map with a string of attention-grabbing concept cars, many harking back to the group's heyday in the 1950s. As he puts it: 'We had to get out there and say: "Hey, we aren't dead".'

From the first concept car 11 years ago, the idea was to do more than just let talented designers exercise their creative skills. 'One thing I felt when I took over design was that we were always a very reactive firm. What I really wanted to do was get us in front.'

The concept cars were meant to underline Chrysler's distinctiveness from General Motors and Ford, and Gale admits: 'I'm just amazed everyone has let us get away with what we've been doing.' Often wacky, they reinforced Chrysler's growing image as a company not run by bean counters in suits but by genuine car enthusiasts. Gale notes that even colleagues who were unconvinced at first 'recognised this was gold. What other medium would have allowed us to gain that much exposure?'

Many of the concepts were sporty exotica, much loved by opinion-forming motoring writers but never designed to take to the road. So, it helped when some – such as the 1989 Viper, a muscular, high-performance coupé – made it from mock-up to real motoring.

The Viper is built in low volumes at a specialist plant. By badging it as a Dodge, Chrysler lifted the image of this rather bland name. 'We needed to put a face on it,' says Gale. Two years ago, the company pulled the same trick with the Prowler, an aptly-named, sharp-nosed convertible redolent of the 1930s. This is sold as a Plymouth.

Because of his corporate responsibilities, Gale has not taken up the sketch pad for some time. But he believes the presence of a designer among the group's top guns was instrumental in giving design a bigger role in Chrysler's corporate affairs. 'I think the concept cars have given a different image to our company than we would have been able to gain otherwise.'

Gale trained as an engineer before switching to styling – something that probably eased his path upward. Starting at GM's AC spark plug subsidiary, he moved to advanced body engineering at Chrysler after gaining his master's degree. Four years later, he transferred to design.

Typically for a Chrysler man, where teamwork is part of the corporate mantra, he stresses the role of that and good management in the design process. 'This is as much about productivity and managing staff smoothly.'

He adds that clear communication and co-operation 'are one of the things that have made us somewhat different. You don't have to tear something down to make something else good'. And he believes that design at other companies is often 'more dictatorial'.

While most praise the design renaissance Gale has inspired, some criticise him for being too 'retro'. Many of Chrysler's concept cars hark back to products from a bygone age, especially a somewhat romanticised 1950s.

Even recent production cars have emphasised such features as the group's once-famous chequerboard radiator grille. Last year, Chrysler went so far as to reintroduce its old corporate badge of the 1920s.

Gale is unmoved by such criticisms. Restoring tradition – such as the bold vertical slats on the radiator grille – was a priority at Jeep which, he feels, had moved too far from its roots under AMC. Dodge, meanwhile, had been affected by a 'lack of identity', something that cars such as the Viper and the more recent Intrepid saloon have helped to restore.

Then, too, reviving the badge had helped to emphasise the heritage of the core Chrysler brand. 'Now,' says Gale, 'you can start to see its identity.'

Foreign buyers, already familiar with Jeep, will be seeing more of Chrysler's products on the road with a new marketing push later this year. Sales of the 300M, a sleek and (for Europe) large saloon, will start in the autumn. Whatever people might think of its aggressive styling, one thing is clear: no one will mistake it for anything but a Chrysler.

The Financial Times, 14 February 1998

Summary of key points

- Good design of products and services is an essential element in satisfying customer needs.
- The major steps in the design process are idea generation, feasibility study, preliminary design and final design.
- Ideas for new products can come from the organisation's research and development (R&D) function, customers, market research data, competitors or technological development.
- The feasibility study consists of a market, economic and technical analysis.
- Preliminary design consists of forming a technical specification of the components of the package.
- The final design will be assessed in the three main areas of functional design, form design and production design.
- Concurrent design can reduce the time and cost involved in the product design process.

- Design for manufacture aims to ensure a product design can be produced easily and at low cost through guidelines on such aspects as simplification, standardisation and modularisation.
- Quality functional deployment (QFD) is a structured process that translates customer needs into technical design requirements.
- Taguchi methods for imposing design quality include robust design, the quality loss function (QLF) and design of experiments (DOE).
- It is often difficult to test the quality levels of a service because it is intangible.

Exercises

1 Outline the role of marketing, engineering and operations in producing a new car design.

2 With an organisation with which you are familiar discuss the method of generating new product ideas.

3 A manufacturer produces a product with the following specification.
Selling price = £15.00/unit
Variable cost = £10.00/unit
Fixed costs = £10,000/week

a) What is the break-even point?
b) How many do they need to sell to make £20,000 profit a week?

4 The following product mix is planned.

	Knives	Forks	Spoons
Product mix	0.4	0.4	0.2
Selling price(£/unit)	0.07	0.08	0.05
Variable cost (£/unit)	0.05	0.06	0.03

a) What is the break-even point?
b) At what volume will profit = £100,000, given the current product mix.
c) If the price of a spoon is reduced by £0.01, what volume is required to make a profit of £100,000.

5 An assembly is made up of four components arranged as shown. The components can be purchased for three different suppliers with the following reliability ratings.

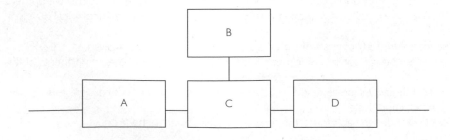

Component	Supplier 1	Supplier 2	Supplier 3
A	0.94	0.95	0.92
B	0.86	0.80	0.90
C	0.90	0.93	0.95
D	0.93	0.95	0.95

a) If only one supplier is chosen to supply all four components, which should be selected?

b) What supplier should be selected for the following configuration?

6 Discuss the objectives of functional design, form design and production design.

7 Explain the role of standardisation, simplification and modularisation in design.

8 Outline the objectives of FMEA.

9 What is the purpose of QFD?

10 An organisation has two suppliers bidding for the supply of a new product. In order to test for quality a sample of 200 is requested from each supplier. The target value is 10 ±2 mm. The quality adjustment cost is £1 per item. The results of the quality sample are as tabulated.

Size (mm)	Supplier A	Supplier B
8	15	20
9	47	54
10	68	67
11	56	36
12	14	23

a) What is the quality loss function (QLF) for each supplier?

b) Which supplier should receive the contract?

11 How do product and service design differ?

References

Behara, R.S. and Chase, R.B., Service quality deployment: quality service by design, in Rakesh V. Sarin (ed.), *Perspectives in Operations Management: Essay in Honor of Elwood S. Buffa*, Kluwer (1993).

Bhote, K.R., A powerful new tool kit for the 21st century, *National Productivity Review*, 16, (4), (1997) pp. 29–38.

Fitzsimmons, J.A., Fitzsimmons, M.J., *Service Management for Competitive Advantage*, McGraw-Hill (1994).

Simonian, H., Car designers: the man who saved Chrysler's skin, *Financial Times*, 14 February (1998).

Taguchi, G. and Clausing, D., Robust quality, *Harvard Business Review*, Jan–Feb (1990), pp. 65–75.

Further reading

Brown, S., *Strategic Manufacturing for Competitive Advantage: Transforming Operations from Shop Floor to Strategy*, Prentice-Hall (1996).

Hope, C., Mühlemann, A., *Service Operations Management: Strategy, Design and Delivery*, Prentice-Hall (1997).

Lovelock, C.H., *Managing Services: Marketing, Operations, and Human Resources*, Prentice-Hall (1988).

Slack, N., Chambers, S., Harland, C., Harrison, A. and Johnston, R., *Operations Management*, Second Edition, Pitman (1998).

Part 2   Management

6 Capacity management and scheduling

Objectives

By the end of this chapter, you should be able to:

- understand the steps involved in medium-term capacity planning;
- understand the differing levels of aggregation involved in the measurement of demand;
- understand the effects of product mix on capacity;
- evaluate the three pure strategies for reconciling capacity and demand;
- understand issues involved in reconciling capacity and demand in service operations;
- understand approaches required for demand management in services;
- understand the use of cumulative representatives to evaluate a level capacity planning approach;
- understand the use of queuing theory to explore the trade-off between the amount of capacity and level of detail;
- understand the limitations of queuing theory in relation to the psychology of customer waiting time;
- understand the use of simulation modelling in capacity planning in manufacturing and services;
- understand the steps involved in a simulation study;
- understand qualitative and quantitative methods of forecasting demand.

Chapter 13 describes the process of forming an operations strategy from corporate objectives. The Hill framework (Hill, 1993) aims to provide a connection between the different levels of strategy making and ensure that there is a degree of fit between the proposed marketing strategy and manufacturing capability. The process of strategy formulation must include developing plans to provide sufficient and appropriate resources (i.e. capacity) in order to execute that strategy. In the long-term capacity decisions relate to considerations of facility location (Chapter 2) and process technology (Chapter 3). For short to medium term planning purposes the physical size of the organisation is considered to be the limiting factor for capacity decisions. Chapter 8 covers the technique of OPT which is an approach to production planning which focuses on the identification of bottlenecks (any resource whose capacity is less than or equal to the demand placed on it). This chapter will focus on capacity management decisions in the short to medium term planing horizon. In addition day-to-day operational decisions are covered in the scheduling section.

A systematic approach to capacity planning

A definition of capacity should take into account both the volume and the time over which capacity is available. Vonderembse (1991) defines capacity as follows:

'Capacity is a measure of an organisation's ability to provide customers with the demanded services or goods in the amount requested and in a timely manner.'

Capacity decisions should be taken using a systematic approach using the following steps:

- Step 1. Measure demand.
- Step 2. Measure capacity.
- Step 3. Reconcile capacity and demand.
- Step 4. Evaluate alternatives and make a choice.

Step 1 requires that future demand be estimated, Step 2 requires the measurement of present capacity, Step 3 requires analysis of capacity planning approaches and Step 4 requires a method of choosing a suitable capacity planning approach. This chapter is structured around this model.

Measuring demand

Capacity planning involves a number of interactions between different levels in the organisation. Figure 6.1 shows the main levels involved in the measurement of demand.

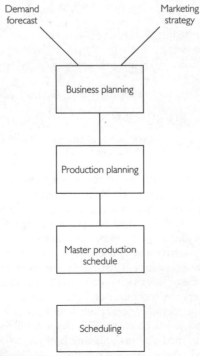

Figure 6.1 Levels in capacity management

There should be a great deal of interaction between the different levels and the process should be an iterative one as plans are refined from long-term business plans to short-term scheduling decisions. The different levels are now described in more detail.

Business planning

The strategic planning process will define the product/service markets in which the organisation will compete in and such factors as the range and volume of product/services in these market segments. The marketing strategy will be evaluated in terms of corporate objectives that are usually expressed in terms of financial measures such as growth or profitability. The role of marketing strategy and operations strategy in meeting corporate objectives is discussed in Chapter 13. Qualitative and quantitative methods of forecasting demand are covered at the end of this chapter.

Based on the marketing strategy and estimates of demand the organisation can formulate a long-range business plan that will include capital budgets for expanding facilities and major equipment investment. Because of the relatively long lead-time of acquiring these facilities they are considered in the short to medium term planning horizon to represent the effective capacity limit of the organisation. It may be possible however to use leasing arrangements or purchase major components from suppliers to increase this capacity limit.

In the medium term (approximately 18 months) planning is undertaken by various functions (manufacturing, marketing, finance etc.) in order to co-ordinate efforts to achieve the business plan within the constraints made by the long-term decisions made in that plan. Planning at this level is a matter of monitoring and control to provide a direction between areas in the organisation and conflicting demand on resource. The planning process can be described as working in cycles, with each cycle confirming detailed plans for the next time period and sketching more tentative plans for the following period. At the next planning meeting these tentative plans are now considered in more detail and the cycle repeats. This process means that the organisation can build on previous plans instead of attempting to devise new plans at each planning cycle. This reduces planning time and leads to more continuity in decision making.

Production planning

The production plan (or operations plan in a service organisation) states the amount of output which will be delivered from the operations function over the medium-term business plan. The output can be expressed in terms of volume, value or units. For example a car manufacturer may commit to an output of 100,000 cars during the next 12-month period. The production plan provides an overall guide to the level of output from the manufacturing/operations department that will be co-ordinated with other functions such as marketing and finance. The aggregate planning process will evaluate the production plan in order to ensure sufficient capacity is available to undertake the output targets.

Master production schedule (MPS)

It is necessary to break the production plan down into a level of detail required for procurement and operational purposes. This means that the demand for each individual product and thus the materials, components and work tasks required to produce it, must be specified. The master production schedule (MPS) states the volume and timing of all products that have a significant demand on manufacturing resources. Further details of the MPS in relation to a materials requirements planning (MRP) system are provided in Chapter 8.

Scheduling

This involves operational capacity management decisions and is dealt with later in this chapter.

Measuring capacity

Measuring capacity may at first seem straightforward, especially when compared to the uncertainty inherent in estimating demand. However capacity is not fixed but is a variable that is dependent on a number of factors such as the product mix processed by the operation and machine set-up requirements. The OPT approach also shows how the level of capacity can be influenced by management decisions (Chapter 8).

Product mix

Only when a narrow product range is involved can capacity be measured reasonably accurately and in this case be quoted in terms of output volume. The effect of product mix on capacity is his highly significant and is illustrated below.

WORKED EXAMPLE

The following assembly times are given for three models of a washing machine.

Model	Assembly time (hours)
Washer (basic)	25
Washer (deluxe)	50
Washer (dryer)	75

The target weekly output is given as 100 units. For a product ratio of 4:2:1 for washer (basic), washer (deluxe) and washer (dryer) the output is as follows:

- Ratio = 4:2:1
- Assembly time for 7 units = $(4 \times 25) + (2 \times 50) + (1 \times 75) = 275$ hours
- Assembly hours available = 4000
- Therefore weekly output = $4000/275 \times 7 = 101$ units

However if the product mix changes to a ratio of 3:2:2 the output is as follows:

- Ratio = 3:2:2
- Assembly time for 7 units = $(3 \times 25) + (2 \times 50) + (2 \times 75) = 325$ hours
- Assembly hours available = 4000

- Therefore weekly output = 4000/325 × 7 = 86 units

Thus a change in product mix from 4:2:1 to 3:2:2 changes capacity output from 101 to 86 units.

When the product mix can change then it can be more useful to measure capacity in terms of input measures, which provides some indication of the potential output. Also for planning purposes when demand is stated in output terms it is necessary to convert input measures to an estimated output measure. For example in hospitals which undertake a range of activities, capacity is often measured in terms of beds available (an input) measure. An output measure such as number of patients treated per week will be highly dependent on the mix of activities the hospital performs.

Design and effective capacity

The theoretical design capacity of an operation is rarely met due to such factors as maintenance and machine set-up time between different products so the effective capacity is a more realistic measure. However this will also be above the level of capacity which is available due to unplanned occurrences such as a machine breakdown.

Reconciling capacity and demand

The organisation's ability to reconcile capacity with demand will be dependent on the amount of flexibility it possesses. Flexible facilities allow organisations to adapt to changing customer needs in terms of product range and varying demand and to cope with capacity shortfalls due to equipment breakdown or component failure. The amount of flexibility should be determined in the context of the organisation's competitive strategy (Chapter 13). Methods for reconciling capacity and demand can be classified into three 'pure' strategies:

- level capacity
- chase demand
- demand management.

Level capacity

This strategy sets the processing capacity at a uniform level throughout the planning period regardless of fluctuations in forecast demand. This means production is set at a fixed rate, usually to meet average demand, and inventory is used to absorb variations in demand. During periods of low demand any overproduction can be transferred to finished goods inventory in anticipation of sales at a later time period. The disadvantage of this strategy is the cost of holding inventory and the cost of perishable items that may have to be discarded.

To avoid producing obsolete items firms will try to create inventory for products which are relatively certain to be sold. This strategy has limited value for perishable goods.

For a service organisation output cannot be stored as inventory so a level capacity plan involves running at a uniformly high level of capacity. The drawback of the approach is the cost of maintaining this high level of capacity although it could be relevant when the cost of lost sales is particularly high.

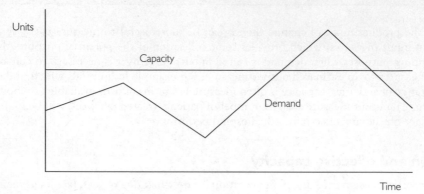

Figure 6.2 Level capacity plan

Chase demand

This strategy seeks to match production to the demand pattern over time. Capacity is altered by such policies as changing the amount of part-time staff, changing the amount of staff availability through overtime working, changing equipment levels and subcontracting. The chase demand strategy is costly in terms of the costs of changing staffing levels and overtime payments. The costs may be particularly high in industries in which skills are scarce. Disadvantages of subcontracting include reduced profit margin lost to the subcontractor, loss of control, potentially longer lead times and the risk that the subcontractor may decide to enter the same market. For these reasons a pure chase demand strategy is more usually adopted by service operations which cannot store their output and so make a level capacity plan less feasible.

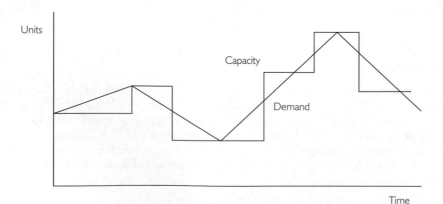

Figure 6.3 Chase demand plan

Demand management

While the level capacity and chase demand strategies aim to adjust capacity to match demand, the demand management strategy attempts to adjust demand to meet available capacity. There are many ways this can be done, but most will involve altering the marketing mix (e.g. price, promotion etc.) and will require co-ordination with the marketing function. Demand management strategies include:

- Varying the price – during periods of low demand price discounts can be used to stimulate the demand level. Conversely when demand is higher than the capacity limit, price could be increased.
- Provide increased marketing effort to product lines with excess capacity.
- Use advertising to increase sales during low demand periods.
- Use the existing process to develop alternative product during low demand periods.
- Offer instant delivery of product during low demand periods.
- Use an appointment system to level out demand.

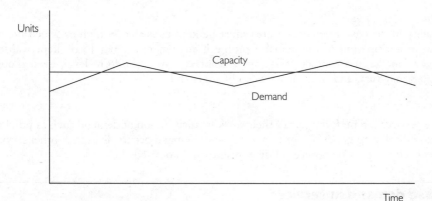

Figure 6.4 Demand management plan

Mixed capacity plans

Due to the complexity of capacity management and the need to optimise a range of performance objectives it is usually necessary to combine the three pure strategies described and form a mixed capacity planning strategy.

Reconciling capacity and demand in service operations

In services the operations manager controls employee actions that directly serve the customer. In manufacturing the manager directs action that produces a product that serves customers' needs. The existence of this intermediate product between employee and customer means that manufacturing and services are managed differently.

Generally services need to be more custom-designed and involve more personal contact in order to meet specific customer needs. Thus customer contact has a number of impacts on the way the service can be run. Customer involvement tends to provide an opportunity for special requests and instructions to be issued by the customer, which tends to disrupt routine procedures and thus efficiency. Capacity may be lost in providing conversation to the customer in addition to delivering the actual service. Quality is closely related to the customer's perception of satisfactory service. Operations employees employed where high levels of customer contact occurs must be skilled in interpreting what the customer really wants. Thus the level of customer/client contact can have a direct effect on the efficiency that an operation can achieve.

Operations has a variety of methods to achieve efficiency and still provide the customer with good service. One way to limit the disruption from unusual requests is to standardise the service, e.g. a fast-food restaurant. A common strategy to improve the overall efficiency of the operation is to keep separate those parts of the operation that do not require direct customer contact. Operations are divided into **front office** – with interaction with the customer and **back office** – where directions are primarily taken from managers, not customers.

The three pure capacity planning strategies are now discussed in a service context.

Level capacity in services

Partitioning demand
Capacity in the customer contact area must be kept consistently high or scaled up and down in anticipation of the demand profile if customers are not to be kept waiting. Capacity in the non-contact areas can be kept at a more uniform level, even though demand may vary, and thus capacity can be more fully utilised.

Inventory
Some services can perform part of their work in anticipation of demand such as purchasing and displaying goods before actual customer demand occurs. For many other services the capacity to provide service is lost if inventory is not used.

Chase demand in services

Good forecasting is very important for service organisations. Estimates of changes in demand, even in time blocks of a few minutes, may be helpful in detailed planning, for example in assigning assistants to supermarket tills. When the operation cannot achieve a demand rate that matches its desired capacity level, its objective usually becomes one of developing a capacity profile that matches its demand profile, to the extent that this is feasible and economically viable. Strategies for achieving this include:

- *Staggered workshift schedules.* Scheduling the availability of capacity to cover demand involves constructing work shifts so that the number of operators available at any one time matches the demand profile, e.g. burger restaurant.
- *Part-time staff.* More flexibility to schedule and smooth the work demand is often available for those parts of a service where the customer is not present and the service is provided by working with some surrogate for the customer. The part-time staff needs to trade-off the cost of not doing some work with the extra cost of employing the staff.
- *Subcontractors.* If there is not enough capacity, additional capacity can be obtained from outside sources, e.g. surgeries employing contract doctor services to cover weekends.
- *Multiskilled floating staff.* Having multiskilled staff increases flexibility in capacity decisions. For example in the case of a hospital it might be desirable to have some floating capacity that can be shifted from one department to another if the number of

patients or the amount of nursing attention required in each department varies.

- *Customer self-service.* With this option, the service capacity arrives when the demand does. Customers at supermarkets and many departments stores select most of their own merchandise.

Demand management in services (yield management)

Yield management is a collection of approaches used to optimise the use of capacity in operations where capacity is relatively fixed and the service cannot be stored in any way. The approach includes:

- *Maintenance of a fixed schedule.* Some services can schedule the times at which the service is available, e.g. airlines, rail, bus. Demand occurs as people purchase tickets to use some of the previously scheduled transportation capacity.
- *Use of an appointment system.* The pattern of demand variations over the longer term can also have a significant influence on the planning of efficient service operations. The ideal would be to achieve uniform utilisation of service capacity, but this is unlikely unless an appointment only policy is operated. Some services are provided by appointment, e.g. dentist. Use of an appointment system permits demand to be moved into available time. The delay between a request for an appointment and the time of the appointment may depend on the backlog or queue of waiting work.
- *Delayed delivery.* Delaying jobs until capacity is available serves to make the workload more uniform, e.g. bank teller. In addition, routine work may be set aside to make capacity available for rush jobs.
- *Providing economic incentives for off-peak demand.* Some operations have a heavy capital investment in the capacity they have to provide their services. The unit cost of capacity that is used only occasionally for peak demand is very high. These operations try to keep demand as uniform as possible by the use of economic inducements, e.g. Economy 7 electricity, off-peak telephone calls.

Evaluating and choosing a capacity planning approach

Capacity planning involves evaluating the capacity requirements and determining the best way to meet these using a capacity planning approach which is feasible and low cost. The term aggregate planning is sometimes used to describe the process of aggregating (i.e. grouping) capacity requirements over a medium-term planning horizon to provide the best way to meet these requirements. In order to choose a capacity plan which meets the above criteria it is necessary to try to predict the consequences of that plan. This can be done with varying levels of accuracy and cost using the following methods:

- cumulative representations
- queuing theory
- simulation modelling.

Cumulative representations

One method of evaluating a level capacity planning approach is to simply plot the cumulative demand and cumulative capacity for a product over the planning time period. An example is shown in Figure 6.5.

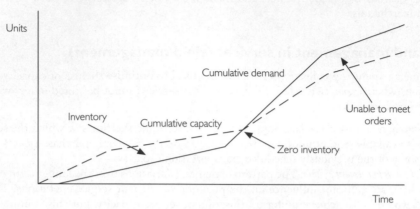

Figure 6.5 Cumulative representation of supply and demand

The graph shows the relationship between capacity and demand over time and thus enables an assessment of the capacity plan. When the cumulative demand line is below the cumulative capacity, the distance between the lines is the level of inventory at that time. If the demand line lies above the capacity line then this represents a shortage of capacity at that time. Because the graph shows the cumulation of capacity and demand, it takes into account the usage of any surplus inventory in periods when demand exceeds supply (i.e. when the graphs meet, inventory is zero). The cumulative representation graph can show if the capacity plan is meeting demand. This occurs when the capacity line is always along or above the demand line over the planning period.

To assess the effect of capacity planning approaches on the capacity plan involves adjusting the gradient of the capacity (for chase demand approach) or demand (for demand management approach) line at the appropriate point at which the change is to take place. The ideal situation would be when the capacity and demand lines follow each other as closely as possible on the graph. However the cost of changing the capacity or demand pattern must be taken into consideration. It should also be noted that it may be cost-effective to only change capacity in certain blocks and the cost of the change may be dependent on the direction of that change (e.g. it may be cheaper to decrease capacity rather than increase capacity for a certain process).

Queuing theory

Cumulative representations rely on the fact that when supply exceeds demand inventory can be stored for use when demand exceeds supply. In service situations however the output of the operation cannot be stored. Waiting time could only be eliminated when customers are asked to arrive at fixed intervals (i.e. an appointment system) and then only if service times are fixed. Thus waiting time in queues is caused by fluctuations in arrival rates and variability in service times. Queuing theory can be used to explore the trade-off between the amount of capacity and the level of demand. Too much capacity and costs will be excessive, but too little capacity will cause long waiting for the customer and loss of service quality leading to loss of business. In a service context queuing theory can provide a useful guide in determining expected waiting time for an arriving customer and the average number of customers who will be waiting for service. This permits an estimate of the amount of capacity that will be needed to keep waiting time to a reasonable level taking into account the expected rate and variability of demand.

Examples of queuing situations include:

- customers at a bank
- aeroplanes circling waiting to land
- patients waiting to see a doctor
- parts waiting for processing at a machining centre.

Queue systems can be classified into a single-channel queuing system consisting of a single queue of customers who wait until a service facility is available and a multiple-channel queuing system that has parallel server facilities in order to increase the service capacity (Figures 6.6 and 6.7).

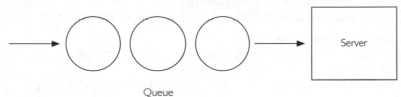

Queue

Figure 6.6 Single channel queue system

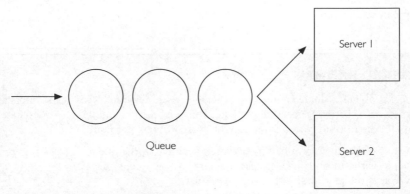

Queue

Figure 6.7 Multiple channel queue system

Arrivals, representing demand for the use of the facility, enter the system at a particular demand rate. If the service facility is already in use the arrival waits in a queue until capacity becomes available. Several factors determine the performance of a queuing system. The timing of customer arrivals into the system are usually assumed to occur randomly according to some probability distribution. A priority system may be used to select the next customer to receive service. In most systems the **first-come first-served** (FCFS) or **first-in, first-out** (FIFO) rule will apply. In some circumstances arrivals may not join the queue if it is too long when they arrive (balking), or they may wait for a time, become impatient and leave (reneging).

Uncertainty in arrival and service times means that even although on average there may be adequate capacity to meet demand, queuing may still occur when a number of successive arrivals or long service times occur. Conversely idle time will occur when arrival rates or service time decreases. Although this behaviour means that full utilisation will not be feasible for this type of system, queuing theory does allow analysis of how much capacity is needed to keep average or maximum queue length or waiting times to an acceptable level. This acceptable level or service quality level will be dependent on the type of operation involved.

Queuing theory equations

There are a number of equations for different queuing structures, but this text will consider the single server and multiple server models only. The following assumptions are made when using the following queuing equations:

- Poisson distribution for arrival rate
- exponential distribution for service times
- first-come first-served (FCFS) queue discipline
- no limit on queue length (i.e. no reneging)
- infinite population (i.e. arrival rate is not dependent on outside factors).

Equations for single server queue system

The mean number of units waiting in the queue, $L_q = \lambda^2/(\mu(\mu-\lambda))$
The mean time spent in the queue, $W_q = \lambda/(\mu(\mu-\lambda))$
The probability that the server is busy (i.e. server utilisation), $p = \lambda/\mu$

where:
l = mean arrival rate
μ = mean service rate

WORKED EXAMPLE

A local shop has a single counter/till at which customers are served. Customers arrive at a rate of 20 per hour according to a Poisson distribution and service times are exponentially distributed with a mean rate of 24 customers per hour.

a) What is the mean number of customers waiting in the queue?
b) What is the mean time a customer spends in the queue?
c) What is the probability that the till is busy?

SOLUTION

$\lambda = 20$ and $\mu = 24$.

$L_q = 20^2/(24 \times (24 - 20)) = 400/96 = 4.17$ customers

$W_q = 20/(24 \times (24 - 20)) = 20/96 = 0.2$ hours

$p = 20/24 = 0.83$

Equations for multiple server queue systems

The mean number of units waiting in the queue:

$$L_q = \lambda\mu(\lambda/\mu)^s P_0/(s-1)!(s\mu-\lambda)^2$$

where:

$$P_0 = 1/\left(\sum_{n=0}^{n=s-1} \frac{\lambda/\mu^n}{n!} + \frac{(\lambda/\mu)^s}{s!(1 - \lambda/s\mu)}\right)$$

The mean time spent in the queue:

$$W_q = L_q/\lambda$$

The probability that the server is busy (i.e. server utilisation)

$$p = \lambda/s\mu$$

where:

λ = mean arrival rate
μ = mean service rate
s = number of servers

WORKED EXAMPLE

Customers queue in a single line in a department store and are served at one of 3 tills on a first-come first-served basis. Customers arrive at a rate of 24 per hour (according to a Poisson distribution) and a service time are exponentially distributed with a mean rate of 10 customers can be served per hour.

a) What is the mean number of customers waiting in the queue?
b) What is the mean time a customer spends in the queue?
c) What is the probability that a till is busy?

SOLUTION

$\lambda = 24; \mu = 10; s = 3$.

$P_0 = 1/((24/10)^0/0! + (24/10)^1/1! + (24/10)^2/2!)$
$= 1/(1 + 2.4 + 2.88) = 0.16$

$L_q = (24 \times 10 \times (24/10)^3/((3-1)! \times (3 \times 10 - 24)^2)) \times 0.16$
$= 3317.76/72 \times 0.16 = 7.37$ customers

$W_q = L_q/\lambda = 7.37/24 = 0.31$ hours

$p = 24/(3 \times 10) = 0.8$

The mathematical equations used in queuing theory make a number of assumptions about the system. They assume steady-state conditions have been reached, that is the effects of an empty system start-up phase have been overcome and the system has reached a steady-state. This may never happen if the mean arrival rate is greater than the service rate. Also the system may shut down for breaks during the day or may not run long enough to reach equilibrium. The equations can also only be used to describe very simple systems and simulation modelling is often used to analyse situations that do not fit adequately the assumed conditions of queuing theory.

The psychology of queues

Maister (1985) points out that although queuing theory has been used successfully to analyse waiting times it does not take into account customer perception of the waiting time itself. Thus depending on the situation a customer may or may not feel that a wait time of 10 minutes is acceptable for instance. Using the concepts of expectation and perception of service levels, Maister has developed a series of propositions about the psychology of queues which can be used by service organisations to influence customer satisfaction with waiting times. The propositions are as follows:

- *Unoccupied time feels longer than occupied time:* the important point here is to try to ensure that unoccupied time is taken up with an activity which is seen as useful by the customer and is related in some way to the forthcoming service.
- *Pre-process waits feel longer than in-process waits:* it is important that human contact is made as soon as possible to convey that the service has started and reduce anxiety in the customer, e.g. handing out the menu in a restaurant immediately a customer arrives ensures that they do not feel they have been overlooked.
- *Anxiety makes waits seem longer:* a particular form of this is when parallel queues are used for a service. What usually happens is that the queue you choose to enter suddenly stops moving while the other queues progress rapidly! Many service organisations (e.g. Post Offices) have a single queue system which seems fairer to customers and reduces anxiety by operating a strict first-come, first-served policy.
- *Uncertain waits are longer than known, finite waits:* it is important to inform the customer how long the wait will be. A particular problem with appointment systems is that they create a specific expectation about when a service should begin and if appointments begin to run behind, anxiety increases as the expectation is not met.
- *Unexplained waits are longer than explained waits:* if the customer understands the reason for a wait they will be more satisfied than if no explanation is given or an explanation which does not provide sufficient justification is given.
- *Unfair waits are longer than equitable waits:* one of the most irritating occurrences for a customer is when someone who has arrived at a later time is served first. This can be eliminated by a single queue system which operates on a first-come, first-served (FCFS) basis.
- *The more valuable the service, the longer the customer will wait:* if the service is seen to be of little value, the tolerance for waiting will diminish greatly. In particular post-process waits, when the required service is over, feel longer than in-process or even pre-process waits.
- *Solo waits feel longer than group waits:* when there is group interaction in a waiting line, perhaps initiated by an announcement of a delay, then waiting becomes more tolerable.

Although the FCFS queue discipline has been mentioned as a possible solution to some of the above problems it cannot always be applied due to factors such as the implications for available space. (e.g. for supermarket customers with trolleys). The single queue also eliminates the possibility of providing custom service points for different customer types (e.g. customer with few items in a supermarket or first-class customers for an airline). Overall the propositions show that in addition to the actual wait or queue time the context of the waiting line will have a significant effect on the level of customer satisfaction.

Simulation modelling

Simulation is a technique using a computer to imitate the operation of various kinds of facilities or processes in order to study their behaviour. The facility or process being studied is treated as a system which can be defined as 'a collection of entities which are related to each other and to their environment so that they form a whole' (Martin, 1991).

Altering the system physically and observing the results is rarely feasible because of cost or disruption to the system. Also the system may not exist but it is desirable to study a proposal in various alternative configurations to see how it should be built in the first place. For these reasons it is usually necessary to build a model as a representation of the system and study it as a surrogate for the actual system. Physical (or iconic) models are not typically used to study engineering or management systems due to their cost and inflexibility. The majority of models are mathematical, representing a system in terms of logical and quantitative relationships which are then manipulated and changed to see how the model, and hopefully system, would react. In some situations a model is constructed as a series of mathematical equations which give an exact representation of model behaviour. This is termed an analytical solution. Most systems however are too complex to be modelled in this way and must be studied by means of simulation.

Classification of simulation models

Simulation models can be classified along the following dimensions:

- **Static vs. dynamic.** A static simulation model is a representation of a system at a particular time, e.g. Monte Carlo models, whilst dynamic systems evolve over time.
- **Deterministic vs. stochastic.** If a simulation does not contain any probabilities (i.e. random) components, it is called deterministic, i.e. only one output state can occur for any input state and set of relationships. Many systems however have some random input components (e.g. customer arrivals) which give rise to stochastic simulation models. This type of model produces an output which is itself random and must therefore be treated as only an estimate of the true characteristic of the model. Various statistical techniques must be employed to assess the accuracy of output measures.
- **Continuous vs. discrete.** Systems can be of two types, discrete and continuous. In a discrete system state, variables change instantaneously at separated points in time while in a continuous system state, variables change continuously over time. Few systems are in practice wholly discrete or continuous but as one type of change predominates it is usually possible to classify in this way. Discrete and continuous models relate to discrete and continuous systems although a discrete model is not always used to model a discrete system and vice versa. This decision depends on the specific objectives of the study. e.g. traffic flow can be measured by the discrete behaviour of individual cars or the aggregate flow of traffic described by differential equations (Law and Kelton, 1991).

Using simulation
It is important to recognise that simulation will not provide the 'best' or 'optimum' combination of input variables for a particular output target. Rather it permits a series of 'what-if' scenarios to be constructed and the results can be observed. This reflects the complexity of real-world systems where the interdependencies between processes and the random variation in process duration makes the state of the system at any time unpredictable.

McHaney (1991) outlines seven advantages of the simulation technique over other design techniques:

1. Allows experimentation without disruptions to existing systems.
2. Concept can be tested prior to installation.
3. Detection of unforeseen problems or bugs.
4. Gain in system knowledge.
5. Speed in Analysis.
6. Forces system definition.
7. Enhances creativity.

All seven of these advantages derive from the reduction of the risk involved in the implementation of a new system or changes to an existing system.

The simulation process
Figure 6.8 shows the major steps which should be taken in a simulation study. These stages will now be outlined in more detail.

Problem definition
Simulation studies are initiated because a decision maker or group of decision makers faces a problem and needs a solution. i.e. An out-patients clinic may have long queues and therefore poor service. The analysis is begun by collecting enough information and data to provide an adequate understanding of both the problem and the system to be studied. The major focus of the planning and orientation period is the determination of the explicit goals or purpose of the simulation project, e.g. identify bottlenecks in systems or identify capacity constraints.

System definition
After the goal of the study is specified the essence of modelling is to identify that small subset of characteristics or features of the system that are required to provide the information required. A model should be designed that neither simplifies the system to the point where the model becomes trivial or misleading nor carries so much detail that it is too complex to identify aspects and relationships. As an example one would not normally model a hospital but a sub-set of it, e.g. ward or operating theatre.

Conceptual model formulation
To show the functional relationship between components in the model we use graphics to describe the system as a logical flow diagram as in Figure 6.9.

Input data preparation
The analyst must decide what data is needed and how to gather it, e.g. types of patient, length of stay of patients.

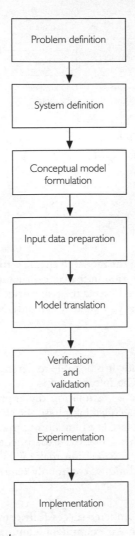

Figure 6.8 Stages in a simulation study

Model translation
The model will normally consist of 'blocks' of computer code that causes the system to change. A variety of ways are available to program the model into a form for use by the computer. General purpose languages (C, PASCAL etc.) are possible but specialised simulation languages, e.g. SIMAN™ (Pegden, 1995), PROMODEL™, have the advantage of reducing the programming task and have features such as automated gathering of statistics.

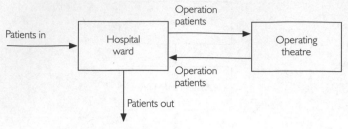

Figure 6.9 Hospital ward conceptual model

Verification and validation
Verification involves debugging the model to ensure errors are eliminated from the model and the code reflects the description in the conceptual model. Validation involves ensuring that the model adequately represents the real world. Because the model is constructed for a specific purpose its adequacy or validity can only be evaluated in terms of that purpose.

Experimentation
By conducting a simulation study it is possible to determine the performance of a system for a given set of conditions. The information is gathered by accumulating data as the simulation is running and then by estimating the appropriate performance measure at the end of the run. For the data collection phase the simulation user must decide under what conditions to run the simulated system, how many replications to perform, and how long each replication should be. Once the experiment has been designed and implemented the simulation user extracts decision-making information from the resulting data using a variety of statistical techniques commonly referred to as **output analysis**.

Implementation
No simulation project can be considered successfully completed until its results have been understood, accepted and used. An example of a animated simulation display is shown in Figure 6.10.

Scheduling

Scheduling concerns capacity planning decisions on an operational or day-to-day basis. The issues concerned will be examined under the three main production types of repetitive, batch and jobbing which represent different volume and variety configurations.

Scheduling for repetitive systems

Repetitive systems produce a standard product in a relatively high volume. These sys-

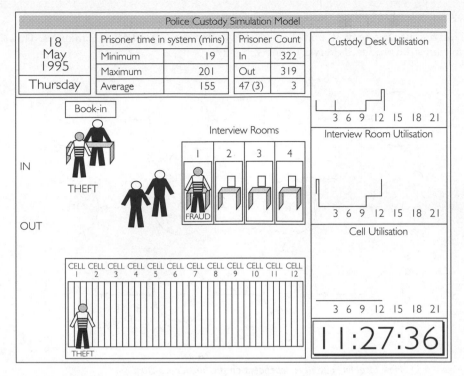

Figure 6.10 Simulation model display

tems which have a characteristic flow (product) layout use specialised equipment dedicated to achieving an optimal flow of work through the system. This is important because all items follow virtually the same sequence of operations. A major aim of flow systems is to ensure that each stage of production is able to maintain production at an equal rate. The technique of line balancing is used to ensure that the output of each production stage is equal and maximum utilisation is attained.

Line balancing

The issue of line balancing is important in a line flow process where a manufacturing operation is broken down into a number of stages. Line balancing involves ensuring that the stages of production are co-ordinated and bottlenecks are avoided. Because of the line flow configuration the output of the whole line is determined by the slowest or bottleneck process. This means an improvement in process time at a non-bottleneck will have no effect on overall output rate. Figure 6.11 shows the concept:

The actual design of the line is guided by the tasks which are involved in producing the product and the required output rate required to meet demand. This provides information which determines the number of stages and the output rate of each stage. The output rate is usually expressed in terms of the cycle time which is the time taken to produce one unit.

Cycle time = 1/ Output rate

Thus an output rate of 30 units/hour gives a cycle time of 1/30/60 = 2 minutes. Thus a unit must be produced every 2 minutes.

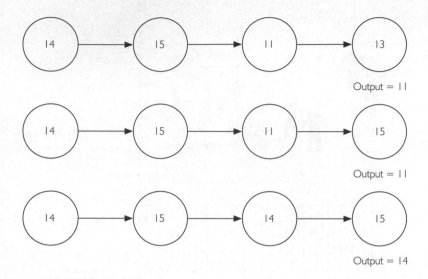

Figure 6.11 How total line output is dependent on the bottleneck stage

A major factor in achieving a proper line balance is to gather accurate estimates of task times in the line flow process. If timings are just based on a average of observations then there is a danger that the effect of variations on task times will not be considered. This can be limited somewhat by keeping a number of job elements in a task which reduces variability and increases flexibility. Simulation modelling can be used to investigate these variations as well as the effect of random variations such as machine breakdown. It should also be noted that the issue of line balancing will be complicated by constraints such as factory layout, material handling between stages and availability of worker skills. The use of a mixed-model line (Chapter 8) to process a range of products, rather than a single product type, also increases the complexity of the line balancing process.

Scheduling for batch systems

Batch systems process a range of product types in batches (groups) thus combining some of the economics of repetitive production with the variety of a job shop. Scheduling in these configurations is a matter of ensuring that the batch of work introduced to the process will be completed to meet customer due dates. Two issues which effect the job completion time and thus the ability to meet due dates are the transfer batch size and the job sequence. The transfer batch size refers to the size of the batch of parts that is processed at a work station before progressing to the next work station. The actual order size may be greater than this, but is divided into a number of transfer batches to decrease the time the jobs take to pass through the production process. The job sequence is the order in which jobs are entered on to the production process. This will not however be the order in which they are completed as different jobs will pass through different work stations and will have different process times. The MRP approach (Chapter 8) is often used to determine the batch size and timing (job sequence) of jobs to meet a projected demand expressed in the form of a **master production schedule** (MPS) that is developed from customer orders and demand forecasts. A closed-loop MRP system will check the feasibility of any schedule against the capacity available over the planning period. An OPT system (Chapter 8) will focus on ensuring that the bottleneck processes are kept busy as they determine the output of the whole process. A problem with batch production control is the tendency for managers to try to keep all work stations busy at all times which leads to work-in-progress (WIP) queues at heavily loaded work stations. Excessive WIP can seriously impede the ability to schedule batch systems successfully by creating long lead times and by making it difficult to determine the correct job priority for new work entering the system. An aim of the JIT system (Chapter 8) is to eliminate this inventory and make the production control process more transparent.

MRP systems use a technique called production activity control to try to ensure that the production system is working to plan. The technique consists of two main components:

- input/output control
- priority control.

Input/output control
This technique helps to control the length of queues in front of work stations and thus the job lead-time (total time spent by the job in the plant). The queue time is the most variable and usually the largest factor in determining job lead time. Typical values for the breakdown of job lead time are:

- **Transportation time**: 20%
- **Set-up time**: 10%
- **Process time**: 15%
- **Queue time**: 55%

Queue time can be as high as 80–95% of the total lead time in some instances. Each one of these factors can be reduced. Set-up time can be reduced by a set-up reduction programme which involves separating internal and external operations (Chapter 8). Process time can be reduced through the use of improvements in technology or learning curve effects. Transportation time can be reduced by improved layout or increased use of material handling equipment such as conveyors. However lead time is most effected by queue time. It is not just the length of the queuing time but the variability which affects the ability to successfully undertake planning and control activities. If the queue time is not known then the lead time cannot be estimated and so it is not known whether the item will meet its scheduled completion. Input/output control attempts to control the size of the queues at work centres in order that queue times are more consistent and predictable. The method measures the actual flow of work into a work centre and the actual flow of work from that work station. The difference is the amount of WIP at that work centre. By monitoring these figures using input/output reports, capacity is adjusted in order to ensure queues do not become too large and average actual lead time equals planned lead time as closely as possible. It is particularly important to provide control at each work station in assembly operations as a delay of a component at one work station may affect the progress of a whole assembly at a subsequent process.

Priority control

Priority control is used to decide which job from a queue of jobs is processed next at a work station. It takes an overall view of the production process so that if an assembly is waiting for one delayed part this part will get priority over jobs arriving earlier at that work station. The priority rule is implemented at each work station by issuing a dispatch list (schedule) for that work station, listing jobs for that operation in order of completion date. Thus jobs further over completion date will get priority. Each time a component leaves a work station it will be added to the dispatch list for the next work station.

Scheduling for jobbing systems

A jobbing system deals with a number of low volume, high variety products. Each product is customised to a customer order and so the production planning and control system must deal with a changing mix of jobs. Because the job may not have been produced before it may be difficult to estimate the elements of lead time for each job. Because each product has a unique routeing and component structure it is also difficult to use systems such as MRP for production planning and control. The pattern of flow through a job shop consists of a number of work stations with queues of work in front of them and what approaches to a random flow paths connecting the work stations.

Job sequencing

Job sequencing is the sequential assignment of jobs to work stations and is also known as dispatching. To attempt to control the progress of a job through the shop, a **job priority system** is used. The priority of jobs queuing at a work centre determines the order in which they are processed. The difficulty lies in determining an appropriate priority rule to obtain the best performance. **Priority rules** include:

- **DDS** – job with nearest customer due-date to the current date.
- **FCFS** – job arriving first at a work centre (i.e. in order of arrival).
- **SPT** – job with shortest process time.
- **LPT** – job with longest process time.

All the rules have different advantages and disadvantages. The SPT rule ensures that jobs with the shortest process time progress rapidly thus the number of jobs processed should be high. However in a heavily loaded job-shop, this may mean a job with a longer process time may have an unacceptably long wait and it is always at the end of the queue. Other rules use a combination of factors to determine the sequence. For instance the **critical ratio (CR)** is the ratio of the time left until the job's due date to the expected elapsed time for the job to be processed through the remaining work centres to its completion.

Critical ratio (CR) = (Due date – Current date) / Days required to complete job

If the ratio is less than 1 the job is behind schedule and should receive priority. **Gantt charts** (Chapter 10) can be employed to show the effect of different job sequencing strategies on the performance of the job shop.

Johnson's rule

An optimal solution to the job sequencing problem has been found for the special case in which all jobs flow through two work centres in the same order. Johnson's rule minimises the overall lead time (start of first job to end of last job) in this case, assuming inventory and set-up costs are not dependent on the job sequence chosen. Set-up times are included in job process times.

The following steps should be followed:

- Step 1. List the processing time for all jobs for both stages of production.
- Step 2. For unscheduled jobs select the job with the shortest time in either stage.
- Step 3. If the shortest time is for the first processing stage, put the job as early as possible in the job sequence; if the shortest time is for the second processing stage, put the job as late as possible in the job sequence; if the time on the first stage for one job equals the time on the second stage for some other job then fill the earliest slot with the job having this amount of time for the first stage and fill the latest slot with the job having this amount of time for the second stage; if both jobs have the same time for both stages they can be placed at either end of the sequence.
- Step 4. Delete the job selected and repeat the steps until all jobs have been sequenced.

WORKED EXAMPLE

A jobshop has five jobs which must be processed on machine 1 and then on machine 2. Determine the sequence that will allow the set of five jobs to be completed in the minimum time.

Job	Process time (mins)	
	Sand	Varnish
A	6	3
B	4	5
C	2	3
D	6	6
E	3	7

SOLUTION
1. Shortest time is 2 minutes for C in sand stage, therefore put as early as possible in job sequence:
2. Next shortest time is 3 minutes for E in stage 1 and 3 minutes for A in stage 2. Therefore put E as early as possible in job sequence and A as late as possible.
3. Next shortest is 4 for B in stage 1. Thus put B as early as possible.
4. The only job remaining is job D, therefore final sequence is as follows.

To find the completion time a Gantt chart is used to total the job completion time. The total completion time is 26 minutes.

Sand	C2	E3	B4	D6	A6		
Varnish		C3	E7	B5		D6	A3	
Time	0	5	10	15	20	25	

It should be emphasised that the rule is only applicable to a flow through 2 work centres in the same order and does not consider individual job due-dates in constructing the schedule.

    CASE STUDY

Pressure Cylinders Ltd

Pressure Cylinders Ltd manufacture a range of cylinders for a global market. Twenty per cent of the production is for the European sector. The cylinders are used for such applications as fire extinguishers and 'sodastream' gas cylinders. The company has been successful in the marketplace through its emphasis on quality and its high level of technical know-how.

The cylinders pass through a number of processes in manufacture:

● *Billet*. Solid metal piping is delivered to order. A small amount of stock is kept of the long delivery items. The billet machining stage cuts the pipe into the correct length for the particular application.
● *Extrusion*. At the extrusion stage the billets are heated to a high temperature and a press stamps the solid billet into a hollow cylindrical shape.
● *Heading*. The hollow end of the cylinder is then heated and pressed to form into a curved top leading to a small opening suitable for fixing an attachment.
● *Heat treat*. The cylinders are then heated in a large heat treat facility which hardens the metal and ensures they can withstand the high pressures involved in holding pressured gas.
● *Final machine*. The final machining stage adds a screw thread and bevel to the top of each cylinder.
● *Hydrostatic test*. Each cylinder is filled with water and tested at the required pressure for a period of time. A sample of cylinders are tested to destruction to determine their operating limits.
● *Finishing*. Each cylinder is cleaned inside and out to ensure no foreign bodies are present.
● *Paint*. If required by the customer the cylinders are painted as appropriate in a large epoxy paint facility.
● *Despatch*. Finally the cylinders are stored for despatch to the customer.

The scheduling process takes place using weekly time baskets. A forecast schedule of demand is made up of expected orders. If an enquiry is received then the forecast demand is confirmed. If the order was not forecast the demand is scheduled for a slack position on the capacity plan. A weekly capacity plan is drawn up three weeks in advance of actual production and aggregated by cylinder diameter. The plan will change if, for example, the production plant has not been able to meet the previous week's demand. Any demand not met is aggregated with the next week's forecast demand. If no cylinders of the same diameter are planned for production that week, the order may be put back another week, or run separately if it is a important order.

The work is then scheduled on to the production plan to give a daily production schedule. The orders are put in order sequence or to ensure no production stages are starved. For instance the heat treat stage capacity is limited by the size of the cylinders. Thus if a long sequence of large cylinders is put through the heat treat process then the production processes after this stage are starved of work because they can process the cylinder faster than the heat treat capacity. Thus the scheduler tends to alternate batches of large cylinders, with small cylinders through the heat treat to ensure a smooth work flow through the plant.

The need to maintain high quality is obvious for such an appliance as a fire extinguisher. A number of tests are undertaken on the cylinders as they pass through the production process. After each test the cylinders are individually stamped to show by whom and when the test was carried out. This allows management to trace any problems due to poor material for example. In addition all cylinders which are exported to the European market must be inspected by a qualified inspector from that country. Because of the difficulty of forecasting when the cylinders will be ready for inspection and the unavailability of inspectors who have to travel to the plant from abroad, cylinders are often stored for long periods of time within the plant awaiting inspection.

Forecasting demand

Accurate forecasts are an important factor in enabling organisations to deliver goods and services to the customer when required and thus achieve a quality service. This is particularly relevant to companies practising JIT supply which relies on the rapid and timely delivery of parts through the supply chain (Chapter 8). Forecasting is also important in relation to anticipating changing customer requirements and meeting them with new product and service designs (Chapter 5). The requirement to be able to understand the needs of the customer is also an important aspect of a TQM initiative (Chapter 11).

In a capacity planning context the business planning process is driven by two elements: the company strategy and forecasts of demand for the product/service the organisation is offering to the market. Demand forecasts will usually be developed by the marketing department and their accuracy will form an important element in the success of any capacity management plans implemented by operations. The demand forecast should express demand requirements in terms of the capacity constraints applicable to the organisation. This could be machine hours or worker hours as appropriate. The demand forecast should permit the operations manager to ensure that enough capacity is available to meet demand at a particular point in time, whilst minimising the cost of employing too much capacity for demand needs. The amount of capacity supplied should take into account the negative effects of losing an order due to too little capacity and the increase in costs on the competitiveness of the product in its market.

Organisations must develop forecasts of the level of demand they should be prepared to meet. The forecast provides a basis for co-ordination of plans for activities in various parts of the organisation, e.g. personnel department employs the right amount of people, purchasing orders the right amount of material and finance estimates the capital required for the business. Forecasts can either be developed through a qualitative approach or a quantitative approach (Figure 6.12).

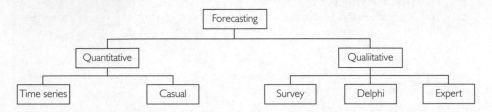

Figure 6.12   Approaches to forecasting

Qualitative methods

The following qualitative techniques will be described:

- market surveys
- Delphi method
- expert judgement.

Market surveys
A market survey collects data from a sample of customers, analyses the responses and makes inferences about the population from which the sample is drawn. They are particularly useful before the launch of a new product when there is limited information on potential customer demand. For the survey to be statistically valid it is necessary to ensure a correct sampling methodology is used and that questions are pertinent and unbiased. Care must also be taken with the analysis of responses. To achieve useful results can be an expensive and time-consuming activity.

Delphi study
This is a formal procedure which aims to bring together the opinions of a group of experts. A questionnaire is completed by a panel of experts which is then analysed and summaries passed back to the experts. Each expert in the group can then compare their forecast with the summarised reply of the others. This process is repeated, maybe up to six times, until a consensus has emerged within the group on which decision to take. The accuracy of the Delphi method can be good, but the cost and effort of organisation may be relatively high.

Expert judgement
This can take the form of an individual or group judgement. An individual judgement relies entirely on a single person's opinion of the situation – which includes both the knowledge and ignorance of the problem. The technique is unreliable and although it may give a good forecast, it can also give a very bad one.

A **group judgement** relies on a consensus being found among a group of people. If the difficulty of finding consensus can be overcome this is a more reliable method than an individual judgement. However it is still relatively unreliable compared to more formal methods and is subject to group processes such as domination of the group by one person and the taking of risky decisions which an individual would not take.

Quantitative methods of forecasting demand

These use a mathematical expression or model to show the relationship between demand and some independent variable or variables. The model that is appropriate for forecasting depends on the demand pattern to be projected and the forecaster's objectives for the model. By constructing a mathematical model of a problem decisions can be made on a more sound and logical basis than relying on a qualitative approach. The following techniques are described:

● time series
● causal models.

Time series

Time series models are adequate forecasting tools if demand has shown a fairly consistent pattern over time and the conditions under which the pattern has occurred are expected to continue. A time series is a sequence of data collected in equal intervals of time and arranged in the order of their occurrence, e.g. monthly sales data.

Time series **smoothing** is appropriate when the random component of a time series has fluctuations that deviate substantially from the average level of demand. Four averaging or smoothing techniques used are:

● simple moving average
● weighted moving average
● single exponential moving average
● double exponential smoothing.

The first three techniques are suitable when the data exhibits no trend (i.e. broadly horizontal demand). Double exponential smoothing can project a trend when the general level of demand is changing over time.

Simple moving average
A simple moving average is a method of computing the mean of only a specified number of the most recent data values in a series. For example we might compute a 3-month moving average at the end of each month to smooth out random fluctuations and get an estimate of the average sales per month.

To compute a three-month moving average, at the end of each month we add sales for the latest three months and divide by three. See Figure 6.13.

Averaging multiple periods helps smooth out random fluctuations so that the forecast or average has more **stability** or does not fluctuate erratically. A moving average will gain stability if a greater number of periods are used in the average. If the number of periods in the average is too great however, the average will be so stable that it will be slow to respond to non-random changes (trends) in the demand data. **Responsiveness** is the ability of a forecast to adjust quickly to true changes (trends) in the base level of demand.

Both responsiveness and stability are difficult to achieve with a forecasting method that looks only at the series of past demands without considering factors that may have caused (or will cause) a change in that pattern without taking into consideration external causative factors.

Month	Demand	3-month total demand	3-month average demand
20	120		
21	130		
22	110	360	120
23	140	380	126.67
24	110	360	120
25	130	380	126.67

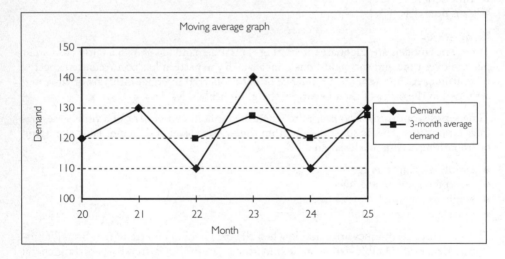

Figure 6.13 Example of three-month simple moving average

Weighted moving average

The weighted moving average assigns more weight (statistical significance) to some demand values (usually the more recent ones) than to others. The rationale for varying the weightings is usually to allow the most recent data to influence the forecast more than older data. See example in Figure 6.14.

Month	Demand	Month 22	Month 23	Month 24	Month 25	Weighted average
20	120	0.2 × 120				
21	130	0.3 × 130	0.2 × 130			
22	110	0.5 × 110	0.3 × 110	0.2 × 110		118
23	140		0.5 × 140	0.3 × 140	0.2 × 140	129
24	110			0.5 × 110	0.3 × 110	119
25	130				0.5 × 130	126

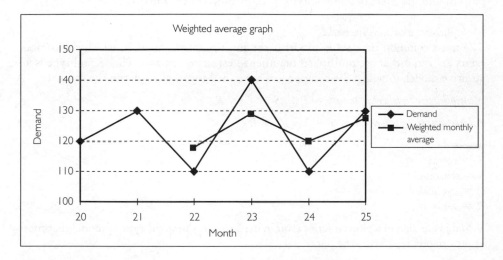

Figure 6.14 Example of a three-month weighted moving average, with the highest weighting factor (0.5) applied to the most recent month

Single exponential smoothing

This method keeps a running average of demand and adjusts it for each period in proportion to the difference between the latest actual demand figure and the latest value of the average. The equation is:

$$SF_{t+1} = SF_t + \alpha (A_t - SF_t)$$

where:
SF_{t+1} = smoothed forecast for time period following t
SF_t = smoothed forecast for period t
α = smoothing constant that determine weight given to previous data
A_t = actual demand in period t

The smoothing constant is a decimal between 0 and 1 where 0 is most stable and 1 is most responsive. Values between 0.1 and 0.3 are often used in practice.

Time series decomposition

Often a pattern cannot be recognised in the raw data and so it must be decomposed into components that show a pattern which is helpful in projecting the data. Four recognised components of a time series are:

- **Trend**: the general movement of the average level of demand over time.
- **Seasonal**: a recurring fluctuation of demand that repeats with a fairly consistent interval, e.g. weather
- **Cyclical**: a recurring fluctuation that repeats with a frequency of longer than 1 year. It may not have a consistent period of repetition, e.g. business cycle.
- **Random**: short, erratic movements that follow no discernible pattern.

Time series decomposition is appropriate if seasonal variation is evident in the demand pattern and the effect of seasonality is to be included in the forecast.

Multiplicative and additive models
The most common time series model is the multiplicative model in which the components are ratios that are multiplied together to estimate demand. The second type is an additive model, in which the components are added together to obtain the estimate.

Multiplicative time series forecast $= T \times S \times C \times R$

Additive time series forecast $= T + S + C + R$

where:
T = trend
S = seasonality
C = cyclical
R = random

Visual inspection of a plotted series is often used to determine the type of model that most appropriately represents the data.

Causal models of forecasting demand
Sometimes demand does not exhibit a consistent pattern over time because the level of one or more variables that have an effect on demand had changed during the period when the demand series was collected. Casual modes are used to identify variables, or a combination of variables, which affect demand and are then used to predict future levels of demand. Models that may be used in this way include linear regression, curvilinear regression and multiple regression.

Regression methods are used when it is desirable to find an indicator that moves before the company's sales level changes (a leading indicator) and that has a significantly stable relationship with sales to be useful as a prediction tool. Linear regression is a means of finding and expressing a relationship. Simple linear regression fits a line to a series of points that indicate past values of one dependent variable (sales) and one independent variable (the indicator). Forecasting techniques are discussed in Vonderembse (1991), Stevenson (1993) and Dennis and Dennis (1991).

Summary of key points _____

- The main elements in capacity planning decisions are the measurement of capacity and demand and the reconciling of the two to form a feasible plan.
- The measurement of demand should take place at an aggregated level and then be refined.

- The measurement of capacity is dependent on factors such as product mix and machine set-up time.
- A level capacity plan sets capacity at a uniform level throughout the planning period.
- A chase demand plan seeks to match production to demand over time.
- A demand management plan attempts to adjust demand to meet available capacity.
- Yield management is a collection of approaches used to optimise the use of capacity in service operations where capacity is relatively fixed and the service cannot be stored in any way.
- Cumulative representations can be used to evaluate a level capacity planning approach.
- In a service context queuing theory can provide a useful guide in determining expected waiting time for an arriving customer.
- Propositions about the psychology of queues can be used by service organisations to influence customer satisfaction with waiting times.
- By conducting a simulation study it is possible to determine the performance of a system for a given set of conditions.
- Scheduling concerns capacity planning decisions at an operational level.
- Demand forecasts can either be developed through a qualitative or a quantitative approach.

Exercises

1 Discuss the procedure for measuring demand in an organisation with which you are familiar
2 Discuss how the product (i.e. course) mix affects capacity at a University.
3 Evaluate ways of reconciling capacity and demand in a manufacturing organisation.
4 Evaluate ways of reconciling capacity and demand in a service organisation.
5 Customers arrive at an automated teller machine (ATM) at a rate of 20 per hour according to a Poisson distribution. The ATM serves customers at a mean rate of 15 customers per hour.
   a) What is the mean number of customers waiting in the queue?
   b) What is the mean time a customer spends in the queue?
   c) What is the probability that the till is busy?
6 Customers arrive at a Post Office serving area at a rate of 60 per hour according to a Poisson distribution. There are 8 tills and the service time of each till is at a mean rate of 10 customers per hour.
   a) What is the mean number of customers waiting in the queue?
   b) What is the mean time a customer spends in the queue?
   c) What is the probability that a till is busy?
7 Discuss how the experience of waiting in a queue can be improved.
8 Provide examples of suitable application areas for the simulation modelling technique.
9 What are the main issues in the scheduling of jobbing, batch and repetitive systems?
10 A job-shop has 5 jobs which must be processed on machine 1 and then on machine 2. Determine the sequence that will allow the set of 5 jobs to be completed in the minimum time, given the following process times for each job.

Job	Machine 1 (hours)	Machine 2 (hours)
A	8	3
B	4	5
C	7	6
D	5	10
E	9	3

11 The following six jobs are to be scheduled on a piece of equipment.

Job No.	1	2	3	4	5	6
Duration (hours)	6	4	2	8	1	5
Due date	6	20	22	24	2	10

    a) Prepare a Gantt chart that will provide a schedule showing when jobs are to be undertaken on the machine. Use the FCFS rule.

    b) Using FCFS how long will it take to complete all the jobs?

    c) Given the due dates shown calculate the average job lateness when FCFS is used.

    d) What schedule of jobs would minimise job lateness?

    e) What would the average throughput time be using FCFS and SPT rules?

    f) In addition to a lower throughput time what additional benefits would a firm get from the superior technique identified in (e)?

    g) What disadvantage is SPT likely to exhibit in a heavily loaded jobshop?

12 A small manufacturer produces custom parts that first require a shearing operation and then a punch operation. There are five jobs to be processed and the processing times are estimated as in the following table.

Job	Shear (hours)	Punch (hours)
1	4	5
2	4	1
3	10	4
4	6	10
5	2	3

Use Johnson's algorithm to identify the processing sequence that will give the lowest overall throughput time. Use a Gantt chart to illustrate the sequence.

13 Discuss the relevance of forecasting demand for an organisation with which you are familiar.

References

Dennis, T.L. and Dennis, W.J., *Management Science*, West Publishing (1991).

Hill, T., *Manufacturing Strategy: the strategic management of the manufacturing function*, Second Edition, Macmillan (1993).

Law, A.M. and Kelton, W.D., *Simulation Modelling and Analysis*, Second Edition, McGraw-Hill (1991).

Maister, D.H., The psychology of waiting lines, in J.A. Czepiel, M.R. Solomon and C.F. Surprenant (eds), *The Service Encounter*, Lexington Press, (1985) pp. 113–123.

Martin, C. and Powell, P., *Information Systems: A Management Perspective*, McGraw-Hill (1992).

Pegden, C.D., Shannon, R.E. and Sadowski, R.P., *Introduction to Simulation using SIMAN*, Second Edition, McGraw-Hill (1995).

McHaney, R., *Computer Simulation: A Practical Perspective*, Academic Press (1991).

Stevenson. W.J., *Production/Operations Management*, Fourth Edition, Irwin (1993).

Vonderembse, M.A. and White, G.P., *Operations Management: Concepts, Methods and Strategies*, Second Edition, West Publishing (1991).

Further reading

Fitzsimmons, J.A. and Fitzsimmons, M.J., *Service Management for Competitive Advantage*, McGraw-Hill (1994).

Greasley, A. and Barlow, S., Using Simulation Modelling for BPR: Resource allocation in a Police Custody process, *International Journal of Operations and Production Management*, 18 (9/10), (1998), pp. 978–988.

Hope, C. and Muhlemann, A., *Service Operations Management: Strategy, Design and Delivery*, Prentice-Hall (1997).

Lovelock, C.H., *Managing Services: Marketing, Operations and Human Resources*, Prentice-Hall (1988).

Russell, R.S. and Taylor, B.W., *Production and Operations Management: Focusing on Quality and Competitiveness*, Prentice-Hall (1995).

7 Inventory management

Objectives

By the end of this chapter, you should be able to:

- understand the trade-off between inventory costs and availability;
- use the EOQ model to calculate inventory order volume and annual inventory costs;
- use the EOQ model to calculate inventory order volume with quantity discounts;
- evaluate the use of the EOQ method in relation to internal batch size;
- use the FOI model to calculate variable inventory order volumes at fixed time intervals;
- use the ROP model to calculate when an order should be placed to replenish inventory;
- use the ABC classification method in order to identify suitable inventory control policies for inventory items;
- understand the use of market demand classification for inventory control.

At the highest level the management of inventory is simply an attempt to match supply and demand at a particular time and so forms part of a capacity management strategy (Chapter 6). Various approaches have been developed towards the management of inventory including MRP, OPT and JIT (Chapter 8) and at a more tactical level various scheduling techniques (Chapter 6) are used to plan and execute day-to-day activities. Inventory management is defined by Slack (1995) as 'the stored accumulation of material resources in a transformation system'. All organisations will carry some inventory or stock of goods at any one time. This can range from items such as stationery to machinery parts or raw materials. The main focus of inventory management is usually on resources that are being transformed, e.g. raw materials, purchased components or customers in a service operation.

Inventory management and demand

The type of inventory management system employed is determined by the nature of the demand for the goods and services on the organisation. Demand can be classified into two categories; dependent and independent.

Dependent demand
A dependent demand item has a demand which is relatively predictable because it is dependent on other factors. For example a fireplace mantel consists of two legs and one shelf. If daily demand for the mantel, derived from the production schedule, is 50 mantels, then a daily demand of 100 legs and 50 shelves can be predicted. Thus a dependent demand item can be classified has having a demand that can be calculated as the quan-

tity of the item needed to produce a scheduled quantity of an assembly that uses that item. MRP systems (Chapter 8) manage dependent demand items by calculating the quantity needed and the timing required (taking into account purchasing and manufacturing lead times) of each item.

Independent demand

Independent demand is when demand is not directly related to the demand for any other inventory item. Usually this demand comes from customers outside the company and so is not as predictable as dependent demand. Because of the unknown future requirements of customers, forecasting is used to predict the level of demand. A safety stock is then calculated to cover expected forecast errors. Independent demand items can be finished goods or spare parts used for after sales service. Inventory planning and control systems that calculate the volume and timing of independent demand items are covered in this chapter.

Types of inventory

Generally inventory is classified as either raw materials, work-in-progress (WIP) or finished goods. The proportion between these inventory types will vary but it is estimated that generally 30% are raw materials, 40% are work-in-progress and 30% finished goods. Waters (1996) points out the arbitrary nature of these classifications as for example someone's finished goods are someone else's raw materials. He also states that the total cost of holding stock is typically 25% of its value over a year.

The location of inventory can be used to define the inventory type and its characteristics. There are various definitions of inventory types. Slack (1995) provides the following.

- **Buffer/safety stock.** This is used to compensate for the uncertainties inherent in the timing or rate of supply and demand between two operational stages.
- **Cycle stock.** If it is required to produce multiple products from one operation in batches, there is a need to produce enough to keep a supply while the other batches are being produced.
- **Anticipation stock.** This includes producing to stock to anticipate an increase in demand due to seasonal factors. Also speculative policies such as buying in bulk to take advantage of price discounts may also increase inventory levels.
- **Pipeline/movement stock.** This is the inventory needed to compensate for the lack of stock while material is being transported between stages, e.g. the time taken in distribution from the warehouse to a retail outlet.

Inventory decisions

The main concern of inventory management is the trade-off between the cost of not having an item in stock against the cost of holding and ordering the inventory. A stock-out can either be to an internal customer in which case a loss of production output may occur, or to an external customer when a drop in customer service level will result. In order to achieve a balance between inventory availability and cost, the following inventory management aspects must be addressed:

- *Volume management:* how much to order.
- *Timing management:* when to order.

- *Choosing the best method:* how should decisions about volume and timing be made for a particular item.

This chapter is structured around these headings.

Volume management

The economic order quantity model

The economic order quantity (EOQ) calculates the inventory order volume required while seeking to minimise the sum of the annual costs of holding inventory and the annual costs of ordering inventory. The model makes a number of assumptions including:

- stable or constant demand;
- fixed and identifiable ordering cost;
- the cost of holding inventory varies in a linear fashion to the number of items held;
- the item cost does not vary with the order size;
- delivery lead time does not vary;
- no quantity discounts are available;
- annual demand exists.

Brown (1996) is critical of the EOQ method where a fixed order number per material type approach is not seen as relevant in a complex and dynamic market. The assumption of one delivery per order, and then the use of that stock over time increases inventory levels and goes against a JIT approach. Also annual demand will not exist for products with a life-cycle of less than a year. However the EOQ and other approaches in this chapter still have a role in inventory management in the right circumstances and if their limitations are recognised.

Before the EOQ model is introduced it is useful to know that various texts use a number of words to describe the cost of holding inventory and the cost of replacing that inventory. These include:

Inventory held	Inventory replaced
Holding cost	Order cost
Carrying cost	Replenishment cost
Storage cost	Delivery cost

Each order is assumed to be of Q units and is withdrawn at a constant rate over time until the quantity in stock is just sufficient to satisfy the demand during the order lead time (the time between placing an order and receiving the delivery). At this time an order for Q units is placed with the supplier. Assuming that the usage rate and lead time are constant the order will arrive when the stock level is at zero, thus eliminating excess stock or **stock-outs**.

The order quantity must be set at a level which is not too small, leading to many orders and thus high order costs, and not too large leading to high average levels of inventory and thus high holding costs.

The **annual holding cost** is the average number of items in stock multiplied by the cost to hold an item for a year. If the amount in stock decreases at a constant rate from Q to 0 then the average in stock is Q/2 (Figure 7.1).

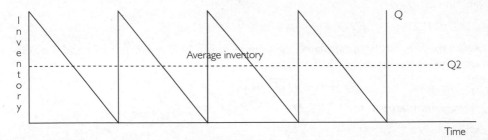

Figure 7.1 Inventory level vs. lead time for the EOQ model

Thus if C_H is the average annual holding cost per unit, the total annual holding cost is:

Annual holding cost $= Q/2 \times C_H$

The annual ordering cost is a function of the number of orders per year and the ordering cost per order. If D is the annual demand, then the number of orders per year is given by D/Q. Thus if C_o is the ordering cost per order then the total annual ordering cost is:

Annual ordering cost $= D/Q \times C_o$

Thus the total **annual inventory cost** is the sum of the total annual holding cost and the total annual ordering cost:

Total annual cost $= (Q/2 \times C_H) + (D/Q \times C_o)$

where:
Q = order quantity
C_H = holding cost per unit
D = annual demand
C_o = ordering cost per order

The total cost and its components of ordering and holding cost are shown graphically in Figure 7.2.

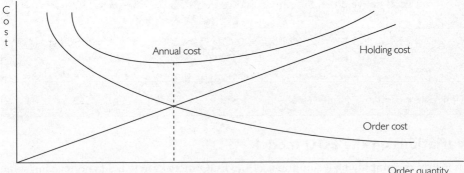

Figure 7.2 Inventory cost vs order quantity for the EOQ model

From the graph it can be seen that the minimum total cost point is when the holding cost is equal to the ordering cost. Mathematically:

$$Q/2 \times C_H = D/Q \times C_o$$

Solving for Q gives:

$$EOQ = \sqrt{2D \times C_o / C_H}$$

Once the EOQ has been calculated the average numbers of orders per year and the average order interval can be calculated:

Average number of orders per year $= \sqrt{C_H D / 2 C_o}$

Average order interval $= \sqrt{2C_o / C_H D}$

where:
C_H = holding cost per unit
D = annual demand
C_o = order cost per order.

WORKED EXAMPLE

The annual demand for a company's single item of stock is 1000 units. It costs the company £6 to hold one unit of stock for one year. Each time that a replenishment order is made the company incurs a fixed cost of £75.

a) Determine the economic order quantity.
b) Suppose that the company's supplier of stock introduces a condition that normally there shall be no more than five orders for replenishment per annum. How much would the company be prepared to pay in order to avoid having to meet this condition?

SOLUTION

a) $D = 1000$, $C_H = 6$, $C_o = 75$.

$$EOQ = \sqrt{2D \times C_o / C_H} = \sqrt{2 \times 1000 \times 75 / 6} = \sqrt{25,000} = 158 \text{ units}$$

b) Total units delivered at one time based on 5 orders per annum = 1000/5 = 200 units.

Total annual cost $= (Q \times C_H / 2) + (D \times C_o / 2) = 200/2 \times 6 + 1000/200 \times 75$
$= 600 + 375 = £975$.

Total annual cost at $EAQ = 158/2 \times 6 + 1000/158 \times 75 = 474 + 474 = £948$

Therefore company would have to pay the difference £975 − £948 = £27.

Variations on the EOQ model

In reality the simplifying assumptions of the EOQ model rarely hold and relaxing some of those assumptions is described below.

EOQ with quantity discounts

Many firms provide discounts for large quantity orders for a number of reasons. These include economies of scale due to fewer set-up times and other production efficiencies. Then the customer must balance the potential benefits of a reduced price against the holding costs incurred by the higher order quantity. The total annual cost with discounts is thus the sum of holding costs + ordering costs + purchasing costs. This can be expressed as the following equation:

$$TC = (Q \times C_H / 2) + (D \times C_0 / Q) + (D \times C_P)$$

where:

Q = quantity ordered
D = annual demand
C_0 = order cost per order
C_H = holding cost per unit for Q being considered
C_P = unit price per unit for Q being considered

Both the unit price and thus holding cost vary with an order quantity that is at a different price **breakpoint**. Thus it may be necessary to calculate the total cost at each price breakpoint to find the lowest value. In addition we need to take into account the fact that we may not be permitted to order the quantity specified at the price discount set. Also it may be that it would be more economical to purchase just a few more units and achieve a more generous price discount at the next breakpoint.

There are two main scenarios that need to be considered. One is where holding costs are considered constant per unit. In this case there will be a single EOQ for all the cost curves at the different breakpoint. In the second case holding costs are expressed as a percentage of purchase price and so each cost curve will increase the EOQ for each breakpoint.

The procedure for finding the best order quantity is:

- Step 1. Begin with the lowest price and solve for the EOQ at this price.
- Step 2. If the EOQ is not within the quantity range for this price, go to Step 3. Otherwise go to Step 4.
- Step 3. Solve for the EOQ at the next higher price. Go to Step 2.
- Step 4. Calculate the total cost for the EOQ that falls within the quantity range and for all the lower price breakpoints. Select the quantity with the lowest total cost.

WORKED EXAMPLE

A company is able to obtain quantity discounts on its order of material as follows:

Price per kilogram (£)	Kilograms bought
6.00	less than 250
5.90	250 and less than 800
5.80	800 and less than 2000
5.70	2000 and less than 4000
5.60	4000 and over

The annual demand for the material is 4000 kg. Holding costs are 20% per year of material cost. The order cost per order is £6. Calculate the best quantity to order.

SOLUTION

Solving the EOQ at the lowest price ($Q = 4000$ and over): $C_o = 6$; $C_H = 20/100 \times 5.6 = 1.12$; $C_p = 5.6$; $D = 4000$:

$$EOQ = \sqrt{(2 \times 4000 \times 6)/1.12} = 207$$

The EOQ is not in the quantity range (4000 and above). It is obvious that the EOQ is lower than the price ranges so jump to the highest price.

Solving the EOQ at the highest price ($Q = 250$ and under): $C_o = 6$; $C_H = 20/100 \times 6 = 1.2$; $C_p = 6$; $D = 4000$:

$$EOQ = \sqrt{(2 \times 4000 \times 6)/1.2} = 200$$

EOQ is in the quantity range so calculate the total cost at the EOQ and all lower price breakpoints, as tabulated.

Q	Order cost	Holding cost	Cost of goods	Total cost
200	120	120	24,000	24,240
250	96	147.5	23,600	23,843.5
800	30	464	23,200	23,694
2000	12	1,140	22,800	23,952
4000	6	2,240	22,400	24,646

Therefore the lowest cost and therefore best order quantity is 800.

EOQ with gradual order replenishment

A major assumption of the EOQ model is that once a replenishment order has been made the order quantity is delivered at one time. Often this is not the case, particularly with internal processes where a machine may deliver a stream of parts as they are produced over time. Thus there is a gradual build-up of inventory up to the maximum stock level allowed. The machine will then be used for other purposes and the stock level will decline to zero. Then another batch of parts are produced continually again. The inventory profile for this system is shown in Figure 7.3.

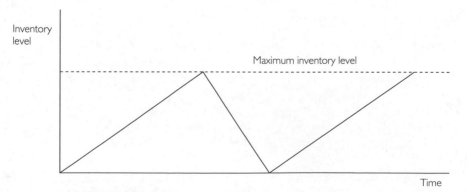

Figure 7.3 Inventory profile for gradual order inventory system

The best order quantity for a gradual order inventory system is called the **economic batch quantity** (EBQ). The maximum inventory level is no longer equal to the best order quantity but is usually considerably lower.

$$EBQ = \sqrt{2DC_o / C_H (1 - D / P)} = EOQ / \sqrt{(1 - D / P)}$$

where:

D = annual demand
C_o = order cost per order
C_H = holding cost per unit
P = delivery (production) rate in units per year
EOQ = economic order quantity

WORKED EXAMPLE

A car manufacturer has a annual demand of 40,000 steering wheels which it produces at a rate of 750 a day. Assuming demand is at a uniform rate through the year, with a holding cost of £2 and set-up cost of £50, Calculate the economic batch quantity. Assume there are 250 working days in a year.

SOLUTION
$D = 40,000; P = 750; C_H = 2; C_o = 50;$ days $= 250$

$EBQ = \sqrt{2 \times 40,000 \times 50 / (2 \times (1 - 40,000 / (750 \times 250)))} = 1594$ units

EOQ and internal processes

When discussing internal processes the ordering cost in the EOQ model can be attributed to the set-up cost in moving from one production lot to a different production lot type. What the model does not take into account is that the set-up cost at a bottleneck process will be much higher than at a non-bottleneck. This is because time lost at a bottleneck will translate as a reduction of capacity for *the whole production system*. In this model the holding cost will also be treated as a function of the production lot size. However while this model holds for finished goods inventory, work-in-progress inventory is more a function of the transfer batch size. In any case higher batch sizes have a number of consequences for costs in terms of:

- more room needed for transportation of large amounts;
- slower progress while waiting for whole batch to be processed before moving to next process;
- quality problems discovered later because of large batch size before quality check.

Another point to bear in mind with work-in-progress inventory is the need to distinguish between short-term inventory produced by imbalances in production rates caused by product mix variations and excessive inventory in the system. Imbalances may occur not only as a result of different production rates for different products but also from differing machine set-up times between products. Large set-up times may lead to an increase in batch size in order to reduce the amount of time lost through machine set-up but this leads to the problems outlined above. A further problem is when the factory is overwhelmed by rush orders leading to excessive expediting of orders, causing additional set-ups and leading to a spiral of deteriorating lead time performance. The just-in-time approach (Chapter 8) to production planning offers one potential solution to these problems by 'pulling' materials through the process to the particular operation only at the point when they are needed.

Fixed order interval (FOI) model

For the EOQ/ROP inventory models, *fixed quantities* of items are ordered at varying time intervals. In a fixed order interval (FOI) model *varying quantities* are placed at *fixed time intervals*. This means that a higher than normal demand will mean a larger order size rather than a shorter time between orders as in a fixed quantity model. The main attribute of the fixed interval model is that it only requires a periodic review of inventory levels to determine the order quantity required. A graph of inventory level over time for a fixed order interval system is shown in Figure 7.4.

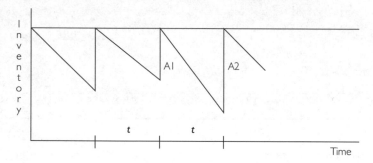

Figure 7.4 Inventory level vs. time for the FOI model

It can be seen that the amount ordered at the fixed interval time period t is determined by the rate of demand during that period. Thus the order amount, A2, is much greater than the order amount A1 due to the relatively high demand during the period leading up to A2.

The main advantage of using this system is that it enables a group of related components to be ordered at any one time, saving the cost of repeat deliveries and simplifying stock control. In addition the need to continuously monitor stock, as in a fixed quantity system, is replaced by a periodic review and so saves monitoring duties. The calculation for the FOI model is dependent on whether demand and delivery lead time are treated as fixed or variable. If it is assumed that deliveries are relatively constant and demand levels are variable, the equation for the amount to order is given as follows:

Amount to order = Expected demand during protection interval + safety stock − amount on

hand at reorder time $= \bar{d} \times (OI + LT) + z \times \sigma_d \times \sqrt{OI + LT} - A$

where:
$\bar{d}$ = average demand rate
OI = order interval (time between orders)

LT = delivery lead time
z = number of standard deviations from the mean
σ_d = standard deviation of demand rate
A = amount of units on hand at reorder time.

(See the ROP model below for an explanation of the formulae for safety stock.)

Variations on the FOI model

A variation on the fixed order interval system is when minimum and maximum levels are set for inventory. Thus at a periodic interval review point, inventory is replenished up to the maximum level only if the inventory level is below a minimum level. A graph of inventory level over time is shown Figure 7.5.

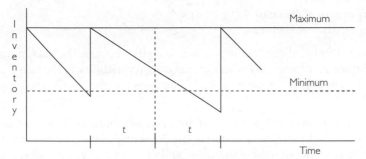

Figure 7.5 Inventory level vs. time for the FOI model with min/max inventory levels

This system is suitable for low-cost items where the additional holding cost incurred when holding higher levels of inventory is offset by reductions in the need to order small amounts more frequently.

Timing management

The re-order point (ROP) model

The EOQ model tells us how much to order, but not when to order. The reorder point model (ROP) identifies the time to order when the stock level drops to a predetermined amount. This amount will usually include a quantity of stock to cover for the delay between order and delivery (the **delivery lead time**) and an element of stock to reduce the risk of running out of stock when levels are low (the **safety stock**).

The previous economic order quantity model provides a batch size that is then depleted and replenished in a continuous cycle within the organisation. Thus the EOQ in effect provides a batch size which the organisation can work to. However this assumes that demand rates and delivery times are fixed so that the stock can be replenished at the exact time stocks are exhausted. Realistically though both the demand rate for the product and the delivery lead-time will vary and thus the risk of a stock-out is high. The cost of not having an item in stock when the customer requests it can obviously be costly both in terms of the potential loss of sales and the loss of customer goodwill leading to further loss of business.

Safety stock and service level

Safety stock is used in order to prevent a stock-out occurring. It provides an extra level of inventory above that needed to meet predicted demand, to cope with variations in demand over a time period. The level of safety stock used, if any, will vary for each inventory cycle, but an average stock level above that needed to meet demand will be calculated.

To calculate the safety stock level a number of factors should be taken into account including:

- cost due to stock-out
- cost of holding safety stock
- variability in rate of demand
- variability in delivery lead time.

It is important to note that there is no stock-out risk between the maximum inventory level and the reorder level. The risk occurs due to variability in the rate of demand and due to variability in the delivery lead time between the reorder point and zero stock level.

The reorder level can of course be estimated by a rule of thumb, such as when stocks are at twice the expected level of demand during the delivery lead time. However to consider the probability of stock-out, cost of inventory and cost of stock-out the idea of a service level is used.

The service level is a measure of the level of service, or how sure, the organisation is that it can supply inventory from stock. This can be expressed as the probability that the inventory on hand during the lead time is sufficient to meet expected demand (e.g. a service level of 90% means that there is a 0.9 probability that demand will be met during the lead time period, and the probability that a stock-out will occur is 10%. The service level set is dependent on a number of factors such as stockholding costs for the extra safety stock and the loss of sales if demand cannot be met.

For example in a variable demand and constant lead time model it is assumed that demand during lead time is composed of independent daily demand that vary approximately to a normal distribution. Thus the total variance is the sum of the daily variances for the number of days in the lead time period.

Total variance = Daily variances × Number of days of lead time $= \sigma_d^2 \times LT$

Standard deviation $= \sqrt{Variance}$

Standard deviation $= \sqrt{\sigma_d^2 \times LT} = \sigma_d \times \sqrt{LT}$

Safety stock $= z \times \sigma_d \times \sqrt{LT}$

where z = service level (e.g. for 1% service level, z = 2.3263 from normal distribution table). The actual service level chosen will depend on a number of factors such as:

- level of competition
- funds available for inventory management
- stock-out costs.

Variations on the ROP model

The re-order problem is one of determining the level of safety stock that balances the expected holding costs with the costs of stock-out. Equations will be derived for the following scenarios:

- constant demand, constant lead time;
- variable demand, constant lead time;
- constant demand, variable lead time;
- variable demand, variable lead time.

Constant demand and constant lead time

Assuming that the delivery lead time and demand rate is constant there is no risk of stock-out so no safety stock is required.

Reorder point (units) $= d \times LT$

where:
d = daily demand
LT = lead time

WORKED EXAMPLE

A company has an demand for an item at a constant of 50 per week. The order delivery lead time is also constant at 3 weeks. What should the reorder point be?

SOLUTION

$d = 50, LT = 3.$

Reorder point $= d \times LT = 3 \times 50 = 150$ units

Variable demand and constant lead time

This model assumes that demand during the delivery lead time consists of a series of independent daily demands and thus can be described by a normal distribution. The average daily demand rate and its standard deviation (measure of variability) are used to determine the expected demand and standard deviation of demand for the lead time period. Thus the reorder point is:

Reorder point (ROP) = *Expected demand during lead time* + *Safety stock* =

$(\bar{d} \times LT) + (z \times \sqrt{LT} \times \sigma_d)$
where:
$\bar{d}$ = average demand rate
LT = delivery lead time
σ_d = standard deviation of demand rate
z = number of standard deviations from the mean

WORKED EXAMPLE

An office supply company sold paper with a variable demand which can be assumed to be normally distributed with an average of 800 boxes per week and a standard deviation of 250 boxes per week. The delivery lead-time has been very consistent at 3 weeks. Determine the recommended re-order level if there is to be no more than a 1% chance that a stock-out will occur in any one replenishment period.

SOLUTION
$\bar{d}$ = 800/week; σ_d = 250/week; LT = 3. At 1% service level, z = 2.3263, from normal distribution table.

$ROP = (\bar{d} \times LT) + (z \sqrt{LT} \times \sigma_d) = 800 \times 3 + 2.3263 \times \sqrt{3} \times 250 = 2400 + 2.3263 \times 433 = 3409$ units

Constant demand and variable lead time

Here the lead time variation is described by a normal distribution and thus the expected lead time is normally distributed. Thus the reorder point is:

Reorder point (ROP) = expected demand during lead time + safety stock = $d \times \overline{LT} + (z \times d \times \sigma_{LT})$

where:
d = constant demand rate
LT = average lead time
σ_{LT} = standard deviation of lead time
z = number of standard deviations from the mean.

Variable demand rate and variable lead time

When both demand rate and lead time are variable, the expected demand during lead time is the average daily demand multiplied by average lead time. Both daily demand and lead time are assumed to be normally distributed.

Reorder point (ROP) = expected demand during lead time + safety stock = $(\bar{d} \times \overline{LT}) + z \sqrt{\overline{LT} \times \sigma_d^2 + \bar{d}^2 \times \sigma_{LT}^2}$

Choosing the best method of inventory control

The ABC inventory classification system

Normally a mix of fixed order interval and fixed order quantity inventory systems are used within an organisation. When there are many inventory items involved this raises the issue of deciding which particular inventory system should be used for a particular item. The ABC classification system sorts inventory items into groups depending on the amount of annual expenditure they incur. This will depend on both the estimated number of items used annually multiplied by the unit cost. To instigate an ABC system a table is produced listing the items in expenditure order (with largest expenditure at the top), and showing the percentage of total expenditure and cumulative percentage of the total expenditure for each item (Table 7.1).

Table 7.1 Example of a ABC classification table.

Item	Annual expenditure (cost usage) (£000s)	Percentage expenditure (%)	Cumulative expenditure (%)
X-76	800	24.1	24.1
X-25	650	19.6	43.7
X-40	475	14.3	58.1
X-22	450	13.6	71.6
X-18	300	9.0	80.7
X-44	200	8.0	86.7
X-42	150	5.4	91.3
X-21	100	3.0	94.3
X-67	75	2.3	96.5
X-88	65	2.0	98.5
X-23	50	1.5	100.0
TOTAL	3315		

By reading the cumulative percentage figure it is usually found, following **Pareto's Law**, that 10–20% of the items account for 60–80% of annual expenditure. These items are called A items and need to be controlled closely to reduce overall expenditure. This often implies a fixed quantity system with perpetual inventory checks or a fixed-interval system employing a small time interval between review periods. It may also require a more strategic approach to management of these items which may translate into closer buyer-supplier relationships. The B items account for the next 20–30% of items and usually account for a similar percentage of total expenditure. These items require fewer inventory level reviews, however, than A items. A fixed order interval system with a minimum order level may be appropriate here. Finally C items represent the remaining 50–70% of items but only account for under 25% of total expenditure. Here much less rigorous inventory control methods need be used, as the cost of inventory tracking will outweigh the cost of holding additional stock.

It is important to recognise that overall expenditure may not be the only appropriate basis on which to classify items. Other factors include the importance of a component part on the overall product, the variability in delivery time, the loss of value through deterioration and the disruption caused to the production process if a stock-out occurs.

Inventory control based on predictability of demand

While the ABC system classifies inventory by sales value, it may also be appropriate to classify by **market demand** characteristics. This will obviously differ between businesses but the idea is to ensure that the mix of inventory types is able to satisfy customer needs and deliver the required profitability and cashflows. The inventory can be classified into the following types (Gattorna, 1996):

- **Base flow products:** have a constant predictable demand and could relate to cycle stock.

- **Wave flow products:** have a seasonal demand variation which is relatively predictable.
- **Surge flow products:** have an unpredictable demand pattern and may not be repeated.

They can be related to an anticipation type of inventory control. Each flow type infers a different inventory management strategy. For instance base flow items can be ordered just-in-time from suppliers with minimum internal stocks due to their high predictability. The strategy for surge flow items needs to take into account the business risk involved in not being able to meet customer demand. Thus the analysis may take into account factors such as the gross margin on the item and the number of stock turns likely in fixing an inventory policy.

Planning and control for demand

The predictability of demand for goods/services can range from a situation of what is essentially dependent demand (i.e. demand can be predicted) to a high level of independent demand (unpredictability). Planning and control strategies to meet this continuum are shown in Table 7.2.

Table 7.2 Planning and control systems for demand types

Demand type	Planning and control system	Resources required in stock
Dependent	Resource-to-order	None
Independent (low variability)	Make-to-order	Transforming
Independent (high variability)	Make-to-stock	Transformed, Transforming

Thus in an dependent demand type situation it is not necessary to activate a planning and control system and acquire resources until a delivery date for an order is received. Both transforming (e.g. staff, machinery) and transformed (e.g. bricks for a house) resources may be acquired at the appropriate time for delivery. In an independent demand situation when demand is relatively predictable the transforming resources such as staff and machinery may be in place on a permanent basis. However the transformed resources, i.e. the raw materials which are used to construct the product, may be acquired on the receipt of a customer order. This is termed a **make-to-order planning and control system**. Finally if demand is unpredictable, the organisation will use a **make-to-stock planning and control system** which produces to a forecast of demand for the product.

Two implications arise from the planning and control system utilised by the organisation. In a make-to-stock system each order must be small compared to total capacity or the risk of making to stock, and not finding a customer for the order, will be too high. In a **resource-to-order system** implies each order is large compared to total system capacity to make the organisation of resources worthwhile. The other implication is that of customer delivery time performance. Whilst the customer will only 'see' the delivery time from stock in a make-to-stock system, in a make-to-order system the delivery cycle will include the purchase, make and delivery stages. This effect is examined using P:D ratios.

P:D ratios

The P:D ratio is a concept derived by Shingo (1981) and compares the demand time D (from customer request to receipt of goods/services) to the total throughput time P of the purchase, make and delivery stages. The relationship between the planning and control systems and the P:D ratio is shown in Figure 7.6.

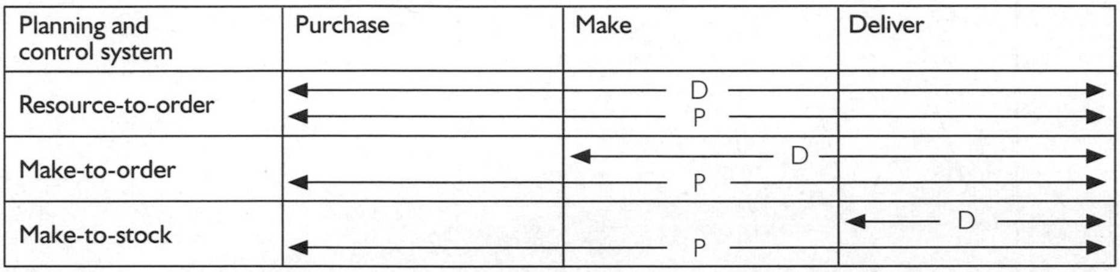

Planning and control system	Purchase	Make	Deliver
Resource-to-order	← D →		
	← P →		
Make-to-order		← D →	
	← P →		
Make-to-stock			← D →
	← P →		

Figure 7.6 The relationship between the P:D ratio and the planning and control system

Thus in a resource-to-order system the demand time and throughput time are essentially the same. The purchase-make-deliver cycle is not triggered until a customer order is received. In a make-to-stock system the demand time is essentially the time of delivery from stock to the customer.

The P:D ratio makes the implications for the delivery time to the customer explicit. In a resource-to-order system the purchase, make and deliver stages all affect delivery performance. In a make-to-stock system however the customer only 'sees' the delivery time. However although delivery performance is improved in a make-to-stock system, the item is being produced to a forecast demand which is subject to error. The risk of producing to this forecast increases with the ratio of P to D, as an increase in throughput times means that the item must be produced to a demand further into the future. Thus reducing the P:D ratio will reduce the risk inherent in the planning and control system.

Inventory location

One of the major issues in inventory management is the level of decentralisation required in inventory distribution. Decentralised facilities offer a service closer to the customer and thus should provide a better service level in terms of knowledge of customer needs and speed of service. Centralisation however offers the potential for less handling of goods between service points, lower control costs and lower overall inventory levels due to lower overall buffer levels required. The overall demand pattern for a centralised facility will be an average of a number of variable demand patterns from customer outlets and so will be a smoother overall demand pattern thus requiring lower buffer stocks (see Figure 7.7). Hence there is a trade-off between the customer service levels or effectiveness offered by a decentralised system and the lower costs or efficiency offered by a centralised system.

One way of combining the advantages of a centralised facility with a high level of customer service is to reduce the delivery lead time between the centralised distribution centre and the customer outlet. This can be accomplished by using the facility of **electronic data interchange** (EDI) which is the direct computer-based exchange between organisations of standard business transaction documents such as invoices and purchase orders. EDI enables automated purchasing, shipping and payment transactions with customers. It may also provide strategic benefits by helping a firm to 'lock-in' customers, offering a ordering service which competitors are not able to match. Chapter 2 provides more information on EDI.

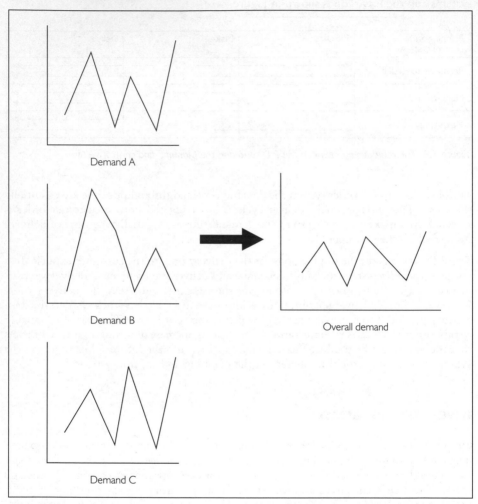

Figure 7.7 The effect of location on inventory level variation

Summary of key points

- Inventory Management is concerned with a trade-off between inventory holding costs and not having inventory in stock.
- In order to achieve a balance between inventory costs and availability the elements of order volume, order timing and classification of inventory items needs to be considered.

- The EOQ model can be useful for calculating an order volume that minimises total inventory costs.
- The EOQ model may not be appropriate to calculate internal batch sizes for production processes.
- The FOI model is useful for calculating inventory volumes at fixed time intervals.
- The ROP model indicates the level at which inventory should be ordered to avoid a stock-out.
- The ROP model can take into consideration variable delivery lead time and variable demand characteristics for an item.
- A classification system is needed in order to identify appropriate inventory control policies for stock items.
- The ABC classification system ranks inventory items by their percentage of cumulative expenditure.
- Items can be classified by their market demand characteristics.
- EDI systems can reduce the delivery lead time between supplier and customer and thus improve the level of customer service.

Exercises

1 Evaluate the EOQ model for inventory control.
2 What are the implications of P:D ratios for an organisation.
3 A typing pool requires 1000 boxes of typing paper each year. Each box is worth £20 and storage costs are 13.5% of stock value a year. The cost of placing an order is £15. For the order quantities 50, 100, 150, 200 and 250, calculate the storage cost, replenishment cost and total cost. Plot these on a graph. Show algebraically that delivery costs and storage costs are equal when 105 boxes are ordered at a time.
4 A company has a demand of 2000 items per annum. Stock ordering costs are fixed at £100 irrespective of the scale of replenishment. It costs £2.50 to hold one item in stock for one year. Calculate the economic order quantity.
5 A company experiences annual demand for 2500 units of the single product that it stocks. The replenishment cost for inventory is fixed at £400 regardless of the size of replenishment. Annual holding costs are £8 per unit. What is the optimum number of replenishments per annum?
6 Computers Ltd. has expanded its range of computers and now requires each year, at a constant rate, 200,000 circuit boards which it obtains from an outside supplier. The order cost is £32. For any circuit board in stock it is estimated that the annual holding cost is equal to 10% of its cost. The circuit boards cost £8 each. No stock-outs are permitted.
   (a) What is the optimal order size, and how many orders should be placed in a year?
   (b) What are the ordering and holding costs and hence what if the total relevant inventory cost per annum?
   (c) If the demand has been underestimated and the true demand is 242,000 circuit boards per annum, what would be the effect on the order quantity calculated in (a) and still meeting demand, rather than using a new optimal level?
7 The purchasing manager of an electrical components retailer, holds a regular stock of light bulbs. Over the past year he has sold, on average, 25 a week and he anticipates that this rate of sale will continue during the next year (which you may assume to be 50 weeks). He buys light bulbs from his supplier at the rate of £5 for 10, and every time he places an

order it costs on average £10 bearing in mind the necessary secretarial expenses and the time involved in checking the order. As a guide to the stockholding costs involved, the company usually value their cost of capital at 20% and as the storage space required is negligible, he decides that this figure is appropriate in this case. Furthermore, the prices charged to customers are determined by taking the purchasing and stockholding costs and applying a standard mark-up of 20%.

(a) Currently the manager is reviewing the ordering and pricing policies and needs to know how many light bulbs he should order each time and what price he should charge. What would be your advice?

(b) If he now finds that he can get a discount of 5% for ordering in batches of 1000 would you advise him to amend the ordering and pricing policy that you have suggested and if so, to what?

8 The manager of a large fishing tackle shop, opens for 50 weeks each year, holds a regular stock of fishing flies. Although the manager has to purchase boxes of these items for £9.60 per box containing 12 flies he is prepared to sell them as single items. Over the past year he has sold, on average, 12 boxes of fishing flies each week and it is likely that this level of sales will continue into the future. Due to telephone, secretarial and transport costs it is estimated that the cost of receiving each order is £16. The annual cost of storage is estimated at 20% of the stock item value and is based on the cost of storage space and the company's cost of capital. The manager of the shop sets a price for his goods by taking the sum of the purchase cost and the appropriately allocated holding cost (storage and delivery) and then applying a mark-up of 50%.

(a) Determine the optimum number of boxes of fishing flies the shop manager should order at a time and the number of orders per year. Show that the selling price per fly that results from this optimum policy is £1.24.

(b) The supplier offers a discount of 4% on the price of each box of flies if the manager is prepared to purchase 500 boxes at a time. It can be assumed that there are no price effects on demand. Show whether or not this discount, assuming it is passed on, is advantageous or not to the customer in terms of shop price.

(c) What percentage discount is required for the order quantity if 500-box deliveries are to be beneficial to the customers?

9 Alarms Ltd, a manufacturer of alarm clocks, used £75,000 worth of LED readout circuits annually in its production process. Cost per order is £75 and the holding charge assessed against this classification of inventory is 20% of the average balance per year. Alarms follows an EOQ purchasing system and to date has not been offered any discount on these circuits. However a supplier has approached Alarms and indicated that if the company would buy its circuits four times a year, a discount of 0.1% off list price would be given in return. Would you advise Alarms to accept this offer or make a counter-offer? If a counter-offer is made, what is the highest price that should be offered for this quarterly purchase?

References

Brown, S., *Strategic Manufacturing for Competitive Advantage*, Prentice-Hall (1996).

Gattorna, J.L. and Walters, D.W., *Managing the Supply Chain: A Strategic Perspective*, Macmillan (1996).

Shingo, S., *Study of Toyota Production Systems*, Japan Management Association (1981).

Slack, N., Chambers, S., Harland, C., Harrison, A. and Johnston, R., *Operations Management*, Pitman Publishing (1995).

Waters, D., *Operations Management: Producing Goods and Services*, Addison Wesley (1996).

Further reading

Mather, K., *Competitive Manufacturing*, Prentice-Hall (1988).

Russell, R.S. and Taylor, B.W., *Production and Operations Management: Focusing on Quality and Competitiveness*, Prentice-Hall (1995).

Stevenson, W.J., *Production/Operations Management*, Fourth Edition, Irwin (1993).

Lamming, R., *Beyond Partnership: Strategies for Innovation and Lean Supply*, Prentice-Hall (1993).

8 MRP, JIT and OPT

Objectives

By the end of this chapter, you should be able to:

- understand the meaning of MRP and MRP II;
- describe the components of MRP;
- understand the MRP process;
- evaluate the MRP technique;
- understand the concept of JIT;
- understand the kanban-based JIT production system;
- evaluate the JIT philosophy and techniques;
- understand the concept of OPT;
- understand the OPT planning and control approach;
- evaluate the OPT technique.

This chapter covers three different approaches to materials management. Materials requirement planning (MRP) aims to ensure that just the right quantity of each item is held at the right time in order to meet the needs of the manufacturing schedule. Just-in-time (JIT) production uses a 'pull' mechanism which provides a trigger when demand occurs and then attempts to supply to this demand. Optimised production technology (OPT) focuses on the system bottleneck – this is a capacity constraint that restricts the actual throughput of goods to the customer.

The above approaches are not mutually exclusive. For example, an EOQ or ROP approach (Chapter 7) could be used to ensure stocks of 'C' category items from an ABC analysis. MRP II could be used to form aggregate capacity plans, OPT to isolate bottleneck processes and optimise throughput and JIT for shop-floor control of non-bottleneck resources.

Materials requirements planning (MRP)

Materials requirements planning (MRP) systems are usually associated with the management of dependent demand items such as raw materials, components or sub-assemblies. MRP aims to ensure that just the right quantity of each item is held at the right time in order to meet the needs of the production schedule taking into account ordering and manufacturing lead times. The different types of MRP systems are now discussed.

Materials requirements planning (MRP I)

MRP is used to refer to slightly different aspects of manufacturing planning and control systems reflecting its development since its first use in the 1960s. The original version of MRP (or MRP I as it is now known) is a technique which works backward from the quantities and due-dates for end items specified in the master production schedule to calculate the volume and timing requirements needed for components to meet that schedule. For organisations with many products all containing parts with various supply lead times and different amounts of inventory, MRP is basically an information system which makes the manual volume and timing calculations unnecessary.

In early MRP systems a production plan was launched based on inventory lead times and the bill of materials without consideration of capacity. Without any information on the capacity of the production unit the system was unable to track the actual status of the production plan. Thus each week a new production plan was generated based on the previous week's performance. With the increase in sophistication of information systems it was possible to develop what is called a **closed-loop MRP system**, which are now the norm. This version of MRP checks the production plans against three levels of capacity using the following plans.

1. **Resource requirements plan (RRP)**. This checks aggregate capacity at the production planning stage (Chapter 6).
2. **Rough-cut capacity plans (RCCP)**. This checks the master production schedule (MPS) against key resource constraints (Chapter 6). Most production plants will have bottleneck resources which constrain the overall production capacity. Checking at this level may save unnecessary detailed planning.
3. **Capacity requirements plan (CRP)**. This plans the schedule against individual work centres or workers. The capacity requirements at this level will most likely be highly variable so infinite capacity would be assumed by the system. The MRP controller can then either decide to allocate extra resources to capacity-constrained cases or to replan the loading over an alternative time-frame.

When MRP includes this feedback loop it can form the basis of a planning and control system for production operations and purchasing.

Manufacturing resource planning (MRP II)

MRP II extends the idea of MRP to other areas in the business such as marketing and finance. Thus central databases hold information on product structure, i.e. the **bill of materials** (BOM) file, which can be updated due to design changes by engineering for example. By incorporating financial elements into item details, inventory cost information can be utilised by finance departments. At a wider level information provided by the MRP II system from simulations of business plans can be used to estimate **plant investment needs and workforce requirements**. This information can then be used to co-ordinate efforts across departments including marketing, financing, engineering and manufacturing.

Components of MRP

MRP is an information system used to calculate the requirements for component materials needed to produce end items scheduled in the **master production schedule** (MPS). The MPS indicates the quantity and timing of each item the organisation produces. The components of an MRP system which use and process this information are shown in Figure 8.1. Each component of the MRP system will be described below.

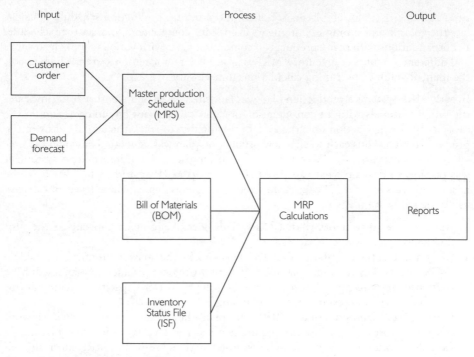

Figure 8.1 Components of an MRP system

Master production schedule (MPS)

An ideal master production schedule (MPS) is one which most efficiently uses the organisation's capacity while being feasible in being able to meet customer due dates. The master schedule provides a plan for the quantity and timing of when orders are required. The MRP system will use this information and taking into account delivery, production and supply lead times will indicate when materials are needed to achieve the master schedule. The MPS will usually show plans based on '**time buckets**' based on for example a day or a week. The length of the time bucket will generally be longer (e.g. a month) for planning purposes and become shorter closer to the present time for detailed production planning tasks.

The MPS will usually contain a mix of both plans for customer ordered items and plans to produce to forecast sales. The forecast is a best estimate of what future demand will be which may be derived from past sales and contact with the customer. These forecasts should be replaced by firm orders as the expected order date approaches. If actual orders exceed the forecast then either the order will be delivered to the customer late or extra capacity must be obtained. (e.g. overtime, subcontracting) to meet the customer delivery date. The mix of forecast and firm orders that a business can work to depends on the nature of the business. Resource-to-order companies (e.g. builders) will only allocate resources and materials to a firm order. Purchase-to-order organisations will not order materials until a firm order is made, but will have labour and equipment permanently available. Make-to-stock businesses however will work mainly to forecast demand. Most operations will actually operate with different P:D ratios (Chapter 7) for different product or service types. The mix between firm orders and forecast demand may also vary over time for a certain business. For example, seasonal effects may increase the number of firm orders taken in certain time periods.

Bill of materials (BOM)

The Bill of Materials (BOM) identifies all the components required to produce a scheduled quantity of an assembly and the structure of how these components fit together to make that assembly. The BOM can be viewed as a product structure tree, similar to an organisation chart (Figure 8.2).

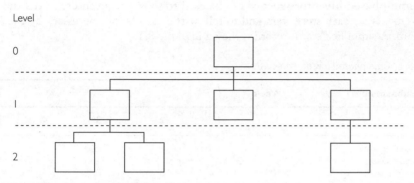

Figure 8.2 Bill of materials (BOM) product structure

The final assembly of the product structure is denoted as level 0, while the structure is 'exploded' to further levels representing subassemblies below this. These subassemblies are then broken down into further levels until the individual order components are reached. Individual order components can either be a single component item or subassemblies purchased from suppliers and thus treated as a single component.

The MRP system holds information on the number required of any item in the structure and the 'parent' item of which it is a component. Usually the product structure is stored in a series of single-level bills of materials, each of which holds a component part number and a list of the part numbers and quantities of the next lower level. The computer will move through all the component BOMs in the product structure to derive a total number of components required for the product. Note the same component may appear in different parts of the product structure if it is used more than once. What is needed is the total number required for each component to make the final assembly. The accuracy of the bill of materials is obviously vital in generating the correct schedule of parts at the right time.

Inventory status file (ISF)

The bill of materials (BOM) indicates the quantity of components needed from the product structure, but this will not be directly translated into demand for components because it is likely that some of the components will be currently held in inventory. The ISF provides information on the identification and quantity of items in stock. The MRP system will determine if a sufficient quantity of an item is in stock or an order must be placed.

The inventory status file will also contain the lead time, or time between order and availability, for each component.

As with the BOM the accuracy of the ISF is vital and some organisations use **perpetual physical inventory** (PPI) checking to ensure that inventory records are accurate. This means a continuous check of inventory records against actual stock are performed, instead of the traditional year-end checks for accounting purposes.

MRP calculations

The **time-phased inventory record** can be used to show the inventory status and data requirements for each stock item and to follow the calculations necessary by the MRP program. A simplified status record is shown in Table 8.1.

Table 8.1 Time-phased inventory record

Item: subassembly 1	Week					
	0	1	2	3	4	5
Gross requirements		100	0	200	0	30
Scheduled receipts				200		
Projected on hand	100	0	0	0	0	–30

In this case weekly time buckets have been used, which is usual for short-term plans. Longer time buckets may be used for long-term planning purposes. The definition of each row is explained below.

Gross requirements
This row simply states the estimated requirements, in this case per week, for the item described. It is assumed that requirements occur during the time bucket (week) so that the scheduled receipts at the beginning of the week will cover them.

Scheduled receipts
This row indicates when the item becomes available for use, from a previously released order. It is assumed that the receipts of the item occur at the start of the time bucket periods.

Projected on hand
Numbers in this row show the number of units to be available at the end of each time bucket based on the balance of requirements and receipts. The formula for projected-on-hand is shown below:

Projected on hand = Inventory on hand + Scheduled receipts – Gross requirements

Net requirements
If the projected on hand is negative it is called a net requirement and means there will not be enough of this component to produce the quantities required to meet the master production schedule. Thus when a negative projected on hand is shown this will increase

the net requirements row by a positive amount equal to the negative on hand. To account for a negative projected on hand, the time phased inventory status record is extended as below in Table 8.2.

Table 8.2 Inventory status file showing net requirements

Item: subassembly 1	Week					
	0	1	2	3	4	5
Gross requirements		100	0	200	0	30
Scheduled receipts				200		
Projected on hand	100	0	0	0	0	−30
Net requirements						30
Planned order release				30		

Planned order release

The planned order release (POR) row indicates when an order should be released to ensure that the projected-on-hand figure does not become negative (i.e. there are enough items to satisfy the MPS). The POR time must take into consideration the lead time between placing the order and the component becoming available. Thus the planned order release is offset by the required time amount to ensure enough items are available to cover net requirements and sometimes to also cover net requirements in future time buckets. It is important that the MRP programme works through all the levels of the assembly before calculating the net requirement for a time bucket as the same item may be needed at different levels of the same assembly or in different assemblies.

MRP reports

A number of reports can be generated by the MRP programme which include information on:

- The quantity of each item to order in the current and future time period.
- Indication of which due dates cannot be met and showing when they can be met.
- Showing changes, either up or down, to quantities of currently ordered items.
- Showing the results of simulation of scenarios for planning purposes. For instance by entering a customer order to the master schedule the effect of this extra work on overall customer due-date performance can be examined. If capacity restrictions mean that the order cannot be completed by the required due-date, a new due-date can be suggested.
- By attaching purchasing and inventory costings to items, total expenditure over time can be estimated thus providing cash flow information.

Distribution requirements planning (DRP)

MRP is traditionally associated with managing dependent demand items which form an assembly which has as independent demand (i.e. the demand is not dependent on other items). However if the concept of MRP is widened from the traditional acquisition, handling and production functions across the supply chain to the customer then another form of dependent demand can be considered between the producer of goods, the regional distribution centre, the local distribution outlets or retailers and the customer. DRP manages these linkages between all these elements on the supply chain beginning with an analysis of demand at each customer service location. These demands are aggregated across distribution centres to form a gross requirement which is fed into the master production schedule. Independent demand items are incorporated into the MRP logic by having a safety stock level below which a replenishment order is triggered. The order amount is determined by a lot sizing calculation. This method is called **time-phased order point**.

Discussion of MRP

MRP can reduce inventory by providing information on the actual inventory required for parent items (rather than stocking enough components for estimated parent demand). It can also help to prioritise orders to ensure delivery due-dates are met, provide information on resource (labour and equipment) requirements for planning purposes and provide financial information on projected inventory expenditure.

However it is not always possible to assess the feasibility of meeting a due-date when they are quoted to a customer. Repeated changes to order due-dates will entail new plans generated from the MRP system which could lead to ever changing schedules. The need to manufacture in batches negates the advantage of only scheduling inventory when needed. If batches are used extensively the component batch size will be a major factor in manufacturing lead time. Also if insufficient capacity is available it is necessary to adjust planned order dates or make available additional resources. The knock-on effect may not be clear until the MRP schedule is regenerated. This may lead to a lengthy process of trying to find a feasible schedule. The MRP system has limited ability to assess the robustness of the schedule to random events (e.g. machine breakdown). Changes to the inputs to the MRP stem may be so rapid (customer needs change, design changes etc.) that the planning function of MRP may be extremely limited. Many of the problems of MRP revolve around the problem of estimating capacity at various time-frames. The RRP, RCCP and CRP discussed earlier help with this.

Just-in-time (JIT) ordering system

Just-in-time (JIT) is an ordering/inventory philosophy originating from the Japanese auto maker Toyota where Taiichi Ohno developed the Toyota production system. The approach may have been developed as a reaction to the lack of natural resources in Japan and a culture abhorrent to the idea of waste. The oil price rise in the 1970s may have also put a focus on the need to provide more efficient ways of working. The basic idea behind JIT is to produce only what you need, when you need it. This may seem a simple idea but to deliver it requires a number of elements in place such as high quality and elimination of wasteful activities.

Bicheno (1991) defines JIT thus: 'JIT aims to meet demand instantaneously, with perfect quality and no waste'. To achieve this aim requires a whole new approach, or philosophy, from the organisation in how it operates.

Different organisations have their own version of JIT. For instance Hewlett-Packard have stockless production and IBM have zero inventory production system (Russell, 1995). Lean production is a term used to describe JIT systems such as the one implemented by Toyota. The name is meant to emphasise the concept of elimination of waste in all its forms and contrast with the traditional buffered systems of mass production. Krafcik presents some of the findings of a study presented in Womack (1988) concerning the effect of location on productivity and quality in the automotive industry. The outcome of the study is that productivity and quality levels in the auto industry were not determined by an assembly plant's location. Generally plants operating with a lean production policy were able to manufacture a wide range of models, yet maintain high levels of quality and productivity (Krafcik, 1988).

Slack (1995) views JIT on two levels. At the first level JIT can be viewed as a philosophy of operations providing direction to the operations function. At the second level JIT can be seen more specifically as a set of tools and techniques which support the philosophy in operation. These elements at both levels will now be examined.

JIT as a philosophy of operations

The JIT philosophy 'is founded on doing simple things well, on gradually doing them better and on squeezing out waste every step of the way' (Ohno, 1988). One aspect of JIT which is lacking in other approaches is the emphasis on people involvement. This is significant because the elimination of waste such as buffer stocks and the emphasis on continuous improvement activities through empowerment means the approach and involvement of personnel is vital to success.

Harrison (1992) defines the core of JIT philosophy as follows:

- elimination of waste
- involvement of everyone
- continuous improvement.

Waste elimination
Waste is considered in the widest sense as any activity which does not add value to the operation. Seven types of waste identified by Toyota are as follows:

1. **Over-production**. This is classified as the greatest source of waste and is an outcome of producing more than is needed by the next process.
2. **Waiting time**. This is the time spent by labour or equipment waiting to add value to a product. This may be disguised by undertaking unnecessary operations (e.g. generating work-in-progress on a machine) which are not immediately needed (i.e. the waste is converted from time to WIP).
3. **Transport**. Unnecessary transportation of WIP is another source of waste. Layout changes can substantially reduce transportation time.
4. **Process**. Some operations do not add value to the product but are simply there because of poor design or machine maintenance. Improved design or preventative maintenance should eliminate these processes.
5. **Inventory**. Inventory of all types (e.g. pipeline, cycle) is considered as waste and should be eliminated.
6. **Motion**. Simplification of work movement will reduce waste caused by unnecessary motion of labour and equipment.

7. **Defective goods**. The total costs of poor quality can be very high and will include scrap material, wasted labour time and time expediting orders and loss of goodwill through missed delivery dates.

Involvement of everyone

JIT embraces the aim to create a new culture in which all employees are encouraged to contribute to continuous improvement efforts through generating ideas for improvements and perform a range of functions. In order to undertake this level of involvement the organisation will provide training to staff in a wide range of areas, including techniques such as statistical process control (SPC) and more general problem-solving techniques.

Continuous improvement

Continuous improvement or **Kaizen**, the Japanese term, is a philosophy which believes that it is possible to get to the ideals of JIT by a continuous stream of improvements over time. Russell (1995) adapts the ten principles given in Hiroyuki (1988) into the following principles for implementing a continuous improvement effort:

- *Create a mind-set for improvement*. Do not accept that the present way of doing things is necessarily the best.
- *Try and try again*. Don't seek immediate perfection but move to your goal by small improvements, checking for mistakes as you progress.
- *THINK*. Get to the real cause of the problem – ask why? five times.
- *Work in teams*. Use the ideas from a number of people to brainstorm new ways.
- *Recognise that improvement knows no limits*. Get in the habit of always looking for better ways of doing things.

Chapter 11 deals with the continuous improvement approach in more detail.

JIT techniques

A wide variety of techniques are considered to be within the JIT philosophy. Some of these are considered below.

Design for manufacture

A major determinant of product quality is its design. Design can also have a major effect on production costs also. It is important that communication takes place at the design stage to ensure production aspects are taken into account to avoid costly changes later on in the design process. These two aspects of quality and product cost should not be viewed as trade-offs because improvements in design can allow better quality at lower costs. Chapter 5 deals in more detail with design for manufacture (DFM).

Cellular manufacturing

To reduce transportation machines are often moved from functional departments (i.e. all similar machines are placed together) to a cell which is a close grouping of different types of equipment, each of which performs a different operation. Cell manufacturing is particularly suited to repetitive JIT manufacturing where it is feasible to dedicate equipment to certain products. Machines are arranged close together in a U-shaped line which reduces transportation and material handling costs, and allows multi-skilled workers to carry out a number of operations simultaneously. Chapter 3 covers cellular manufacturing in more detail.

JIT supplier networks

The JIT system requires a continuous stream of small lot supplies to ensure inventory is minimised within the organisation. To achieve this, close long-term relationships are formed with a small number of suppliers. Because of the frequency of deliveries in JIT supply, suppliers are usually situated relatively near to the organisation. In order to facilitate design for manufacture the organisation will work with suppliers to improve component design and ensure quality. It is necessary for JIT suppliers to practise JIT supply themselves or to avoid inventory being 'pushed' back to them. Russell (1995) outlines the trends in supplier policies since the advent of JIT:

- Locate near the customer.
- Use small, side-loaded trucks and ship mixed loads.
- Consider establishing small warehouses near to the customer or consolidating warehouses with other suppliers.
- Use standardised containers and make deliveries according to a precise delivery schedule.
- Become a certified supplier and accept payment at regular intervals rather than upon delivery.

Supply chain issues are dealt with in more detail in Chapter 9.

Total preventative maintenance (TPM)

Because of the lack of inventory providing a buffer, it is essential that there is minimum disruption to the production system to avoid loss of production. TPM aims to prevent machine breakdown by undertaking preventative maintenance activities. Many activities are undertaken by process owners who are in the best position to monitor machine performance. Chapter 12 covers TPM issues.

Set-up reduction (SUR)

In order to achieve small-lot production it is necessary to reduce set-up time drastically (the time taken to adjust a machine to work on a different component) because of the increased number of set-ups needed. Originally some operations such as stamping car door panels with a press die were done in very large lot sizes, and the output stored in inventory, because the set-up time for the press could be measured in hours or even days. Shigeo Shingo was hired by Toyota to study how press die set-up could be reduced and he achieved impressive results. For example he reduced the set-up time on one 1000 ton press from 6 hours to only 3 minutes. The system he developed became known as the Single Minute Exchange of Dies (SMED) and is based on the following principles:

1. *Separate internal set-up from external set-up.* Set-up tasks are classified as internal – they must be performed while the machine is stopped and external – they can be performed in advance whilst the machine is running. Performing external set-up tasks during operation and then delaying only for the internal set-up tasks can reduce set-up times by 30–50%.
2. *Convert internal set-up to external set-up.* This means ensuring any tasks normally undertaken during the internal set-up phase (e.g. gathering tools, preheating an injection mould) are undertaken during the external phase.
3. *Streamline all aspects of set-up.* This can be achieved by organising tools near to the point of use and simplifying or eliminating operations.

4. *Perform set-up activities in parallel or eliminate them entirely*. Deploying extra people to a set-up can reduce set-up time by a considerable amount, maybe by more than double. Standardisation of parts and raw materials can reduce or even eliminate set-up requirements.

Visual control

Visual control is one of the factors that makes continuous improvement work. **Visibility** is about maintaining an orderly workplace in which tools are easily available and unusual occurrences are easily noticeable. This is achieved through what is called the five S's (seiri, seiton, seiso, seiketsu, shitsuke) which roughly translate as organisation, tidiness, cleanliness, maintenance and discipline. To achieve these factors visibility measures include Andon signs (coloured lights), control systems such as the kanban and performance charts such as **statistical process control** (SPC) charts. Chapter 12 covers the SPC method.

JIT planning and control

The kanban production system operationalises the **pull system** which is a major feature of the JIT approach. The idea of a pull system comes from the need to reduce inventory within the production system. In a push system a schedule pushes work on to machines which is then passed through to the next work centre. A production system for an automobile will require the co-ordination of thousands of components, many of which will need to be grouped together to form an assembly. In order to ensure that there are no stoppages it is necessary to have inventory in the system because it is difficult to co-ordinate parts to arrive at a particular station simultaneously. The pull system developed by Ohno (1988) comes from the idea of a supermarket in which items are purchased by a customer only when needed and are replenished as they are removed. Thus inventory co-ordination is controlled by a customer pulling items from the system which are only then replaced.

Kanban production control system

To implement a pull system a kanban (Japanese for 'card' or 'sign') is used to pass information through the production system. Each kanban provides information on the part identification, quantity per container that the part is transported in and the preceding and next work station. kanbans in themselves do not provide the schedule for production but without them production cannot take place as they authorise the production and movement of material through the pull system. Kanbans need not be a card, but something that can be used as a signal for production such as a marker, or coloured square area. There are two types of kanban system, the single-card and two-card.

The **single-card system** uses only one type of kanban card called the conveyance kanban which authorises the movement of parts. The number of containers at a work centre is limited by the number of kanbans. A signal to replace inventory at the work centre can only be sent when the container is emptied.

Toyota use a **dual-card system** (Figure 8.3) which in addition to the conveyance kanban, utilises a production kanban to authorise the production of parts. This system permits greater control over production as well as inventory. If the processes are tightly linked (i.e. one always follows the other) then a single kanban can be used.

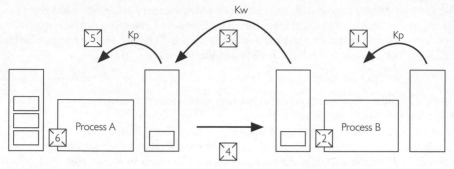

Figure 8.3 Dual card kanban system

In order for a kanban system to be implemented it is important that the seven operational rules that govern the system are followed. These rules can be summarised as follows:

- *Move a kanban only when the lot it represents is consumed.* This means the whole of the lot (batch) of parts must be processed before the kanban is sent to the preceding process to ask for more parts.
- *No withdrawal of parts without a kanban is allowed.* No process can move parts without the authorisation of a kanban request.
- *The number of parts issued to the subsequent process must be the exact number specified by the kanban.* This means a kanban must wait until sufficient parts are made before the lot of parts is moved.
- *A kanban should always be attached to the physical product.* The kanban should travel with the parts themselves and be visible.
- *The preceding process should always produce its parts in the quantities withdrawn by the subsequent process.* Processes should never overproduce parts in any quantity.
- *Defective parts should never be conveyed to the subsequent process.* A high level of quality must be maintained because of the lack of buffer inventory. A feedback mechanism which reports quality problems quickly to the preceding process must be implemented.
- *Process the kanbans in every work centre strictly in order in which they arrive at the work centre.* If several kanbans are waiting for production they must be served in the order that they have arrived. If the rule is not followed there will be a gap in the production rate of one or more of the subsequent processes.

In the dual card kanban system (Figure 8.3):

1. A production kanban arrives at process B, attached to an empty container. Process B is activated to fill the container.
2. Process B requests inputs, from process A, to fulfil Step 1.
3. A withdrawal kanban is sent to process A to fulfil Step 2.
4. A full container is sent from process A to process B.
5. The production kanban, which was attached to the container in Step 4, is placed on a empty container, activating process A.
6. Process A requests inputs to fulfil Step 5. A withdrawal kanban is not activated as sufficient stock is present.

The kanban system is similar to the re-order point inventory system but has the objective of the continual reduction of inventory. The amount of inventory can be reduced over time by reducing the number of kanbans in the system. The formula suggested by Hall (1987) for the number of kanbans at each production stage is given below:

$$y = D\,(T_W + T_p)(1 + X)/\,a$$

y = total number of kanbans (production and conveyance) for a part
D = planned usage rate (units/day)
T_W = average waiting time for replenishment of part (fraction of a day)
T_p = average production time for a container of parts (fraction of a day)
X = a policy variable corresponding to possible inefficiencies in the system
a = capacity of a standard container in units (should usually be less than 10% of daily usage for that part).

Setting X to zero provides just enough inventory ($y \times a$) to cover the time required to produce and move a container of parts.

The system is implemented with a given number of cards in order to obtain a smooth flow. The number of cards is then decreased, decreasing inventory and any problems which surface are tackled. Cards are decreased, one at a time, to continue the continuous improvement process.

Levelled scheduling

The approach to scheduling which has been followed in traditional manufacturing systems is to make a large number of one product before switching to another. Unfortunately this approach will lead to high levels of finished goods inventory at some times (the end of a production run) with the possibility of not being able to satisfy customer demand at other times (when long production runs of other goods are being manufactured). A level assembly schedule attempts to overcome this problem by producing the smallest reasonable number of units of each product at a time.

Mixed model scheduling

This attempts to spread the production of several different end items evenly throughout each day. If, say, three different products are to be produced then the ideal schedule would be to produce the products in sequence throughout the day. Usually however the products in the sequence will be needed in different quantities so that the sequence will need to be adjusted to reflect that.

When a level assembly schedule has been achieved the production of each item will closely match demand. However because the flow of component parts must be adjusted to match the rate at which finished goods will be produced it is necessary to match the **production cycle time** (the rate of production) at the work centres with the **demand rate**.

For example, if total demand for 3 products is 80 units a day and production is available for 8 hours (480 minutes) a day the cycle time is as follows:

Cycle time = Working time per day/Units required per day = 480/80 = 6 minutes/unit

The cycle time for each product is then considered in a mixed-model sequence.

Product	Daily demand	Cycle time (minutes)
A	40	480/40 = 12
B	10	480/10 = 48
C	30	480/30 = 16

One possible assembly sequence in this example could be ACACBACA. One unit of product A will be produced every 12 minutes on average throughout the day to a level assembly schedule. This means that components must be supplied to product A to match this cycle time. Also the system must be co-ordinated to produce either A, B or C once every 6 minutes. To achieve these results requires that sufficient machines and labour are configured and set-up times minimised.

JIT in service and administration systems

JIT is usually associated with manufacturing applications because this is the setting in which it was developed and has been applied most frequently. However, many of the ideas behind JIT can be employed in service settings. This is important because direct administration services can account for as much as 35% of the total cost of a product to a customer (Funk, 1989). In addition to JIT manufacturing principles, Schniederjans (1993) presents introductory implementation strategies that can be applied to almost all administration organisations.

- *Worker or department responsibility for quality control workers.* Everybody in an administration department should serve as a customer service agent. Service quality is everybody's responsibility in a JIT administration. When poor quality is observed in the delivery of an administration service that can be corrected the individual worker or department that is responsible should be made to implement the correction.
- *Scheduling administration work at less than full capacity.* Management should be willing to sacrifice production for improved quality and allow workers extra time for JIT activities such as quality control
- *Increased worker flexibility.* All employees should be multifunctional to increase worker flexibility and help workers understand more of the operation.
- *Restructure the administration facility layout to simplify work methods and to improve the application of JIT principles.* Walls and departmental barriers cause greater routeing, filing, walking and proofing and should be re-structured into various groups of workers or **group technology** (GT) cell work stations with multifunctional skills. Multiple cells allows more than one channel through which work can flow, increasing flexibility to better balance work load with variable capacity. In a departmental system if one department is backlogged other offices will become idle and inefficiencies can occur. Also elimination of departments decreases much duplication and can substantially reduce the amount of commonly used equipment, filing cabinets and storage areas.
- *Increase standardisation of product processing.* Standardising work procedures can save time in training and improve operational efficiency by removing a job complexity. Standardising order forms and routeing system can also reduce complexity and helps workers understand processes and thus suggest improvements.

Problems in administration areas can be many and the result of long-standing policies and procedures. Schniederjans (1993) suggests using techniques such as cause-effect diagrams and Pareto analysis (Chapter 12) in order to identify and prioritise problems in administration areas.

JIT and MRP

JIT is associated with a pull type production system and MRP as a push system anticipates future demand levels. Despite this difference in approach there are circumstances when these systems can work together. For instance MRP can deal with complex parts requirements from products that are made infrequently and in low volumes, while JIT performs best with stable demand pattern. Situations when JIT and MRP can co-exist include:

- *Using MRP/JIT for different volume products.* Using JIT for common parts among the product range controlled by a stable weekly demand forecast and utilising MRP for low volume parts. This has the advantage of reducing the complexity of the MRP and allowing JIT to focus on the repetitive production processes.
- *Using MRP for long-term and JIT for short-term planning.* This involves using MRP to plan the supply of materials which are pulled into the JIT production planning system as needed. This can improve response to demand changes while retaining the simplicity of the JIT/pull system for local control.

For organisations which have been using MRP and MRP II systems and wish to incorporate JIT to increase flexibility and efficiency, need to make a number of changes successfully to achieve this strategy. Schiederjans (1993) lists four tactics to implement this change:

- increased flexibility in purchasing policies with vendors;
- increased flexibility with workers;
- a synchronised layout;
- an alternative ordering policy with customers.

Discussion of JIT

JIT has been covered in this chapter both as a philosophy and as a set of techniques.

From the viewpoint of JIT as a philosophy of the **elimination of waste** it can be seen as applicable to all organisations, small or large, manufacturing or service. At this level JIT requires organisational systems to be developed around identifying and eliminating waste. The main implementation issues concern the requirement of a problem-solving culture of trust and co-operation within the workforce. It is also likely that problem-identification and problem-solving activities will be more successful at a higher volume of output which gives a better chance for learning to occur.

Regarding JIT as a collection of tools and techniques, therefore, JIT is more likely to be applicable to a medium to high volume of product and one which has reached a mature development phase in the market. JIT techniques include the kanban production control system. Prerequisites for the implementation of this type of system include aspects such as facility design (e.g. cell manufacturing), set-up time reduction, line balancing and statistical process control.

Environmental factors influencing the success of JIT are discussed in Chapter 9 under 'Green logistics'.

Optimised production technology (OPT)

Optimised production technology is based on the identification of **bottlenecks** within the production process. Goldratt (1992) defines these bottlenecks as 'any resource whose capacity is less than or equal to the demand placed on it'. In identifying bottlenecks, OPT views the production process as a whole with respect to the market and the business within which it operates. OPT makes the assumption that all manufacturers have the aim of making money as their overriding objective. This 'goal' is defined in terms of three performance measures (Goldratt, 1992):

- throughput
- inventory
- operational expense.

Throughput is the rate at which the production system generates money through sales. Throughput however does not equal manufacturing output as any output not sold is seen as waste in the long run. OPT therefore does not consider 'finished goods' stocks as assets. Inventory is defined as all the money that the system has invested in goods that it intends to sell. OPT excludes labour costs and indirect expenses from inventory valuation. Operational expense is that which the system spends in order to turn inventory into throughput. This includes all expenses, both direct and indirect.

Goldratt (1992) uses these performance criteria to restate the goal of a manufacturing organisation as:

'To reduce operational expense and reduce inventory whilst simultaneously increasing throughput.'

To understand why OPT focuses on bottlenecks it is necessary to understand how OPT differs from traditional approaches to production planning. The traditional approach is to balance (i.e. make equal) capacity at all the work stations in response to anticipated demand from the master production schedule. However there are two reasons why a production facility cannot be balanced to the demands of production. These are:

- non-determinance
- interdependence.

Non-determinance simply refers to the fact that the information used to derive the production schedule may not be of a fixed nature. For example the process time for an activity may vary each time it is performed. The rate usually quoted will be the average of these times. However it can be shown that statistical fluctuations around the average can have a significant bearing on plant performance.

Interdependence refers to the fact that most stages in production are connected in some way to other stages, e.g. stage A cannot start until stage B has finished, which cannot start until stages C and D have finished, etc. The effect of interdependence is to accumulate the fluctuations caused by non-determinance from stage to stage downstream of the production process. This is because the ability to go faster than average depends on the ability of all others in front of the process while there is no limit to go slower. Therefore fluctuations don't average out but accumulate and the end of the line has to make up for the accumulation of all the slowness.

This behaviour has led Goldratt (1981) to suggest the following recommendation for dealing with an unbalanced plant:

- Bottlenecks must be identified, and since they determine the rate of throughput for the whole plant, must be carefully protected from disturbances and potential delays to assure full utilisation.
- The resources must be organised so the bottleneck resource is used primarily at one of the earliest stages of production.
- Instead of trying to eliminate at random overcapacity of non-bottlenecks, we must strive to arrange some resources such that one has sufficient overcapacity to fully support the bottleneck. Ideally this would involve a gradual increase of overcapacity as we go downstream.

These recommendations move away from trying to level capacity with demand to managing the whole system to the pace set by the bottlenecks. The principles underlying this approach are as follows:

- *Balance the flow, not capacity.* By trying to maintain flow in a balanced capacity plant means that all stages are expected to work to full capacity. In a non-balanced system (i.e. all systems) inventory will accumulate at bottleneck resources. Thus capacity should be used only when necessary, as in JIT.
- *Constraints determine non-bottleneck utilisation.* Bottlenecks should pace production and determine the level of utilisation for non-bottleneck resources. The only machine to be working at 100% capacity is the bottleneck.
- *Activation is not always equal to utilisation.* To activate a resource not needed at the bottleneck is a waste.
- *An hour lost at a bottleneck is an hour lost for the entire system.* In effect an hour lost at the bottleneck is an hour lost of factory output, as it can never be made up.
- *An hour saved at a non-bottleneck is a mirage.* An hour saved at a non-bottleneck will not actually increase output of the whole system.
- *Bottlenecks govern throughput and inventory.* Inventory will accumulate at the bottleneck. There is no point in inventory after this stage because throughput is determined by the rate of production at the bottleneck.
- *The transfer batch size should not always equal a process batch size.* At non-bottlenecks transfer batches can be small to speed the flow of WIP as an increase in total set-up time is not critical. At bottleneck resources these transfer batches then accumulate into larger process batches to save set-ups and maximise output.
- *Process batches should be variable, not fixed.* The process batch should not be determined by some fixed lot-sizing rule for instance but should be varied to balance the flow of the manufacturing cycle.
- *Set the schedule by examining all the constraints simultaneously.* MRP II systems predetermine batch size, lead times and set schedules accordingly. OPT suggests that all the constraints of a complex network are considered simultaneously using the simulation capabilities of the OPT software.

The OPT planning and control approach uses the terminology of 'drum', 'buffer' and 'rope'.

The drum

The drum determines the rate of production which corresponds to the master production schedule (MPS). In MRP and JIT the MPS is determined primarily from market demand but with OPT the bottleneck resources are used to develop the schedule ensuring that bottleneck capacity is not exceeded. Other non-bottleneck resources are scheduled to serve the bottlenecks by varying process batch and transfer batch sizes. Thus the bottle-neck resource sets the drumbeat for the entire process.

The buffer
Buffers are placed at certain locations to prevent unforeseen events disrupting output of finished goods. There are two types of inventory buffer. Time buffers are determined by the amount of output the system could produce during the period of time it takes to correct a disruption. They are generally placed before bottleneck resources. Stock buffers are inventories of finished goods determined by forecasts of possible demand fluctuations.

The rope
The rate of operation of processes which come after the bottleneck are determined by the rate of output from the bottleneck machine. To control the rate of processes before the bottleneck there is a linkage between the bottleneck and the processes that feed it termed the 'rope'. The rope can take the form of a planned production schedule or an informal discussion between employees at the bottleneck and employees at other work stations.

Discussion of OPT

This JIT operation is based on the final assembly schedule, implying this is the bottle-neck and sufficient capacity is available at other work stations. OPT does not make this assumption and uses a computer-based package that aims to identify bottlenecks, max-imise the flow through these resources and thus maximise the throughput of the whole plant. OPT is flexible in that it can react to changes in product mix and demand derived from the master production schedule. OPT acknowledges that lead times are determined by the schedule and thus waiting time is taken into account when estimating lead time. OPT also takes a flexible approach to batch sizes. Batch splitting means that transfer batches can be used to minimise lead time, while set-ups are reduced at bottlenecks.

Although OPT can be relatively quickly implemented it needs expertise for correct imple-mentation which may not be available for small organisations. The OPT software may also be expensive for some organisations. OPT could also be criticised for not containing contin-uous improvement activities of JIT although these could be incorporated and the two approaches could be used in combination to form a continuous improvement effort.

Summary of key points _____

- MRP systems calculate the volume and timing of components needed to meet the mas-ter production schedule.
- MRP II extends the concept of MRP to other areas in the organisation such as marketing and finance to form an integrated business system.
- MRP calculations are based on information from the master production schedule (MPS), the bill of materials (BOM) and inventory status file (ISF).
- JIT can be seen on one level as a philosophy and on a second level as a set of tools and techniques.
- The core of the JIT philosophy is the concept of elimination of waste, involvement of everyone and continuous improvement.

- JIT planning and control is based on the kanban production control system.
- OPT is based in the identification of bottlenecks within the production process.
- The OPT planning and control approach uses the terminology of drum, buffer and rope.
- The MRP, JIT and OPT approaches can be used in combination.

Exercises

1 Identify and explain the role of the main components of an MRP system.
2 What are the main factors in the successful implementation of a materials requirement planning system?
3 Evaluate the advantages and disadvantages of the MRP approach to production planning.
4 Identify and explain the main elements of the JIT philosophy.
5 Provide an analysis of the techniques used to implement a JIT philosophy in a manufacturing organisation.
6 Explain how you would utilise the concepts of JIT in a service operations environment.
7 Evaluate the advantages and disadvantages of the JIT approach to production planning.
8 Evaluate the advantages and disadvantages of the OPT approach to production planning.

References

Funk, J.L., A comparison of inventory cost reduction strategies in a JIT manufacturing system, *Int. J. Production Research*, **27** (7), (1989), pp. 1065–1080.

Gattorna, J.L. and Walters, D.W., *Managing the Supply Chain: A Strategic Perspective*, Macmillan (1996).

Goldratt, E.M., The unbalanced plant, *APICS 1981 Intl. Conf. Proc.*, (1981), pp. 195–199.

Goldratt, E.M. and Cox, J., *The Goal: A Process of Ongoing Improvement*, Second Edition, Gower (1997).

Hall, R.W., *Attaining Manufacturing Excellence*, Irwin (1987).

Harrison, A., *Just-in-Time in Perspective*, Prentice-Hall (1992).

Hiroyaki, H., *JIT Factory Revolution*, Productivity Press (1988).

Krafcik, J.F., Triumph of the lean production system, *Sloan Management Review*, (Fall, 1988) pp. 41–52.

Ohno, T., *Toyota Production System: Beyond Large Scale Production*, Production Press, (1988).

Russell, R.S. and Taylor, B.W., *Production and Operations Management: Focusing on Quality and Competitiveness*, Prentice Hall (1995).

Schniederjans, M.J., *Topics in Just-in-Time Management*, Allyn and Bacon (1993).

Skinner, W., *Manufacturing in the Corporate Strategy*, Wiley (1978).

Slack, N., Chambers, S., Harland, C., Harrison, A. and Johnston, R., *Operations Management*, Pitman Publishing (1995).

Vonderembse, M.A. and White, G.P., *Operations Management: Concepts, Methods, and Strategies*, Second Edition, West Publishing (1991),.

Womack, J.P., Jones, D.T. and Roos, D., *The Machine that Changed the World*, Rawson Associates (1990).

Further reading

Goldratt, E.M., *It's Not Luck*, Gower (1994).

Goldratt, E.M. and Fox, R., *The Race*, North River Press (1986).

Mather, K., *Competitive Manufacturing*, Prentice-Hall (1988).

Shingo, S., *Study of Toyota Production System*, Japanese Management Association (1981).

Srikanth, M.L. and Cavallaro, H.E., *Regaining Competitiveness: Putting the Goal to Work*, Second Revised Edition, North River Press (1993).

9 Supply chain management

Objectives

> By the end of this chapter, you will be able to:
>
> - discuss the origin and the evolution of supply chain management;
> - explore the supply chain management concept and explain how it differs from traditional approaches of resource acquisition and movement;
> - demonstrate an understanding of the environmental changes that are influencing the evolution of supply chain management;
> - discuss the nature and types of relationships in the supply chain;
> - describe the activities that are undertaken in the supply chain pipeline;
> - explore the strategic changes in the supply chains (emphasis on speed/time, quality, asset productivity and customer satisfaction) that firms have developed to respond to the changes in the environment.

This chapter introduces the scope and the importance of supply chain management (SCM) to a business from both macro and micro perspectives. In many companies, especially service industries, the management of materials is not as visible as other functions within the business, such as marketing and manufacturing. However all firms, as part of the input/transformation/output system, use materials of one form or another. The importance of material to the business of a washing machine manufacturer is clear. Of equal importance, in a hospital, are the materials used to provide health care (bandages, medicines, food, linen) although these are not as obvious, and are often consumed in the process of producing the product, a healthy person. Given that in many firms materials are a major element of cost, it is unusual to find a single department that is devoted to the management of them. Most firms have people whose duties include the purchasing, movement and storage of items that the firm uses and people who are concerned with the products the firms sells, but often they are in separate departments. In an increasingly competitive world market, for some companies the ability to move materials and products effectively gives them a competitive edge, in terms of lower costs and dependability over their rivals. For other firms, the ability to build and sustain relationships within the supply chain gives competitive advantages in the form of quality and product development areas.

Defining supply chain management

Supply chain management (SCM) is concerned with:

the efficient and effective *flow* of physical items, in the form of *materials* from *suppliers*, through the *production chain*, to the *customer*, in the form of a *finished product*. Synergetic relationships between the firm, customers and suppliers, who share *information*, co-operate in product *development* and aid in *decision making*, benefit all parties in the production of a product that enables the supply chain to conform to *customer requirements*.

The essential elements of the definition imply the far-reaching consequences of the SCM concept. If we break the definition down into these elements, we see that it means doing the right things (effective) well (efficient) by having close links (relationships) with the people supplying the materials (suppliers) and the people receiving our product (customers). It is an integrating concept that requires complete understanding of the internal and external needs (environment) of the firm.

The chapter begins by addressing the dynamics affecting the supply chain system. It then looks at the activities that occur within the supply chain. The chapter then discusses the integrating concept of a supply chain management, and finally focuses on customer service as the ultimate objective of supply chain management.

Historical development

Supply chain management is an evolving concept within the sphere of operations management. The armed forces have recognised for a long time the importance of keeping troops well supplied with human needs, arms and fuel, together with the intelligence that determines where they are needed and how they will get there. The Gulf War of 1990/91 is sometimes referred to as the Logistics War. General Gus Pagonis commanded a force of 100,00 trucks and 50,000 workers at a cost of £500,000 per day. Distribution of people and materials quickly to the right location was an important factor in the war. The principles that apply to conducting a military campaign transfer readily into business concepts.

Historically many companies have split the responsibility for flow of these items between a number of departments in the firm, the main divisions being between purchasing, production and distribution departments. Companies have constantly looked for improvements in the way in which they work, to reduce costs and improve the quality of the products they produce. This improvement process has traditionally been inward looking, examining how the firm manages its own transformation processes. For example, purchasing is often conducted in an adversarial fashion, trading off one supplier against another, based on low cost. It is only recently that suppliers have been viewed to some extent as partners, both supplier and customer benefiting from each other's success. Companies are examining the organisation of the management process associated with the supply chain. Figure 9.1 illustrates the integration of the processes involved in the supply chain, and identifies some of the essential terms used in the process. Some of these terms are defined as follows.

Logistics management
Although sometimes used synonymously with supply chain management, it has in the UK been used primarily in connection with distribution of products and the information associated with managing distribution channels. The term is commonly used at a micro level to describe the gathering of resources and delivery of a resource within part of a larger system. The logistics war described earlier is essentially how to manage and distribute resources already in the system.

- *Materials management* is concerned with the inbound logistics systems and includes purchasing systems, traffic (inbound transportation), materials handling and warehousing.

- *Physical distribution* is a common term used to cover outbound logistics processes such as transportation and distribution channels.

Within this chapter, we will use the term logistics to describe the management of resources at points within the supply chain.

Business logistics
Developments in both materials management and physical distribution have occurred in parallel over the last few years, mirroring a greater awareness of customer needs and taking advantage of developments in technology, such as **electronic data interchange** (EDI). The prime movers have been the retail sector, who have questioned their core competencies and who were one of the first businesses to sell off the distribution related activities such as transportation fleets and warehouses.

Figure 9.1 illustrates the structure of firm with regard to material and distribution management. The structure of firms in the 1960s has some obvious disadvantages. Each department or function requires information to operate effectively. This meant that either duplication of effort occurred in obtaining and collating this information, or inadequate information was used. This often led (and still leads) to incorrect levels of inventory, poor quality, late deliveries, and slow product development. (Estimates from the European Commission indicate that some 80% of information is duplicated, errors cost 80 m euros p.a. and information leading to better use of transport could save 390 m euros p.a.)

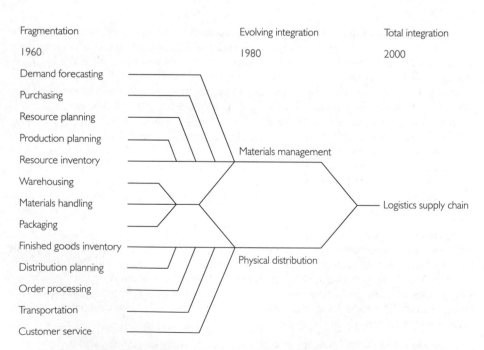

Figure 9.1 Evolution of supply chain organisation (adapted from Coyle, Bardi and Langley (1996) p. 7)

During the 1980s it was recognised that additional opportunity for increased business performance could be obtained through internal integration of inbound and outbound logistics. As we approach the 21st century companies are integrating further by including customers and suppliers as integral partners in the management of the supply chain. The additional forces of a global market further enhance the need for partnerships.

Porter (1985) has indicated that certain activities within a business add value. Porter's basic model has been expanded by Gattorna (1994 p.7), to include the relationships between activities, function and price within a firm (see Figure 9.2). The activities that are deemed to add value are those that are associated with the transformation of the resources – people, equipment, money and materials – into a product. Each element within the value chain affects other elements and will determine overall profitability. For example, we need to buy the best materials, but what does 'best' mean? Porter was essentially advocating an adversarial system, where value could be maximised through vertical integration. This view has been replaced largely by a recognition of core competencies and an appreciation of the value of firms working together for mutual benefits.

In Chapter 11 we introduce the idea of **cost/quality trade-offs**. Take for example the humble safety pin. The safety pin is a piece of bent wire. To reduce costs we could reduce the thickness of the wire. This will result in a loss of strength and durability, but it could be sold at a lower price. We gain in one area, lower costs, and lose in another, some of the qualities of the product. To know what is 'best' we need to know what our customers expect, but we also need to know what our suppliers can provide. It may be that we can achieve the reduction in thickness without losing strength by using different steel, and the best people to advise us may be the steel suppliers.

Figure 9.2 Transformation value chain, based on Gattorna (1994) p. 7

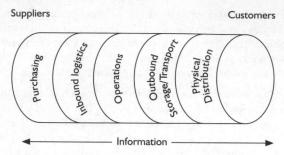

Figure 9.3 The supply chain pipeline

An analysis of the pipeline is also useful (see Figure 9.3). At each stage in the supply chain we need to ask Who, Why, What and How questions around issues such as:

- Who makes the replenishment decision?
- How is the size determined?
- How often is the decision made?
- What product range is carried?
- How are deliveries handled and received?
- How are products stored?
- How scarce are materials?
- When is stock rotated?
- What are the ideal storage conditions?
- Why are our warehouses here?
- How close are they to the market?
- How efficient is our order processing?
- What equipment is used for picking?
- Why do we use that method for packing?
- What is the organisational structure?
- How do we administer the supply chain activities?

The first step to developing a successful SCM strategy is developing an understanding of the process.

The supply chain environment

The growth in logistics expenditures throughout the supply chain, which are estimated to reach $2.1 trillion (16% of world wide GNP) by 1999 indicates the importance of supply chain issues to the economy as a whole (Coyle *et al.* (1996, p. 483)). The trend to seek low cost sources of supply and meet the needs of dispersed and high growth markets creates complex supply chains.

The supply chain environment is changing in response to six pressures:

- **Market demands**. Customers require a wider range of products and services; markets are becoming more segmented. In the past limited product ranges meant that customers had fewer choices. Now companies compete in offering variations of both product and service.
- **Financial constraints**. Companies have examined their core business and chopped out any unnecessary bits. To maintain effective distribution channels costs money. Strategic alliances with logistical providers have enabled many companies to restructure and direct valuable capital to the parts of the business that add most value, which means they need less capital and pay less interest.
- **Technology revolution**. The advances in information, manufacturing, and transport technologies are changing the way that companies manage the supply chain. If components are in stock then it is possible to offer companies lead-times of one day anywhere in the UK. For example, to implement just-in-time systems it is imperative to have excellent communications between the customer, manufacturer, and supplier. Some Japanese companies now work on lead-times as low as ½ hour.
- **Globalisation and demographic shifts**. Many companies have a global philosophy. The geographic availability of raw materials and demand for products is expanding.
- **Retail outlets**. Locally consumption may be shifting away from cities to out-of-town shopping centres and industrial parks. Internet trading is now a reality.
- **Regulation**. World trade is becoming more deregulated, whereas regulation related to modes of transport change in respect to environmental considerations such as pollution.
- **Management practices**. The way in which we manage businesses is changing in response to the needs and demands of stakeholders. Managers are becoming more familiar with ethical, technological, sociological and integrated systems, and of the need to involve many interests in these decision-making processes.

There are three major components of supply chain costs, inventory cost, transportation cost and packaging. We can subdivide these further depending on the part of the supply chain we are examining. Inventory costs generally tend to be the greatest. The quality of the information systems that link the structure is crucial in meeting customers' needs. Any methods of supply chain management that can reduce the levels of inventory held will be of the greatest value to the company, although as we see later, supply chain management goes beyond the short-term cost factor.

Supply chain activities

The supply chain **pipeline** helps to illustrate the links between suppliers and customers. The smoother the flow the greater the effectiveness of the company. If the pipe is full of kinks and bends, the flow will become erratic, like water in a hose-pipe. Inventory size is equivalent to the volume of water in the pipe, capacity the amount of water flowing per minute. If we reduce the diameter of the pipe we decrease the volume of water, but we then need to increase the speed of flow to achieve the same capacity. A closer analogy is shown in Figure 9.4, where we have pools of inventory in between the transformation processes. Whenever a pool of inventory occurs, we lose value, as

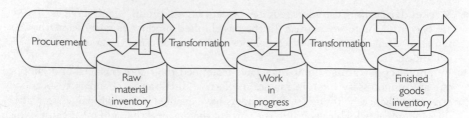

Figure 9.4 Broken pipe

explained in Chapter 7. The pipeline is sometimes referred to as the **value chain**. It is important that value is added at each stage. The customer must perceive this value, either in the form of price or service.

The pipeline links the Vendors to the customers, material travelling one way and information both ways. Customer dissatisfaction can occur if any one part of the chain fails. We can apply the pipeline approach to all activities within the supply chain and even extend the principles to supporting activities, such as the management of spare parts and capital purchases.

Excellent logistics processes are founded on the same principle that applies to other activities within the firm: conformation to customers' requirements. We need to be aware of the requirements whoever the customer is. For example, a company producing widgits has external customers such as individuals, retailers, and internal customers in the form of workers in the production chain and in the supporting services.

The logistics function of a company often deals with the following activities:

- Procurement and delivery of consumable items (oil, paper, bandages).
- Procurement and delivery of raw materials and component parts (ball bearings, books, prosthesis).
- Procurement and delivery of capital assets (machines, computers, ultrasound monitors).
- Assembly of labour force (welders, clerks, nurses).
- Internal distribution of all these items.
- Clearance of production lines.
- Distribution of finished products (products, students, treated patients).
- The exchange of finished product for a monetary payment.
- The rendering of the service (maintenance, careers advice, aftercare).

Customer service
Customer service represents the output and the measure of effectiveness of the supply chain system. How successfully we implement strategies to achieve it, be they quality management, restructuring or new operational initiatives, depends on how well the firm manages change.

CASE STUDY
Dinner at 7-Eleven

Three times a week Toshifumi Suzuki, the chairman, and other managers of the 7-eleven company sit down to a meal comprising of the products sold in their stores. 7-Eleven is Japan's largest convenience chain store; it made $680 million dollars on sales of $1.44 billion in 1990. The meal will consist of anything from instant noodles to boiled octopus; nothing that does not taste good or is stale will be on the menu in future. The stores are linked in to one of the most advanced product tracking systems in the world. Details such as the customer's sex and approximate age are collected for every purchase. This information is transmitted to suppliers and manufacturers, to enable rapid response to falling inventory levels. Slow moving items are removed and product innovations based on customer trends enhanced.

Reprinted from 1992 *Reinventing America* issue of Business Week by special permission © 1992 by McGraw-Hill companies

The concept of customer service has evolved out of the post-World War II marketing movement. The three-pronged **marketing concept** states that businesses should be:

- customer rather than production focused;
- customer satisfaction comes from integrated efforts;
- corporate goals can only occur if customers are satisfied.

LaLonde *et al.* (1988, p. 5) define customer service as:

> '...a process which takes place between buyer, seller, and third party. The process results in a value added to a product or service exchanged. This value added in the exchange process might be short term as in a single transaction or longer term as in a contractual relationship. The value added is also shared, in that each of the parties to the transaction or contract is better off at the completion of the transactions than they were before the transaction took place. Thus in a process view: Customer service is a process for providing significant value-added benefits to the supply chain in a cost-effective way.'

LaLonde and Zinster (1976) have classified three ways to view customer service: as an activity, in terms of performance levels, and as a management philosophy. To some extent, the opening illustration of 7-Eleven illustrated these; the philosophy is inherent in the company and visible by the chairman's actions, the company manage the development of customer satisfaction by ensuring that information is collected and acted upon, and finally the company will record performance indicators, such as profit to see how well they are providing the service.

The aim of customer service is to provide customers with what they expect, not just with the physical product, but with the process by which they purchase and receive it. The product may be the best available, but without good customer services, it will not sell. The elements that provide customer service will differ between companies. Coyle *et al.* (1996, p. 114) have identified some of the customer service elements for the food industry, as reproduced in Table 9.1.

Table 9.1 Customer service elements for the food industry

Element	1995	2000
Product availability	98%	99%
Order cycle time	9 days	7 days
Complete orders shipped	90%	94%
Accurate invoices provided	90%	93%
Damaged products	1%	0.5%

In many respects, customer service and quality management overlap. In the opening section of this chapter, the definition of supply chain management referred to conforming to customer requirements, an objective of **quality management**. Within the supply chain system there are three elements that contribute importantly to customer satisfaction or the quality of the system:

● availability
● performance
● reliability.

Logistics quality

Logistics can create customer value in three general areas:

● **Performance:** the efficiency of the system to deliver quickly and at low cost.
● **Effectiveness:** the ability to deliver the correct order on time.
● **Differentiation:** the ability to adapt to the needs of differing customer requirements.

The elements and importance of customer service measures will vary between industries. The common ingredients are:

● time
● accuracy
● the ease of interaction between customer and supplier.

Time is an important element. The time between the customer making his request for a product, and the time he receives it, the **order cycle time**, or speed. Within this we are concerned with the way in which the customer makes his request, the way that we process and prepare the order and the way that the order is shipped. Time **reliability**, is how well we deliver at a point in time. We are also concerned with **time flexibility**, how well as an organisation we can react to changes in customer delivery requirements.

Dependability is very important to the customer. If we say we can supply a product within a particular lead-time, the customer can minimise their inventory and organise any special receiving procedures. The condition of goods is important; the customer wants undamaged goods. Condition is associated with the quality of packaging and materials handling techniques. It is costly for everyone to be involved in returns, but if we are, how effective is the **claims procedure**? It is important to send the correct order. **Complete orders filled**, measures this. **Inventory availability** influences the speed of order processing and the number of incomplete orders shipped.

Convenience is important for many firms that deal directly with the public. The company must try to provide the product in the form the customer requires it. For example, one customer may require a particular pallet; another may want special packaging. These issues have to be balanced with the operational problems of achieving them. How flexible are we on **order size**? Communication is very important; the advent of EDI is helping to ensure that accurate information is being passed between supplier and customer. **Invoice procedures and accuracy, order status information** and the **accessibility** of the firm's ambassadors, who may be the sales team, or the drivers of the transportation fleet, all have a bearing on how easy we are to work with.

Using strategic analysis we identify those elements above of **customer service** that are important to the company. We can estimate the costs of poor service and set customer service standards that can be monitored and improved. We can then target those areas of the firm that are the bottlenecks to service improvement. Listen to the case of the customer who never was:

'Most of you will have met me. I am the person who waits patiently in the clothes shop for the assistants to stop chatting about their friends, only to find they do not have the jacket in my size. I am the person who orders moules marinières, only to find it is not on the menu today. I wait patiently in the electronics shop, while the assistant tries to sell me a video that (they say) is similar to the one I have spent a month reading up on, but they are out of stock with that model. I have just taken last week's copy of the TV guide back to the newsagent and been accused of not looking at the date on the cover, it was my fault the shop was selling the out of date magazine! I am the person who has just gone back to the furniture store, to get the pack of screws that must have fallen out of package for the do-it-yourself bookcase. I avoid travel, because I am fed up with throwing away the sawdust sandwiches sold by travel operators. You all know me, I am that nice person, who listens, waits and does not cause much fuss. I am also the person you do not see again.'

Systems approach

The previous section introduced the activities that are associated with the firm's supply chain. The philosophy of supply chain management moves on from this inward analysis to include the whole system within which the firm conducts its logistics activities. It takes an organisational and environmental perspective that recognises that suppliers and customers have an influence over the firm's cost, revenue and quality. The integration of operations and marketing functions are of particular importance. If the firm does not have a logistics function, we must examine how the supply chain processes are managed between these functions. In addition to the dynamic relationships between direct contributors in the supply chain, a systems approach takes into account other factors such as the social, economic and political considerations that may affect logistics performance.

How we control the movement of material will be largely dependent on the type of demand that we are dealing with, push or pull. This is dealt with in detail in Chapter 8, where we discuss materials planning and just-in-time philosophies.

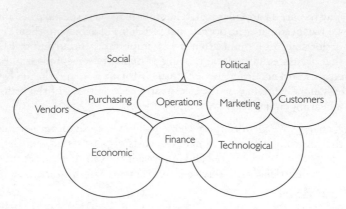

Figure 9.5 The supply chain system

Problems to overcome

One major reason why it is difficult to establish an efficient logistics system is because there is often a complex interaction of influences that all lead to inefficiencies, natural and manmade. In some industries, there is also a tendency towards over capacity of people and resources, which leads to a logistics subculture working hard to minimise the effects of this additional capacity. These effects are spread between different functions within a firm and can be classed as:

- Organisational, such as structure, accountability, and communication.
- Operational, such as poor facilities and equipment.
- Administrative, such as a poor and inefficient ordering systems.
- Financial, such as incorrect inventory levels.

One should not loose sight of the fact that while many functions benefit from integrated philosophies, functions themselves do not integrate. Each function will have specific duties to perform within a set budget. It is the people within the functions that enable integration to occur and the resultant synergy.

Inbound logistics

This section begins the process of examining the chain of activities that link suppliers to customers. The focus for this section is on inbound logistics, and explores the role of **purchasing** and **materials management**. It is important to understand that for the whole supply chain there are common activities and processes; similar information requirements and similar resource requirements relate to the decision-making activities. For example, the information used to decide on the number and placement of warehouses is essentially the same for both raw materials and for finished goods; both need to take into account demand, service and cost.

Once we have decided that there is a need for a product and that we can fulfil that need, we gather the resources satisfy it. The first stage then in the supply chain is to obtain the resources, in the form of consumables, parts, and assets. The firm should have systems in place that enable them to seek out the best deal and then monitor the performance of the supplier once selected.

   CASE STUDY

Purchasing in British Coal

British Coal in its heyday had a large purchasing function. Its relationships with suppliers were often adversarial, although for many of the more specialist mining equipment, joint development, delivery and service contracts were established. Purchase orders were placed dependent on the type and volume of material required. Some items were ordered through: 'blanket orders', where regular delivery of items was made, based on established demand, for example, timber products; 'call offs' where the items were ordered as required by a colliery from a central store; 'one-off' items were ordered directly by the colliery, when it had the authority to do so. In almost every case the items purchased were from suppliers who had undertaken a rigorous selection procedure, and then monitored through a national stores database of information. A central office that employed around 1000 staff controlled the purchasing process. Purchase requisitions often followed a paper trail that perpetuated the empire. The organisation could afford to be and was on occasion, dynamic in the development of new systems. One such development harnessed the power of technology in the form of local area networks, which enabled colliery engineers to initiate a purchase request. This information then travelled along an electronic trial that checked for availability of items and availability of funds. Although the system was based on the existing paper system, it enabled orders to be processed faster and provided for a greater level of management information. The purchasing system itself formed part of a large integrated management information system that was open to most officials and staff at the colliery. In addition to the general purchasing system a system for managing the provisioning of a coal-face was under continual development. Figure 9.6 shows some of the main elements of this system. Coal-face equipment costs millions of pounds. It was vital that British Coal used its assets to the fullest. To aid in the coal-face provisioning a combination of local systems designed for specific tasks was linked to national systems to provide a very comprehensive system.

The mainframe systems included:

- DAPPER: Direct Access Plant Pool Equipment Register. This contained records of all pieces of capital machinery at all collieries, their availability and state of repair.
- Stores: an extensive purchasing and stores system that was designed to meet all ordinary purchasing requirements.
- Project ledger: contained financial details pertaining to assets at a colliery and was used to create the profit and loss accounts for a colliery.

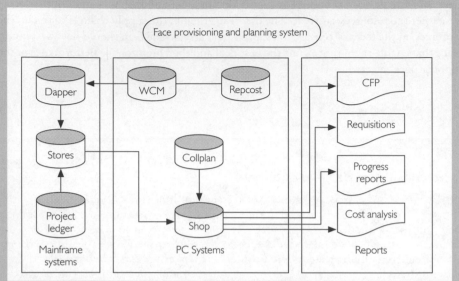

Figure 9.6 Coal-face provisioning system

The PC systems included:

- WCM: Workshops Cost Monitoring. This monitored all maintenance work conducted on capital machinery.
- REPCOST: repair cost. This collated maintenance costs, running costs, causes of failure, and provided guidance on maintenance schedules.
- COLLPLAN, Colliery Planning System. A network analysis system that provided comprehensive planning data in the form of Gantt charts that were used as one of the main items that managers were held accountable for.
- SHOP: shopping list. This system collated data from the other systems to provide information on asset locations and purchasing requirements. It also monitored the progress of the purchasing project and the costs associated with it.

Numerous reports were available including CFP – the coal-face provisioning master plan, requisitions for purchase and monitoring information.

Resources once purchased need to be transported to the firm, unloaded, stored or moved to the production area. For example, in the case of a supermarket the production area is the shop floor. Many shops have a warehouse, or storeroom, where some items are held in bulk storage. It is far more efficient to have goods deliveries go straight on to the shop floor, rather than into the storeroom where they are not adding value.

One does not immediately associate a predominantly manufacturing-based system of control with the management of a service industry. Can systems such as materials requirements planning, scientific inventory control and just-in-time be useful within a service industry? For many services, the control of inventory per se does not contribute substantial cost benefits. However, the philosophy behind the concept can reveal hidden rewards, such as quality improvements and increases in resource utilisation.

CASE STUDY
Just-in-time in a hotel

The Warren Buckley Hotel in the heart of London's Knightsbridge area has 235 bedrooms, a restaurant, coffee shop, cocktail bar, conference suites and a number of shops. In the bars, an average of 108 days of stock was held at an annual cost of £2,233. Existing suppliers were able to deliver at least once a week, but were limited in their ability to meet the requirements of a JIT approach to delivery. After a process of systems analysis, staff training and communication, supplier selection and technology review, a JIT system was implemented. The system enabled a reduction in stock days to 39 coupled with an improvement in customer service in terms of product availability from an average of 9.7% to 1.9% unavailable. However, the cost savings that resulted from the implementation of JIT are perhaps secondary to the improvements in other aspects of the management of the hotel. Staff became more committed to the hotel. Management became more aware of operational bottlenecks, and of problem-solving methods. It was hoped that space saved both in the cellar and from better utilisation of bed linen (a subsequent study) would enable more space to be utilised for revenue-generating activities (Barlow, 1995).

The purchasing process

The co-ordination of material supply with customer demand is important. It is often difficult to predict customer demand; it is independent of the activities of the firm. Using **forecasts** of sales we can then plan our strategy for meeting demand. Demand can be met from finished goods inventory, or from new production. In the later case, the production planner uses sales forecasts to develop a production schedule. As discussed in Chapter 8 many firms use demand to pull production through the firm. Customers buying products will generate a need to produce more, and a resultant demand for raw materials.

We need a system to enable effective purchasing to be undertaken, so that we, as customers, get the right product, and for the supplier so that they know exactly what we require. There is an increasing trend to purchase as many of the resources we require, rather than make them in-house. Purchasing expertise is important. The complex needs of a modern operations facility requires a number of items to be sourced externally to the organisation, because of the specialist knowledge and capability required to produce them competitively. It is important that a company has reliable suppliers that can supply within our quality and cost constraints.

The purchasing process has the following stages.

Defining purchase specifications for the goods or service
Purchase decisions are initiated as a response to the needs of a customer, within or outside the firm. Once we have recognised a new need or have to re-evaluate an existing need, we begin the **procurement process**. We need to specify the item we want from the supplier. It is not always possible to provide a full specification, in which case it is necessary to specify any possible variations. It is important to get things right at the product design stage. Suppliers should be involved to add their expert advice on the materials

available for a product, the prices, tolerances and availability. While marketing may desire a certain finish or ingredient in a product it may not be economical to provide it. For example, a student would like each course to provide all the course materials for all the subjects that they are studying. If university marketing staff offered this material without consultation with the 'suppliers', the academic staff, it would cause operational problems, as well as increasing the cost of the course.

Apart from specifying the materials required, there needs to be an effective **coding system** that uniquely identifies each item. This system needs to be acceptable to both the supplier and the purchaser. The costs of development of such systems can sometimes be shared between a consortium of interested companies, especially in respect to the development of an electronic system.

Obtaining price quotations

The quotations should include the charges that will be made to the company if a deviation from the original specification should occur. For some businesses, for example the construction industry, the work will vary over time. When builders tender for a job, they have to include an estimate of charges for any additional or unusual work that may be encountered. For example, a new shopping centre may find that its foundations will lie over some important archaeological relics or an area of unstable ground and alternative foundation techniques must be applied. The builder should state or estimate the cost for these eventualities.

Quotations can be found from a variety of sources. Yellow pages, trade directories, business libraries and industry journals have contact details for commonly occurring items. To establish prices for services and to establish longer lasting relationships we could ask firms to tender for the work.

Developing criteria for supplier selection

It is important for reasons, other than simply price, to get the right supplier. The issues examined include:

- **Price** – including discounts for bulk deliveries.
- **Quality** – conformance to agreed specifications.
- **Terms** – cash discounts, credit periods.
- **Deliveries** – reliability and speed of response to order requisitions.
- **Service** – general co-operation, continuity of supply.

The supplier once selected will have considerable influence on the company's success. Issues such as quality, and reliability, will affect productivity. If poor quality materials are used, poor quality products will result. If late deliveries occur either production will stop, customers orders will be late, or you will have to hold large inventories as insurance. **Quality** has become a qualifying, rather than competitive criterion for many firms. Most companies look for firms that can provide an assured service or product. If you manage a restaurant one of the success factors will be in the quality of food you prepare. If a delivery of fish has been tainted, or is late, fish may be off the menu for the evening, which may result in lost sales, or lost customers. Firms must have in place systems that indicate and control the conformance of the product to the customers' requirements. However, it may be acceptable to have a product that conforms to requirements 99% of the time, rather than one that conforms 99.5% of the time at twice the cost, as long as the supplier can demonstrate the ability to maintain an agreed specification, or service level.

The time spent selecting a supplier depends on the importance of the commodity to the business. A useful rule of thumb, developed by Tomes and Hayes (1993 p.99), is as shown in Figure 9.7.

Suppliers competition

	Low	High
Low	Do not waste negotiating time where the benefits are low, dispose of decision quickly.	Impose your systems (e.g. ask for tenders or quotes).
High	The supplier has the upper hand and will attempt to impose their procedures, neglect, or impose higher costs. Have an alternative supplier.	Both parties need to negotiate and haggle.

Importance of purchase

Figure 9.7 Supplier vs purchaser power (Thomes and Hayes, 1993, p. 99)

Order placement

When the order is placed it provides a record of the transaction that can later be monitored or used for checking deliveries. We should avoid loose specifications, for example an order for 'three crates of Coke'. We need to specify the pack type, size and grade: three cases of 500 ml cans of diet Coke.

Order progression

Once an order has been placed, it is necessary to follow it up to ensure that it has been received and accepted. **Expediting** is the monitoring of supplier deliveries of materials and speeding up the process if necessary. In an ideal world, an order, once placed, would arrive in full on the date expected. In reality things occasionally go wrong, so we monitor the state of orders to alleviate problems before they become serious threats to the firm. The need to expedite is caused through a breakdown in the system; the world is not perfect. For example, lecturers not informing the bookshop of book requirements, or lecturers not being informed of the numbers of students on the course, or the bookshop not placing the order. This may then leave a student in the position of having to chase for a copy of the book.

Receive goods

Traffic is involved with getting material from the vendor to the firm. **Traffic management** uses similar techniques and data to those required for physical distribution and hence will be dealt with under the section on outbound logistics. We are concerned that deliveries are made as quickly as possible and that the process of unloading and transfer to store, or production is made as simple as possible. When the materials have arrived we become involved with **goods received**. When we receive goods we must verify that they are the type, size and grade of goods ordered and in the quantity required. An examination of the goods is usually made, to check for damage and for the correct quality standards.

Once we have established a degree of trust with the supplier then the need to monitor becomes less important. Companies involved in just-in-time operations minimise the need for quality checks, by ensuring that suppliers send materials that are 'always' perfect in quality and quantity. We may not have perfect relationships, all of the time, so companies need to develop quality assessment techniques that monitor and test deliveries to a suitable standard and frequency.

Payment
The final act is one of payment in line with the terms of the supplier's contract.

Strategic purchasing

The importance and role of the purchasing function depends primarily on the type of value-adding activity the firm is involved with. For example, in a supermarket the high turnover of products means that fractions of pence saved through effective purchasing will result in dramatic increases in profits. Retailers need to spend considerable effort in monitoring and controlling the stock. In a manufacturing industry such as a car company that operates a just-in-time philosophy, routine purchasing is dealt with automatically and the purchasing department is concerned as much with establishing strategic collaborative ventures with suppliers, to help improve quality and reduce costs.

It is becoming more frequent that firms are creating formal alliances or **partnerships** with suppliers and customers. The partnership movement has developed from customers moving towards JIT principles of manufacture and is sometimes known as JIT supply. Many companies realise that if they involve their suppliers at an early stage in the business cycle everyone benefits. Suppliers can help design the product, by advising on suitable materials and production. Suppliers can also help with the design of the logistics systems that will enable rapid delivery of the product in a state fit for use. Suppliers benefit from a long-term stable market that enables them to confidently invest in new capital. The firm benefits from an increase in quality, which is a prerequisite for a purchasing relationship to be established. Even if the market is not stable the interchange of information together with flexible manufacturing systems enable more markets to be serviced. For example, if Lucas, who manufacture electrical equipment, are aware that the Ford Motor Company have sold fifty cars, they will be able to dispatch a hundred headlamp units to the Ford assembly plant and commence their own operations to manufacture another hundred units.

Cherrett (1995 p. 403) has identified some benefits associated with **partnership sourcing**. Partnership sourcing can help organisations:

- achieve world class quality standards;
- cut lead times and increase flexibility in response to market fluctuations;
- slash stock and administration costs and bolster cash flow;
- improve planning through long-term, information-rich relationships with customers and suppliers;

- reduce production downtime and increase capacity;
- cut time-to-market, the time lag between identifying a market and introducing a new service or product on to that market;
- innovate through better information from customers and supplier, and gain access to the technical resources of both.

To enable this, a partnership needs to be established between the two companies. Traditionally the purchasing cycle involved accurate specification of the materials, shopping around for the best supplier and then monitoring their performance against agreed quality and cost criteria. The cycle is still valid, although has been adapted to meet the requirements of the competitive market.

Relationships in supply chains

Figure 9.8 illustrates the supply chain between a frozen food company and numerous customers. The company would like all of its customers to feel part of and contribute to the company's success. Each customer, apart from maybe the final consumer, has his or her own business to manage. Trying to meet, match and agree on how the chain will function for the benefit of all parties is inevitably going to be fraught with some difficulties. For most of the chain, all we need is a friendly working relationship; the benefits from maintaining close partnerships with everyone concerned are likely to be less than the costs of maintaining them. The closest relationships are found when we own parts of the chain. **Vertical integration** was fashionable in the 1980s when 'big' was, largely, viewed as beautiful. Some companies over-extended the scope of their businesses and lost sight of their area of core competence, i.e. what they did best. Now firms are refocusing their activities, by down-scoping and selling off those parts of the chain that do not add to their main activities whilst entering into relationships with new suppliers.

Figure 9.8 Lean supply

In many companies, especially small and medium sized ones, the benefits of formal relationships with all suppliers are not always realisable. We may be involved, for instance, in irregular purchase of materials for special jobs and apply simple selection criteria to those suppliers. It is in this situation that companies are most vulnerable. For example, a building contractor has located suppliers and informed the client of anticipated start and finish dates, which form part of his contract to construct an extension to a house. The work progresses to a point where delivery of materials for a conservatory are expected, a week before the work is due to commence. The materials do not arrive, so the builder contacts the glazing firm. A day goes by before contact is made and this is with a person who says they are only temporary and that the managers are off site; a message will be left for them to contact him. Two more days go by without any form of contact being made. The builder, who by this time is getting worried, because of the penalty clause for late completion in his contract, drives to the head office of the firm. After meeting the staff at the glazing firm, he is promised delivery the following day. This does not happen. What should the builder do?

In this case, it is evident that the supplier is either incompetent, incapable, or disinterested in the customer. As soon as tell-tale signs, such as temporary staff, lies, buck-passing, late delivery and poor quality become evident, it is probably best to re-order with another supplier quickly. This may cost more, but a legal action against the original supplier may recoup the extra costs. In any event, it is likely to be more costly for your own company to bear the hidden costs of inefficient supply than to tolerate it in any form at all.

The types of relationships found in supply chains have been classified by Slack *et al.* (1995 p. 536). Many relationships exist in the supply chain and all are important. A company would not have just the one type of relationship. For example, no business can be a truly **integrated hierarchy**, because they could never have the capability to produce everything they need for the business to succeed. For example all businesses need paper – very few grow trees!

Integrated hierarchy
A fully integrated firm that manages all operations from raw materials sources to delivering the final product to the consumer. This is not as common as it used to be. An example would be a farmer who grows the wheat, mills the grain, bakes the bread and delivers it to the customer.

Semi-hierarchy
In a semi-hierarchy all the major parts of the chain are owned by the same company, but operate as separate business units. Public utilities such as the National Health Service operate partly as semi-hierarchies. Hospitals are independent units, but benefit from corporate services, such as regional supply centres.

Co-contracting
Co-contracting refers to close alliances between companies, where an interchange of competencies, resources, assets and equity takes place. It encompasses the essence of supply chain management, when companies form equal partnerships. Lamming (1993) has developed the idea of **lean supply** that links together total quality management concepts, global markets, information technology and management control issues. (See Figure 9.8.)

Co-ordinated contracting

Co-ordinated contracting involves long-standing intermittent relationships between companies such as builders who employ subcontractors to do parts of the work for them. Many firms who are involved in project work are involved in this type of relationship. For example, an information technology consultancy operation may have a central body of staff who generate work (projects) and then hire people to do the fieldwork. It is a relationship type that is on the increase as companies attempt to become virtual. (A **virtual company** is one that exists only for as long as it is required; it has no fixed assets, hires and fires at will, and appears whenever there is a market opportunity.)

Co-ordinated revenue links

These types of relationships exist commonly in franchised and licensed operations, where the franchiser does not want to manage every single operation, but wishes to retain the quality of the brand name. In return for a fee paid to the franchiser, the business will be given rights to buildings, territories, training, equipment, and quality procedures. It will also benefit from national advertising campaigns, which are often beyond the means of smaller firms. Examples include car repair centres, fast food outlets and dry cleaners.

Medium/long-term trading commitment

When companies have been trading together for some time, an informal relationship develops that is not formally written down in a contract. The relation develops with a mutual understanding and, in some ways, the firms develop systems that are mutually beneficial. An example is the blanket order described in the British Coal illustration.

Short-term trading commitment

Short-term arrangements are characterised by a lack of formal contact between the supplier and customer. There is little interchange of information and assistance other than that connected with the immediate purchase.

Other materials management activities

Materials management traditionally covers all the activities associated with the supply and handling of raw materials and products including storage, and movement of them. Warehouse operations include many of these activities.

Materials handling

Materials handling is important in all aspects of operations, within many types of firms. Accidents involving the movement of materials or incorrect use of equipment are common and, for that reason alone, it is an important topic. A poorly planned handling system will result in overstaffing, delays and damage to the materials being moved. Materials handling is associated with the short distance movements that take place within the confines of a building, or between a building and a transport agency. There are four basic components influencing the design of materials handling systems:

- movement
- time
- quantity
- space.

The management objectives are to:

- *Increase capacity*. The capacity objective involves minimising operating cost by utilising as much space as possible. This includes using the building height and minimising aisle space.
- *Improve efficiency*. The objective of improving operating efficiency involves reducing the number of times goods are handled. Additional handling must be avoided. Materials handling design must minimise movements to, within, and from a warehouse or node.
- *Improve working conditions*. Materials handling systems are increasingly **sociotechnical**, a blend of automated and manual processes. Workers must be motivated to get the job done. The system should be safe to operate but designed to enhance productivity. Monotonous and heavy manual work should be eliminated, with the aim to replace people as much as possible.
- *Improve service*. Logistics service should be improved by quickening response times to customers. Materials handling requirements should be integrated with company departmental needs, and customer needs.
- *Reduce cost*. The reduced cost objective will be a natural consequence of achieving the first four objectives.

There are four main activities within materials handling:

- the receiving and shipping stages;
- material handling devices;
- storage devices;
- intelligent warehousing systems.

Receiving and shipping permits the rapid flow of material in and out of the facility. Ideally materials coming in should proceed without undue delay to the production line; products leaving the production line should go straight to the customer. In reality though, it is necessary to have storage areas for both.

Equipment and packing

There is a proliferation of equipment available to companies for moving materials about. These range from forklift trucks and overhead cranes to docking equipment that enables trucks to load effectively. The choice of equipment depends on the physical properties of the item and the nature of the movement. Automated guided vehicles, AGVs, are robots that connect receiving, storing, manufacturing and shipping, carrying items to a pre-programmed destination. Materials tend to travel around in packs until they arrive at the machine, or person that is going to use them. The choice of equipment to use involves a comparison of the performance of existing equipment with the possible benefits of changing

There are numerous designs of pallets for different stacking and storage systems. The substance the pallet is made of is important. The grocery industry, which uses primarily wooden pallets, repairs sixty-eight million pallets each year. If the product is hazardous or a high degree of cleanliness is required then pallets made of plastic or metal are sometimes used.

Storage devices are used to enable materials parts to be stacked in a neat and easily retrievable manner. There are two categories: those designed for the picker to get the item and those where the item goes to the picker. (A picker is the person who fetches the item for order make-up.)

Packaging is extremely important to a logistics manager. It enables them to get the product to the customer in the right condition; people expect to purchase goods in perfect condition – no bruised apples or dented tins. It also plays a part in transportation costs by influencing the size and shape of the product.

Packaging has three functions:

- protection
- information
- containment.

Packaging is split into two types: **primary packaging**, that which is seen by the customer (consumer) and **secondary packaging** (exterior, industrial), that which is used for transportation and storage. Marketing managers are concerned with consumer packaging, the primary packaging, which provides the confinement for the product. It may involve one or more layers, the outer layer containing the product description and advertising. Containment is required to enable shops to provide goods in a self-service environment. Secondary packaging is of concern to the logistics manager, although the two areas overlap. Many bulk products now come with a minimum amount of packaging. For example, it is only fairly recently that nails have become available pre-packed.

To develop appropriate packaging it must be considered that the product is going to be in five basic locations during its life:

- the plant
- the warehouse
- in transit
- the retail outlet
- the home or place of use.

Ease of handling is important; package design includes shape, strength, and size as well as consumer appeal. In addition, the design should be compatible with handling equipment. Colour coding, universal product codes, computer readable labels, either printed or as chips which convey information on the content of the package. Package labelling is also used as a major form of communication to the intermediaries who will be handling the product on its journey from the firm to the customer.

Most packaging ends up in the bin. The majority of the refuse is paper, and there are many millions of trees being used each year in packaging. As consumers and conservationists, we should all put pressure on companies to reduce the amount of packaging to a minimum, and encourage effective recycling wherever possible. By the year 2000 it is estimated that 220 million tonnes of municipal waste will be produced in the United States. Figure 9.9 illustrates the type of waste to be disposed of, a considerable proportion of which will be packaging.

Scrap
If municipal waste reflects the potential burden to society of getting rid of redundant packaging materials, then scrap represents the burden to an individual company of its own trash-producing process. Some scrap is an unavoidable by-product of the company's business. As the marketing department has its major responsibility in getting the finished product to the customer, it is often the materials management function to get rid of waste products. Some products have a value, such as used oil from garage service centres, which

can be recycled, or used as fuel. Some products need special disposal facilities, such as hazardous waste. Collieries, for example, produce almost as much shale and mud as they do coal. Some of this can be sold to construction companies, some of it has to be dumped in old quarries, but it poses a major logistical problem however it is disposed.

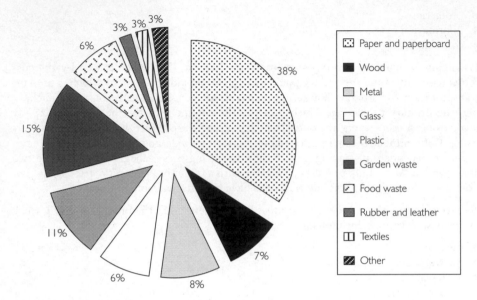

Figure 9.9 Solid waste types

Reverse logistics: recycling

Reverse logistics is the process of continuously taking back products and/or packaging materials to avoid further waste disposal in landfills or high energy consumption through the incineration process. As firms are put under increased pressure to become environmentally friendly, the concept of recycling is gaining in importance. There is increasing pressure from stakeholders, such as customers, workforce and local communities as well as increased legislation, which forces some changes, but ideally firms should be proactive, and continually look for improvement. To be economically viable, reverse logistics needs to be embedded in the firm's strategy, so that the issues concerned are connected with the firm's environmental and product strategies. Basically, reverse logistics is dealing with rubbish or products that have reached the end of their useful lives, hence the value of them is low. For firms to profitably re-use rubbish the stages of collection, sorting and re-processing need to be efficient and effective. Firms can assist in this in the product design stage by **designing for disassembly**. **Retro-manufacturing** can be defined as: 'the use of recycled commodities in a manufacturing process'. The final event in the recycling chain is the reuse of the materials, where recycled items again enter the production process.

Warehousing

Warehouses are used throughout the supply chain either as storage areas for raw materials or for finished products; as such, they are part of both inbound and outbound logistics activities. However, warehousing plays an increasingly important part in reducing a company's supply chain expense, mainly transportation, and in improving customer service. Rather than transporting the goods in perhaps small loads to a number of outlets, large loads are transported to a centralised warehouse, where they are then broken down into smaller loads. Warehouses are located close to customer demand and customers are then served with shorter lead times. If a company knew exactly what the demand for their product will be, and could supply that demand immediately, then there would not be a need for warehouse storage. This however is not the case. The need for warehousing stems from the need to supply customers quickly, and the inability to meet demand instantly.

A warehouse is a fixed point or a node in the logistics system. In the past warehousing has been viewed negatively, a 'soak' for costs, i.e. increased inventory, and as an interruption of the flow of materials between the firm and the customer. However warehouses can add value by:

- lowering transportation costs;
- offering product mixing;
- improving service;
- providing contingency protection;
- smoothing production.

In deciding our strategy for materials and product movement and storage, we need to decide how to manage the use of warehouses. Warehousing decisions include: ownership, number, size, location, and stocking.

Ownership involves a choice between private or public warehousing, with the option of having both, depending on circumstances. Whether the company uses its own and operates a private warehousing system, or contracts out to a public system, is a make-or-buy decision. Generally, the greater the volumes dealt with, the cheaper it will be to use an internal system. Public warehouses are open to anyone to store items for any period. They can be designed for specific types of products, such as frozen goods, or household furniture, or as general storage. The firm is not involved in the capital costs of owning their own warehouse and they can offer firms some flexibility in terms of changing location. Public warehouses offer a wide range of services. They can add value to the basic service of storage. They can be used for short time periods, and have a competitive price structure. However, products stored in them may be stored with other incompatible products that may either damage the goods, or in the case of foods, taint the flavours.

Contract warehousing combines the benefits of both public and private systems. Long-term relationships are established, risks are shared and costs are reduced. The number of warehouses is a function of the costs associated with running them and the increased levels of inventory incurred. Figure 9.10 illustrates the nature of these costs. Increasing the number of warehouses decreases transport costs, and costs of lost sales, but increases inventory and warehousing costs.

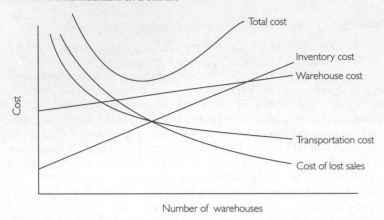

Figure 9.10 Cost of warehouses

Four non-cost factors affect the number and location of warehouses:

- the need for rapid customer service;
- inadequate transportation systems;
- customers need for small quantities and short lead-times;
- poor customer inventory management resulting in stockouts and urgent deliveries.

The main purposes of the warehouse are: to hold stocks (inventory to buffer the imbalance of supply and demand), consolidate, to bring together many products from many sources, and to break bulk and offer mix. Figure 9.11 illustrates these basic functions.

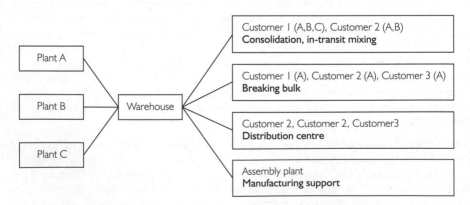

Figure 9.11 Warehouse functions

Consolidation might be the main function of a supermarket's warehouse. Breaking bulk may not actually involve storage, the facility just being geared up to take advantage of bulk transportation methods for long distances then splitting the product up for local delivery. Warehousing also increases customer service, it is easier to maintain good service levels in large systems then smaller ones, because the deviations of demand cause a relatively smaller impact. A smoother service with greater protection against unforeseen factors will occur.

Movement and storage are the basic on-site warehouse operations. Movement operations involve short distances and include:

- receipt and checking;
- unpacking/repacking/resizing/regrading/mixing;
- transfer to storage area;
- inventory checks/disposal of obsolete goods;
- selection of goods/materials for orders/production;
- loading for shipment.

The layout of the warehouse is determined by its functions, that of receiving, storing and shipping goods, and the nature of the goods in question. As one of the purposes of warehousing is to reduce cost, warehouses must be run with the minimum of effort. Efficient materials handling must be in use. The maximum use must be made of the warehouse's volume. The layout must be planned with ease of extracting products, or picking, as required. In determining the space requirement for the warehouse, a forecast of the future demand for the company's products is required. This is then used to determine the numbers of products to be kept to meet customer requirements. This number is then converted into square footage. Other space is required to allow for aisles, offices and personnel spaces, roughly about ⅓ of the space. Modern warehouses make use of intelligent systems that can be controlled remotely, with various types of robots.

A number of general design principles are applied to the warehouse:

- use single storey facility;
- use straight lines for flows of goods;
- use efficient materials handling equipment;
- keep up-to-date and accurate storage plans;
- minimise isle space;
- make maximum use of facility height
- separate bulky and hazardous materials;
- safeguard from pilferage;
- ensure special needs are catered for (heat, refrigeration, fragility).

We can evaluate the efficiency of the warehouse in terms of two aspects:

- utilisation of space;
- utilisation of labour.

This can be measured by looking at three variables:

- activity levels;
- size of items;
- comparison of load size and order size.

When it comes to improving productivity within the warehouse five things are recommended:

- reduce distances travelled;
- increase the unit sizes handled;
- round-trip use of warehouse equipment;
- improve cube utilisation of storage space;
- utilise technology.

Many warehouse activities benefit from bar-coding, from receiving to shipping and for stock counts. There are a variety of systems that can be used from hand held scanners to automatic systems. The most visible use of the system can be seen at the local supermarket, when goods are essentially logged out of the store. This coupled with information on deliveries gives an instant indication of inventory levels, barring those items that are damaged or are stolen.

Chapter 2 discussed the importance of facility location. The siting of warehouses is one of the more common subjects of this type of decision.

Outbound logistics

Outbound logistics is primarily concerned with establishing an effective distribution strategy, which fulfils customer requirements. The system needs to be able to respond rapidly to changing customer needs and the tendency to move towards pull methods of demand management. Historically, and still so for many companies, outbound logistics has been associated with the marketing function. This section introduces the main activities within the distribution system, the control methods employed, and the strategies adopted.

Channels of distribution

It is useful at this point to introduce another definition of logistics management, one that perhaps illustrates the role of any logistics activity. Sometimes called the layperson's definition, the **Seven Rs of distribution** defines logistics as:

> Ensuring the availability of the *right product*, in the *right quantity* and the *right condition*, at the *right place*, at the *right time*, for the *right customer*, at the *right cost*.

It is a useful exercise to break down each of the 'rights' and examine what it implies. For example, right condition implies that we have chosen an appropriate mode of transport, and that the packaging has provided sufficient protection. Each element refers to either the spatial or the temporal aspects of logistics and has an underpinning of cost and customer service. Each of the 'rights' in the Seven Rs definition of logistics indicate what they might mean in terms of information, transportation, packaging, customer service, and management control.

Many firms use a number of channels through which they get their product to the consumer. Figure 9.12 illustrates a possible channel structure for a frozen food company. Sometimes these chains have many levels between the producer and the final customer. You can consider that in some ways the wholesaler is taking away some of the burdens of the logistics function from the manufacturer. Their business is one of maximising the value-added part of the logistics function. They are well placed to do it as they are dealing with a large number of products from a number of suppliers.

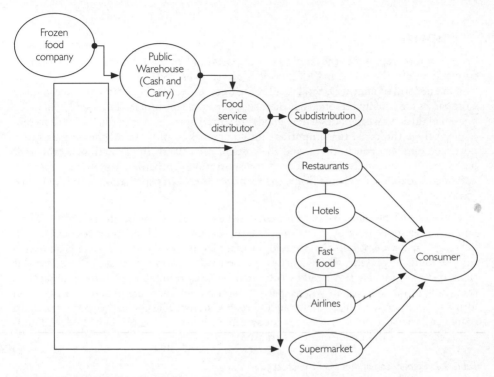

Figure 9.12 A distribution channel for a frozen food company

A channel is the route taken by a commodity between the point of production and its point of sale or consumption. Some channels have historical set-ups; for example, shops will buy potatoes from a potato merchant, who will obtain potatoes from a number of farmers, as well as importing them. There are a number of possible configurations of the chain, some of which are quite complex. The simplest is direct from the manufacturer to the customer, although this is quite rare. Most manufacturers do not have the organisation to deal directly with large numbers of customers; you would not go to the baked bean factory to buy a tin of beans! More commonly, warehouses are used as intermediators.

A danger with complex distribution channels is in the breakdown of communication between the customer and the manufacturer. To avoid this effort needs to be made in developing vertical marketing systems to enable all parties to work towards the same goal. The nature of relationships is discussed in detail in a later section.

Each member of the channel must work in co-operation with the others to achieve a goal or set of goals that are of mutual concern. If **conflict** occurs then the optimal operation for the whole channel is difficult. For example where sales areas overlap. Another issue to address within a supply chain is that of **competition**. Often elements within the channel will be competing with each other; the competition and its impact on the channel must be evaluated.

Transportation

Transportation represents the single most important element in logistical costs for most firms. Typically about one half of logistics costs are absorbed by transport. Transportation in one form or another is vital to all companies, especially in today's global economy. Companies are usually remote from their suppliers and consumers. The supply chain is a system of links between nodes where goods are stored or transferred. Transportation companies bridge the gaps. It is important for companies to understand the various transportation options open to them, and the costs of each. With the growth of world trade has come an increase in the number of transportation companies. For these companies and of course public transport firms, the management of transportation activities is vital to the business.

The selection of the transportation system depends largely on the products moved. Water and rail often move bulk products such as coal, ore, and gravel. In countries with a well-developed rail system, rail is often used for manufactured products. Britain is an exception, tending, at present, to concentrate on the road networks, because of the relatively short distances involved. Airfreight is limited by cost to high value items compared to their bulk or for those items where speed is paramount. There are of course many other forms of transport which combine rail and road systems. The challenge to the transport manager is to select the most appropriate system for the firm and product. Table 9.2 illustrates the uses of the major modes of transport.

Table 9.2 Comparison of modes of transport

Transport mode	Normal usage
Pipeline	Liquid/gaseous products, large distances, for example water and oil.
Air freight	Technically all types of products, but high cost/volume penalty limits its use to high value/low volume products, such as electrical goods.
Water (shipping, barge)	All types of product can be carried. It offers high volume/low cost, but the long lead-times limits its use to non-perishable, low value products such as timber, coal and road-stone.
Rail	All products can be carried. It has high volume and is fast. Rail systems have few nodes, so they tend to be used in conjunction with other modes that are used at transfer depots. Transfers and storage facilities required.
Road	All products, low volume, fast.

Strategically being able to command a low transport cost, enables some companies to compete globally. Take for example the coal industry. A colliery in Scotland mines coal at a cost of £30 per tonne. It is sold at the pithead for around £42 per tonne. The transport cost to the power station to move it a short distance would be in the region of £2 per tonne. The total cost to the generator being about £45 per tonne. Coal from Columbia can be purchased at Rotterdam for £35 per tonne, the transport cost, from there to the power station, being approximately £6 per tonne, making imported coal cheaper than the Scottish product. The product from Columbia has been produced at a much lower cost and the majority of the cost is in the transportation to Rotterdam. If this cost were to increase for some reason (e.g. fuel costs increasing, or exchange rate fluctuations) then this coal would become uncompetitive. Low cost producers in the global market must manage and control transport costs to gain this competitive advantage.

Even on the microeconomic scale, those companies that can realise saving in transportation costs will gain a competitive advantage. Many companies are using third-party carriers, who can move products in bulk for a number of customers and reduce overall transport costs. Customers are often faced with a purchasing decision that relies not on the product price, as companies tend to be competitive on product price, but on the delivery cost of the product. For example, if tempted to buy from mail order companies, always check that the delivery charge is reasonable. Computer software, for example, may be advertised at £25 but delivery charges may vary between £2–£7.

The transport selection decision

The choice of carrier can be split into a number of operating steps. Firstly, we must decide on the appropriate mode of transport; modes such as rail, motor, water, air or intermodal. Figure 9.13 illustrates the relative carrying capacities of the main modes of transport. The figure shows how effective water transportation is in carrying huge loads. However, the nature of the product to be moved often dictates the type of carrier to be used, see Table 9.2.

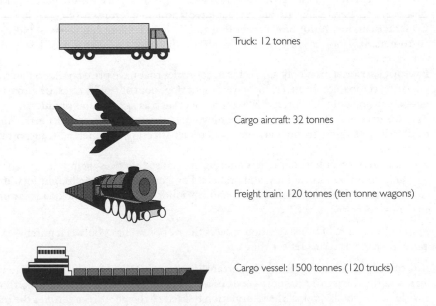

Truck: 12 tonnes

Cargo aircraft: 32 tonnes

Freight train: 120 tonnes (ten tonne wagons)

Cargo vessel: 1500 tonnes (120 trucks)

Figure 9.13 Carrying capacities of various modes of transport

Intermodal transportation is common where large distances are to be covered. Most intermodal combinations involve a motor carrier as part of the chain. Intermodal combinations are referred to by some quaint terminology, such as 'piggyback' for truck/rail, 'birdyback' for truck/air and 'fishyback' for truck/water; it is debatable what trains and pigs have in common!

The transport service can be judged on factors that are similar to all services, Table 9.3 indicates the relative performance of each mode.

Table 9.3 Performance rating of modes of transport (1 = best/lowest; 5 = worst/highest)

	Road	Rail	Air	Water	Pipe
Delivery speed	2	3	1	4	1
Delivery reliability	1	2	3	4	1
Cost	4	3	5	2	3
Route flexibility	1	2	3	4	5
Capability	2	1	3	4	5
Accessibility	1	2	3	4	3
Frequency	1	3	2	3	1
Composite score	12	16	19	25	19

Carrier legal relationships

The choice of carrier, the type of contract and the nature of the journey to be undertaken for the materials or products are, from a legal aspect, a complex consideration. The firm needs to consider the legal standing of the carrier. There are five groups:

- **Common carrier**. These carriers are used as a 'for hire' service by any person, or firm that requires them. They are highly regulated and liable for losses of goods in transit.
- **Contract carrier**. A 'for hire' carrier that tailors its service to the needs of individual customers. It is not used by the public, although offers a similar service level, to the common carrier.
- **Exempt carrier**. This is only applicable in countries that have price regulation on transportation companies. In effect, the government does not control its rates, or it may gain tax benefits by only hauling specialised products such as agricultural products.
- **Private carrier**. These are the companies which own transportation fleets. Again, these are not subject to any national regulations affecting commercial transportation companies.
- **Special carriers**. A host of carriers offering specialised services including: freight forwarding, shipping associations, and brokers. For example domestic freight forwarders collect small shipments from shippers and consolidate them into truckloads for inter-city movements.

The pricing structure of transportation reflects the responsibilities between purchaser and supplier. A range of terms reflect this.

- **Bill of lading**. The single most important document. It is the contract between the firm and the carrier to transport goods to a customer. It sometimes has the certificate of title to the goods, and all the information related to the goods. Sometimes the terms of sale will be included on the Bill.

- **Ex-works**. The price of an item at the site of manufacture. The purchaser accepts all responsibility for organising transport to their required location.
- **Free alongside**. The price of the item includes transport to the port of loading. The purchaser has to pay all cots beyond that, insurance, loading on to the vessel and subsequent costs.
- **Free on board**. The price of the item includes all costs associated with getting the item on board a vessel.
- **Delivered**. The price of the item includes all delivery costs until they are delivered and accepted by the customer.

The pricing structure can be further refined by including greater or lesser elements of the transportation operation, such as insurance cover for the whole journey.

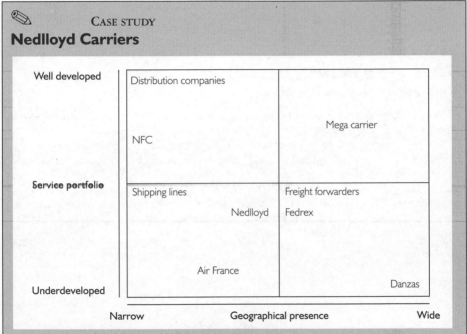

CASE STUDY
Nedlloyd Carriers

Figure 9.14 Mega-carrier classification (Cooper, Brown and Peters, 1991, p. 204)

Nedlloyd is one carrier approaching mega status. Figure 9.14 illustrates its relative position in terms of product range and geographical presence. Its strengths and weaknesses include:

- Potential for global logistics – liner shipping and road freight interests.
- Originates from a country with a powerful trading base.
- Good reputation with Dutch hauliers.
- Dutch business culture perceived to be neutral.
- Underdeveloped in some areas – express and dedicated work.
- Coverage of EC not complete.
- Financial and managerial resources are stretched because of rapid expansion.

Transportation management

Transportation issues are often the subjects of debate in local and national forums.

- The desire of the EU to create an integrated European rail network is influenced by structural issues such as differing track gauges, and signalling systems, between countries.
- The environmental effects of companies choosing to operate JIT methods of production. This could increase the number of journeys, unless it is managed effectively. One solution is the use of nominated carriers.
- The development of new ships that can reduce journey times between countries as a consequence of increased global trade and the need to reduce logistics costs.
- The rise of the mega carrier.

A number of changes are occurring within the transportation industry. The changes are being prompted by deregulation, political, economic and social influences.

 CASE STUDY

Rail track standardisation

The EU is keen to create a unified transport system. This has many implications and many costs. The rail network for example has different gauges of rail track. In the 1830s there were 5 gauges of rail track in England ranging in size from 1.3 to 2.1 m. The standard gauge in England is now 1.5 m. Australia created a standard track only in June 1995. In Europe there are four different power systems and three different signalling systems, illustrated in Figure 9.15. Trains need to be designed to work within these different standards. The information systems involved in traffic need to be standardised. The telematics infrastructure that is being created will cost the EU £7.8b over the next 10 years.

- 1 DC 3000v
- 2 DC <1500v
- 3 AC 25kv/50hz
- 4 AC 15kv/16hz

Figure 9.15 European railway electrification

CASE STUDY

The tuned-in traveller

A consortium of German companies (Siemens, BMW, Philips, and Daimler) will, by the year 2005, have developed the personal trip organiser, PTA. This system will connect numerous databases containing information on railway timetables, hotel room availability, car hire availability and so on. The information will be updated with on-line current information relating to delays and congestion. Cars will be equipped with satellite navigation and geographical information systems (GIS) to pin-point the exact position of the vehicle. An executive travelling from Liverpool to Lisbon for a meeting will be plugged into the system. At Leicester the system warns them of a two-hour delay on the M1 at Luton. The system will advise that the best way to meet the deadline would be to drive to the Railway station at Loughborough catch the 11:14 am train to London. It will book the tickets arrange for a hire car/taxi to the airport and provide a hotel booking. The implications for business, for freight forwarder say, are that the quickest and cheapest passage for products will be found. Information on availability of warehouse, truck, vessel, and rail space will be available.

Green logistics

Transport is the main area of logistics that suffers from criticism on environmental grounds: pollution, road damage, building programmes and noise are causes of local disputes. The site of the warehouse, or production centre needs to reflect these possibilities. Research into fuel type, efficiency and pollution are of interest to the transport company. Cooper and Tweddle (1990) show that fuel consumption decreases at night by about 5% and if aerodynamic aids are fitted to a vehicle, by another 5%. This coupled with the better use of assets is making some companies move towards 24-hr warehousing and transport. Intelligent warehousing systems reduce the labour costs associated with 24-hr working.

JIT is in danger of dying through choking on congested roads. Just-in-time deliveries are costly to the environment, because of the increase in fuel consumption due to the increase in road congestion. For some companies, it may be a good marketing ploy to actually state that JIT deliveries are not done on environmental grounds. Good planning and the effective use of transport may well take the place of the JIT supply, but other JIT principles (such as eliminating waste) will still be as valid. If companies were truly altruistic, they would already be recognising that JIT supply is in many respects wasteful. One way in which companies will get round frequent small deliveries will be to use nominated carriers who will collect materials from a number of suppliers, but this will inevitably increase lead-times.

Global supply chain relationships

This section examines the complex topic of supply chain relationships. The supply chain concept extends the idea of integration of logistics activities such as procurement, manufacturing support and physical distribution to include customers and suppliers. The supply chain perspective shifts the channel arrangements from a loosely linked group of independent business to a co-ordinated effort focused on increased competitiveness. These broad-based channel structures and dynamics can go beyond national boundaries.

Global logistics

World trade is being influenced by a number of factors. Communication technology has improved so that it is easier to promote products globally. It is also easier to communicate with related organisations.

Trade barriers are being removed as in the development of the General Agreement on Tariffs and Trade (GATT) agreement and the European Union (EU) initiatives. The US/Canada agreement is of similar importance to those countries and similar trade deals have been made between America and Mexico under the Macuiladora scheme.

The Single European Market has removed the physical, technical, and fiscal barriers to trade in the European Union countries. The European Union itself is expanding; countries that are currently under the European Free Trade Association (EFTA), which is largely Scandinavian countries and Comecon, which is largely eastern European Countries are being included in the Union.

The Treaty of Rome, the document that laid the foundation for the European Community, has specific sections devoted to a **common transport policy**. Some of the provisions of the policy are:

1. That common rules shall apply.
2. Member states cannot introduce legislation that will interfere detrimentally with carriers used by other member states. For example the UK has expressed concern that minibuses for passenger transport should be fitted with seatbelts; this involved a rule change that legally needs to be sanctioned by the European Parliament.
3. Tariffs shall reflect the economic state of the transport industry.
4. Transportation in any form should not be subsidised. Unless authorised by the union (e.g. East Germany).
5. The rules only apply to inland transportation, not air or sea.

The European Community is keen to develop an international rail network. This will require central planning that will co-ordinate the various rail bodies. An important consideration for Britain will be in the impact of the Channel Tunnel. The tunnel links England, with the mainland of Europe. Four hundred trains per day will travel through the tunnel (20/hr) and an estimated 7 million tonnes of freight cargo will be carried annually. How the tunnel will affect the UK transport policy, if at all, remains to be seen. Rail is environmentally friendly, but requires a lot of capital investment to bring it in line with mainland European standards. In our free market, it is cheaper now to use road transport, hence rail has lost volume and the costs of using it are now high. Without some form of subsidy, its use, as a major transport option within this country seems remote at least in the short term. The completion of the tunnel is prompting some firms to examine their location and the economics of producing in this country.

Asia is emerging as an important player in the global economy. In the past they have primarily been involved with the supply of raw materials but they are now involved with much of the processing of these into finished products. Countries such as Japan are transplanting their operations into the Western economy. China is becoming more open to

Western ideas and is inevitably going to be influenced to some extent by them. Singaporean companies are establishing bases in South Eastern China that will lead to greater opportunities for other companies from other nations.

World trade and logistics expenditure is expanding rapidly, more than twice as fast as world output. Global markets are a direct consequence of the acknowledgement and homogenisation of global needs and wants. Communications enable people around the world to learn of and express their need for many of the same products. Australians are just as likely to want to eat peanut butter from America as they will drink vodka from Poland. Many companies have a global presence, partly because location decisions require them to be close to sources of supply, or markets. A multinational company is distinct from a global company as each location may be serving a distinct market need. Global companies try to create the homogeneous market and then serve the needs of that market from the most advantageous world-wide locations. Global companies create standardised yet customised marketing, shortened product life cycles of say one year, greater out-sourcing, and better co-ordination of manufacturing activities and strategies. A global strategy is formulated where the company strategically sources materials and components world-wide, and select warehouses and distribution centres in global locations. There are a number of important differences between national and international supply chain management.

- **Lead times**. Whereas in national systems one might be working to lead times of three to five days, in global terms we are talking about lead times of three to four weeks. In some industries lead times of one to two years are not uncommon (for example in pharmaceuticals). The time difference is due to: communication problems, customs formalities, time zones, scheduling for shipping, and increased distance.
- **Operations**. Culture, language, product segmentation, transportation and inventory dynamics all tend to decrease the effectiveness of the operations function. In Europe alone language differences mean than inventory levels for a single product are increased if the product requires labelling in separate languages. There are few integrated global transportation companies, and shipping itself does not lend itself to establishing alliances and relationships. (Reliable shipping companies often belong to a Conference, a collection of shipping companies. Whilst a firm may undertake negotiations with an individual shipper, the contract itself will be with the conference the shipper belongs to.)
- **Systems integration**. Information is an essential aspect of effective supply chain management. Information systems have evolved to meet the needs of the domestic economy. European integration of EDI systems is a goal of the EU, a world-wide standard EDI system is still some time away.
- **Alliances**. Alliances are of crucial importance to global operations. Without alliances, the firm would find itself attempting to manage a multitude of contacts with retailers, wholesalers, suppliers and service providers. International alliances would provide greater access to markets, expertise as well as reducing the risks involved. In some countries it is impossible to establish an operation without a national partner.

Summary of key points

- Supply chain management is concerned with the efficient and effective management of materials used in the transformation process.

- The concept of SCM has evolved from both military and business practices.
- The management of the supply chain relies increasingly on alliances and strategic relationships.
- The pipeline concept illustrates the main activities and interactions within the supply, namely, suppliers, inbound logistics, operations, outbound logistics, and customers.
- Changes in the environment, such as economic, political technological and social issues have an important influence of the development of supply chain strategies.
- The importance of SCM varies with the type of company, but all firms need to be aware of the variety and type of relationships that exist within the supply chain, so that they can be managed effectively.
- Purchasing is important to a firm as it has a direct bearing on profitability.
- Purchasing is important as it links the firm with suppliers, who have an influence on the success of the company.
- Materials handling is important as it can waste resources. It needs to be managed to reduce time, distance, and human interaction.
- Warehousing is important as it adds value and customer service.
- Transportation is important, because many items are located away from the point of consumption.

   CASE STUDY

Caremore Hospital

The National Health Service spends approximately £125m per annum on sterile services. This equates to about £275 per bed and £28 per operation, each district spending about £865,000 per annum. Caremore Hospital in Illshire is a large general hospital that acts as a focal point for health care for the surrounding district. The hospital is reviewing its sterile services provision. Caremore's general manager, William (call me Willy) Getwell, has contracted some consultants to advise on the future strategy for the service. Willy is concerned that its supply chain management could be improved in various areas. At present two aspects are being investigated. Firstly the supply of sterile dressings that are used during surgery, within the accident and emergency department and routinely on wards. Secondly the use of reusable items, such as surgical instruments. The sterile service unit (SSU) works two eight-hour shifts, with eight staff on each shift. The unit is managed by an ex-ward sister, who reports to the hospital's hotel manager, R.T. Lett. Mr Lett is due to retire next year. Although the hospital currently produces much of its own requirements, it is possible to buy-in dressing packs from suppliers such as Smith & Nephew.

The majority of sterile dressings are manufactured within the SSU at the hospital. The SSU obtains its raw materials from a regional supplies depot (RSD), which supplies a range of items, such as swabs, cotton wool balls, and paper bags, as well as food items to all of the hospitals in the region. The RSD obtains the materials direct from manufacturers, and claims to offer value in the form of economies of scale. Within the SSU two manufacturing lines are used.

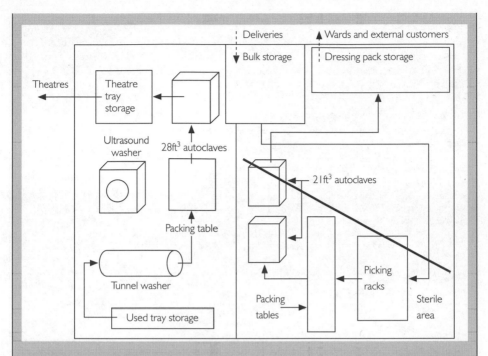

Figure 9.16 Caremore Hospital SSU layout

Figure 9.16 illustrates the process. The dotted lines indicate material flow. Raw materials are used to create dressing packs. A dressing pack will consist of a number of items that nurses and doctors have identified as being needed for certain operations and injury types. For example a nose pack would consist of some cotton wool balls, a clamp, two rubber bungs, some swabs, some cotton buds and be wrapped in a paper bag. The cost of this pack would be £1.56. A list of some of these and the average usage is shown in Table 9.5. The hospital manufactures 676 different types of pack.

Table 9.5 Stock in sterile pack store

Description	Cost (£)	Holding cost (£)	Average use	Standard deviation	Re-order level
Basic Dressing	0.49	0.074	74	57	456
Catheterisation	0.66	0.099	46	35	368
Oral Hygiene	0.53	0.079	28	22	224
Nose Pack	1.56	0.205	4	3	32
Normal Delivery	1.27	0.191	67	52	536
Basic Maternity	0.96	0.144	35	27	280
A/E Dressing	0.89	0.134	253	194	2024
Chest Aspiration	1.27	0.195	3	2	25
Plastic Stitch R	1.060	0.159	9	7	72
Minor ENT	2.040	0.215	140	108	1120

The other main operation of the SSU is in the recycling of reusable items, such as surgical operating trays. The hospital has over half a million pounds invested in instruments. The contents of one such tray in shown in Table 9.6. The hospital has 180 different tray types and 890 trays. Table 9.7 shows a sample of trays and their weekly usage.

Table 9.6 Contents of orthopaedic general set

Instruments	Quantity
S. Well Artey FCP COF B/J 6	10
Kochers Art FCP CVD 15 cm	1
Kochers Art FCP CVD 20 cm	1
Janson Gouge FCP 18 cm	1
Ramsey Diss FCP plain 18 cm	1
Braithwaites Th Diss 1/2 FCP	2
Bonney Diss FCP 1/2 th 18 cm	2
Mayo towel grip	6
Hills nasel rasp	1
Lanenbeck Ret 4.5cm x 1.3 cm	2
Volkman Scoop D/E medium	1

Table 9.7

Tray description	Cost (£)	Number of sets	Weekly usage
Basic orthopeadic	123	17	6
Cardiac catheter	60	21	0
Cardiac bypass	250	10	12
Medium	110	25	20
Child hernia	70	2	6
Small	80	23	21
Large	120	34	33
Plastic basic	70	19	19
Tracheostomy	12	6	2
Cystoscopy	6	6	10

Take on the role of the consultant and respond to the following questions:

1. What factors do you need to consider when reviewing the provision of these services?
2. What choices or options are open to Caremore, Is Just-In-Time an appropriate strategy?
3. If the hospital continues with its own manufacturing process how could this be improved?
4. How might the hospital optimise its use of theatre trays?

Case study

Private Eye

John Dory is managing director of an expanding electronic consumer goods firm, Private Eye. They manufacture a revolutionary new surveillance system that is cheap and easy to install. John's firm although relatively small is experiencing very fast growth and he is struggling to maintain quality and meet demand. Consultants have been advising the firm on general operations improvements. Last week John sent the following note to the consultants:

To: S.C. MANCON (consultants)
From:J. Dory
Date: 12/9/98
Subject: Supply chain improvements
Ref: SCM 1

Company	Mean lead time (days)	Reliability (lead time)	Order quantity satisfied
Minunasu	12	85%	90%
Reading Plastics	18	75%	70%
Finner	20	80%	100%
Charlie's Engineering	17	85%	75%
Tawdry Corporation	21	70%	85%

We source our materials from both local and remote businesses. Some of them small like ours and others which are part of multinational companies. We have had problems in the past relating to delivery reliability, and material quality. I suspect that we could partly be to blame for this, as far as our checking and storage procedures are concerned. I recently saw a television programme on strategic alliances between companies. The programme specifically mentioned the liaison between The Body Shop and the Lane Transport Group. Could such alliances be useful to our firm?

We have collected some information on the supply chain, which includes a blueprint of the supply system from supplier to dispatch. This process is typical for all our suppliers. A transcript of a conversation with Pauleen Pike, who is responsible for administration, is also provided. Pauleen works part-time Thursdays and Fridays and deals with all orders, and the accounts.

Figure 9.17 illustrates the order process. Customer orders are received by post, or by telephone. The order is then checked against customer records. If it is a regular customer, such as a retailer, then credit details are entered on the form. (Some retailers are operating on a sale or return system, others on a purchase system.) If the customer is a debtor then delivery is not authorised until they are contacted further.

If the order is cleared for preparation, then an invoice is prepared and a packing note is sent to the finished goods inventory store. The packing note indicates the quantity and types of unit required, and customer address details. The units are packed using expanded polystyrene loose fill, plastic bags and cardboard boxes. The invoice is

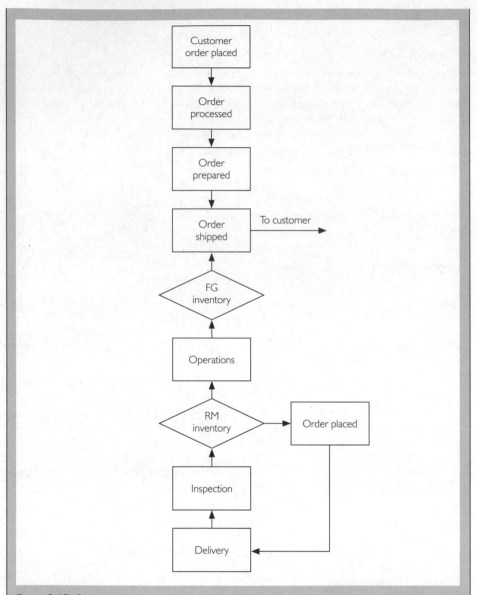

Figure 9.17 Order process

placed inside the box. The delivery details are attached to the box in a clear plastic wallet.

The order is normally delivered using Parcelforce, part of the Post Office. If the order is required urgently then an express delivery firm, such as Securicor, is used; this cost is passed on to the customer.

A stock check is made visually and, if a model appears to be getting low then, more are made to bring the numbers up again. Material is collected from the raw material store as required. This has led to a number of problems with some items running out quicker than expected. We have started to keep a record of their usage to try to avoid shortages in these.

When inventories of materials are low then an order is placed for more. This is invariably done using the telephone. Most of the companies deliver within a lead time of three weeks. On delivery the quantity is checked.

Pauleen Pike made the following comments about the system.

'When I arrive on Thursday my first task is to untangle the mess that the office seems to get in when I'm not there. We started getting problems a while ago, with every Tom, Dick, or Harry dealing with the telephone orders. They would take the order on a scrap of paper, then leave it on the desk for me to find. As a result orders were lost, or information was missing on the paper. The form has helped in this, but it is still not very good, because the orders get mixed up with other messages, such as complaints about the units, or late deliveries. Once I've checked the orders, I make an estimate of the material required to make them. I have a rough idea of the amount of materials in the store, which I keep on a card index system. If the amount used takes us below a certain level, then I will order some more. For some reason that I cannot work out, the inventory records on the index system are always wrong, but I have not the time to do a stock check every week; as a result we sometimes run out of materials. My biggest problem is dealing with complaints, and these seem to be increasing. The majority of complaints seem to be related to late delivery of orders. We normally offer delivery within a week. Another source of complaints are damaged, or faulty units. The damage to units is primarily cracking of the VDU screen case. The problems with faulty units seem to be the sensor heads not working, or parts missing from the unit. When the units are returned the workforce seem to get most of them working by stripping the sensor heads down then using the compressed air hose on them. Roger Carp says that the only thing wrong with them is dust getting in, either during construction, or in transport. With the increase in the number of orders we have been getting recently we should get a proper system of control in place that clearly identifies what we expect from our suppliers, and what we intend to offer our customers.'

Take on the role of the consultants and advise John Dory on a possible supply chain strategy you may wish to advise on. Comment on the materials management and control system. Should the firm develop a strategic partnership with any of the suppliers?

Project: Supply chain description exercise

Once a system has been described it is possible to determine why the system works well, or poorly and to recommend improvements. Describe and analyse a supply chain system with which you are familiar, for example, a shop, restaurant, transport system, hospital, are possible examples. In doing so answer the following questions:

1. What are the important aspects of the supply chain?
2. How are inventories controlled?
3. Create a flow chart of part of the delivery system. In other words describe in diagrammatic form the processes that enable the business to deliver its product to the customer. The flow chart should indicate where the system may fail and should form the basis for much of your analysis.
4. Can the customer/provider interface be changed to include more technology, or more self service?
5. What measures are being used to evaluate and measure the service?

The report should be in the region of 3,000 words, with appropriate analysis, tables and figures. Tip: imagine you are a consultant with a brief to evaluate the current supply chain strategy of the business and offer recommendations to improve its operation. This is an academic exercise and will be judged on its academic rigour in terms of analysis, criticism and research methods, as well as its application to logistics theory and management practice. A good report will contain the following elements:

- clear aims objectives and methodology;
- well structured and presented in a report format;
- evidence of a range of secondary research, using texts, journals, magazines, newspapers, and computer-based information sources;
- be critical and analytical;
- offer alternative original opinions;
- illustrate issues with real life examples, as well as a clear focus on a particular operation within an organisation.

Exercises _____

1. What are the issues facing Bulgarian companies trying to compete on the world market from a supply chain perspective?
2. What service issues do firms who supply beverages to customers at a garden party face?
3. What strategies are open to a company to provide accurate deliveries on time to customers who are not technologically aware?
4. How might the JIT supplier philosophy be beneficial to a hospital?
5. What are the differences between logistics and supply chain management?
6. What customer service issues, from a supply chain perspective, would be important for the following type of company?
   (a) bank
   (b) restaurant

(c) oil refinery

(d) car manufacturer

(e) cosmetics company

7 The transport manager of a major personal computer manufacturer is determining the future transportation policy for the company. The average value of the PC's is £500, each PC is packaged separately and occupies 0.25 m³ of space. The transportation costs per 100 miles per m³ and optimum capacities are: Truck £6 (100 computers), Rail £4 (500 computers), Water £2 (1000 computers). The lead times are 2 days, 4 days and 10 days respectively. The inventory cost is £2.5 per day per computer. The firm sells 1000 computers per week to customers an average of 500 miles away. All of the customers have access to all three modes of transport. Which mode should the manager favour and why?

References

Barlow, G., JIT implementation within a service industry: a case study, *Proc. 2nd Int. Symp. Logistics*, The University of Nottingham (1995).

Cherret, K., Building customer/supplier relationships, *The Financial Times Handbook of Management*, ed. Crainer, S., Pitman Publishing (1995) p. 403.

Cooper, J., Brown, M. and Peters, M., *European Logistic*, Blackwell Business (1991) p. 103, 204.

Cooper, J.C. and Tweddle, G., Distribution round the clock, Cooper J.C, ed., *Logistics and Distribution Planning: Strategies for Management* (revised edition) London: Kogan Page (1990).

Cowe, R., Supermarkets give manufacturers fright with own brand of success, *The Guardian*, (28th Oct, 1992) p. 13.

Coyle, J., Bardi, E. and Langley, J., *The Management of Business Logistics* 6th ed, West Publishing (1996) pp. 7, 114, 483.

Gattorna, J., Adding value through managing the logistics chain, in *The Gower Handbook of Logistics and Distribution Management*, ed. Gattorna J., 4th ed., Gower Publishing Company (1994) p. 7.

Kreth, F., *Handbook of Solid Waste Management* New York: McGraw-Hill (1994).

LaLonde, B. and Zinszer, P., *Customer Service: Meaning and Measurements*, Chicago: Council of Logistics Management (1976).

LaLonde, B., Cooper, M. and Noordewier, *Customer Service: A Management Perspective*, Chicago: Council of Logistics Management (1988) p. 5.

Miller, K., Listening to shoppers' voices, *Business Week*, Special Issue – Reinventing America (1992) p. 69.

Porter, M., *Competitive Advantage: Creating and Sustaining Superior Performance*, New York: The Free Press and London: Collier Macmillan Publishers (1985).

Slack, N., Chambers, S., Harland, C., Harrison, A. and Johnston, R., *Operations Management*, London:. Pitman Publishing (1995) p. 536.

Tomes, A. and Hayes, M., *Operations Management: Principles and Practices*, Prentice-Hall (1993) p.99.

Further reading

Crainer, S., *The Financial Times Handbook of Management*, Pitman Publishing (1995).

LaLonde, B., Cooper, M. and Noordewier, *Customer Service: A management perspective*, Chicago: Council of Logistics Management.

Motor Transport, 25 October 1990.

10 Project management

Objectives

By the end of this chapter, you should be able to:

- understand the main elements of the project management approach;
- evaluate how projects can relate to the structure of an organisation;
- understand the role of the project manager;
- understand the major network analysis techniques;
- undertake the construction of a network diagram using the activity-on-node method;
- understand the benefits and limitations of the network analysis approach.

Projects are unique, one-time operations designed to accomplish a specific set of objectives in a limited time-frame. Examples of projects include a building construction or introducing a new service or product to the market. Large projects may consist of many activities and must therefore be carefully planned and co-ordinated if a project is to meet cost and time targets. However, not all aspects of implementation can be controlled or planned, but the chance of success can be increased by anticipating potential problems and by applying corrective strategies. Network analysis can be used to assist the project planning and control activities.

Project management activities

The project management process includes the following main elements:

- estimate
- plan
- control.

Estimate

At the start of the project a broad plan is drawn up assuming unlimited resources. Once estimates have been made of the resources required to undertake these activities it is then possible to compare overall project requirements with available resources. If highly specialised resources are required then the project completion date may have to be set to ensure these resources are not overloaded. This is a **resource-constrained** approach. Alternatively there may be a need to complete a project in a specific time-frame (e.g. due date specified by customer). In this case alternative resources may have to be utilised (e.g. sub-contractors) to ensure timely project completion. This is a **time-constrained** approach.

The next step is to generate estimates for the time and resources required to undertake each task defined in the project. This information can then be used to plan what resources are required and what activities should be undertaken over the life cycle of the project. Statistical methods should be used when the project is large (and therefore complex) or novel. This allows the project team to replace a single estimate of duration with a range within which they are confident the real duration will lie. This is particularly useful for the early stage of the project when uncertainty is greatest. The accuracy of the estimates can also be improved as their use changes from project evaluation purposes to approval and day-to-day project control. The PERT approach described later in this chapter allows optimistic, pessimistic and most likely times to be specified for each task from which a probabilistic estimate of project completion time can be computed.

Once the activities have been identified and their resource requirements estimated it is necessary to define their relationship to one another. There are some activities that can only begin when other activities have been completed. This activity is termed a **serial relationship** and is shown as:

$$A \rightarrow B \rightarrow C$$

The execution of other activities may be totally independent and thus they have a **parallel relationship** shown as:

$$A \rightarrow$$
$$B \rightarrow$$
$$C \rightarrow$$

For a project of a reasonable size there may be a range of alternative plans which may meet the project objectives. Project management software can be used to assist in choosing the most feasible schedule by recalculating resource requirements and timings for each operation.

Plan

The purpose of the planning stage is to ensure that the project objectives of cost, time and quality are met. It does this by estimating both the level and timing of resources needed over the project duration. These steps may need to be undertaken repeatedly in a complex project due to uncertainties and to accommodate changes as the project progresses. The planning process does not eradicate the need for the experience of the project manager in anticipating problems or the need for skill in dealing with unforeseen and novel incidences during project execution. However, the use of plans which can be executed sensibly will greatly improve the performance of the project.

The project management method uses a systems approach to dealing with a complex task in that the components of the project are broken down repeatedly into smaller tasks until a manageable chunk is defined. Each task is given its own cost, time and quality objectives. It is then essential that responsibility is assigned to achieving these objectives for each particular task. This procedure should produce a **work breakdown structure** (WBS) which shows the hierarchical relationship between the project tasks.

Control

Project control involves the monitoring of the project objectives of cost, time and quality as the project progresses. It is important to monitor and assess performance as the project progresses in order that the project does not deviate from plans to a large extent. Milestones or time events are defined during the project when performance against objectives can be measured. The amount of control will be dependent on the size of the project. Larger projects will require development of control activities from the project leader to team leaders. Computer project management packages can be used to automate the collection of project progress data and production of progress reports.

The type of project structure required will be dependent on the size of the team undertaking the project. Projects with up to six team members can simply report directly to a project leader at appropriate intervals during project execution. For larger projects requiring up to 20 team members it is usual to implement an additional tier of management in the form of team leaders. The team leader could be responsible for either a phase of the development or a type of work. For any structure it is important that the project leader ensures consistency across development phases or development areas as appropriate. For projects with more than 20 members it is likely that additional management layers will be needed in order to ensure that no one person is involved with too much supervision.

The two main methods of reporting the progress of a project are by written reports and verbally at meetings of the project team. It is important that a formal statement of progress is made in written form, preferably in a standard report format, to ensure that everyone is aware of the current project situation. This is particularly important when changes to specifications are made during the project. In order to facilitate two-way communication between team members and team management, regular meetings should be arranged by the project manager. These meetings can increase the commitment of team members by allowing discussion of points of interest and dissemination of information on how each team's effort is contributing to the overall progression of the project.

Projects and organisational structure

There are three main ways of structuring an organisation. The reasons for choosing a particular structure are outlined below.

The project structure

This consists of an organisation which not only follows a team approach to projects, but has an organisational structure based on teams formed specifically for projects. The approach delivers a high focus on completing project objectives but can involve duplication of resources across teams, an inhibition of diffusion of learning across teams, a lack of hierarchical career structure and less continuity of employment.

Examples of organisations which utilise this approach include many professional service firms such as management consultancies.

The functional structure

Here a project is given to the most appropriate functional department. Thus the organisational structure remains in the standard hierarchical form.

The approach ensures there is limited disruption to the normal organisational activities but can lead to a lack of focus on project objectives. A lack of co-ordination can result, especially if outside help is required and there can be a failure to meet customer needs if other departmental activities are taking priority over project work.

The matrix structure

Here a series of project teams are overlaid on a functional structure in an effort to provide a balance between functional and project needs. There are three different forms of matrix structure:

- **Functional matrix**. Here the project manager reports to functional heads to co-ordinate staff across departments.
- **Balanced matrix**. Here the project manager manages the project jointly with functional heads.
- **Project matrix**. Here functional staff are seconded to a project team for a fixed period of time.

The role of the project manager

The project manager bears the ultimate responsibility for the success or failure of the project. Included in the functions of the project manager is to provide clearly defined goals to project participants and to ensure that adequately skilled and experienced human resources are employed on the project. Throughout the project it is necessary to manage the elements of time, cost and quality. Because of the unique nature of projects and the potentially high number of interrelated tasks involved an effective way is needed to communicate project plans and progress across the project team. Network analysis methods can provide a valuable aid to the monitoring and control of projects and will be described below.

Network analysis

This section describes the major stages in the construction of the critical path method (CPM) and programme evaluation and review technique (PERT) project networks. The CPM method described here was developed by DuPont during the 1950s to manage plant construction. The PERT approach was developed by the US Navy during the development of the Polaris Submarine Launched Ballistic Missile System during the same decade (Sapolsky, 1972). The main difference between the approaches is the ability of PERT to take into consideration uncertainty in activity durations.

The first two stages of network analysis of identifying project activities and estimating activity durations relate to the estimated element of project management. The remaining stages relate to the plan and control elements.

Identifying project activities

In order to undertake network analysis it is necessary to break down the project into a number of identifiable activities or tasks. This enables individuals to be assigned responsibility to particular tasks which have a well-defined start and finish time. Financial and resource planning can also be conducted at the task level and co-ordinated by the project manager who must ensure that each task manager is working to the overall project objectives and not maximising the performance of particular tasks at the expense of the whole project.

The project is controlled by allocating the performance objectives of time, cost and quality with each activity.

Estimating activity durations

The next stage is to retrieve information concerning the duration of the tasks involved in the project. This can be collated from a number of sources, such as documentation, observation, interviewing etc. Obviously the accuracy of the project plan will depend on the accuracy of these estimates. There is a trade-off between the cost of collecting information on task durations and the cost of an inaccurate project plan.

Identifying activity relationships

It is necessary to identify any relationships between tasks in the project. For instance a particular task may not be able to begin until another task has finished. Thus the task waiting to begin is dependent on the former task. Other tasks may not have a dependent relationship and can thus occur simultaneously.

Critical path diagrams are used extensively to show the activities undertaken during a project and the dependencies between these activities. Thus it is easy to see that activity C for example can only take place when activity A and activity B has completed. Once a network diagram has been constructed it is possible to follow a sequence of activities, called a path, through the network from start to end. The length of time it takes to follow the path is the sum of all the durations of activities on that path. The path with the longest duration gives the project completion time. This is called the critical path because any change in duration in any activities on this path will cause the whole project duration to either become shorter or longer. Activities not on the critical path will have a certain amount of slack time in which the activity can be delayed or the duration lengthened and not affect the overall project duration. The amount of slack is a function of the difference between the path duration the activity is on and the critical path duration. By definition all activities on the critical path have zero slack. It is important to note that there must be at least one critical path for each network and there may be several.

There are two methods of constructing critical path diagrams: **activity-on-arrow** (AOA) method, where the arrows represent the activities and activity on node (AON) method, where the nodes represent the activities. The issues involving which one to utilise will be discussed later. The following description on critical path analysis will use the AON method.

Drawing the network diagram

For the activity-on-node notation each activity task is represented by a node with the format as given in Figure 10.1.

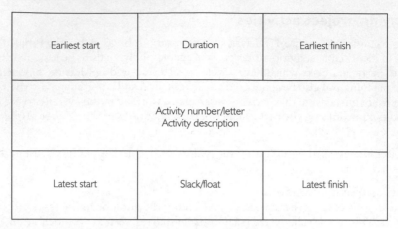

Earliest start	Duration	Earliest finish
	Activity number/letter Activity description	
Latest start	Slack/float	Latest finish

Figure 10.1 Activity on node notation

Thus a completed network will consist of a number of nodes connected by lines, one for each task, between a start and end node as in Figure 10.2.

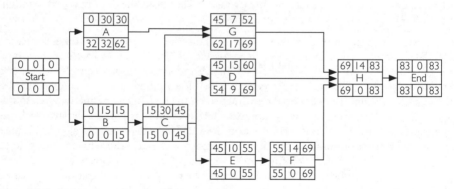

Figure 10.2 Activity on node network diagram

Calculating the earliest start/finish times (forward pass)

From the duration of each task and the dependency relationship between the tasks it is possible to estimate the earliest start and finish time for each task as follows. (You move left to right along the network, forward through time.)

1. Assume the start (i.e. first) task begins at time = 0.
2. Calculate the earliest finish time where: *Earliest finish = Earliest start + Duration.*
3. Calculate the earliest start time of the next task where: *Earliest start = Earliest finish of task immediately before.*
4. If there is more than one task immediately before take the task with the latest finish time to calculate the earliest start time for the current task.
5. Repeat Steps 2 and 3 for all tasks.

Calculating the latest start/finish times (backward pass)

It is now possible to estimate the latest start and finish time for each task as follows. (You move right to left along the network, backward through time.)

1. Assume the end (i.e. last) task end time is the earliest finish time (unless the project end time is given).
2. Calculate the latest start time where: *Latest start = Latest finish – Duration*.
3. Calculate the latest finish time of the previous task where: *Latest finish = Latest start of task immediately after*.
4. If there is more than one task immediately after take the task with the earliest start time to calculate the latest finish time for the current task.
5. Repeat Steps 2 and 3 for all tasks.

Calculating the slack/float times

The slack or float value is the difference between the earliest start and latest start (or earliest finish and latest finish) times for each task. To calculate the slack time:

1. *Slack = Latest start – Earliest start OR Slack = Latest finish – Earliest finish*.
2. Repeat Step 1 for all tasks.

Identifying the critical path

Any tasks with a slack time of 0 must obviously be undertaken on schedule at the earliest start time. The critical path is the pathway connecting all the nodes with a zero slack time. There must be at least one critical path through the network, but there can be more than one. The significance of the critical path is that if any node on the path finishes later than the earliest finish time, the overall network time will increase by the same amount, putting the project behind schedule. Thus any planning and control activities should focus on ensuring tasks on the critical path remain within schedule.

WORKED EXAMPLE

A particular project comprises the following activities.

Activity	Duration (days)	Immediate predecessor(s)
A	30	–
B	15	–
C	30	B
D	15	C
E	10	C
F	14	E
G	7	A,C
H	14	D,F,G

(a) Draw an AON diagram for this project.
(b) Calculate the earliest start, earliest finish, latest start, latest finish and slack times for each activity.
(c) Identify the critical path.

SOLUTION
(a) The AON diagram is constructed by using the predecessor information contained in the table to connect the nodes as appropriate. For instance activity G has two predecessors, A and C, so both these nodes must point to the start of activity G. The completed network diagram is shown in Figure 10.2.

(b) The earliest start/finish times are calculated by a forward pass (left to right) through the network. For instance, activity A earliest start = 0, duration = 15, therefore earliest end = 15–0 =15. Activity G, earliest start = 45 (= earliest finish of activities immediately before; A = 30, C = 45).

The latest start/finish times are calculated by a backward pass (right to left) through the network. For instance activity H latest end = 83, duration = 14, therefore latest start = 83 – 14 = 69. Activity C, latest end = 45 (= latest start of task immediately after; G = 62, D = 54, E = 45).

The slack time is the difference between the earliest and latest start times for each activity. For instance slack for G =17 (= latest start – earliest start = 62–45 = 17).

(c) The critical path is the path or paths through the network with all nodes having a zero slack time. In this case there is one critical path; B, C, E, F, H.

The activity-on-arrow method
The format for the activity-on-arrow method will now be described. The symbol used in this method is shown in Figure 10.3.

Rather than considering the earliest and latest start and finish times of the activities directly, this method uses the earliest and latest event times as below:

● *Earliest event time.* This is determined by the earliest time at which any subsequent activity can start.

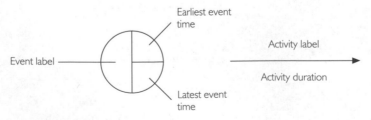

Figure 10.3 Activity-on-arrow notation

- *Latest event time*. This is determined by the latest time at which any subsequent activity can start.

Thus for a single activity the format would be as shown in Figure 10.4.

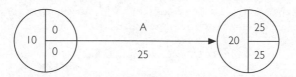

Figure 10.4 Calculating event times for a AOA network

As stated earlier, there are two methods of constructing network diagrams. Historically there has been a greater use of the activity-on-arrow (AOA) method, but the activity-on-node (AON) method is now being recognised as having a number of advantages including:

- Most project management computer software uses the AON approach.
- AON diagrams do not need dummy activities to maintain the relationship logic.
- AON diagrams have all the information on timings and identification within the node box, leading to clearer diagrams.

Identifying schedule constraints

Gantt charts

Although network diagrams are ideal for showing the relationship between project tasks, they do not provide a clear view of which tasks are being undertaken over time and particularly how many tasks may be undertaken in parallel at any one time. The Gantt chart provides an overview for project managers to allow them to monitor project progress against planned progress and so provides a valuable information source for project control.

To draw a Gantt chart manually undertake the following steps:

1. Draw a grid with the tasks along the vertical axis and the time-scale (up to the project duration) along the horizontal axis.
2. Draw a horizontal bar across from the task identifier along the left of the chart starting at the earliest start time and ending at the earliest finish time.
3. Indicate the slack amount by drawing a line from the earliest finish time to the latest finish time.
4. Repeat Steps 2 and 3 for each task.

WORKED EXAMPLE

Draw a Gantt chart for the AON network shown in Figure 10.2.

SOLUTION
Scale the Gantt chart to the project duration (i.e. 83 days) on the horizontal axis and place the activity labels on the vertical axis. Then take the earliest start and finish times for each activity and draw a horizontal bar. Indicate the slack times for relevant activities with a line extending to the latest finish time. (Figure 10.5.)

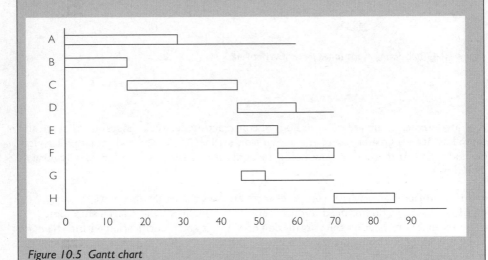

Figure 10.5 Gantt chart

Capacity loading graphs

The basic network diagram assumes that all tasks can be undertaken when required by the earliest start times calculated from the node dependency relationships. However resources required to undertake tasks are usually limited and the duration of an individual task or the number of parallel tasks may be limited. In order to calculate the capacity requirements of a project over time the capacity requirements associated with each task are indicated on the Gantt chart. From this a capacity loading graph can be developed by projecting the loading figures on a time graph.

To manually construct a capacity loading graph undertake the following steps (referring to Figure 10.6):

1. Draw a Gantt chart for the project. Each task bar should indicate the capacity requirements for that task.
2. Draw a capacity loading graph immediately below the Gantt chart. The graph should have an identical horizontal time scale. The vertical axis should be scaled to the estimated highest capacity loading level from the Gantt chart.

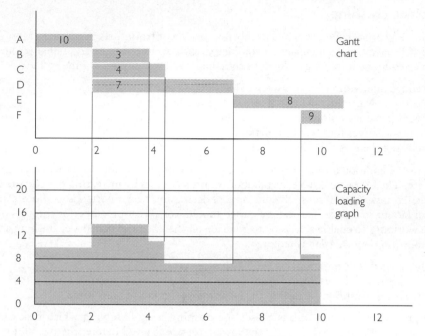

Figure 10.6 Constructing a capacity loading graph from a Gantt chart

3. Start at time 0.
4. Calculate the capacity loading requirement by totalling the loading figures for all parallel tasks. Move along the time-scale until a task finishes or a new task begins.
5. Mark the capacity loading level on the graph,
6. Repeat Steps 4 and 5 for each change in loading figure.

Project cost graphs

The previous discussion has concentrated on the need to schedule and control activities in order to complete the entire project within a minimum time-span. However there are situations in which the project cost is an important factor. If the costs of each project are known then it is possible to produce a cost graph which will show the amount of cost incurred over the life of the project. This is useful in showing any periods when a number of parallel tasks are incurring significant costs leading to the need for additional cash flow at key times. In large projects it may be necessary to aggregate the costs of a number of activities, particularly if they are the responsibility of one department or subcontractor.

As a control mechanism the project manager can collect information on cost to date and percentage completion to date for each task to identify any cost above budget and take appropriate action without delay.

Project crashing

Within any project there will be a number of **time/cost trade-offs** to consider. Most projects will have tasks which can be completed with an injection of additional resources, such as equipment or people. Reasons to reduce project completion time include:

- Reduce high indirect costs associated with equipment.
- Reduce new product development time to market.
- Avoid penalties for late completion.
- Gain incentives for early completion.
- Release resources for other projects.

The use of additional resources to reduce project completion time is termed *crashing the network*. The idea is to reduce overall indirect project costs by increasing direct costs on a particular task. One of most obvious ways of decreasing task duration is to allocate additional labour to a task. This can be either an additional team member or through overtime working. To enable a decision to be made on the potential benefits of crashing a task the following information is required.

- the normal task duration;
- the crash task duration;
- the cost of crashing the task to the crash task duration per unit time.

The process by which a task is chosen for crashing is by observing which task can be reduced for the required time for the lowest cost. As stated before, the overall project completion time is the sum of the task durations on the critical path. Thus it is always necessary to crash a task which is on the critical path. As the duration of tasks on the critical path are reduced however other paths in the network will also become critical. If this happens it will require the crashing process to be undertaken on all the paths which are critical at any one time.

WORKED EXAMPLE

Software Ltd has established a project team to undertake some important market research work. It is possible to reduce the expected or 'normal' times for certain activities in units of 1 week (but not in fractions of a week), but at an extra cost. The relevant information is given below. In addition to the costs shown there is a cost of retainer fees and administration overheads of £10,000 for each week that the project lasts.

(a) What is the normal expected duration of the project, and its total cost? What is the critical path?

(b) What would be the cost of completing the project using the normal durations?

(c) What would be the duration of the project if costs are to be minimised? What is the optimal cost?

Activity	Predecessor	Normal Duration (weeks)	Cost of weeks (£)	Crash Duration (weeks)	Extra cost per week saved (£)
A	–	5	4,000	3	2,000
B	–	4	3,000	4	–
C	A	2	6,000	1	15,000
D	C	4	1,000	4	–
E	B	5	4,000	3	3,000
F	B	5	7,000	1	7,000
G	B,C	4	4,000	2	20,000
H	F	3	5,000	2	10,000

SOLUTION

a) Construct the AON diagram by using the predecessor information in the table. From the diagram the duration of the project is 12 weeks. The critical path is B, F, H. (Figure 10.7.)

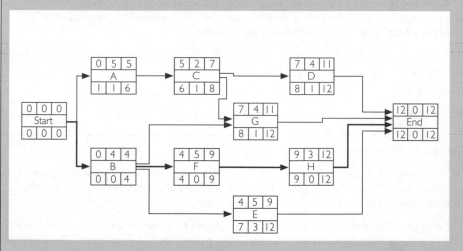

Figure 10.7 AON diagram

(b) The total project cost = Cost of activities + other costs = £34,000 + 12 × £10,000 = £154,000

(c) The minimum cost solution can be found by looking at the normal time solution.

- Ignore B and D because they cannot be reduced.
- Ignore C, G and H because it is too expensive to reduce these activities. This leaves A, E and F.

- F is the only activity on the critical path, so reduce this activity from 5 weeks to 4 weeks.
- This costs £7,000 but saves £10,000, net saving £3,000.
- Reduce E by 2 and A by 2, thus reducing the overall project duration to 9 weeks.
- This costs 2 × £5,000 but saves 2 × £10,000, net saving of £10,000
- No more time can be saved for less than the relevant cost.
- Therefore the optimal duration is 9 weeks, optimal cost is £141,000.

Dealing with uncertainty

Project evaluation and review technique (PERT)

The PERT approach attempts to take into account the fact that most task durations are not fixed but vary when they are executed. A beta probability distribution is used to describe the variability inherent in the processes. The probabilistic approach involves three time estimates for each activity:

- **Optimistic time**. The task duration under the most optimistic conditions.
- **Pessimistic time**. The task duration under the most pessimistic conditions.
- **Most likely time**. The most likely task duration.

As stated the beta distribution is used to describe the task duration variability. To derive the average or expected time for a task duration the following equation is used.

Expected duration = (Optimistic + (4 × Most likely) + Pessimistic)/6

To calculate the degree of uncertainty associated with the duration of a task we computer the task variance.

Variance = (Pessimistic − Optimistic)² /36

By summing the variance for each task on a path through the network it is possible to calculate the variance for the path. The square root of the variance is taken to calculate the standard deviation for a particular network path.

The combination of the expected time and standard deviation for the network path allows managers to compute probabilistic estimates of project completion times. The probability of completing any path through the network in a specified time is calculated using the following equation:

z = *(Specified time − Expected time)/Path standard deviation*
Thus if the specified time = 20 and the expected time = 19, with a path standard deviation of 1.00, z = (20 − 19)/1.00 therefore z =1. Looking up the value of z on a standardised normal curve (Appendix), gives an area under the curve of 0.8413. Thus the probability of finishing the project in 20 weeks = 84.13%.

A point to bear in mind with these estimates is that they only take into consideration the tasks on the critical path and discount the fact that slack on tasks on a non-critical path could delay the project. Therefore the probability that the project will be completed by a specified date is the probability that all paths will be completed by that date, which is the product of the probabilities for all the paths.

WORKED EXAMPLE

Stone Ltd has just accepted a project that can be broken down into the following eight activities. The project must be completed in 141 days, otherwise severe penalties become payable. You are required to find the critical path and to estimate the probability of the critical path time exceeding 141 days.

		Estimated duration (days)		
Activity	Predecessor	Optimistic	Most likely	Pessimistic
A	–	4	11	12
B	–	45	48	63
C	B	13	33	35
D	B	25	29	39
E	A,C	14	21	22
F	D,E	18	32	34
G	A,C	17	19	27
H	G	15	20	25

SOLUTION

First calculate the mean and standard deviation for each activity:

Mean = (optimistic + 4 × most likely + pessimistic) /6

Standard deviation = (pessimistic – optimistic)^2 /36

Activity	Mean	Standard deviation
A	10	1.33
B	50	3
C	30	3.67
D	30	2.33
E	20	1.33
F	30	2.67
G	20	1.67
H	20	1.67

Next draw the AON network diagram (Figure 10.8).

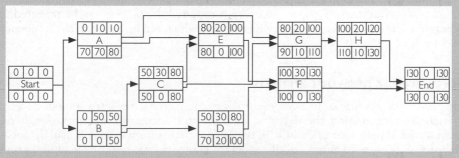

Figure 10.8 AON daigram

This gives a critical path of B, C, E, F giving an expected time of 130 days. Assuming that the distribution of the total project time is normal, the probability of the project time exceeding 141 days can be found using the following table. There are 5 routes through the network.

Route	Mean duration	St. dev.	(141–mean)	z	Prob. within 141 days
BCEF	130	5.6	11	1.96	97.5%
BDF	110	4.6	31	6.63	100%
BCGH	120	5.3	21	3.96	100%
AEF	60	3.3	81	24.55	100%
AGH	50	2.7	91	33.7	100%

Since the only route likely to exceed 141 days is BCEF, the probability that the company will become liable to pay the penalties is $(100 - 97.5) = 2.5\%$.

Project network simulation

In order to use the PERT approach it must be assumed that the paths of a project are independent and the same tasks are not on more than one path. If a task is on more than one path and its actual completion time was much larger than its expected time it is obvious that the paths are not independent. If the network consists of these paths and they are near the critical path time then the results will be invalid.

Simulation can be used to develop estimates of a project's completion time by taking into account all the network paths. Probability distributions are constructed for each task derived from estimates provided by such data collection methods as observation and historical data. A simulation then generates a random number within the probability distribution for each task. The critical path is then determined and the project duration calculated. This procedure is repeated a number of times (maybe more than 100) until there is sufficient data in order to construct a frequency distribution of project times. This distribution can be used to make a probabilistic assessment of the actual project duration. If greater accuracy is required the process can be repeated to generate additional project completion estimates which can be added to the frequency distribution.

Software for network analysis

For projects of any size or in a commercial situation, computer software will be used to assist in constructing the network diagram and calculating network durations. From a critical path network and with the appropriate information it is usually possible for the software to automatically generate Gantt charts, resource loading graphs and cost graphs. A screen display for the Microsoft Project™ charts are shown in Figure 10.9.

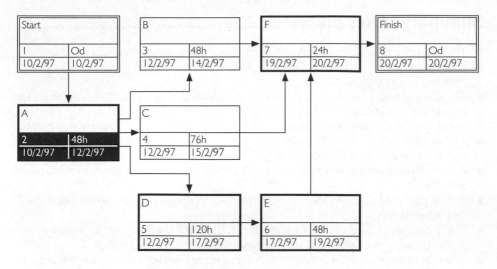

Figure 10.9 Network chart generated by Microsoft Project™

Benefits of the network analysis approach

The following benefits can be attained by using the network analysis approach in project management:

1. It requires a structured analysis of the number and sequence of tasks contained within a project, so aiding understanding of resource requirements for project completion.
2. It provides a number of useful graphical displays which assist understanding of such factors as project dependencies and resource loading.
3. It provides a reasonable estimate of the project duration and the tasks which must be completed on time to meet this duration (i.e. the critical path).
4. It provides a control mechanism to monitor actual progress against planned progress on the Gantt chart.
5. It provides a means of estimating any decrease in overall project time by providing extra resources at any stage.
6. It can be used to provide cost estimates for different project scenarios.

Limitations of the network analysis approach

There are however a number of limitations to bear in mind when using network analysis:

1. Its use is no substitute for good management judgement in such areas as prioritising and selecting suppliers and personnel for the project
2. Any errors in the network such as incorrect dependency relationships or the omission of tasks may invalidate the results.
3. The task times are forecasts and are thus estimates which are subject to error.
4. PERT and simulation techniques may reduce time estimation errors, but at the cost of greater complexity which may divert management time away from more important issues.
5. Time estimates for tasks may be greater than necessary to provide managers with slack to ensure they meet deadlines.

Summary of key points

- The main elements of project management are estimate, plan and control
- Projects are unique, one-time operations designed to accomplish a specific set of objectives in a limited time frame.
- There is a move to using project work in organisations due to the need to bring together people with a wide range of skills across functional boundaries.
- There are three main ways of structuring an organisation; Project, Functional and Matrix.
- The function of the project manager is to provide clearly defined goals and ensure adequate resources are employed on the project.
- A work breakdown structure splits the overall project task into a number of more detailed activities.
- Critical path analysis shows the activities undertaken during a project and the dependencies between them.
- The critical path is identified by making a forward, then a reverse pass, through the network calculating the earliest and latest activity start/finish times respectively.
- The activity-on-node (AON) method provides a number of advantages over the activity-on-arrow (AOA) method of network construction.
- Gantt charts provide an overview of what tasks are being undertaken over time.
- Capacity loading graphs provide an indication of the amount of resource needed for the project over time.
- Cost graphs provide an indication of monetary expenditure over the project period.
- Project crashing consists of reducing overall indirect project costs (e.g. by reducing the project duration) through increasing expenditure on a particular task.
- The PERT approach provides a method of integrating the variability of task durations into the network analysis.
- Project network simulation can be used to estimate the project duration when probability distributions are used to generate task durations.

Exercises

1 For an organisation with which you are familiar evaluate the organisational structure in terms of the project approach.
2 A company has identified the following activities that will make up a project.
   (a) Draw an AON diagram for this project.
   (b) Calculate the earliest start, earliest finish, latest start, latest finish and slack times for each activity.
   (c) Identify the critical path.

Activity	Duration (hours)	Immediate predecessor(s)
A	1	—
B	1	A
C	3	B
D	2	B
E	2	D
F	1	E
G	3	C
H	2	E,F,G
I	1	H
J	1	I
K	1	I
L	1	J,K

3 A company has identified the activities and resource requirements for the following projects.
  (a) Draw an AON diagram for this project.
  (b) Calculate the earliest start, earliest finish, latest start, latest finish and slack times for each activity.
  (c) Identify the critical path.
  (d) Draw a Gantt chart of the project indicating the slack times for each activity.
  (e) Draw a capacity loading graph based on the Gantt chart.

Activity	Duration (days)	Immediate predecessor	Members required (day)
A	2	—	10
B	2	A	3
C	3	A	4
D	5	A	7
E	2	D	8
F	1	B,C,E	9

4 A company has identified the following and activities and resource requirements for the following project.
  (a) Draw an AON diagram for this project.
  (b) Calculate the earliest start, earliest finish, latest start, latest finish and slack times for each activity.
  (c) Identify the critical path.
  (d) Draw a Gantt chart of the project indicating the slack times for each activity.
  (e) Draw a capacity loading graph based on the Gantt chart.

Activity	Duration (days)	Immediate predecessor	Members required (day)
A	3	—	4
B	4	—	3
C	9	—	4
D	4	A,B	7
E	5	B	8
F	6	D,C	9
G	6	E,C	5
H	10	F,G	2

5 The following table describes the introduction of a new product to be manufactured by a firm. The product has been developed and market-tested by the R&D centre, but the manufacturing processes required to produce the product have yet to be developed. The process engineering group has been assigned the responsibility of the design project and have been given a target of 60 days to arrive at an overall process design. Although 60 days seemed very short to the process engineers at first, after some discussion it was concluded that they could probably pull it off because the product and its processes were so similar to the present processing technologies in use at their plant. These activities, their precedence relationships, and their durations were estimated by the engineers as given in the table.

(a) Draw an AON diagram for this project.

(b) Calculate the earliest start, earliest finish, latest start, latest finish and slack times for each activity.

(c) Identify the critical path.

Activity	Description	Precedence	Duration (days)
A	Initial product design study	–	12
B	Preliminary product redesign for production	A	10
C	Preliminary facility redesign for product	A	15
D	Preliminary process technologies study	A	9
E	Facility modification for product redesign	B	6
F	Intermediate facility redesign	C,E	12
G	Intermediate product redesign	B	14
H	Specific process machinery design	B,D	21
I	Final facility, product and process design	F,G,H	10

6 The following outlines the installation of a new computer system in an organisation. There are two main areas involved in this procedure, namely computer hardware order, delivery and installation and computer staff training to operate the system. The relative durations of each of these tasks will determine the overall project length. Different strategies can be applied in both areas to obtain the quickest implementation. Hardware can be delivered and installed by a third-party supplier or installed by people in the organisation after suitable training. On the software side staff can be either trained or specialist staff employed to gain a quicker implementation but with obvious cost consequences. In this case training of present staff was implemented and the network was constructed with the following activities and dependencies.

(a) Draw an AON diagram for this project.

(b) Calculate the earliest start, earliest finish, latest start, latest finish and slack times for each activity.

(c) Identify the critical path.

Activity	Description	Precedence	Estimated duration (days)
A	Select system	–	10
B	Obtain finance	A	30
C	Order equipment	B	7
D	Appoint training staff	B	10
E	Buy software	B	5
F	Delivery	C	28

G	Set up training	C,D	30
H	Prepare data	E,G	20
I	Install equipment	F	14
J	Run courses	G	15
K	Test system	I,J,H	14
L	Commission	K	7

7 The HairCare Company manufactures a range of hair care products, including a range of hair styling gels. A competitor has recently introduced a new hair gel, which in the last six months, has taken a significant share of the market, with adverse effects on HairCare's sales. The management at HairCare has decided that a competitive product must be introduced as quickly as possible and has asked Walter Dobie, the management accountant, to draw up a plan for developing and marketing the new product. As the first step in planning the project, Walter has identified the following major tasks which will be involved in the new product launch. He has also estimated how long each task will take and what other tasks must precede each one.

Activity	Description	Precedence	Estimated duration (weeks)
A	Design new product	–	8
B	Design packaging	–	4
C	Organise production facilities	A	4
D	Obtain production materials	A	2
E	Manufacture trial batch	C,D	3
F	Obtain packaging	B	2
G	Decide on test market area	–	1
H	Package trial batch	E,F	2
I	Distribute product in test area	H,G	3
J	Conduct test market	I	4
K	Assess test market	J	3
L	Plan national launch	K	4

(a) Draw an AON diagram for this project and determine how long it will be before the new product can be launched.

(b) Calculate the slack time available for all the activities.

(c) The time taken to complete tasks A, B, D, K and L is somewhat uncertain and so the following optimistic and pessimistic estimates have also been made to supplement the most likely figure given above. The additional estimates are given below. What now is the expected time until the product can be launched and what is the probability of this time exceeding 35 weeks? (You should assume that the overall project duration follows a normal distribution.)

Activity	Optimistic time (weeks)	Pessimistic time (weeks)
A	5	13
B	2	6
D	1	4
K	2	6
L	2	8

8 A computer system has recently been installed in the accounts department of a manufacturing company. The activities involved in introducing the system are listed below together with their normal durations and costs. Since it would be possible to shorten the overall project duration by crashing certain activities at extra cost, the relevant details are also included. In addition there will be a weekly charge of £2,500 to cover overheads. The crash time represents the shortest time in which the activity can be completed given the use of more costly methods of completion. Assume that it is possible to reduce the normal time to the crash time in steps of one week and that the extra cost will be proportional to the time saved.

(a) Using the normal durations and costs construct an activity network for the introduction of the new computer system. Determine the critical path and associated cost.

(b) Activities E and F have to be supervised by the chief accountant who will not be available for the first seven weeks of the project period. Both activities, however, can be supervised simultaneously. Determine whether or not this will affect the completion date and, if so, state how it will be affected.

(c) Assuming the chief accountant will be available whenever required and that all resources necessary to implement the crashing procedures will also be available, determine the minimum cost of undertaking the project.

Activity	Predecessor	Normal duration (weeks)	Cost (£)	Crash duration (weeks)	Cost (£)
A	–	3	3,000	2	4,000
B	–	6	6,000	–	–
C	A	4	8,000	1	11,000
D	B	2	1,500	–	–
E	A	8	4,000	5	5,000
F	B	4	3,000	2	5,000
G	C,D	2	2,000	–	–
H	F	3	3,000	1	6,000

9 The following case study outlines the erection of a new building. After demolition of the present structure the site is excavated, foundations are sunk and the structural skeleton and concrete structure is formed. The various tasks can be carried out inside and outside the building. Inside the building the plumbing, electrical and heating systems can be installed before the construction of interior partitions and finally the installation of lighting fixtures. Outside the building over the same time period the construction of the exterior skin can take place. The timings and precedence for the relationships are as follows.

(a) Draw an AON diagram for this project.

(b) Calculate the earliest start, earliest finish, latest start, latest finish and slack times for each activity.

(c) Identify the critical path.

Activity	Description	Precedence	Duration (weeks)
A	Demolition	–	4
B	Excavation	A	5
C	Foundations	B	5
D	Steel skeleton	C	6
E	Concrete structure	D	8

F	Exterior skin	E	12
G	Plumbing system	E	5
H	Electrical system	E	3
I	Heating system	E	4
J	Interior partitions	G,H,I	3
K	Lighting fixtures	J	5

References

Sapolsky, H.M., *The Polaris System Development: Bureaucratic and Programmatic Success in Government*, Harvard University Press (1972) pp. 118, 119.

Further reading

Dingle, J., *Project Management: Orientation for Decision Makers*, Arnold (1997).

Lockyer, K. and Gordon, J., *Critical Path Analysis and Other Project Network Techniques*, 5th ed., Pitman (1991).

Maylor, H., *Project Management*, Pitman (1996).

Peters, T., *Liberation Management: The Basic Elements*, Macmillan (1992).

Russell, R.S. and Taylor, B.S., *Production and Operations Management: Focusing on Quality and Competitiveness*, Prentice-Hall (1995).

Yeates, D., *Project Management for Information Systems*, Pitman (1991).

Part 3　Improvement

11 Improving performance

Objectives

By the end of this chapter, you should be able to:

- understand the philosophy of total quality management (TQM);
- understand customer expectations of quality;
- be aware of the TQM implementation models of the quality gurus;
- evaluate the costs of quality;
- understand the objectives of the ISO 9000 quality standard;
- understand the need for organisational learning;
- understand the levels of organisational learning;
- understand the role of environment, involvement and problem solving in the implementation of continuous improvement;
- understand the concept of business process re-engineering (BPR);
- To evaluate the relationship between BPR and continuous improvement (CI) initiatives.

Hayes (1988) has recognised that **competitive performance** at any one time is less important than the rate of improvement of **competitive position** in relation to competitors. This emphasises the fact that any move to improve performance relative to competitors will most likely be met by moves by those competitors to improve performance also. Thus to achieve higher levels of performance than competitors whose own performance is improving requires a combination of rapid improvement and continuous improvement to stay ahead.

Continuous improvement

Continuous improvement programmes are associated with incremental changes within the organisation whose cumulative effect is to deliver an increased rate of performance improvement. They are often associated with a **total quality management** (TQM) approach which attempts to instil a culture which recognises the importance of quality to performance. Continuous improvement is also associated with the concept of the **learning organisation** (Senge, 1990) which aims to create an environment which builds knowledge within the organisation and can utilise that to improve performance. The important point about continuous improvement is that it can deliver improvements that are difficult to copy by competitors. For instance a culture which recognises and delivers quality and reliability is a long-term project which may not show immediate financial benefits.

In order to catch up or overtake competitors it has been realised that continuous improvements may not be enough, but step changes in performance are required. These are associated with innovations in areas such as product design or process design. The technique of **business process re-engineering** (BPR) has been widely cited as an approach which locates suitable areas for change and delivers improvements to them.

Chapter 8 briefly outlined principles for implementing a continuous improvement culture (kaizen) in the context of the JIT philosophy. This chapter looks more closely at two major elements of continuous improvement efforts: TQM and learning organisations.

Total quality management

Total quality management (TQM) is a philosophy and approach which aims to ensure that high quality, as defined by the customer, is a primary concern throughout the organisation and all parts of the organisation work towards this goal. TQM does not prescribe a number of steps that must be followed in order to achieve high quality but rather should be considered as a framework within which organisations can work. The TQM process will be dependent on such factors as customer needs, employee skills and the current state of quality management within the organisation.

Defining quality

In order to understand TQM it is first necessary to consider more closely the meaning of quality itself. If the objective of a business is to produce goods and services that meet customers' needs then the concept of quality should be related to how well these needs are met from the customers' point of view. Since different customers will have different product needs and requirements it follows that they will have different quality expectations. Garvin (1984) defines eight dimensions of quality or quality characteristics which the customer looks for in a product:

- performance
- features
- reliability
- conformance
- durability
- serviceability
- aesthetics
- other perceptions.

The customer will trade-off these quality characteristics against the cost of the product in order to get a value-for-money product or what they have paid for. From the producer's point of view it is important that marketing can identify customer needs and then operations can meet these needs at the quality level expected. Once the product design has been determined then quality during the production process can be defined by how closely the product meets the specification required by the design. This is termed the **quality of conformance** and the ability to achieve this depends on a number of factors such as the performance level of the machinery, materials, and training of staff in techniques such as statistical process control. In addition the product cost is an important design consideration. If the production process cannot produce items at a cost that conforms to the product price, then the price will be more than the customer is willing to pay for the quality characteristics of the product. Thus the organisation must consider quality both from the producer and customer point of view and product design must take into consideration process design in order that the design specification can be met at the required cost.

The principles of total quality management

TQM has evolved over a number of years from ideas presented by a number of quality Gurus. People such as W. Shewhart developed many of the technical methods of **statistical process control** such as control charts and sampling methods which formed the basis of **quality assurance**. In the early 1970s however this technical focus was subsumed by more of a managerial philosophy. A.V. Feigenbaum introduced the concept of **total quality control** to reflect a commitment of effort on the part of management and employees throughout an organisation to improving quality. There is a particular emphasis on strong leadership to ensure everyone takes responsibility for control and there is an emphasis on quality improvement as a continual process – giving rise to the term continuous improvement. TQM encompasses both the techniques of quality assurance and the approach of total quality control. A number of implementation models have been put forward by what are known as the quality gurus, who include Deming, Juran and Crosby.

Deming proposed an implementation plan consisting of 14 steps which emphasises continuous improvement of the production process to achieve conformance to specification and reduce variability. This is achieved by eliminating common causes of quality problems such as poor design and insufficient training and special causes such as a specific machine or operator. He also places great emphasis on **statistical quality control** techniques and promotes extensive employee involvement in the **quality improvement programme**. Deming's 14 steps (Deming, 1985) are summarised as follows:

1. Create a constancy of purpose towards product improvement to achieve long-term organisational goals.
2. Adopt a philosophy of preventing poor-quality products instead of acceptable specified levels of poor quality as necessary to compete internationally.
3. Eliminate the need for inspection to achieve quality by relying instead on statistical quality control to improve product and process design
4. Select a few suppliers or vendors based on quality commitment rather than competitive prices.
5. Constantly improve the production process by focusing on the two primary sources of quality problems, the system and workers, thus increasing productivity and reducing costs.
6. Institute worker training that focuses on the prevention of quality problems and the use of statistical control techniques.
7. Instil leadership among supervisors to help workers perform better
8. Encourage employee involvement by eliminating the fear of reprisal for asking questions or identifying quality problems
9. Eliminate barriers between departments, and promote co-operation and a team approach to working together.
10. Eliminate slogans and numerical targets that urge workers to achieve higher

performance levels without first showing them how to do it.

11. Eliminate numerical quotas that employees attempt to meet at any cost without regard for quality.

12. Enhance worker pride, artisanry and self-esteem by improving supervision and the production process so that workers can perform to their capabilities.

13. Institute vigorous education and training programmes in methods of quality improvement throughout the organisation, from top management down, so that continuous improvement can occur.

14. Develop a commitment from top management to implement the previous thirteen points.

Juran put forward a 10-step plan in which he emphasises the following elements.

- **Quality planning** – designing the product quality level and ensuring the process can meet this.
- **Quality control** – using statistical process control methods to ensure quality levels are kept during the production process.
- **Quality improvement** – tackling quality problems through improvement projects.

Crosby suggested a 14-step programme for the implementation of TQM. He is known for changing people's perceptions of the **cost of quality** when he pointed out that the costs of poor quality far outweigh the cost of preventing poor quality, a view not traditionally accepted at the time.

Oakland sees the approaches of the quality gurus as essentially complementary and has suggested his own 11-step process (Oakland, 1993).

The main principles of TQM covered in these plans can be summarised in the following three statements:

1. *The customer defines quality and thus their needs must be met.* Earlier it was stated that the organisation must consider quality both from the producer and customer point of view. Thus product design must take into consideration the production process in order that the design specification can be met. Thus it means viewing things from a customer perspective and requires that the implications for customers are considered at all stages in corporate decision making.

2. *Quality is the responsibility of all employees in all parts of the organisation.* In order to ensure the complete involvement of the whole organisation in quality issues TQM uses the concept of the internal customer and internal supplier. This recognises that everyone in the organisation consumes goods and services provided by other organisational members or internal suppliers. In turn every service provided by an organisational member will have an internal customer. The implication is that poor quality provided within an organisation will, if allowed to go unchecked along the chain of customer/supplier relationships, eventually lead to the external customer. Therefore it is essential that each internal customer's needs are satisfied. This requires a definition for each internal customer about what constitutes an acceptable quality of service. It is a principle of TQM that the responsibility for quality should rest with the people undertaking the tasks which can either directly or indirectly affect the quality of customer service. This requires not only a commitment to avoid mistakes but actually a capability to improve the ways in which they undertake their jobs. This requires management to adopt an approach of empowerment with people provided with training and

the decision-making authority necessary in order that they can take responsibility for the work they are involved in and learn from their experiences.

3. *A continuous process of improvement culture must be developed* to instil a culture which recognises the importance of quality to performance and conformance.

The cost of quality

All areas in the production system will incur costs as part of their TQM programme. For example the marketing department will incur the cost of consumer research in trying to establish customer needs. Quality costs are categorised as either the cost of achieving good quality – the *cost of quality assurance* or the cost of poor-quality products – the *cost of not conforming* to specifications.

The cost of achieving good quality

The costs of maintaining an effective quality management programme can be categorised into prevention costs and appraisal costs. Prevention reflects the quality philosophy of 'doing it right the first time' and includes those costs incurred in trying to prevent problems occurring in the first place. Examples of prevention costs include:

- The cost of designing products with quality control characteristics.
- The cost of designing processes which conform to quality specifications.
- The cost of the implementation of staff training programmes.

Appraisal costs are the costs associated with controlling quality through the use of measuring and testing products and processes to ensure that quality specifications are conformed to. Examples of appraisal costs include:

- The cost of testing and inspecting products.
- The costs of maintaining test equipment.
- The time spent in gathering data for testing.
- The time spent adjusting equipment to maintain quality.

The cost of poor quality

This can be seen as the difference between what it actually costs to provide a product or service and what it would cost if there was no poor quality or failures. This can account for 70% to 90% of total quality costs and can be categorised into internal failure costs and external failure costs. Internal failure costs occur before the goods are delivered to the customer. Examples of internal failure costs include:

- The scrap cost of poor quality parts that must be discarded.
- The rework cost of fixing defective products.
- The downtime cost of machine time lost due to fixing equipment or replacing defective product.

External failure costs occur after the customer has received the product and primarily relate to customer service. Examples of external failure costs include:

- The cost of responding to customer complaints.
- The cost of handling and replacing poor-quality products.
- The litigation cost resulting from product liability.
- The lost sales incurred because of customer goodwill affecting future business.

The quality/cost trade-off

The classical economic trade-off between costs shows that when the cost of achieving good quality (i.e. prevention and appraisal costs) increases, the cost of poor quality (internal and external failure costs) declines. This relationship is shown graphically below in Figure 11.1.

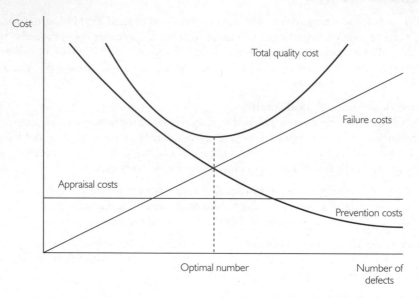

Figure 11.1 The traditional quality/cost trade-off

Adding the two costs together produces the total cost curve. The optimal quality level is thus at the point when quality costs are minimised. However many Japanese organisations did not accept assumptions behind the traditional model and aimed for a zero defect performance instead. The two views on the costs of quality can be seen by comparing the traditional and zero defect cost of quality (Figure 11.2) graphs. According to the traditional view the costs of prevention rises substantially as the zero defect level is approached. This is based on the assumption that the last errors are the hardest to find and correct. The **zero defect approach** assumes that it costs no more to remove the last error as the first. It may take longer to determine what the source of the last error is but the steps to correct it are likely to be simple. While there is debate about the shape of the cost-quality curves and if zero defects is really the lowest cost way to make a product it is beyond doubt that the new approach to quality performance is beneficial.

Many of the benefits of a quality programme are difficult to measure such as the positive reputation from customers that follows from good quality and increased motivation and productivity gains from a **quality improvement programme**. However, the establishment of a zero defect approach does have many implications for the organisation. It means that all involved in the delivery of the product must not only strive to minimise errors but eliminate them, by a change in how they are undertaking their tasks if necessary. This means identifying and removing the cause of errors in order to obtain a 'right first time' performance every time. This will require a proactive role from workers involved in the processes in finding solutions to quality problems. It is not enough for management to issue directives on quality but the workforce must be given the tools and training in order to improve the processes which they are the most familiar with. There must also not be a **blame culture** when defects are found but a recognition of the need to work together to solve the cause of the problem. There must also be an increased awareness of the cost of quality through widely available statistics. Suppliers also need to be educated in order to ensure quality problems are not 'imported' into the organisation. Other aspects include the need to ensure that quality is designed into the product to eliminate costly problems later at the manufacturing stage.

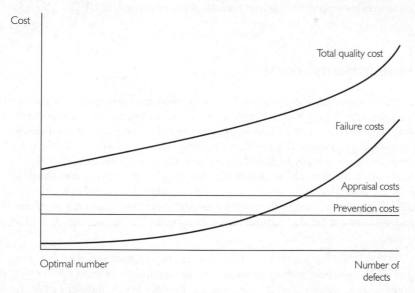

Figure 11.2 The zero defects quality/cost trade-off

Quality systems

ISO 9000 provides a quality standard between suppliers and a customer. Having a predefined quality standard reduces the complexity of managing a number of different quality standards when a customer has many suppliers. Many countries have adopted ISO 9000 and so it is particularly useful in standardising the relationship between customers and suppliers on a global basis. The UK equivalent is called BS 5750. ISO 9000 is a series of standards for quality management and assurance and has five major subsections as follows:

- **ISO 9000** provides guidelines for the use of the following four standards in the series.
- **ISO 9001** applies when the supplier is responsible for the development, design, production, installation, and servicing of the product.

- **ISO 9002** applies when the supplier is responsible for production and installation.
- **ISO 9003** applies to final inspection and testing of products.
- **ISO 9004** provides guidelines for managers of organisations to help them to develop their quality systems. It gives suggestions to help organisations meet the requirements of the previous four standards.

The standard is general enough to apply to almost any product or service, but it is the specific organisation or facility that is registered or certified to the standard. To achieve certification a facility must document its procedures for every element in the standard. These procedures are then audited by a third party periodically. The system thus ensures that the organisation is following a documented, and thus consistent, procedure which makes errors easier to find and correct. However the system does not improve quality in itself and has been criticised for incurring cost in maintaining documentation while not providing guidance in quality improvement techniques such as **statistical process control** (SPC).

Learning organisations

The need for organisational learning has been identified as a consequence of the need for organisations to continually produce innovations in order to maintain a competitive edge. The ability to generate a continuous stream of ideas for improvement and implement them is seen as a sustainable competitive advantage for organisations. To consider how an organisation learns is really to consider how learning of individuals within that organisation takes place and how the results of that learning are integrated into the practices, procedures and processes of the organisation. The transfer of knowledge from individual to organisational system means that the knowledge becomes independent of the individual and is possessed by the organisation and is replicable by individuals within that organisation.

Pedler (1991) describes a learning organisation as 'an organisation that facilitates the learning of all its members and continuously transforms itself'. Probst (1997) states that the outcome of an organisational learning process is qualitatively different from the sum of the individual learning processes. This is because learning is the outcome of human interactions and the sharing of experiences between individuals. For example a decision made by a group can have outcomes which are totally different from the outcomes of the sum of individual decisions.

The learning process

There is a range of definitions of the levels of organisational learning. Probst (1997) distinguishes between three different levels. The alternative definitions of Argyris and Schon (1978) are given in brackets.

- adaptive (single-loop)
- reconstructive (double-loop)
- process (deutero).

Adaptive learning

This is when an organisation adapts to its environment by means of members of that organisation identifying problems in the environment, developing strategies for dealing with them and implementing these strategies. Thus the organisation is making a correction in order to align behaviour towards existing goals. 'Thus the organisation adjusts to environmental factors, but existing norms and values are not questioned; they remain directed towards the existing purpose of the company' (Probst, 1997).

Reconstructive learning

Reconstructive or double-loop learning occurs when there is a more significant change in the relationship between the organisation and its environment for which a process of adaptation is insufficient. Here changes at the more fundamental level of the values of individuals or groups within the organisation must be changed in order to align behaviour towards attainment of an organisation's goals. In fact this questioning of the organisation's 'theories of action' leads to a questioning of the original organisational goals, which are then changed.

Process learning

A formidable obstacle to the successful learning process is **defensive routines** which individuals, groups and organisations have built up to protect them from the threat of change (Argyris, 1990). 'Fundamental rules develop which ensure that errors are ignored, or not discussed, and that their non-discussability is also not discussed' (Probst, 1997). This means that even if individuals recognise the need for learning, these defensive routines prevent them from doing so. Thus a process of 'learning to learn' – the study of the process of learning itself – must take place. This process is the highest level of learning and is in fact the act of learning to understand adaptive and reconstructive learning. 'The learning process is directed not towards the procedures, principles or goals in themselves, but towards understanding the meaning of the organisation' (Probst, 1997).

Implementation of continuous improvement (CI)

Continuous improvement requires creating the right environment in which the importance of continuous improvement is recognised and rewarded, ensuring the involvement of all the members of the organisation and ensuring that organisational members have the problem-solving skills necessary to achieve worthwhile improvements. Thus the following issues will be explored:

- environment
- involvement
- problem-solving skills.

Environment

In order to create the right environment in which improvement can take place it is important to have a set of procedures for the improvement process which formalises actions so that progress can be monitored and measured. A procedure for an improvement study could follows the steps of the **plan-do-check-act cycle (PDCA)** as follows:

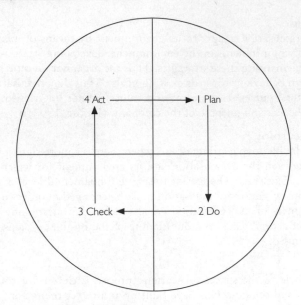

Figure 11.3 The plan-do-check-act (PDCA) cycle

1. What change is needed in order to gain continual improvement?
2. Analyse appropriate data. Carry out suggested change to the process.
3. Evaluate the results of the changes to the process.
4. Make the changes permanent, or try another step (i.e. go to Step 1).

Involvement

The idea behind continuous improvement is to utilise the skills and knowledge of all the workforce in a sustained attempt to improve every aspect of how the organisation operates. Gilgeous (1997) outlines the following factors which should be present in order to ensure that this involvement is facilitated:

- suggestions being made;
- evidence of housekeeping and organisation;
- meetings both formal and informal;
- management presence and participation;
- training and education provided;
- use made of procedures and standards;

It is useful to disseminate information around the organisation regarding progress on various performance measures in order to emphasise the importance of the improvement effort. This can be done in the form of newsletters and boards displaying charts. The most common objectives used are the **QCDSM measure** of quality, cost, delivery, safety and morale.

Suggestion schemes

The idea behind suggestion schemes is to offer the person closest to the work activity the opportunity to suggest improvements to the process. Suggestions by employees are evaluated and if they are assessed as providing a significant saving then a cash award may be paid by the employee. The award could be a fixed amount for all suggestions or a percentage of net savings over a specific time period. Suggestion schemes are most likely to be successful when employees are given training in aspects such as data collection and the scheme is promoted, rather than the size of any award payments.

Continuous improvement teams

Process improvement teams or **quality circles** are using the different skills and experiences of a group of people in order to solve problems and thus provide a basis for continual improvement. In order to do this the team should be aware of the tools available for measuring and thus improving performance, which is covered in Chapter 12, such as **statistical process control (SPC)** and **cause and effect diagrams**. A group can be particularly effective at working through a cause and effect diagram to find the root cause of a particular problem. Expertise outside the group can also be used to contribute to group effectiveness. A quality circle is a small group of people (6–12) who meet voluntarily on a regular basis. The process improvement teams are usually made up of experienced problem-solvers from departments affected by the process and are appointed by management.

CASE STUDY

Productivity and technology: Lessons in improvement

John Griffiths examines a 'kaizen breakthrough' at Perkins, where a continuing programme of examining production methods is reaping many rewards.

Perkins Engines, the UK-based diesel engine maker sold for $1.3bn recently by Lucas-Varity Corporation to Caterpillar of the US, invited in a few outsiders just before Christmas to help Perkins tear itself apart. Large mobile cranes, forklift trucks and anything else that might be needed were placed to hand. Then the management stood back – well, almost – and let them get on with it.

The outsiders came from a diversity of companies; some to which it is a supplier of engines; others in the financial services and accountancy fields. They came from a variety of working backgrounds, with few having close connections with process engineering.

Yet just four days after they had first started walking purposefully towards key areas of Perkins' production lines, to embark on what was formally named a 'Shopfloor Kaizen Breakthrough', the transformations they had achieved in terms of improved efficiency and productivity could be described accurately as radical. In the four production areas which the outsiders, formed into teams with a mix of Perkins' own workers, tackled, few of the processes in place just four days earlier were immediately recognisable

A large area devoted to machining of engine connecting rods had been completely reconstructed, including the reshuffling of process machinery weighing several tonnes. The floor space needed for all the processes had been cut by 72 per cent.

Work-in-progress had been reduced by 93 per cent. The labour force required to carry out the processes had been reduced by 40 per cent, and the number of machine tools required from eight to five.

The results, according to Perkins' general manager and divisional director, Brian Amey, were even better than the company has come to expect from the ongoing series of 'kaizen breakthrough' taskforces it has now set into action in some 150 areas of the plant.

Until the most recent four-day exercise in 'kaizen' – the Japanese term for continuous improvement – the teams had consisted always of Perkins' own employees, but from different areas of the company from that being targeted. The 'breakthrough' idea is that the teams, comprising usually a dozen or so, bring a fresh and critical eye to long-entrenched, but not necessarily efficient, production processes in the space of a short, highly concentrated exercise lasting just a few days.

This time round, however – an occasion regarded by Perkins as a big first – was to be a public kaizen, opening the company's doors and its processes to wider critical scrutiny.

The productivity and cost-saving gains were made by all teams involved in the exercise, with empirical evidence of the improvements when the four teams of the public kaizen made formal presentations to Perkins management at the end of the exercise.

Another team of a dozen or so which examined the core build area of Perkins' four-litre engine range made sweeping changes. Much process plant was shifted around, with parts for assembly made to fall more easily to hand by opening up both sides of the assembly line and reducing radically the number of movements required of operators. Result:

- A 41% improvement in operator productivity.
- A 79.5% reduction in inventory.
- Floor space reduced by 45%.
- Cycle time reduced by 25%.
- Total distance travelled by employees between process functions for a complete cycle reduced from 350 m to 50 m.

Previously, the team had found 'workers hopping around the production line like rabbits'.

The process meets no apparent resistance from the shop floor. To the contrary, most of the company's several thousand employees, many of whom have themselves now been involved in internal kaizen breakthrough, say they have found the exercises stimulating as well as surprising.

However, part of the ground rules set down by North Carolina-based TBM Consulting Group, which has overseen Perkins' kaizen activities, is that employees receive pledges of no redundancies arising from the exercises. In Perkins' case such assurances have not been difficult to give. The company has embarked on a number of expansion programmes expected to result in engine production doubling to around 500,000 units a year by early next decade.

Some of the public kaizen solutions were relatively obvious and clearly had been in the back of managers' minds as needing improvement even before it began. For most of the teams, indeed, the pre-exercise discussions with plant managers gave some clear pointers as to where some improvements might come. Nonetheless, Perkins managers are adamant that the teams were not merely following up ideas for improvement planted by managers themselves.

Much of the teams' attention was taken up with dismantling 'pipeline' processes – so restricted and sequential that they can only move at the speed of the slowest operator or piece of equipment – and putting in their place a system which could flow around obstructions.

In all operations like this, says Anand Sharmah, TBM's president and chief executive, the idea is 'to lower the water around the process to make any efficiencies visual and painful. If you let people continue to hide problems then you cannot manage those problems.'

Mr Amey, who joined Perkins in late 1995 from Nissan, where he had been deeply involved in ongoing improvements of production systems, knew very substantial production increases were in prospect for Perkins when he joined, and one of his first acts was to start kaizen activities. Factory floor space started appearing as if from nowhere. 'It proved time and time again that we already had the space capability to double production,' recalls Mr Amey.

But can kaizen breakthroughs work for everyone? Mr Sharmah agrees that this is not the case, but says that what he would regard as companies failing to get a serious grip on kaizen-type improvements represent no more than 5 per cent of the more than 100 US and more than 20 UK companies with which TBM has worked.

Kaizen, stresses Mr Sharmah, is surprisingly easy to make gains initially. 'But it is much more difficult to sustain.'

The Financial Times, 23 February 1998

Problem-solving skills

Information technology has had a particular impact on the level of problem solving and hence decision-making skills required in the organisation. The decision-making activity is often classified in order that different decision processes and methods can be adopted for the common features of decisions within these choices. Martin (1992) classifies decision types into strategic, tactical and operational relating to top, middle and supervisory management levels. The main variables across these levels being the time-span over which decisions are taken and the amount of money involved in the choice of option.

An alternative definition is the categorisation by Simon (1960) of decisions along a continuum ranging from programmed (i.e. repetitive and routine) and relating to supervisory and middle management to non-programmed (i.e. unique with no definite procedure for handling them) relating to top management. The routine nature of programmed decisions makes them easily programmable (i.e. automated) into a computer. The uncertainty inherent in non-programmable decisions means they must be either moved towards the programmable end of the continuum (by the work of information systems analysts for instance) or be solved by managers with optional support provided by an information system (i.e. a decision support system).

These classifications although useful have been criticised (Mintzberg, 1987) in that they miss important aspects of how complex decisions are made, e.g. many strategic decisions emerge as the result of numerous small low-level decisions (Gore, 1992). They also fail to recognise the changes that are taking place with the introduction of information systems causing many former 'production' workers to become 'knowledge' workers (Scott-Morton, 1991).

Shoshana Zuboff (1988) describes the changes that took place within continuous process factories in the United States which changed to computer-controlled systems. The extra information produced by these systems required a different kind of conceptual grasp by the person concerned in order to recognise patterns and understand the consequences of actions on the overall process. This represents a major change from just the monitoring of information on the computer screen. In other words these more sophisticated computer applications, rather than simply replacing repetitive and mechanical tasks, often serve as a sophisticated decision-support tool that is most valuable in the hands of a sophisticated user with broad responsibilities. This implies that the link between information and management level may become increasingly inappropriate as the job scope and responsibility of many people within the organisation increases with the advent of information systems aimed at increasing effectiveness rather than the historical emphasis on efficiency and subsequent de-skilling (Scott-Morton, 1991).

A more useful classification may be of workers engaged in Type I and Type II **information activities** (Sprague, 1987).

- *Type I activities* are characterised by large volumes of low value transactions, based on structured data and processed using well-defined procedures. The output from the process is easily measurable, being iterative in nature, and so the emphasis is on performing the activity efficiently.
- *Type II activities* are characterised by a few high value transactions, based on less well structured data, processed using procedures designed for the activity. Output is not easily measurable because it consists of problem solving and goal attainment and will be accomplished differently by different people.
- The *Type I/Type II classification* is similar to the programmed/non-programmed breakdown used by Simon. However instead of concentrating on the management level at which the task is undertaken it argues that the nature of the task itself is the most important characteristic in determining what kind of support is required for information systems. It is clear that most of the use of information systems in the past has been for the repetitive and routine tasks of Type I work. 'It is easiest and most natural to use a process engine (computer) to support process driven tasks' (Sprague, 1987). It is also clear that the challenge of the future is to support Type II tasks as the ability to analyse information assumes greater importance in developing market opportunities.

CASE STUDY

Computer simulation: a model of efficiency

Computer controls are cutting costs in process industries, writes Michael Kenward. Running a chemical plant at a higher pressure or with the temperature turned up can do wonders for output. But go too far and the whole thing just might explode.

One way to find the optimum operating level is through trial and error. A less risky alternative is to simulate the operation of the chemical plant in a computer. If a human operator does something silly, a computer model will tell them off. The only damage is to their self-esteem.

The same computer models that simulate the operation of complex processing plants can also help in their design and in the control of their operation. Aspen Technology, the US process software company, has become the leader in the growing market for process modelling software. It has achieved this by its ability to capture the working of a plant in computer models. It can take thousands of mathematical equations to describe all the chemical and physical processes that go on in a complex processing plant. AspenTech's strength has been in capturing this mass of detail in software – effectively a computer model of the plant. The software then enables computers to carry out complex calculations to improve the plant's design and range of operation.

Set up in 1981, AspenTech {http:www.aspentech.co] supplies software and services to the process sector. Based in Cambridge, Massachusetts, the company grew out of a US government-funded research project set up in response to the energy crisis of the 1970s. A team of researchers at the Massachusetts Institute of Technology set out to develop ways of describing in software the complex chemical reactions that happen in refineries and other processing plants. The aim was to create software tools to design the synthetic fuel plants that were expected to replace conventional oil refineries. But the approach turns out to have wide-ranging applications, from power stations to refineries and even food processing plants.

A computerised model of a plant can replace the notebooks full of rules and experience that people rely on for manual control operations. Models are more efficient than humans, because the software can assess many more variations and operating conditions.

While this may seem to be a step towards eliminating operator skills, it could have the opposite effect. Ideally a model should adjust its behaviour in response to market conditions – to changing demand for particular products, for example. Relieved of the need to deal with minute-by-minute operations, the plant's operators can become a part of the company's wider management process.

The growing availability of inexpensive computer power has opened the way for computer control of process plants. Sensors can collect information on the state of the various stages in the plant, feeding data to the software models. These can work on-line to optimise the plant's performance.

Adding modern control systems can bring the benefits of computer control to even the oldest of plants. 'Many of today's plants were originally designed with slide rules,' says Larry Evans, AspenTech's chairman and chief executive. 'They have not had the benefit of today's technology.'

Dr Evans estimates that process industries – oil refineries, chemical plants, paper-makers, glass manufacturers, food processors and so on – with a combined turnover in excess of $6,000bn (£3,600bn) – could save between 15 per cent and 20 per cent of their production costs. DuPont the US chemicals company, has estimated that it could save between $5bn and $8bn a year by bringing the operation of its processing plants up to the industry's best practice.

Richard Schmotzer, a principal consultant with BP Oil based in Cleveland, Ohio, says advanced control and automation could increase the profits from every barrel processed by between 10 and 20 cents. That is just the beginning. Full implementa-tion of 'model centric' process control and business management might achieve as much as 50 cents more profit per barrel of feedstock that goes through the company's refineries. 'There is a significant amount of money available with this technology,' he explains.

Hoechst, the German chemicals company, also has an alliance with AspenTech. Horst Glich of Hoechst says the company is convinced of the value of the model-based approach to plant operation.

Hoechst has combined software work and laboratory experiments to develop models of a ketene plant, a standard part of many chemicals complexes. This resulted in a 5 per cent increase in the plant's capacity, says Dr Glich. Hoechst is transferring the technology to a plant in India and estimates that it will take less than a year to recover the cost of the work.

AspenTech has started to integrate its various software packages. It is also con-necting process control systems to a plant operator's information management sys-tems. Dr Evans describes the combined approach as 'plantelligence'. The idea is to produce what is, in effect, the process plant equivalent of the office suite of desk-top computing.

The Financial Times, 25 February 1998

Business process re-engineering (BPR)

This section looks at the major approach to **breakthrough improvement**: business process re-engineering.

Business process re-engineering (BPR) can be seen in the context of business improve-ment approaches over the last 100 years. F.W. Taylor formalised the idea of product inspection as the final stage in the manufacturing process. This involved little change in the process itself, but simply the rejection of poor quality goods. Deming and others then developed the idea of quality control in the 1930s which studied the manufacturing process and measured variations through the use of statistical process control (SPC) (Chapter 12). This was followed by total quality management (TQM) which took a broad view of quality across functions but still focused on incremental change in the form of continuous improvement and minimising variation in existing processes. Hayes and Wheelwright (1984) outline how manufacturing companies were the first to pursue breakthrough business improvements in the 1980s. Towards the end of the 1980s the idea of re-designing or re-engineering business processes gained popularity.

Business process re-engineering became popular largely as the result of articles by Hammer (1990) and Davenport and Short (1990). BPR calls for an analysis of a business from a process rather than a functional perspective and then the re-engineering of these processes to optimise performance. A process is a set of activities designed to produce a desired output from a specified input. Armistead (1996) discusses how this process orientation matches the idea of the main objectives of the operations function as the management of the transformation process of inputs (resources) into outputs (goods and services) covered in Chapter 1. The operations management concepts and techniques for designing, managing and improving operational processes are also seen as relevant to BPR.

An example of the process perspective taken in operations management is the product design process (Chapter 5) which takes design ideas from the R&D function, undertakes customer tests in the marketing function and produces a prototype and final design in the engineering and manufacturing functions. Focusing on the whole product development process ensures that activities within the process are orientated to the customer. This requires each function to examine the contribution to the performance of the whole process, not just to their own functional tasks. An example of this is the need at the design stage to take account of the manufacturability of the product at the manufacturing stage. A design must not just meet the standard design criteria set down by other functions if the overall process performance is to be optimised. Focusing on the whole product development process in this way will improve quality, speed up time to market and reduce costs.

Davenport (1993) provides the following approach to a BPR study:

- identifying processes for innovation
- changing process levers
- developing process visions
- understanding existing processes
- designing and prototyping the new processes.

Identifying processes for innovation

The organisation should select a process or processes which are critical to the organisation and so provide a potentially large increase in performance in return for the re-engineering effort. The scope and number of process redesign projects must be compatible with the organisation's ability and experience to undertake them.

Identify change levers

Davenport (1993) outlines three main enablers or levers of change.

- information technology (IT)
- information
- organisational/human resource.

Information technology

Davenport provides the following categories in which information technology (IT) can provide **process innovation**:

- **Automational** – e.g. robotics in manufacturing, workflow in services.
- **Informational** – the ability of IT to provide additional information about a process which can be used for improvement (see Zuboff, 1988).
- **Sequential** – transform process execution (e.g. concurrent engineering).
- **Tracking** – knowing the status of components (e.g. mail delivery systems).
- **Analytical** – providing additional information for decision making.
- **Geographical** – using world-wide communications system (e.g. linked CAD).
- **Integrative** – case management approach: needs database of information from around the organisation.
- **Intellectual** – database of company knowledge of processes.
- **Disintermediating** – connects buyers and sellers without intermediaries.

Information

Much information is not handled by IT resources in the organisation, but may still be a powerful lever in making process innovation possible. Examples include the visible display of information on the shop floor in lean production organisations and the market information used by executives in making strategic decisions.

Organisational/human resource

The need to align the organisational culture with technological change is discussed in Chapter 4 on Job Design. For example many process innovations will lead to increased worker empowerment which may require an adjustment in organisational culture to ensure successful implementation. The successful use of teams is also essential in implementing cross-functional processes.

Developing process vision

It is essential that the process innovation effort is consistent with the organisation's strategy. A process vision consists of measurable objectives and provides the link between strategy and action. A shared vision is essential to ensure true innovation, rather than standard improvement efforts such as simplification and rationalisation. A vision allows conventional wisdom about how processes are undertaken to be questioned. Key activities in developing a process vision include:

- assessing existing business strategy for process direction;
- consulting with process customers;
- benchmarking process performance targets;
- developing process performance objectives and attributes.

Understanding existing processes

This step is necessary to enable those involved in the innovation activities to develop a common understanding of the existing processes, understand complexities, avoid duplicating current problems and provide a benchmark against which improvements can be measured. Traditional process-oriented approaches such as flow-charting can be used for this task, but do not contain the elements necessary for the implementation of radical change.

Designing and prototyping the new processes

The design of new processes requires a team with a mix of members who can deliver creative and innovative process solutions and ensure that they are implemented. Key activities in the design and prototype phase are the brainstorming of design activities, assessing the feasibility risk and benefit of these alternatives, prototyping the new process design, developing a migration strategy and implementation of the new organisational structure and systems. **Simulation modelling** (Chapter 6) can be a valuable tool in assessing new process design.

Combining BPR and CI

Davenport (1990) summarises the differences between BPR and continuous improvement (CI) and how they can exist. BPR and CI are quite different but arise out of the same tradition. They share:

- orientation to process as the unit of improvement;
- orientation to strategy execution rather than strategy itself;
- belief in the importance of measurement and analysis;
- focus on external criteria (e.g. benchmarking) as the basis for judging improvement.

When BPR and CI coexist within an organisation they should be perceived as being related aspects of an overall performance improvement initiatives. Figure 11.4 shows how the two approaches could be combined in an improvement initiative to outperform an organisation using only one of the approaches.

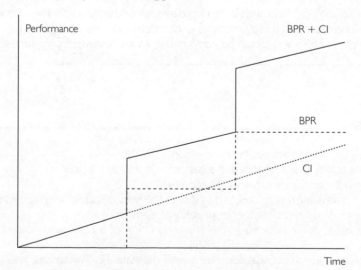

Figure 11.4 Combining business process re-engineering (BPR) and continuous improvement (CI) initiatives

The focus on continuous improvement (CI) is on the implementation of a stream of ideas from the workforce which together produce a substantial improvement over time. This approach can generate a highly motivated workforce as a large percentage of suggestions are accepted and implemented. The business process re-engineering (BPR) approach however requires major change initiatives, often covering cross-functional processes, which means a higher proportion of ideas are rejected which may lead to a drop in involvement. A possible way of combining the advantages of both approaches is to have a company-wide scheme for incremental improvements and form groups to investigate areas for potential breakthrough innovations.

Summary of key points

- Total quality management (TQM) should be considered a framework within which organisations can work.
- Different customers will have different quality expectations.
- TQM has evolved over a number of years from ideas presented by a number of quality gurus.
- Quality costs can be categorised as either the cost of achieving good quality or the cost of poor quality.
- ISO 9000 provides a quality standard between suppliers and customers.
- Organisational learning has been identified as a consequence of the need for organisations to continually produce innovations in order to maintain a competitive edge.
- Implementation of continuous improvement requires attention to the organisational environment, involvement of organisational members and development of problem solving skills.
- BPR calls for an analysis of a business from a process rather than functional perspective and then the re-engineering of these processes to optimise performance.
- The approaches of BPR and CI can be combined in an improvement programme.

Exercises

1 What is the purpose of total quality management (TQM)?
2 Describe the quality characteristics that a customer looks for in a product.
3 What as the main principles of the TQM approach?
4 Contrast the traditional quality/cost trade-off with the zero defects quality/cost trade-off.
5 Evaluate the three different levels of organisational learning.
6 Discuss the main issues involved in the implementation of a continuous improvement effort.
7 Identify tools and techniques that could be used to facilitate a BPR initiative.
8 Discuss the factors behind the integration of the BPR and CI improvement approaches.

References

Argyris, C. and Schön, D.A., *Organizational Learning: A Theory of Action Perspective*, Addison-Wesley (1978).

Argyris, C., *Overcoming Organizational Defenses: Facilitating Organizational Learning*, Allyn & Bacon (1990).

Armistead, C. and Rowland, P., *Managing Business Processes: BPR and Beyond*, Wiley (1996).

Davenport, T.H., *Process Innovation: Reengineering Work through Information Technology*, Harvard Business School Press (1993).

Davenport, T.H. and Short, J., The new industrial engineering: information technology and business process redesign, *Sloan Management Review*, (Summer, 1990) pp. 11–27.

Deming, W.E., Transformation of Western-style management, *Interfaces*, **15**, (3), (May–June, 1985), pp. 6–11.

Garvin, D.A., What does quality really mean? *Sloan Management Review*, **26**, (1), (1984) pp. 25–43.

Gilgeous, V., *Operations and the Management of Change*, Pitman Publishing (1997).

Gore, C., Murray, K. and Richardson, B., *Strategic Decision Making*, Cassell (1992).

Hammer, M., Re-engineering work: don't automate, obliterate, *Harvard Business Review*, (July–August, 1990) pp. 104–112.

Hayes, R.H. and Wheelwright, S.C. *Restoring Our Competitive Edge*, Wiley (1984).

Hayes, R.H., Wheelwright, S.C. and Clark, K.B., *Dynamic Manufacturing*, Free Press (1988).

Martin, C. and Powell, P., *Information Systems: A Management Perspective*, McGraw-Hill (1992).

Mintzberg, H., Crafting strategy, *Harvard Business Review*, (July–August, 1987) pp. 65–75.

Oakland, J.S., *Total Quality Management*, Second Edition, Butterworth-Heinemann (1993).

Pedler, M., Burgoyne, J. and Boydell, T., *The Learning Company: A Strategy for Sustainable Development*, McGraw-Hill (1991).

Probst, G. and Büchel, B. *Organizational Learning: The Competitive Advantage of the Future*, Prentice-Hall (1997).

Scott-Morton, M.S., (ed.) *The Corporation of the 1990s: Information Technology and Organisational Transformation*, Oxford University Press (1991).

Senge, P.M., *The Fifth Discipline: The Art and Practice of the Learning Organization*, Century Business (1990).

Simon, H.A., *The New Science of Management Decision*, Prentice-Hall (1960).

Sprague, R.H., *DSS in Context, Decision Support Systems*, 3, pp. 197–202.

Zuboff, S., *In the Age of the Smart Machine: The Future of Work and Power*, Heinemann Ltd (1988).

Further reading

Crosby, P.B., *Quality is Free*, McGraw-Hill (1979).

Deming, W.E., *Out of the Crisis*, MIT CAES (1986).

Feigenbaum, A.V., *Total Quality*, 3rd Edition, McGraw-Hill (1983).

Garvin, D.A., *Managing Quality*, Macmillan (1988).

Ishikawa, K., *Guide to Quality Control*, 2nd Edition, Krans International (1986).

Juran, J.M. and Gryna, F.M., *Quality Planning and Analysis*, 2nd Edition, McGraw-Hill (1980).

Taguchi, G., *Introduction to Quality Engineering*, Asian Productivity Organisation (1986).

12 Measuring performance

Objectives

By the end of this chapter, you should be able to:

- understand the use of statistical process control (SPC);
- utilise control charts for variable and attribute data;
- understand the relationship between tolerance, control limits and process capability;
- understand the use of acceptance sampling;
- understand the use of sampling plans;
- understand the use of total preventative maintenance (TPM);
- evaluate preventative maintenance activities;
- understand the concept of benchmarking;
- understand the concept of Pareto analysis;
- understand the use of cause and effect diagrams.

Traditionally performance measures in operations have focused on indicators such as productivity which divides the value of the output by the value of the input resources consumed. This can be a valid tool for the operations manager and provides an indication of the level of utilisation of resources. However it has been criticised, not only because of the difficulty of finding appropriate input and output parameters but its failure to consider customer and competition issues (Schefczyk, 1993). This failure to consider external factors has also been directed to traditional financial measures of success of organisations such as return on investment and market share. These measures are criticised for measuring past performance, while strategic performance needs a more forward looking measure, and for the need to provide at least minimal satisfaction to all stakeholders, reflecting the need to simultaneously maintain several performance parameters within safe limits (Ashby, 1971). Chakravarthy (1986) states that the necessary conditions for excellence cannot just be based on current financial performance but the ability of the organisation to transform itself in response to changes in its environment. The frequent change in the leading organisations underlines the point that current financial success is not a guaranteed of future competitive success.

This discussion leads to a view of moving away from the traditional view of the operation's function as a buffer between other functions within the organisation to one directly in touch with those functions and in particular stakeholders such as the customer. This requires a redefinition of the performance objectives of the operation's function to a more customer-based and strategic viewpoint. This is reflected in the five **performance objectives** of quality:

- quality
- dependability
- speed
- flexibility
- cost

These are explored in Chapter 13. The concept of operations with a customer focus leads to the need to be involved in the design process to ensure the five performance objectives. Chapter 5 covers product and service design and methods for measurement of design quality such as **failure mode and effect analysis (FMEA)**. This chapter investigates measurement tools of process performance. **Statistical process control** (SPC) is a particularly important technique in ensuring that the process of delivering the product/service is performing satisfactorily. Acceptance sampling is relevant to organisations which have not yet achieved TQM quality levels and has also been traditionally used when the cost of inspection is high relative to the cost of the defective being identified. The idea behind **total preventative maintenance** (TPM) is to anticipate equipment failures through a programme of routine maintenance which will not only help to reduce breakdowns, but also to reduce downtime (time not in operation) and lengthen the life of the equipment. Other process measurement tools discussed include benchmarking against competitor performance, Pareto analysis and cause and effect diagrams.

Statistical process control (SPC)

Statistical process control is a sampling technique which checks the quality of an item which is engaged in a process. Thus SPC should be seen as a quality check for process rather than product design. Quality should be built in to the product during the design stage and techniques which can assist this are covered in Chapter 5. SPC works by identifying the nature of variations in a process, which are classified as being caused by 'chance' causes or 'assignable' causes.

Chance causes of variation

All processes will have some inherent variability due to factors such as ambient temperature, wear of moving parts or slight variations in the composition of the material that is being processed. The technique of SPC involves calculating the limits of these chance/cause variations for a stable system, so any problems with the process can be identified quickly. The limits of the chance/cause variations are called control limits and are shown on **an SPC control chart**, which also shows sample data of the measured characteristic over time. There are control limits above and below the target value for the measurement, termed the **upper control limit** (UCL) and **lower control limit** (LCL) respectively. An example control chart is shown in Figure 12.1.

The behaviour of the process can thus be observed by studying the control chart. If the sample data plotted on the chart shows a random pattern within the upper and lower control limits then the process is 'in control'. However if a sample falls outside the control limits or the plot shows a non-random pattern then the process is 'out of control'.

Assignable causes of variation

If an out-of-control process is discovered, then it is assumed to have been caused by an assignable cause of variation. This is a variation in the process which is not due to random variation but can be attributed to some change in the process, which needs to be

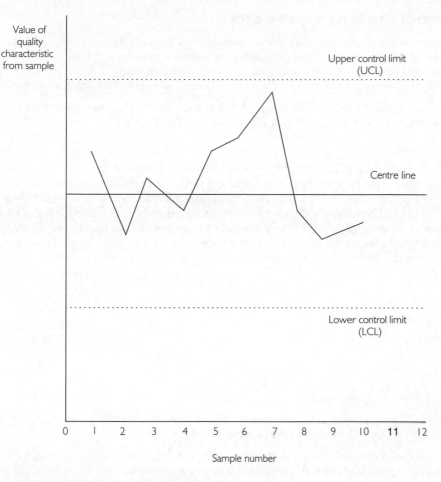

Figure 12.1 Statistical process control chart

investigated and rectified. However in some instances the process could actually be working properly and the results could have been caused by sampling error. There are two types of error which can occur when sampling from a population:

- *Type I error* – an error is indicated from the sample output when none actually occurs. The probability of a Type I error is termed α.
- *Type II error* – an error is occurring but has not been indicated by the sample output. The probability of a Type II error is termed β.

Thus Type I errors may lead to some costly investigation and rectification work which is unnecessary. It may even lead to an unnecessary recall of 'faulty' products. Type II errors will lead to defective products as an out-of-control process goes unnoticed. Customer compensation and loss of sales may result if defective products reach the marketplace. The sampling methodology should ensure that the probability of Type I and Type II errors are kept as low as reasonably possible.

Control charts for variable data

Control charts for variable data display samples of a measurement that can vary over a range of possible values. Values will fall in or out of a range around a specified target value. Examples of variable data could be a customer transaction time in a bank or the width of an assembly component. Two control charts are used in measuring variable data:

- $\overline{X}$ -chart: shows the distance of sample values from the target value (central tendency)
- R-chart: shows the variability of sample values (dispersion)

$\overline{X}$ chart

The $\overline{X}$ (x-bar) chart consists of a series of tests on a sample of data to check that the mean value of the process aligns with the target value. The sample size tends to be small, say four or five. The $\overline{X}$ -chart uses the central limit theorem which states that the sample means will be normally distributed if the process distribution is also normal. Otherwise if the process does not follow a normal distribution the distribution of the sample means will be normally distributed if the sample size is sufficiently large. Thus to construct control limits for an $\overline{X}$ -chart the following calculations can be used:

$$\text{UCL} = \mu + z \times \sigma_x$$

$$\text{LCL} = \mu - z \times \sigma_x$$

where:
μ = process average
$\sigma_x = \sigma/\sqrt{n}$
σ = process standard deviation
n = sample size
z = 3 (for a 3-sigma chart).

When the process mean, μ, is not known, the average of the sample means, $\overline{\overline{X}}$, can be used instead and substituted in the previous equation.

A z value of 3 corresponds to a normal probability of 99.74%. Sometimes the z value is 2, giving a probability of 95%, thus giving more narrow control limits. A smaller value of z increases the risk that the process sample will fall outside the control limits due to normal random variations. Conversely a large value of z means that non-random process deviations may not be discovered. Traditionally control charts use z = 3, called 3-sigma (3σ) or 3 standard deviation limits.

Using $\overline{X}$ with R-charts

Usually the $\overline{X}$ and R-charts are used together and in this case the sample range is used as a measure of process variability. Thus the control limits can be calculated as follows:

$$CV = \overline{\overline{X}}$$

$$\text{UCL} = \overline{\overline{X}} + A_2 \overline{R}$$

$$\text{LCL} = \overline{\overline{X}} - A_2 \overline{R}$$

where:
$\overline{\overline{X}}$ = average of sample means
$\overline{R}$ = average sample range.
Values of A_2 vary with the sample size and are shown in Table 12.1, column 2.

Table 12.1 Factors for determining control limits for $\overline{X}$- and R-charts

Sample size n	Factor for $\overline{X}$-chart A_2	Factor for R-chart D_3	Factor for R-chart D_4
2	1.88	0	3.27
3	1.02	0	2.57
4	0.73	0	2.28
5	0.58	0	2.11
6	0.48	0	2.00
7	0.42	0.08	1.92
8	0.37	0.14	1.86
9	0.34	0.18	1.82
10	0.31	0.22	1.78
11	0.29	0.26	1.74
12	0.27	0.28	1.72
13	0.25	0.31	1.69
14	0.24	0.33	1.67
15	0.22	0.35	1.65
16	0.21	0.36	1.64
17	0.20	0.38	1.62
18	0.19	0.39	1.61
19	0.19	0.40	1.60
20	0.18	0.41	1.59
21	0.17	0.43	1.58
22	0.17	0.43	1.57
23	0.16	0.44	1.56
24	0.16	0.45	1.55
25	0.15	0.46	1.54

R-chart

Control limits for range limits are found using the following calculations:

$$CV = \overline{R}$$

$$UCL = D_4\,\overline{R}$$

$$LCL = D_3\,\overline{R}$$

where: $\overline{R}$ = average sample range; values of D_3 and D_4 vary with the sample size and can be found in Table 12.1, columns 3 and 4.

It is usual to plot both a $\overline{X}$ and a separate R-chart for a process to provide perspectives on both movements in the process mean and movements in process dispersion respectively.

WORKED EXAMPLE

As part of its process control activities a bakery wishes to monitor the weight of dough portions being measured out prior to baking. The company has specified that the mean weight of portions should be 376 grams.

Below are given the weight of six samples each of five portions, taken at intervals while the machine was known to be 'in control'.

(a) Use the data to initiate control charts for mean and range.
(b) The subsequent weights given are of samples taken thereafter at half hourly intervals. Plot these data on to the appropriate charts and comment on the stability or otherwise of the process.

Initial samples   *Subsequent half-hourly samples*

1	2	3	4	5	6	7	8	9	10	11	12	13
375	375	375	373	375	378	375	379	378	374	378	374	379
378	374	375	376	379	373	373	374	378	376	376	379	380
376	376	378	377	376	376	377	376	375	373	380	379	379
378	379	377	376	378	375	376	376	377	376	379	376	377
377	376	376	375	376	378	377	379	378	377	377	379	379

SOLUTION

Sample	1	2	3	4	5	6	7	8	9	10	11	12	13
$\overline{X}$	376.8	376	376.2	375.4	376.8	376	375.6	376.8	377.2	375.2	378	377.4	378.8
R	3	5	3	4	4	5	4	5	3	4	4	5	3

Taking the first six samples: $\overline{X} = 376.2$ and $R = 4$

For the means chart: sample size is 5 therefore A_2 is 0.58 (Table 12.1).

LCL $= 376.2 - 0.58 \times 4 = 373.88$; CV $= 376.2$; UCL $= 376.2 + 0.58 \times 4 = 378.52$.

For the ranges chart: sample size is 5 therefore $D_3 = 0$ and $D_4 = 2.11$ (Table 12.1).

LCL $= 4 \times 0 = 0$; CV $= 4$; UCL $= 4 \times 2.11 = 8.44$.

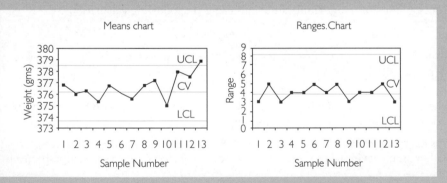

Figure 12.2

From the means chart in Figure 12.2, it can be seen that the machine is overfilling.

Control charts for attributes data

Attributes control charts measure discrete values to determine if a component value is defective or not. Thus there are no values as in a variable control chart, from which a mean and range can be calculated. The data will simply provide a count of how many items conform to a specification value and how many do not. Two control charts will be described for attribute data.

- *p*-chart – shows the proportion of defectives in a sample;
- *c*-chart – shows the number of defectives in a sample.

p-chart

The *p*-chart is used when it is possible to distinguish between defectives and non-defectives for each sample item, and thus calculate the number of defectives as a percentage of the whole (i.e. the proportion).

A *p*-chart takes samples from a process over time and the proportion of defective items is calculated to see if it falls within the control limits on the chart. Assuming a significant sample size and a 3-sigma chart the calculations can be based on a normal distribution to calculate the control limits as follows:

$$CV = p$$

$$UCL = p + 3\sqrt{p(1-p)/n}$$

$$LCL = p - 3\sqrt{p(1-p)/n}$$

where:
p = population proportion defective (process mean);
n = sample size.

When the process mean, p, is not known the proportion defective, $\bar{p}$, can be calculated from the samples and substituted in the previous equation.

WORKED EXAMPLE

The following table gives the results of daily inspections of 500 units of a standard design electronic device produced during the months of June 1998.

(a) Estimate the total proportion of rejects during this month.
(b) Establish a single set of control limits for the daily fraction of rejects based on these figures and plot a control chart, showing the daily results.
(c) Comment on the stability of the manufacturing process. What appears to have happened to cause the sudden change between 19th and 20th June?
(d) Based on the records of this month, what would you recommend as the central value, p, to use for the following month's control chart for fraction rejects?

Date in June	3	4	5	6	7	10	11	12	13	14
Number of rejects	10	14	18	10	14	21	17	12	15	16

Date in June	17	18	19	20	21	24	25	26	27	28
Number of rejects	16	25	26	12	14	17	15	9	10	14

SOLUTION

(a) The number of inspections in June 1998 is 500 units per day for 20 days, totalling 10,000 units. During this month a total of 305 units are rejected. Hence the proportion rejected, p, is: $p = 305/10,000 = 0.0305$ (3.05%)

(b) The control limits are as follows: $p = 0.0305$; $n = 500$.

UCL $= 0.0305 + 0.02306 = 0.0536$; CV $= 0.0305$; LCL $= 0.0305 - 0.02306 = 0.0074$.

The proportion of rejects over the 20 working days of June 1998 are as follows:

Date	3	4	5	6	7	10	11	12	13	14
Proportion defective	0.02	0.028	0.036	0.02	0.028	0.042	0.034	0.024	0.030	0.032

Date	17	18	19	20	21	24	25	26	27	28
Proportion defective	0.032	0.050	0.052	0.024	0.028	0.034	0.030	0.018	0.020	0.028

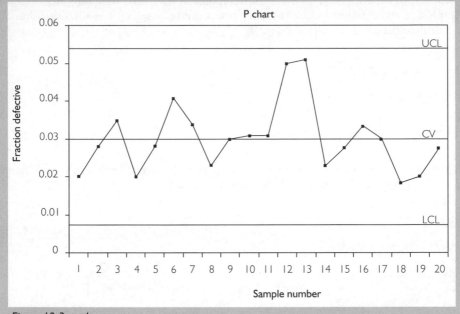

Figure 12.3 p-chart

(c) The manufacturing process appears to be under control for the first half of June, and again over the last few days of the month. However it seems clear that the process was interrupted between the 19th and 20th of June. It seems likely that the process controller decided that the process had gone out of control during the 18th and 19th of June, with two consecutive observations so close to the upper control limit. This fault was rectified so that the later results were an improvement.

(d) When recommending a central value for the following month it would seem sensible to only use those days in June when the process was stable. Hence the results of the 18th and 19th of June would be ignored. The recommended value for p for the following month is:

$p = (305 - (25 + 26))/(10,000 - 1000) = 254/9000 = 0.0282$

Alternatively we might use the results of just the last 7 days of June (the days after adjustment) to form the basis of the recommendation. This gives:

c-chart

A c-chart counts the actual number of defects when the proportion cannot be calculated. For example if the quality of paint on a car body panel is being inspected, the number of blemishes (defects) can be counted, but the proportion cannot be calculated because the total number is not known. The Poisson distribution is theoretically used to represent the probability of a defect from an extremely large population, but the normal distribution is used as a substitute for the c-chart. Assuming a 3-sigma chart the control limits can be calculated as follows:

$$CV = c$$
$$UCL = c + 3\sqrt{c}$$
$$LCL = c - 3\sqrt{c}$$

where:
c = mean number of defects per sample.

When the process mean, c, is not known the sample mean, $\bar{c}$, can be estimated by dividing the number of defects by the number of samples and substituting in the previous equation.

Investigating control chart patterns

Apart from the plots on the control charts that lie outside the control limits it is still possible that the process may be out-of-control due to non-random behaviour within the control limits. If the behaviour is random then the plots should follow no discernible pattern and occur either side of the centre line. Referring to Figure 12.4, there are several guidelines for identifying non-random behaviour including the following examples:

Pattern A: 8 consecutive points on one side of the centre line
Pattern B: 8 consecutive points either moving up or moving down
Pattern C: 14 points alternating up and down
Pattern D: 2 out of 3 consecutive points between $2\sigma_x$ and $3\sigma_x$.
Pattern E: 4 out of 5 consecutive points between $1\sigma_x$ and $2\sigma_x$ or beyond $1\sigma_x$.

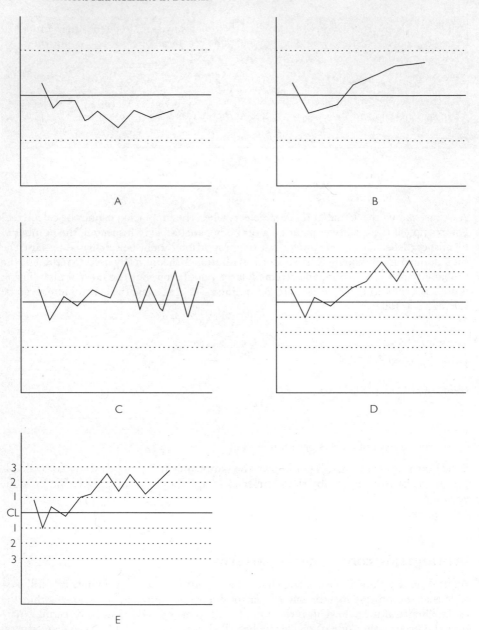

Figure 12.4 Control chart patterns

Run patterns

It is possible to use a z pattern test or run test to determine the probability of certain plot patterns occurring. The general form of the calculation for the z test is as follows:

z_{TEST} = (Observed runs − Expected runs)/ σ

where:

σ = standard deviation

From this the following calculation is derived for a run of sample values that consistently go up or down within the control limits:

$Z_{U/D} = r - ((2n-1)/3)/\sqrt{(16n - 29)/90}$
where:
r = observed number of runs
n = sample size

For a run of sample values which are above or below the centre line, the calculation is as follows:

$Z_{A/B} = r - ((n/2)+1)/\sqrt{(n - 1)/4}$

where:
r = observed number of runs
n = sample size.

The z test values are compared to a z value for a particular level of variability. Thus at a 95% probability level the z value will be ±1.96. (from z value table in the Appendix). This means if the $Z_{A/B}$ or $Z_{U/D}$ is not within ±1.96 then there is a 95% chance that the variability is not due to random variation.

WORKED EXAMPLE

A company wants to perform run tests to see if there is a pattern of non-randomness exhibited within the control limits. It wants to use a test statistic consistent with a 95% probability that the non-random patterns exist. The following run pattern has been identified.

Sample	Above/below	Up/down
1	B	−
2	A	U
3	B	D
4	A	U
5	B	D
6	B	D
7	A	U
8	B	D
9	A	U
10	B	D

SOLUTION

$r = 9$; $n = 10$:

$Z_{A/B} = 9 - ((10/2) + 1)/((10 - 1)/4) = 2.00$

$r = 8$; $n = 10$:

$Z_{U/D} = 8 - ((20 - 1)/3)/((160 - 29)/90) = 1.38$

At a 95% probability $z = \pm 1.96$. The above/below test is slightly over this limit at $+2.00$, indicating that there may be some non-random pattern in the samples and the process should be checked.

Determining the sample size for variable and attribute control charts

It is important to note that the required sample size for each plot for a variable or attribute control chart is quite different. For $\overline{X}$- and R-charts sample sizes are usually 4 or 5 and can be as low as 2. This is because even 2 observations should provide a reasonable measure of the sample range and sample average. For p-charts and c-charts sample size are usually in the hundreds to achieve a useful quality measure. For example, for a proportion defective of 5% this would require 5 defective items from 100. In practice sample size is also kept to a minimum to save operator time in observation. This however, permits more observation points to be implemented which will assist in finding the cause of any quality problem. Also observations of output from a mix of machines may make it difficult to identify which machine is the source of the error.

Tolerances, control limits and process capability

It is important to distinguish between the above terms, referring to the variability of process output. They can be defined as follows:-

- **Tolerance** – a specified range of values (e.g. from customer needs) in which individual units of output must fall in order to be acceptable.
- **Control limits** – statistical limits on how sample statistics (e.g. mean, range) are allowed to vary due to randomness alone.
- **Process capability** – The inherent variability in a process.

The relationship between control limits and process capability can be expressed in the following formula:

Control limits = Process mean $\pm z \times$ (Process capability/ $\sqrt{n}$)

where:
z = number of standard deviations from the mean
n = sample size.

Thus it can be seen that control limits are based on the variability of samples of process output whose variability is a function of the process capability. Tolerances however are product/service specifications and are not specified in terms of the process by which the product/service is generated. Thus a process which is performing statistically in control may not necessarily be conforming to the external tolerance specifications imposed. Therefore it is essential to ensure that the process is capable of meeting the required specifications and then ensure it can meet this tolerance consistently over time using process control. Conversely if the natural variation of the process exceeds the designed tolerances of the product the process cannot produce the product according to specifications as the process variations which occur naturally, at random, is greater than the designed variation. To avoid this situation it is important that process capability studies are undertaken during the product/service design stage.

6-sigma quality

If the process output is normally distributed within 3-sigma limits then the probability of a good item is 0.9973. Thus when the process is in control there should only be a maximum of 0.0027% or 2700 defects per million. However this may still represent an unacceptable quality goal and for this reason some organisations have adopted an aim of 6-sigma quality. Six-sigma control limits correspond to a rate of 3.4 defective parts per million (ppm) as opposed to 2700 ppm for 3-sigma. Thus in a total quality management (TQM) environment quality is measured, not in defects per thousand but in parts per million (ppm).

Acceptance sampling

Acceptance sampling consists of taking a random sample from a larger batch or lot of material to be inspected. The quality of the sample is assumed to reflect the overall quality of the lot. If the sample has an unacceptable amount of defects the whole lot will be rejected. The point at which the defect level becomes unacceptable is based on an agreement between the customer and supplier of the goods. Because acceptance sampling is based on the traditional approach which assumes that a number of defects will be produced by a process, it is usually associated with the receiving inspection process from external suppliers. Although the acceptable defect rate may be quoted as a percentage the comments on 6-sigma quality levels above apply here also. Thus many organisations who take a TQM approach would expect defect levels measured in parts per million. Indeed if suppliers have successfully achieved a TQM philosophy and are in a stable partnership with the supplier the receiving inspection process may be eliminated.

Acceptance sampling is however still relevant to organisations which have not yet achieved TQM quality levels and has also been traditionally used when the cost of inspection (e.g. destructive testing, sampling food etc.) is high relative to the cost of the defect or defective part being identified. As in SPC when the product is inspected to see if it conforms to a specification the measurement can be a process variable or in the form of a product attribute.

The sampling design includes the following aspects:

- the operating characteristic curve
- producer's and consumer's risk
- average outgoing quality.

The operating characteristic curve

Because we are only using a sample to estimate the actual number of defects in the lot, this may lead to errors in accepting or rejecting a lot due to sampling error. For example if there is a target of 2% fraction defectives in a lot, a particular sample may contain a higher percentage than this even though the whole lot may not. Therefore the lot will be incorrectly rejected. The operating characteristic curve (**OC curve**) indicates how effective the sampling plan is in discriminating between good and bad lots by showing the probability of accepting a lot for different quality levels for a given sample size and acceptance level. The shape and location of the OC curve is determined by the sample size (n) and the acceptance level (c) for the sampling plan. A selection of OC curves for different values of n and c is shown in Figure 12.5. Note when the sample size is the same as the lot size the curve is a vertical line indicating 100% inspection with no risk.

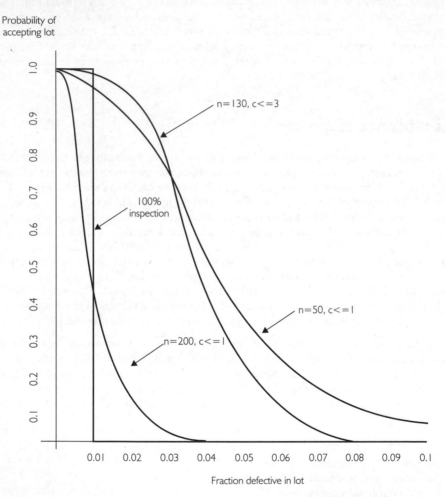

Figure 12.5 OC curves for different sample size (n) and acceptance number (c)

Producer's and consumer's risk

As discerned for the OC curve, sampling error may mean either that a good lot is rejected (Type I sample error) or that a bad lot is accepted (Type II sample error). The acceptable quality level (AQL) is the maximum percentage (fraction defective) that is considered acceptable. The probability of rejecting a lot that has an acceptable quality level is termed the producer's risk and is related to α_x, the probability of a Type I error.

Due to sampling error there may be a sample taken that does not accurately reflect the quality level of the lot and thus a lot that does not meet the AQL is passed on to the customer. The upper limit of defective items which the customer will accept is termed the **lot tolerance per cent defective** (LTPD). The probability of accepting a lot in which the quality level (fraction defective) exceeds the LTPD is termed the consumer's risk and relates to ß, the probability of a Type II error.

Usually the customer will prefer the quality of lots to be as good or better than the AQL but is willing to accept some lots with quality levels no worse than the LTPD. A common scenario is to have a producer's risk (α) at 5% and consumer's risk (β_x) at 10%. This means the customer expects to reject lots that are good or better than the AQL about 5% of the time and to accept lots that exceed the LTPD about 10% of the time.

A sampling plan is devised from these measures by using the OC curve. The α and AQL measures specifies a point on the probability of acceptance axis and the β and LTPD measures define a point on the proportion defective axis. However a trail and error process is required to determine the sample size (n) and acceptance number (c) to achieve these performance measures. This involves determining the probabilities of accepting a lot for various lot percentage defective values. A typical OC curve is shown in Figure 12.6.

From Figure 12.6 in this case it can be seen that if a lot has 3% defective items, for example, the probability of accepting a lot is 0.95. If management defines the AQL at 3%, then the probability that the lot will be rejected (α) is 1 minus the probability of accepting a lot (i.e. $1 - 0.95 = 0.05$). If management is willing to accept lots with a percentage defective up to 15% (LTPD), this corresponds to a probability that the lot will be accepted (β) of 0.10.

To avoid the time-consuming task of using a trial-and-error method to construct OC curves, standardised tables, called the **Dodge-Romig Inspection Tables**, can be used based on a given set of risks. Also computer software is available which will develop sampling plans based on values for AQL, LTPD, α and β.

Average outgoing quality (AOQ)

Even though the probability of accepting a lot containing defects may be very small, all lots, whether they are accepted or not, will pass on some defects to the customer. The expected number of these defective items is measured by the AOQ. Assuming that defective items rejected (and thus completely inspected) lots are replaced the defective items that are passed on to the customer are contained in the lots that are accepted. Thus

$$AOQ = pP_a \, ((N - n)/N)$$

where:
p = percentage defectives (horizontal axis in OC chart)
Pa = possibility of accepting a lot (vertical axis in OC chart)
N = lot size
n = sample size

Values for AOQ against fraction defectives are shown in Figure 12.7.

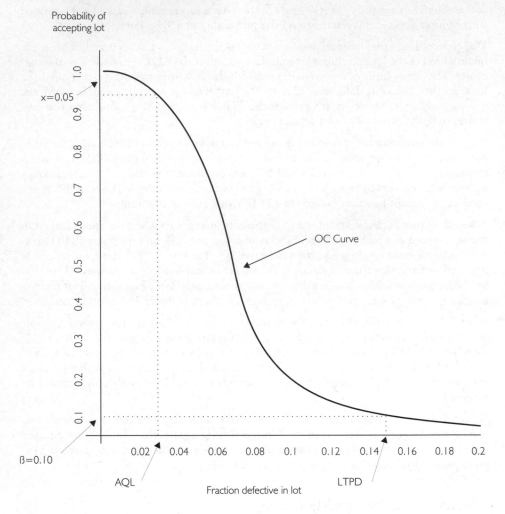

Figure 12.6 An operating characteristic curve

From the graph it can be seen that the AOQ rises to a point from the origin and then falls back again. The peak is termed the **average outgoing quality limit** (AOQL) and represents when the sampling plan does its worst job of upgrading quality, i.e. below this there are few defects accepted, above this there are more defects, but they are rejected and replaced. Each sampling plan will have a different AOQ curve and the AOQL can be used to select a suitable sampling plan.

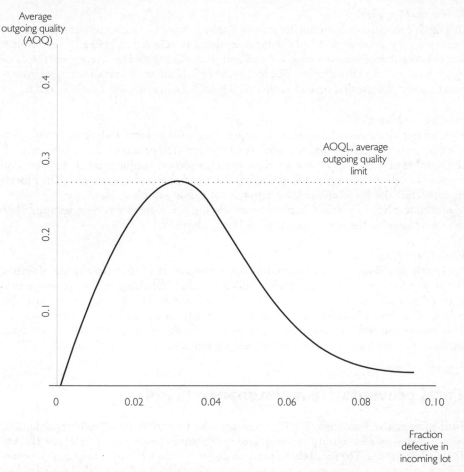

Figure 12.7 Average outgoing quality vs. fraction defectives

Sampling plans

The method of sampling or sampling or sampling plan can take a number of forms including the following.

- single sampling
- double sampling
- multiple sampling
- variable sampling.

Single sampling plan
For a single sample attribute plan the method consists of selecting a sample at random from a larger lot and determining if the goods are defective or not (i.e. a discrete decision).

Double sampling plan

In a double sampling plan a smaller sample is taken than in a single sampling plan. If the quality is very good or very bad the lot is accepted or rejected as before. If the result is inconclusive then a second sample is taken and the lot is rejected or accepted on the combined results of the two samples. The technique should allow an overall saving of inspection costs by the use of a smaller sample which will usually provide a definite result.

Multiple sampling plan

Here an initial sample (which can be as small as one unit) is taken. If the number of defectives is above or below a specified limit the lot is rejected or accepted as appropriate. If the number of defectives is between these limits, a second sample is taken and the total number of defects is compared to an increased set of upper and lower limits. The process repeats until the lot is accepted or rejected. Multiple sampling plans are particularly appropriate when inspection costs are relatively high, e.g. for destructive testing, when the cost of testing the whole sample would be prohibitive.

Variable sampling plan

A variable sampling plan takes samples from a measure that can take a range of values, as opposed to an attribute plan which is a discrete value. Variable sampling plans are constructed in a similar way to attribute plans but instead of the binomial and Poisson distribution, a normal distribution is assumed (especially for a sample size greater than 30). This means the trial-and-error approach to develop the plan is not needed, but standardised variable tables are available to develop plans for various AQL values.

Total preventative maintenance (TPM)

Total preventative maintenance (TPM) combines the practice of preventative maintenance with the ideas of total quality and employee involvement which form part of the JIT and TQM philosophies. The idea behind preventative maintenance is to anticipate equipment failures through a programme of routine maintenance which will not only help to reduce breakdowns, but also to reduce downtime (time not in operation) and lengthen the life of the equipment. It has been realised that the cost of a maintenance programme can be outweighed by the more consistent output of a better quality product. In a TPM programme all employees are encouraged to use their knowledge to improve equipment reliability and reduce variability in performance. When considering the cost implications of maintenance activities it is important to consider not just the cost of lost production due to poor maintenance but the costs associated with loss of business due to poor customer service.

Maintenance activities

TPM includes the following activities:

- *Regular maintenance* activities such as lubricating, painting, cleaning and inspection. These activities are normally carried out by the operator in order to prevent equipment deterioration.

- *Periodic inspection* to assess the condition of equipment in order to avoid breakdowns. These inspections are normally carried out at regular time intervals by either operator or maintenance personnel.
- *Preventative repairs*, due to deterioration, but before a breakdown has occurred. Normally carried out by maintenance personnel but ideally by the operators.

TPM thus emphasises the equipment operator's role in maintenance and considers preventative maintenance to be more than preventative repairs, but the execution of regular maintenance and inspection activities which ensures the equipment is in the best possible environment and is not allowed to deteriorate. This will require a programme of training of operators to maintain equipment over its life span. The TPM approach embraces the philosophy of continuous improvement in that the idea is not just to keep equipment operational but to make improvements to eliminate breakdowns (i.e. **zero defects**). To do this requires the design of products to include aspects such as the ease of maintenance of equipment used to produce that product.

Predictive maintenance

Preventative maintenance uses a system of routine inspection and replacement of parts. This may lead to the equipment being out of service for periods of inspection or even replacement of parts during what could be productive time. Predictive maintenance uses a system of monitoring performance measures of equipment to predict failures, rather than a periodic check. Thus by predicting problems in advance the maintenance activity may take place when the machine is not in use saving production output. Also overtime payments and component expediting costs may be saved. Predictive maintenance is undertaken using sensors which monitor variables such as vibration at critical points. These readings are tracked by computer which identifies trends in performance. Analysis of particles in lubricants and examination of equipment parts by fibre optics, eliminating the need for disassembly, can also help to predict problems and thus help plan maintenance outputs in advance.

Evaluation of preventative activities

The amount of preventative maintenance undertaken can be considered as a trade-off between the cost of preventative maintenance and the cost of breakdown maintenance. The amount of preventative maintenance will depend on a variety of factors such as the age of equipment (see notes on reliability, Chapter 5) but there is a point when too much preventative maintenance (e.g. rebuilding equipment every day) can be too costly in labour and downtime. The relationship between cost and preventative maintenance is shown graphically in Figure 12.8.

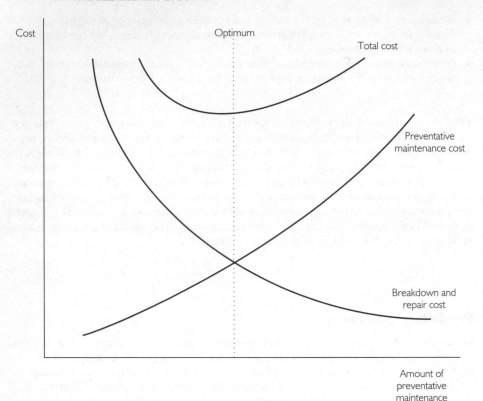

Figure 12.8 Cost vs. amount of preventative maintenance

Measurement tools

Benchmarking

Benchmarking as a **measurement tool** can be defined as the continuous measurement of an organisation's products and processes against a company recognised as a leader in that industry. The analysis of competitor products is an older technique which forms part of the product design process (Chapter 5). Benchmarking was initially restricted to the comparison of direct competitors in the manufacturing sector. Now it is practised in the service sector (e.g. banks), in all functional areas (e.g. marketing) and in comparison with a wide variety of companies from which relevant lessons can be learnt (i.e. not just the 'best in its class'). Because of the widespread use of the technique and the requests by many organisations to visit the same high performance firms, much benchmarking data is held in databases for general use. A number of models for implementing a benchmarking programme have been developed. The main activities involved in benchmarking are summarised below:

- **Planning**. Understand your own processes, identify key processes and form benchmarking teams.

- **Analysis**. Conduct research on possible competitors and other relevant companies and formulate questions to elicit the required information. Establish a relationship with a partner organisation and collect and share information.
- **Implementation**. Implement and monitor improvements suggested by analysis

It is important that the relevant processes in the organisation are benchmarked before comparison with a competitor. Processes are benchmarked in terms of metrics (numeric measurements) and procedures (process flows). For example a payment process could be measured by the time taken from receiving the request to delivery of the payment. The technique would also measure the type and amount of personnel involved in each step of the process. Problems with some benchmarking programmes has been the necessary focus on developing metrics and the lack of energy put into implementing changes suggested by the benchmarking process. Other problems are the difficulty in obtaining direct competitor information and the fact that if the process is simply used to emulate a competitor, competitive advantage may be short-lived as the aware competitor makes further improvements.

Benchmarking may best be seen as used in conjunction with a programme of continuous improvement (CI) to sustain competitive advantage and business process re-engineering (BPR) which focuses on improvement of whole business processes across functions to gain significant performance improvements (Chapter 11).

Pareto analysis

It has been found that the cost of a large percentage of poor quality can be attributed to a single category of defects. Pareto analysis assists in the identification of these major causes. The technique is undertaken by constructing a tally of different possible causes of quality and then converting the tally into a cumulative percentage (by dividing each tally by the total tally count). This frequency distribution is then displayed on a bar chart or Pareto diagram which identifies the relative causes of poor quality (Figure 12.9).

The Pareto diagram shows which cause should be tackled to achieve the greatest return on investment. Other causes can then be addressed as part of a continuous improvement programme.

Cause and effect/fishbone diagrams

Although the Pareto diagram may identify the cause of a quality problem, the reasons behind that problem needs to be identified. Cause and effect or fishbone diagrams are used as a problem-solving tool to identify the root cause behind a particular quality problem. An example fishbone diagram is shown in Figure 12.10.

The idea is to work back from the quality problem and identify individual causes on lines radiating from each category branch, associated with the problem in each major category (categories may differ from those shown in the example). The tool helps structure and identify the underlying causes of the problem.

Cause	Number of defects	Percentage
Poor product design	85	65%
Defective components	20	15%
Operator error	13	10%
Defective materials	8	6%
Incorrect tooling	5	4%
	131	100%

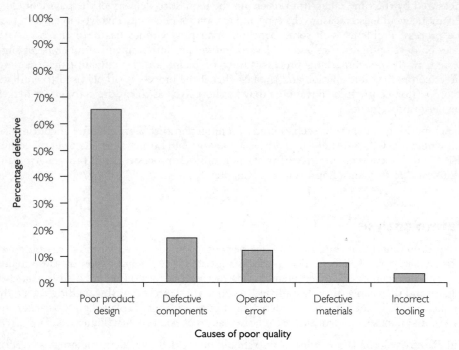

Figure 12.9 Pareto table and chart

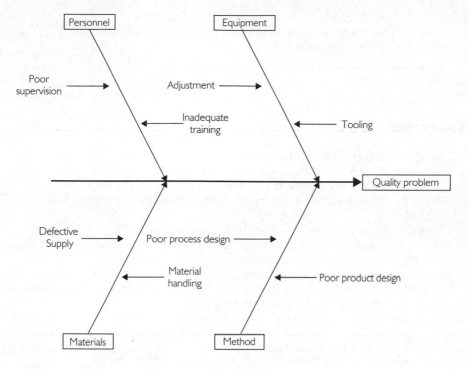

Figure 12.10 A general cause and effect (fishbone) diagram

Summary of key points _____

- Statistical process control (SPC) is a sampling technique which checks the quality of an item which is engaged in a process.
- Chance causes of variation are caused by the inherent variability in the process.
- Assignable causes of variation can be attributed to some change in the process which need to be investigated and rectified.
- An $\overline{X}$-bar chart shows the distance of sample values from the target value.
- An R-chart shows the variability of sample values.
- A p-chart shows the proportion of defectives in a sample.
- A c-chart shows the number of defectives in a sample.
- Control chart limits are based on the variability of samples of process output whose variability is a function of process capability.
- Acceptance sampling consists of taking a random sample from a larger batch or lot of material to be inspected.
- Sampling plans can be in the form of single, double, multiple or variable sampling plans.
- Total preventative maintenance (TPM) involves regular maintenance, periodic inspection and preventative repairs.
- Benchmarking can be defined as the continuous measurement of an organisation's products and processes compared against a company recognised as a leader in that or a related industry.

- Pareto analysis can identify the major causes of poor quality.
- Cause and effect diagrams can be used as a problem-solving tool to identify the root cause behind a particular quality problem.

Exercises

1 Distinguish between chance causes of variation and assignable causes of variation.
2 What is the difference between an attribute control chart and a variable control chart?
3 Discuss the determination of the sample size for attribute and variable control charts.
4 What is the difference between the means chart and the ranges chart for a variable control chart?
5 Distinguish between tolerances, control limits and process capability.
6 The following table gives the number of defectives in successive samples of 100 final assemblies removed at random from that day's production.
   (a) Estimate the total proportion of rejects.
   (b) Establish a single set of control limits for the daily fraction of rejects based on these figures and plot a control chart, showing the daily results.
   (c) Comment on the stability of the manufacturing process.

Day	Number of defectives	Day	Number of defectives
1	6	11	11
2	8	12	8
3	7	13	13
4	10	14	14
5	11	15	15
6	5	16	12
7	13	17	7
8	9	18	34
9	9	19	29
10	10	20	8

7 The following table gives the means and ranges, from a sample size of 10, for the diameter of a machined part.

Use the data to set up a control chart for means and for ranges.

Mean $\bar{X}$	Range R	Mean $\bar{X}$	Range R	Mean $\bar{X}$	Range R
0.52	0.03	0.5	0.11	0.57	0.1
0.53	0.1	0.53	0.08	0.52	0.07
0.57	0.09	0.52	0.05	0.52	0.12
0.49	0.08	0.48	0.09	0.51	0.11
0.48	0.12	0.54	0.03	0.49	0.09

8 A machine produces components to a specified average length of 9.03 cms. Every hour a random sample of five components is selected from the process and their lengths measured. After 10 hours the data given below have been collected.

Use the data to set up a control chart for means and for ranges.

Sample number	Measurements (cm)				
1	9.00	9.10	9.00	9.05	8.95
2	9.10	9.10	9.00	9.05	9.05
3	9.00	9.05	9.00	9.05	9.00
4	9.00	9.00	8.95	9.00	9.05
5	9.00	9.10	9.05	9.05	9.00
6	9.00	9.10	9.10	9.05	9.00
7	9.00	9.10	9.05	9.15	9.05
8	9.00	9.10	9.10	9.00	9.05
9	9.00	9.00	8.95	9.00	9.00
10	9.00	9.05	9.00	9.10	8.95

9 The following table gives the crimes per 1000 residents for various parts of a city in the last month. The mean number of crimes has stayed around four for several years.

Draw a c-chart to determine if there is any reason to believe that any of the city areas are out of line in terms of numbers of crimes.

City area	Crimes per 1000 residents
1	2
2	4
3	3
4	6
5	5
6	11
7	9
8	3
9	2
10	4

10 When is the technique of acceptance sampling appropriate?

11 What is the function of the operating characteristics curve?

12 Explain the concepts of producer's risk and consumer's risk in acceptance sampling.

13 Why is it important to determine the average outgoing quality limit (AOQL) in acceptance sampling?

14 Outline the differences between single and multiple sampling plans in acceptance sampling.

15 What is the role of total preventative maintenance (TPM) in operations performance improvement?

16 Distinguish between preventative and predictive maintenance.
17 Evaluate the role of benchmarking.

References

Ashby, W.R., *An Introduction to Cybernetics*, Chapman & Hall (1971).

Chakravarthy, B.S., Measuring strategic performance, *Strategic Management Journal*, 7, (1986) pp. 437–458.

Schefczyk, M., Operational performance of airlines: an extension of traditional measurement paradigms, *Strategic Management Journal*, 14, (1993) pp. 301–317.

Further reading

Besterfield, D.H., *Quality Control*, Fourth Edition, Prentice-Hall (1994).

Dodge, H.F. and Romig, H.G., *Sampling Inspection Tables – Single and Double Sampling*, 2nd Edition, Wiley (1959).

Wilkinson, A., Redman, T., Snape, E. and Marchington, M., *Managing with Total Quality Management: Theory and Practice*, Macmillan (1998).

Field, S.W. and Swift, K.G., *Effecting a Quality Change: An Engineering Approach*, Arnold (1996).

Holloway, J., Lewis, J. and Mallory, G., (eds.) *Performance Measurement and Evaluation*, Sage Publications (1995).

13 Operations strategy

Objectives

> By the end of this chapter, you should be able to:
>
> - understand the role of operations in strategy development;
> - understand the concept of focused manufacturing;
> - understand the significance of the operations performance objectives in measuring operations performance in achieving its strategic goals;
> - be familiar with approaches to strategy development;
> - be aware of tools available to assist in strategy implementation.

This chapter describes the role and formulation of operations strategy in the organisation. Firstly the nature of strategy is investigated. It is seen to be concerned with the long-term direction of the organisation and exists at three main management levels. The increasing importance of the role of operations strategy is discussed. The idea of focus in meeting strategic needs is also discussed. The role of operations in strategy development can be assessed by using the Hayes and Wheelwright 4-stage model. In order to ensure strategic goals are being met it is necessary to develop measures of operation's performance. Performance objectives that can be used are those of quality, speed, dependability, flexibility and cost. Three approaches to strategy development are considered which are concerned with matching internal operations capability with external competitive market requirements. Implementation of strategic change must take account of many factors. Some of the tools to assist the manager in implementing strategic change are considered.

What is strategy?

Johnson and Scholes (1993) provide the following definition of strategy:

> 'Strategy is the *direction* and *scope* of an organisation over the *long term*: ideally, which matches its *resources* to its changing *environment*, and in particular its *markets*, *customers* or *clients* so as to meet *stakeholder* expectations.'

Thus strategic decisions occur as a result of an evaluation of the external and internal environment. The external evaluation may reveal market opportunities or threats from competitors. The evaluation of the internal environment may reveal limitations in capabilities relative to competitors.

Strategy is seen as complex in nature due to:

- A high degree of uncertainty in future consequences arriving from decisions.

egration is required of all aspects and functional areas of business.
Major change may have to be implemented as a consequence of strategic choices made.

Levels of strategy

Strategy can be seen to exist at three main levels within the organisation.

At the highest or corporate level the strategy provides very general long-range guidance for the whole organisation, often expressed as a statement of its mission. The mission statement describes in general terms what key decision-makers want the company to accomplish and what kind of company they want it to become. Thus the mission focuses the organisation on specific market areas and the basis on which it must compete.

The second level of strategy is termed a business strategy and may be for the organisation or at the strategic business unit (SBU) level in larger diversified companies. There the concern is with the products and services that should be offered in the market defined at the corporate level.

The third level of strategy is termed the operational or functional strategy where the functions of the business (e.g. operations, marketing, finance) make long-range plans which support the business strategy. Since the operations function is responsible in large part for the delivery of the product/service it has a major responsibility for business strategy formulation and implementation. A typical focus for three strategy levels is given in Table 13.1.

Table 13.1 Levels of strategy

Strategy level	Focus
Corporate	What business do we operate in (in five years' time)?
Business	How do we compete (this year)?
Functional	What needs to be done (next) to meet the business plan?

This simple model implies a 'top-down' approach to strategy formulation in which corporate goals are communicated down to business and then functional areas. Although there has always been interaction within this hierarchy in both directions in this model the role of functional areas such as operations in setting the framework for how a company can compete is being recognised. The increasing importance of operations strategy development is discussed in the following section.

The role of operations in strategy development

The importance of the role of operations/manufacturing function in the formulation and delivery of the organisation's strategy has become recognised (Brown, 1996). Market conditions have changed from a mass production era with an emphasis on high volume, low cost production to an environment demanding performance on measures such as quality and speed of delivery as well as cost. In addition the rapid pace of change in markets means the basis of how the organisation will compete may change quickly over time.

The traditional approach to strategy development has been for senior managers to establish corporate objectives, develop a strategy for meeting these objectives and then to acquire resources necessary to implement the chosen strategy. This approach is intended to ensure that resources are directed efficiently at the areas identified as 'strategically' important from the strategic analysis. The approach is based on the firm's ability to forecast future market conditions and thus identify gaps between future market needs and organisational capability. However in dynamic markets the ability to forecast far enough into the future in order to build a competitive advantage will be limited. Hayes (1995) outlines another potential problem that has emerged with the traditional approach to strategy development and implementation. The method has encouraged an ends-based approach to change, which emphasises the use of projects led by senior managers to achieve objectives through such 'structural' changes as new equipment installations, new product introduction and changes to the design of the organisational structure. Specifically it can also be reflected in an approach where the implementation of improvement programmes such as JIT and TQM are seen in the short term as solving a specific manufacturing problem identified in the strategic plan. Thus this approach has led to an emphasis on relatively short-term objectives and a lack of emphasis on 'behavioural' factors such as performance evaluation systems and selection and development of the workforce. The idea is that in dynamic market conditions the strategic plan should indicate the general direction that the organisation should follow based on the capabilities and values it possesses. Thus strategic advantage will derive from developing capabilities across a range of areas and matching these capabilities to emerging technologies and market opportunities (Hayes and Pisano, 1994). For instance a key role of strategy should be to guide the selection of improvement programmes such as JIT and TQM and to see them in terms of the type of skills and capabilities they bring to the organisation which are relevant to meeting future market needs.

Focused manufacturing

One approach to providing a 'fit' between the manufacturing strategy task and the internal process capability and infrastructure is called focused manufacturing (Skinner, 1974). The idea is to focus particular market demands on individual facilities. This should reduce the level of complexity generated when attempting to service a number of different market segments from an individual plant. Hill (1993) states that focus, or the act of concentrating on a manageable set of structural elements (e.g. product, technologies, volume) and supporting infrastructure (e.g. management planning and control systems) can overcome the following complexities in markets:

- markets of low volume and dynamics where economies of scale are not appropriate;
- different order-winning criteria required for a range of products;
- complexity of large plant size (e.g. bureaucracy);
- lack of focus on manufacturing strategy because of a range of needs;
- utilisation of plant more important than suitability of manufacturing task;
- important initiatives (e.g. TQM, JIT) not developed to fit the market needs of the business.

Potential advantages of the focus approach include improved communications, orientation to agreed business objectives, simpler and more appropriate management style, higher levels of employee participation, higher levels of employee motivation, shorter process lead times, lower WIP inventory, reduced complexity of production control tasks and more accurate assessment of financial performance.

Disadvantages include an increase and duplication of processes and infrastructure and the loss of possible economies of scale.

The relative importance of these advantages and disadvantages will determine the approach to focusing facilities. Hill (1993) provides three approaches:

● *Based on products/markets.* The focus is based on the forecast sales of customer or product groups. This implies that manufacturing is aligned with the marketing view of the business.
● *Based on process.* The focus is based on the process needs (e.g. line, batch) of the products. The products needing the same process will go to the same manufacturing unit thereby avoiding the potential duplication of investment. The organisation within a plant on the basis of process type is known as group technology (Chapter 3).
● *Based on order-winners.* The focus is based on the different order-winners and qualifiers which manufacturing needs to provide. This approach aims to ensure that the conditions are created where manufacturing can excel at the criteria which are necessary for market success, i.e. the external (market) competitive factors are translated into internal performance objectives for manufacturing. For example if the order-winning criteria is fast delivery then an emphasis on cycle-time reduction is necessary from the manufacturing unit. Focus based in this way will need to reflect changes in the relative performance objectives in meeting market-place demands in customer needs, competitor actions and the stages of the product life cycle.

JIT production facilities often use the idea of the focused factory as outlined by Skinner (1974). These factories organise their functions around a relatively narrow range of products or product family (a group of products that share similar production requirements) in order to ensure simple and consistent operations. This may be the outcome of splitting a large manufacturing plant that has developed a large product range over time into two or more focused plants. In terms of JIT flow, concentrating on a narrow range of products will simplify layout reducing transportation time and reduce WIP inventories. The concept of focus is connected with the JIT philosophy of keeping work methods simple and reducing system complexity. To sustain flexibility, however, there will be less automation used than is generally associated with the focused factory which is often associated with computer-integrated manufacturing (Chapter 3).

Judging and measuring the contribution of operations to strategy

Hayes and Wheelwright (1988) asserts that the success of manufacturing companies is dependent on their overall manufacturing capability and so provides a model which enables managers to identify manufacturing's current strategic role and the changes needed in order to improve competitiveness. The four-stage model traces the contribution of the operations function from a largely reactive role in Stage 1 to a proactive element in competitive success in Stage 4. The stages are described as follows:

- **Stage 1: Internal neutrality.** Here the operations function has very little to contribute to competitive success and is seen as a barrier to better competitive performance by other functions. The operations function is simply attempting to reach a minimum acceptable standard required by the rest of the organisation whilst avoiding any major mistakes, thus the term 'internal neutrality'. However a major mistake by operations could still have serious consequences for the rest of the organisation (e.g. product recall).
- **Stage 2: External neutrality.** Here the operations function begins to focus on comparing its performance with competitor organisations. Although it may not be innovative enough to be in the 'first division' of companies in its market, by taking the best ideas and attempting to match the performance of competitors it is attempting to be externally neutral.
- **Stage 3: Internally supportive.** Here the operations function is one of the best in their market area and aspires to be the best in the market. The operations function will thus be organising and developing the operations capabilities to meet the strategic requirements of the organisation. Thus operations is taking a role in the implementation of strategy and being 'internally supportive'.
- **Stage 4: Externally supportive.** In Stage 4, the operations function is becoming central to strategy making and providing the foundation for future competitive success. This may be delivered through the organisation of resources in ways that are innovative and capable of adapting as markets change. When operations is in the role of the long-term driver of strategy it is being 'externally' supportive.

Performance objectives

The five basic operations' performance objectives allow the organisation to measure its operation's performance in achieving its strategic goals. The performance objectives outlined by Slack (1995) are:

- quality
- speed
- dependability
- flexibility
- cost.

Each one of these objectives will be discussed in terms of how they are measured and their significance to organisational competitiveness.

Quality
Quality covers both the quality of the product/service itself (Chapter 5) and the quality of the process that delivers the product/service (Chapter 11). Quality can be measured by the 'cost of quality' model covered in Chapter 11. Here quality costs are categorised as either the cost of achieving good quality (the cost of quality assurance) or the cost of poor quality products (the costs of not conforming to specifications).

The advantages of good quality on competitiveness include:

- *Increased dependability* – fewer problems due to poor quality means a more reliable delivery process.
- *Reduced costs* – if things are done right first time expenditure is saved on scrap and correcting mistakes.

- *Improved customer service* – a consistently high quality product (product quality) delivered on time (process quality) will lead to high customer satisfaction.

Speed

The time delay between a customer request for a product/service and then receiving that product/service is the delivery time. To a greater or lesser extent the delivery speed is important to the customer in making a choice about which organisation to use. The concept of P:D ratios (Chapter 7) compares the demand time D (from customer request to receipt of goods/services) to the total throughput time P of the purchase, make and delivery stages. Thus in a make-to-stock system D is basically the delivery time, but for a customer-to-order system the customer demand time is equal to the purchase, make and delivery stages (P). In this case the speed of the internal processes of purchase and make will directly affect the delivery time experienced by the customer.

Although the use of a make-to-stock system may reduce the delivery time as seen by the customer, it has the disadvantages associated with producing for future demand. These include the risk of the products becoming obsolete, inaccurate forecasting of product demand leading to stock-out or unwanted stock, the cost of any stock in terms of working capital and the decreased ability to react quickly to changes in customer requirements. Thus the advantage of speed is that it can be either be used to reduce the amount of speculative activity and keep the delivery time constant or for the same amount of speculative activity it can reduce overall delivery lead time. Thus in competitive terms speed can be used to both reduce costs (making to inaccurate forecasts) and reduce delivery time (better customer service).

Dependability

Dependability refers to consistently meeting a promised delivery time for a product/service to a customer. Thus an increase in delivery speed may not lead to customer satisfaction if it is not produced in a consistent manner. Dependability can be measured by the percentage of customers that receive a product/service within the delivery time promised. In some instances it may even be important to deliver a product not too quickly, but only at the time required. (e.g. a consignment of wet concrete for construction). Dependability leads to better customer service when the customer can trust that the product/service will be delivered when expected. Dependability can also lead to lower costs, in that progress checking and other activities designed to ensure things happen on time can be reduced within the organisation. Key activities needed to increase dependability include planning and control mechanisms to ensure problems are uncovered early, and making dependability a key performance measure.

Flexibility

Flexibility is the ability of the organisation to change what it does quickly. This can mean the ability to offer a wide variety of products/services to the customer and to be able to change these products/services quickly. Flexibility is needed so the organisation can adapt to changing customer needs in terms of product range and varying demand and to cope with capacity shortfalls due to equipment breakdown or component shortage. The following types of flexibility can be identified:

- *Product/service* – to be able to quickly act in response to changing customer needs with new product/service designs.
- *Mix* – to be able to provide a wide range of products/services.
- *Volume* – to be able to decrease or increase output in response to changes in demand.

Volume flexibility may be needed for seasonal changes in demand as services may have to react to demand changes minute by minute.

- *Delivery* – this is the ability to react to changes in the timing of a delivery. This may involve the ability to change delivery priorities between orders and still deliver on time.

Flexibility can be measured in terms of range (the amount of the change) and response (the speed of the change). Table 13.2 outlines the range and response dimensions for the four flexibility types of product/service, mix, volume and delivery, based on Slack (1995).

Table 13.2 The range and response dimensions for the four system flexibility types

Flexibility type	Range flexibility	Response flexibility
Product flexibility	The range of products/services which the company has the capability to produce	The time necessary to develop or modify the product and processes to the point where regular delivery can start
Mix flexibility	The range of product/services which the company can deliver within a given time period	The time necessary to adjust the mix of products/services being delivered
Volume flexibility	The absolute level of the aggregated output which the company can achieve for a given product/service mix	The time taken to change the aggregated level of output
Delivery flexibility	The extent to which delivery dates can be brought forward	The time taken to reorganise the delivery system so as to replan for the new delivery date

The range and response dimensions are connected in the sense that the more something is changed (range) the longer it will take (response). The relationship between the two can be observed by constructing range-response curves. In general the benefit of flexibility from the customer's point of view is that it speeds up response by being able to adapt to customer needs. The ability of the internal operation to react to changes will also help maintain the dependability objective.

Cost

If an organisation is competing on price then it is essential that it keeps its cost base lower than the competition. Then it will either make more profit than rivals, if price is equal, or gain market share if price is lower. Cost is also important for a strategy of providing a product to a market niche, which competitors cannot provide. Thus cost proximity (i.e. to ensure costs are close to the market average) is important to maximise profits and deter competitors from entering the market.

The major categories of cost are staff, facilities (including overheads) and material. The proportion of these costs will differ between operations but averages are for staff 15%, facilities 30% and material 55%. Thus it can be seen that the greatest scope for cost reduction lies with reduction of the cost of materials. A relatively small proportion of costs is usually assigned to direct labour. The level and mix of these costs will be dependent on the following factors:

- volume and variety of output
- variation in demand.

Increased volume means that cost per unit will decrease as resources can be dedicated to the production or delivery of a particular service. However diseconomies of scale can still occur due to increased organisational complexity which can lead to poor communication as volumes or activities increase. Increases in volume may either be achieved with present resources or require significant investment in equipment and labour. The cost implications of increases in volume must therefore be considered carefully.

Variety of output will increase complexity and thus costs. However this complexity can be reduced by using such techniques as design simplification and standardisation, or increased mix flexibility in moving from one product to another. The focused factory concept (Skinner, 1974) can be used to separate the organisation into units dedicated to different product types. These techniques can assist a firm in achieving both the variety and low cost that customers require.

Finally cost is dependent on the other performance objectives. As noted earlier, increased flexibility can lead to a decrease in the cost of product/service design. In fact all the performance objectives can lead to a reduction in cost. Thus improving the four performance objectives externally the customer will actually reduce internal costs and thus achieve this performance objective also. In fact it has been suggested that a improvement strategy should tackle the performance objectives in the order of quality, dependability, speed, flexibility and finally cost (Slack, 1995).

Approaches to operations strategy

The following approaches to operations strategy provide useful guidelines in dealing with the issue of aligning operations to competitive needs. Three approaches to strategy development will be outlined:

- Hill framework
- Platts-Gregory procedure
- Slack procedure.

Hill framework

The emphasis of the Hill methodology is that strategic decisions cannot be bound solely on information regarding customer and marketing opportunities addressed solely from a marketing function's perspective, but the operations (manufacturing) capability must also be taken into account. Thus the Hill framework is based around the idea of developing the operation's strategy from the customers' view of competitive factors.

Hill proposes that the issue of the degree of 'fit' between the proposed marketing strategy and manufacturing's ability to support it is resolved at the business level in terms of meeting corporate (i.e. strategic) objectives. Thus Hill provides an iterative framework that links together the corporate objectives; which provide the organisational direction, the marketing strategy; which defines how the organisation will compete in its chosen markets, and the operations strategy; which provides capability to compete in those markets. The framework consists of five steps (Hill, 1993):

- Step 1. Define corporate objectives.
- Step 2. Determine marketing strategies to meet these objectives.
- Step 3. Assess how different products win orders against competitors.
- Step 4. Establish the most appropriate mode to manufacture these sets of products – process choice.
- Step 5. Provide the manufacturing infrastructure required to support production.

In traditional strategy formulation the outcome of Step 3 is 'passed on' to Steps 4 and 5 and no further feedback occurs between steps in the process. The Hill methodology requires iteration between all five steps in order to link manufacturing capability into decisions at a corporate level. This model is shown graphically in Table 13.3.

Table 13.3 The Hill methodology of operations strategy formulation (Slack et al., Operations Management, Pitman, Financial Times Management, 1995)

Step 1 Corporate objectives	Step 2 Marketing strategies	Step 3 Competitiveness	Step 4 Operations strategy	Step 5 Supporting infrastructure
• growth • profit • ROI • other financial measures	• product/service markets and segments • range • mix • volumes • standardisation or customisation? • innovation • leader or follower?	• price • quality • delivery speed • delivery dependability • product/service range • product/service design • brand image • technical service	• process technology • trade-offs embodied in process • role of inventory • capacity • size • timing • location	• functional support • operations planning and control systems • work structuring • payment systems • organisational structure

The steps in the Hill methodology are now described in more detail.

Step 1. Corporate objectives

Step 1 involves establishing corporate objectives that provide a direction for the organisation and performance indicators that allow progress in achieving those objectives to be measured. The objectives will be dependent on the needs of external and internal stakeholders and so will include financial measures such as profit and growth rates as well as employee practices such as skills development and appropriate environmental policies.

Step 2. Marketing strategy

Step 2 involves developing a marketing strategy to meet the corporate objectives defined in Step 1. This involves identifying target markets and deciding how to compete in these markets. This will require the utilisation of product/service characteristics such as range, mix and volume that the operations activity will be required to provide. Ot~ ~issues considered will be the level of innovation and product development and the cl~ or 'follower' strategies in the chosen markets.

Step 3. How do products win orders in the market place?

This step provides the link between corporate marketing proposals and th~

ecessary to support them. This is achieved by translating the
ge of **competitive factors** (e.g. price, quality, delivery speed)
wins orders. Hill distinguishes between **order-winning fac-**
to winning business from customers) and **qualifying factors**
order to be considered for business from customers). The com-
most important indicator as to the relative importance of the
tives discussed earlier in this chapter. The performance objec-
bility of operations to meet the customer-defined competitive
factors. Table 13.4 provides examples of how different (external) competitive factors will
require a focus on the corresponding (internal) performance objectives.

Table 13.4 *The relationship between competitive factors and performance objectives*

Competitive factor	Performance objective
High quality	Quality
Fast delivery	Speed
Reliable delivery	Dependability
Wide product/service range	Flexibility (mix)
Low price	Cost

Slack (1995) outlines three main influences on the relative importance of the competitive
factors:

- customer needs
- competitor needs
- stage of the product life cycle.

Customer needs
Customers will value a range of competitive factors for any particular product/service;
thus it is necessary to identify the relative importance of a range of factors. The concept
of 'order-winning' and 'qualifying factors' of Hill helps distinguish between those factors
that directly contribute to winning business and those that are necessary to qualify for
the customer's consideration between a range of products/services. The importance of this
is that while it may be necessary to raise performance on some factors to a certain level
in order to be considered by the customer, a further rise in the level of performance may
not achieve an increase in competitiveness. Instead competitiveness may then depend on
raising the level of performance of different 'order-winning' factors. It may also be the
case that the order-winning and qualifying factors will differ for different customer
groups that the organisation may be serving. One strategy for dealing with divergent customer demands is to use the idea of the focused factory and to break the plant into units
allocated on the basis of 'order-winner' and 'order-qualifying' criteria.

Competitor actions
Competitor actions will also influence the basis on which competition is based and may
require a change in priorities of the competitive factors used by the organisation: e.g. if
an organisation is competing on price and a competitor enters the market and takes market share by competing on faster delivery, the organisation may need to consider that as

a new competitive factor. The significance of this influence is that the initiative for change had been provided by a competitor, not the customer.

The stage of the product life cycle

The **product/service life cycle** (PLC) is an attempt to describe the change or trend in sales volume for a particular product or service from when it is introduced into a market until its withdrawal. The model shows sales volume passing through the four stages of introduction, growth, maturity and decline. The model is useful in that each stage in the life cycle requires a different approach from the operations function and thus emphasises the need for a range of capabilities from the operations function. The drawback of the approach is that it may be difficult to predict when the product/service will enter the next stage of the cycle or even determine what stage of the cycle the product/service is currently in! The main stages of the PLC can be described as follows:

- **Introduction**. On introduction the product/service specification may frequently be changed as feedback is received from customers. Operations will need to maintain flexibility in terms of design changes and response to changes in demand levels. Quality levels need to be maintained, despite frequent design changes, in order to ensure customer acceptance.
- **Growth**. If the introduction of the product/service has been successful then a period of sales growth occurs. Competitors may also enter the market. The main concern of operations will be to meet what may be a rapid increase in demand whilst maintaining quality levels.
- **Maturity**. After a period of growth, customer demand will be largely satisfied and demand will level off. The market may be dominated by a few organisations offering a standard product/service. Competition on price will be important and so the main issues for operations will be minimising costs and maintaining a dependable supply.
- **Decline**. After a certain time the need for a product/service will be satisfied, or a new product/service will be introduced undertaking the tasks of the original. At this point sales will decline, competitors will drop out of the market and remaining competition will be focused on price, indicating a need for operations to minimise costs.

Table 13.5 provides a graphical description on the effect of the product/service life cycle on the organisation (Slack *et al.*, 1995).

Table 13.5 The effects of the product/service life cycle on the organisation (Slack et al., *Operations Management, Pitman, Financial Times Management, 1995)*

	Introduction	Growth	Maturity	Decline
Volume	Low	Rapid growth	High level	Declining
Customers	Innovators	Early adopters	Bulk of market	Laggards
Competitors	Few/none	Increasing number	Stable number	Declining number
Variety of product/service designs	Possible high customisation or frequent design changes	Increasingly standardised	Emerging dominant types	Possible move to commodity standardisation
Likely order winners	Product/service characteristics, performance or novelty	Availability of quality products/services	Low price; dependable supply	Low price
Likely qualifiers	Quality; range	Price; range	Range; quality	Dependable supply
Dominant operations performance objectives	Flexibility; quality	Speed, dependability; quality	Cost, dependability	Cost

Step 4. Process choice

This step involves the choice of process relating to the volume and variety mix of the product or service as outlined in Chapter 3. The main process types in manufacturing are project, jobbing, batch, line and continuous in order of increasing volume and decreasing variety. The step also considers other process issues such as the size, timing and location of capacity (Chapter 6).

Step 5. Manufacturing infrastructure

While Step 4 investigates manufacturing capabilities required for the process design, Step 5 considers the capabilities required of supporting infrastructure such as planning and control systems, quality assurance and organisational structure.

The crucial stage in Hill's methodology is Step 3, where any mismatches between the requirements of the organisation's strategy and the operation's capability are revealed.

The Platts-Gregory procedure

The Platts-Gregory procedure (Platts and Gregory, 1990) uses a profile analysis to identify any gaps between the needs of the market and operation's performance. The procedure has three stages:

- Stage 1 involves making a comparison between what the market wants (e.g. price, delivery) and how the operations performs (e.g. cost, delivery). An example profile analysis is shown in Figure 13.1.
- Stage 2 involves assessing the capabilities of the operation to achieve the desired market characteristics identified in Stage 1.
- Stage 3 involves reviewing the various strategic options open to the organisation and selecting a strategy which best satisfies the criteria identified in the previous stages.

The Slack procedure

The Slack procedure (Slack, 1991) combines features of both the Hill and Platts-Gregory approaches and follows a four-step process.

Step 1: Setting manufacturing objectives

This step aims to clarify how the organisation will compete in its chosen markets. Outcomes should be a ranked set of performance objectives for each product group and an assessment of the level of development of manufacturing capabilities necessary to meet these objectives. The relative performance objectives can be determined by using a 9-point scale of degrees of order-winning, qualifying and less important customer-viewed competitive factors. By ranking each performance objective on this scale their relative importance can be determined.

Step 2: Judging achieved performance

The next step ranks manufacturing's achieved performance against competitor achievement. Benchmarking in this way clarifies the competitive position of the organisation and helps identify where performance should be improved. A 9-point performance scale (rating from consistently better than the nearest competitor to consistently worst than most competitors) is used for each performance objective.

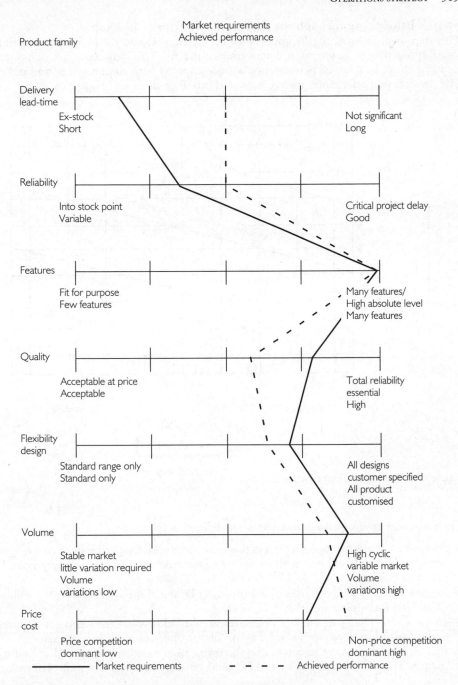

Figure 13.1 Platts-Gregory analysis (Gilgeous, G., Operations and the Management of Change, Pitman, Financial Times Management, 1997)

Step 3: Prioritising through the importance/performance gap

This step involves bringing the importance rating (Step 1) and the performance rating (Step 2) together in an importance/performance matrix. This indicates what customers find important in achieved performance when compared with competitor performance. The importance/performance matrix is divided into four zones (see Figure 13.2).

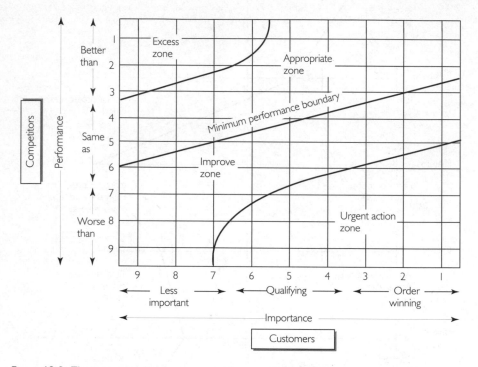

Figure 13.2 The importance/performance matrix

The Slack importance/performance zones are defined as follows:

- *Appropriate*. Performance objectives in this zone are satisfactory in the short to medium term, but there should be a wish to improve performance towards the upper boundary of the zone.
- *Improve*. Performance objectives below the lower bound of the appropriate zone will be candidates for improvement.
- *Urgent action*. Here performance objectives are far below what the customer requires and so should be improved to 'same as' or 'better then' competitor performance.
- *Excess?* Here too, many resources may be being used to achieve this level of performance. There is a possibility that they could be deployed to a less well performing area.

Although the main thrust of the operations function will be to move the performance objectives up the vertical scale and so outperform competitors, horizontal movement (i.e. changing customer perceptions of the relative importance of competitive factors) should be considered. The position of the performance objectives on the matrix will change, without any actions from the organisation, as customer preferences change and competitor performance improves. Thus improvement strategies should take the dynamic nature of the variables onto account.

Step 4: Develop action plans
The next stage shows how the performance objectives should be improved. This means ranking the performance objectives in priority of change (from Step 3) and asking what contribution to improvement could be derived from changes in:

- the operation's process technology;
- the operation's organisation and the development of its human resources;
- the operation's network of supply both in terms of information flows and material flows.

Strategy implementation

Garvin (1992) outlines six tools that will assist the operations manager in implementing strategic change.

Measurement systems
The importance of using a range of performance measures to translate strategy into action has become increasingly clear. Chapter 1 outlines how a range of measures can be used to assess performance and thus the competitive position of the organisation, using the balanced scorecard approach. The performance objectives outlined earlier in this chapter facilitate measurement of the performance of the operations function.

Technology
Implementation of technology can provide many benefits including improved productivity, superior quality and increased flexibility. However change in this area must be aligned with the organisational strategy and consider aspects such as the organisational structure and changes in work organisation. The stakeholder model (Chapter 1) can be used to consider the needs of interested parties in the introduction of new technology.

Organisation
Organisation decisions cover configuration of facilities, managing the network of operations but also aspects such as the use of teams and the form of organisational structures that allocate responsibility.

People
Different people will need to take on different roles during the implementation process. Garvin (1992) states the need for the following roles:

- **Sponsors** – these are usually senior managers that secure resources for the project and provide protection from outside influences.
- **Champions** – these take a participative role and act as change agents. Champions may need to be single-minded in pursuit of their goals in order to overcome opposition.
- **Implementers** – these put the ideas into reality and are involved in daily operations. One of their prime responsibilities is to gain co-operation of the workforce.

Leadership signals

It is important that a clear direction is given so that employees know the relative importance of a company's initiatives. These signals may be in the form of written directives, changes in management style or precedent setting decisions.

Culture

Culture can be seen as 'the way things are done around here' and shapes employees' norms, values and behaviour. The organisational culture may be a considerable barrier to strategy implementation. Managers may need to re-shape the culture of the organisation so that it can survive in new markets. For example a new strategy of innovation may require more of a risk-taking culture to be present.

Summary of key points

- Corporate strategy should provide a framework for the development and exploitation of organisational capabilities.
- The operations function may provide many of the capabilities on which an organisation can compete and thus should play an important role in corporate strategy development.
- Focused manufacturing aims to reduce the level of complexity in the manufacturing strategy task by focusing particular demands on individual facilities
- The five basic operations performance objectives are quality, speed, dependability, flexibility and cost.
- The performance objectives allow an operation to measure its performance in achieving strategic goals.
- The Hill methodology for strategy development provides an iterative framework that links together corporate objectives, the marketing strategy and the operations strategy.
- Tools to assist in implementing strategic change include measurement systems, technology, organisation, people, leadership signals and culture.

Exercises

1 Evaluate strategy development at the corporate, business and functional levels of an organisation.
2 Indicate how a major investment decision could be analysed in terms of its effect on the capability of the operations function.
3 Evaluate the potential advantages and disadvantages of focused manufacturing.
4 How can the relative significance of the five performance objectives be determined in formulating the organisation's strategic direction?
5 Discuss the main types of business flexibility
6 Explain the significance for management of linking operations strategy, marketing strategy and corporate objectives.

References

Brown, S., *Strategic Manufacturing for Competitive Advantage: Transforming Operations from Shop Floor to Strategy*, Prentice-Hall (1996).

Garvin, D.A., *Operations Strategy: Text and Cases*, Prentice-Hall (1992).

Gilgeous, V., *Operations and the Management of Change*, Pitman Publishing (1997).

Johnson, G. and Scholes, K., *Exploring Corporate Strategy*, 3rd Edition, Prentice-Hall (1993).

Hayes, R.H., Strategic planning – forward in reverse? *Harvard Business Review*, (Nov–Dec, 1985).

Hayes, R.H. and Pisano, G.P., Beyond World-Class: the New Manufacturing Strategy, *Harvard Business Review*, (Jan–Feb, 1994).

Hayes, R.H. and Wheelwright, S.C., *Restoring our Competitive Edge: Competing through Manufacturing*, Wiley (1988).

Hill, T. (1993) *Manufacturing Strategy*, 2nd Edition, Macmillan.

Platts, K.W. and Gregory, M.J., Manufacturing audit in the process of strategy formulation, *Int. J. Operations and Production Management*, 10, (9), (1990).

Slack, N., *Manufacturing Advantage: Achieving Competitive Manufacturing Operations*, Mercury (1991).

Slack, N., Chambers, S., Harland, C., Harrison, A. and Johnston, R., *Operations Management*, Pitman Publishing (1995).

Skinner, W., The Focused Factory, *Harvard Business Review*, (May–June, 1974), pp.113–121.

Further reading

Flaherty, M.T., *Global Operations Management*, McGraw-Hill (1996).

Pisano, G.P. and Hayes, R.H., *Manufacturing Renaissance*, Harvard Business School (1995).

Womack, J.P., Jones, D.T. and Roos, D., *The Machine that Changed the World*, Macmillan (1990).

Appendix

Areas under the standardised Normal Curve from 50% to 99.9% for values of z from 0 to 3

z	.00	.01	.02	.03	.04	.05	.06	.07	.08	.09
.0	.5000	.5040	.5080	.5120	.5160	.5199	.5239	.5279	.5319	.5359
.1	.5398	.5438	.5478	.5517	.5557	.5596	.5636	.5675	.5714	.5753
.2	.5793	.5832	.5871	.5910	.5948	.5987	.6026	.6064	.6103	.6141
.3	.6179	.6217	.6255	.6293	.6331	.6368	.6406	.6443	.6480	.6517
.4	.6554	.6591	.6628	.6664	.6700	.6736	.6772	.6808	.6844	.6879
.5	.6915	.6950	.6985	.7019	.7054	.7088	.7123	.7157	.7190	.7224
.6	.7257	.7291	.7324	.7357	.7389	.7422	.7454	.7486	.7517	.7549
.7	.7580	.7611	.7642	.7673	.7704	.7734	.7764	.7794	.7823	.7852
.8	.7881	.7910	.7939	.7967	.7995	.8023	.8051	.8078	.8106	.8133
.9	.8159	.8186	.8212	.8238	.8264	.8289	.8315	.8340	.8365	.8389
1.0	.8413	.8438	.8461	.8485	.8508	.8531	.8554	.8577	.8599	.8621
1.1	.8643	.8665	.8686	.8708	.8729	.8749	.8770	.8790	.8810	.8830
1.2	.8849	.8869	.8888	.8907	.8925	.8944	.8962	.8980	.8997	.9015
1.3	.9032	.9049	.9066	.9082	.9099	.9115	.9131	.9147	.9162	.9177
1.4	.9192	.9207	.9222	.9236	.9251	.9265	.9279	.9292	.9306	.9319
1.5	.9332	.9345	.9357	.9370	.9382	.9394	.9406	.9418	.9429	.9441
1.6	.9452	.9463	.9474	.9484	.9495	.9505	.9515	.9525	.9535	.9545
1.7	.9554	.9564	.9573	.9582	.9591	.9599	.9608	.9616	.9625	.9633
1.8	.9641	.9649	.9656	.9664	.9671	.9678	.9686	.9693	.9699	.9706
1.9	.9713	.9719	.9726	.9732	.9738	.9744	.9750	.9756	.9761	.9767
2.0	.9772	.9778	.9783	.9788	.9793	.9798	.9803	.9808	.9812	.9817
2.1	.9821	.9826	.9830	.9834	.9838	.9842	.9846	.9850	.9854	.9857
2.2	.9861	.9864	.9868	.9871	.9875	.9878	.9881	.9884	.9887	.9890
2.3	.9893	.9896	.9898	.9901	.9904	.9906	.9909	.9911	.9913	.9916
2.4	.9918	.9920	.9922	.9925	.9927	.9929	.9931	.9932	.9934	.9936
2.5	.9938	.9940	.9941	.9943	.9945	.9946	.9948	.9949	.9951	.9952
2.6	.9953	.9955	.9956	.9957	.9959	.9960	.9961	.9962	.9963	.9964
2.7	.9965	.9966	.9967	.9968	.9969	.9970	.9971	.9972	.9973	.9974
2.8	.9974	.9975	.9976	.9977	.9977	.9978	.9979	.9979	.9980	.9981
2.9	.9981	.9982	.9982	.9983	.9984	.9984	.9985	.9985	.9986	.9986
3.0	.9987	.9987	.9987	.9988	.9988	.9989	.9989	.9989	.9990	.9990

Index